Cook

Cook

The Extraordinary Voyages
of Captain James Cook

NICHOLAS THOMAS

WALKER & COMPANY
NEW YORK

First published in the United States of America in 2003 by
Walker Publishing Company, Inc.; published simultaneously in
Canada by Penguin Group (Canada) and in Great Britain, as
Discoveries: The Voyages of Captain James Cook, by
Penguin Books Ltd. First paperback edition published by
Walker Publishing Company, Inc. in 2004.

For information about permission to reproduce selections from
this book, write to Permissions, Walker & Company,
104 Fifth Avenue, New York, New York 10011

Library of Congress Cataloging-in-Publication Data
Thomas, Nicholas.
Cook : the extraordinary voyages of
Captain James Cook / Nicholas Thomas.
p. cm.
Published simultaneously under the title:
Discoveries : the voyages of Captain James Cook.
Includes bibliographical references (p.).
ISBN 0-8027-1412-9 (alk. paper)
1. Cook, James, 1728–1779—Travel.
2. Explorers—England—Biography. 3. Voyages
around the world. 4. Oceania—Discovery and exploration.
I. Title: Extraordinary voyages
of Captain James Cook. II. Title.

G420.C65T56 2003
910'.92—dc22
[B]
2003057648

ISBN 0-8027-7711-2 (paperback)

Visit Walker & Company's Web site at www.walkerbooks.com

Typeset by Rowland Phototypesetting Ltd, Bury St. Edmunds,
Suffolk, England

Printed in the United States of America

2 4 6 8 10 9 7 5 3

for Annie Coombes
with all my love

Contents

PART 4:
TO THE NORTH PACIFIC

Epilogue:
Cook's afterlives

List of illustrations

Introduction: The *Resolution* in Antarctic waters: William Hodges's *Ice Island*, 1773–4, wash and watercolour, Mitchell Library, New South Wales.
Part 1: Detail from *A Chart of the West Coast of Newfoundland, Surveyed by Order of Commodore Pallisser, Governor of Newfoundland, Labradore &c.*, by James Cook, London, 1768.
Part 2: Tupaia, *A Scene in Tahiti*, 1769, pencil and watercolour, British Library, London.
Part 3: William Hodges, *Tongan Canoe*, 1774, pen and Indian ink, British Library, London.
Part 4: John Webber, *A Night Dance by Men in Hapaee*, 1777, Dixson Library, State Library of New South Wales, Sydney.
Epilogue: The Milbi Wall, Cooktown (photo: Mark Adams).

List of maps

Introduction:
History's man

In January 1774 James Cook wrote that his ambition led him 'not only farther than any other man has been before me, but as far as I think it possible for man to go'. Forty-five years old, he had been a seaman for twenty-five years, a naval man for nearly twenty, and a man engaged in the specialized and unusual business of maritime exploration for around five. Now, at the edge of a vast field of ice well to the south of the Antarctic circle, he was in search of the Great South Land that had preoccupied geographers for centuries. The morning of 30 January was fine. Light reflected off the ice filled the southern half of the sky. Snow-white clouds near the horizon merged into ice mountains – or perhaps just fog. The distance and the glare made it hard for the eye to separate frozen water from water vapour, but what was apparent was that there was no inhabitable country here. There might be land somewhere closer to the pole, beyond or beneath the ice, but it was impossible to 'proceed one Inch farther South'. So Cook tacked and took the *Resolution* and his exhausted crew back.

The aim of Cook's second voyage was to establish once and for all whether any southern continent existed. His method was to undertake a series of extended forays towards the South Pole over three successive summers. During the intervening periods, refreshments were obtained and people encountered among the islands of the Pacific. The Antarctic cruises were gruelling. For the most part Cook writes matter of factly about the intense cold, fog, snow and sleet. The seamen had been issued special jackets and trousers made of 'a thick woollen stuff called Fearnought', yet these proved inadequate. Not long before Christmas 1772, during their first venture into the Antarctic, Cook found it necessary to have the sleeves lengthened with baize, and also supplied the men with canvas and baize caps. The sailors had no gloves; they are not much use if one has to handle rope all day. Yet the ship's sails and rigging were frequently encased in ice; how knots were tied and untied and what these sailors' hands were like, I try and fail to imagine.

A couple of weeks before the sight of the huge ice sheet, Cook alluded to 'excessive hard gales' in his journal. His brilliant but cranky naturalist, Johann Reinhold Forster, elaborated upon what misery an 'excessive' gale could cause.

Our ship is tossed backwards & forwards, up & down the mountainous waves: each summit, from which you may overlook the vast extent of the Ocean, follows again a deep abyss, where we get hardly any light in our Cabins . . . At 9 o'clock, there came a huge mountainous Sea & took the Ship in her middle, & overwhelmed all her parts with a Deluge. The table in the Steerage, at which we were sitting, was covered with water, & it put our candle out: the great Cabin was quite washed over & over by the Sea coming through the Sides of the Ship . . . I did not sleep all night, my cabin was now below full of water, & I could not stir without being in water to my Ankles . . . The Ocean & the winds raged all night.

The tempest passed, but the wetness of sheets, clothes and everything exacerbated Forster's assorted ailments and the incipient scurvy that troubled a good few of the crew members, which Cook would not acknowledge or mention.

At this latitude, at this time of year, the sun barely set – but it was often dark anyway in the dense fog. William Hodges, the voyage artist, went to some pains to capture the peculiarities of light and atmosphere in the many places visited in the course of the three-year expedition and produced extraordinary watercolours during these frigid midsummer weeks. His sea was not blue or green but a gloomy grey, suspended beneath broken black cloud. The monotony of this ocean was interrupted only by icebergs, or 'ice islands', as the mariners called them. Far bigger than those known to Greenland whalers, they were unexpectedly irregular and grotesque. While remarkable and curious, they also constituted a natural minefield. Shortly before Christmas 1773 the *Resolution* had come close to being wrecked upon one. The officer of the watch had foolishly thought to sail to its windward, but the ship slowed and 'got so near that he could get neither one way nor the other'. Destruction appeared imminent, and – as one of the lieutenants wrote – 'to discribe the horrour depicted in every person's face at the awful situation in which we stood is impossible'. Sails were hastily adjusted and somehow the vessel passed clear, though 'we were actualy within the backsurge of the Sea from the Island . . . her stern just trailing within the Breakers'.

Cook had taken his men to this extremity in order to make discoveries. His claim that he had been as far as it was possible for man to go was no expression of idle hubris. The *Resolution* had not only gone further south than any ship before, but had travelled right around the Antarctic, its whole course much farther south than those of notable predecessors such as Tasman, Halley and Bouvet. Towards the end of this same voyage, Cook restated his claim, writing that 'the risque one runs in exploring a coast, in these unknown and icy seas, is so very great, that I can be bold enough to say that no man will ever venture farther than I have done; and that the lands which may lie to the South will never be explored'. He was eventually proved wrong, but it was well over a century before any explorer went further, and then only with a technological base that lay beyond his epoch's imagination.

Cook's history-making, however, lay in discovering nothing. His unprecedented expedition found no great land in the south. One of the last of the few inhospitable islands he did discover was South Georgia, a mass of jagged and frozen mountains. Even at the height of summer, the ice extended right to the water's edge. This was hardly 'that Land or Islands of Great extent, hitherto unvisited by any European Power . . . in Latitudes convenient for Navigation, and in Climates adapted to the production of Commodities useful in Commerce' that had been the object of the Admiralty's programme of exploration. After two and a half years at sea, Cook was exhausted and appalled by the lifelessness of the place. But he was unlike Columbus, Cortés or Quiros – unlike even his celebrated predecessor George Anson, whose mid-eighteenth-century voyage into the 'South Sea' had been disastrous for its loss of ships and life, but in the end triumphant for its capture of Spanish gold. What drove Cook was not the prospect of naval victory, or the spoils of conquest and colonization. Cook liked a point or a line on a chart. The map of the southern hemisphere engraved at the front of his *Voyage Toward the South Pole* may have mattered more to him than the book as a whole, though the lavishly illustrated book was one of the publishing events of 1777. His chart of an unfamiliar half-globe, bottom up, the South Pole at its centre, was the most succinct expression of his expedition's findings. It showed his tracks criss-crossing a formerly unknown part of the world. It dispatched one of the most longstanding imperial fantasies and a favourite object of geographic speculation.

One of the men who must have eagerly awaited Cook's return was Alexander Dalrymple. He'd spent his life sifting the muddled accounts of Dutch, Portuguese and Spanish navigators, collecting the sightings of capes and distant mountains that might have represented edges and extensions of a great south land and making maps with suggestive and capacious blank spaces. He would have been profoundly disappointed. The capes turned out to be islets. The mountains were inventions or banks of cloud. The empty spaces on the charts were sailed through, yielding no coastlines. Cook's sense of accomplishment did not hinge on the presence or absence of the continent, but on the distance he ventured and the precise record he kept of his route and his findings. He saw himself as making history by making geography. His account of his own importance was accepted during his own life and has been, for the most part, since. He is still commonly regarded as the greatest sea explorer of all time.

Out of this kind of story comes our sense of Cook as the lone director of a remarkable mission. We envisage him as a single-minded, rational man who arrived at a plan and made that plan work. But Cook's voyages and his life had passages quite unlike this heroic probing of the Antarctic. Elsewhere, he was not author of the script and director of the action. He was in the midst of a crowd, playing roles he had not chosen. He was a witness and a reporter – sometimes of things that had gone wrong.

Cook found not only lands and islands unknown to Europeans, but also people who already knew these islands intimately, whose ancestors had lived and died on them. Cook was a master of techniques that enabled him to determine the orientation of a coast, the height of a mountain and the position of a reef – and to transcribe the whole on to a chart. But he lacked devices that might measure or describe a meeting with men, women and children. Distinctive bodies, unfamiliar practices, exotic rites and alien art forms were not susceptible to plotting or precise delineation. Cook wrote, of course, and one of this book's voyages is through the prose he produced, through his efforts to make sense of indigenous peoples who were different to Europeans, different from each other and different in their dealings with him.

A person is not an object that remains still and silent as its characteristics are recorded. Knowing involves interaction and interaction has consequences. A person being inspected or interviewed may present themselves in a particular way, in response to questions, because they are threatened by an intruder, or because they find an intruder curious. Knowing was never a one-way activity. The Oceanic peoples Cook discovered themselves discovered Europe, or rather they discovered peculiar floating samples of European society. These encounters were replete with surprises, and were mutually exciting – but were also confusing, unpredictable and injurious. Some meetings brought Cook and his fellow-voyagers into contact with human behaviour that repelled them; some of what he and they wrote denigrated peoples. Cook and his men could also idealize indigenous bodies, behaviours and societies; these positive evaluations were often just as partial and ethnocentric as their negative judgements. But it is notable that the mariners' responses – like those of the people they met – were not often either simply positive or negative, rather they were unsure and ambiguous.

Cook was perplexed not only by people he encountered, but also, in a way, by his own mission. Voyaging was never as simple a matter as surveying a passage and putting a line on a chart. It had effects – on himself, on his crew and on other people – that he could neither anticipate nor control.

The mariners had been told that the island was called Te Wai Pounamu, which can be translated as 'the greenstone land'. It has mostly been known, more prosaically, as the South Island. It is the bulkier but colder and more sparsely occupied of the two main landmasses of New Zealand. Its northern end breaks into a scatter of finger-like peninsulas and islets. Above their protected shingle beaches are hillsides covered in tree-ferns. Further inland are huge and gaunt mountains.

Among the bodies of water is Totaranui, or Queen Charlotte Sound. Within it is a broad but usually calm bay known as Motuara, or Ship Cove. Cook visited this place five times in the course of his three voyages. Like his first port, Whitby Harbour, the naval yards at Deptford, and places such as Funchal, Madeira and Table Bay at the Cape of Good Hope, it was a place he knew at different times and seasons, a place which became familiar, but which changed, as the places do that grow older with us.

His second visit was during the southern winter of 1773. The *Resolution* had been separated from the *Adventure* four months earlier in the Antarctic fog. Cook was no doubt relieved to find the other ship here, at the agreed rendezvous. He seems to have been anxious to get to sea again, to make further investigations in the ocean to the east, but he had something else, something quite different to do. Vegetable gardening is hardly an activity we associate with maritime exploration, but it was one that had a place in Cook's project and one he seems to have found satisfying. On 31 May he was busy clearing and digging ground on the small island of Motuara, not far from Ship Cove, 'and planting it with Wheat, Pease and other Pulse Carrots Parsnips and Straw berries'. A couple of days earlier he had been across to this island with a Maori man called Teiratu, to whom he was pleased to point out the potatoes brought from Cape Town and planted by an officer from the *Adventure*. 'There seems to be no doubt of their succeeding as they were in a very thriving state, the man was so pleased with them that he immidiately began to hough the earth about the plants, I called them Coumalla . . . I explained to him as well as I could the nature of the Turnips, Carrots & Parsnips roots together with Potatoes that will be of more use to them than all the other vegetables.'

When Cook introduced these plants to Maori land and introduced a Maori man to them, his gesture was both decidedly modern and strangely nostalgic. Transplantation had in one sense been going on for millennia. Cultivated plants were always being spread through piecemeal adoption from place to place. But as the European colonization of the Americas and elsewhere gained momentum, plants and animals began to be shipped about in an increasingly deliberate way, and the mid eighteenth century was distinctive for the emergence of a more concerted and scientifically based approach. Cook's companion on the first voyage, Joseph Banks, had learned some of his botany from Phillip Miller, who ran the Physic Garden beside the Thames at Chelsea. Miller was enthusiastically interested in the business of collecting plants and seeds in one place and establishing them in research gardens in Britain, and anywhere else in the empire where they might be made to flourish. Banks devoted much of his later career to the expansion of the former royal garden at Kew into the scientific botanical garden it became, and advocated the transplantation of breadfruit from Tahiti to the West Indies and the breeding of Spanish merino for wool in Australia. Cook's turnips and 'Straw berries' were small instances of an ambitious programme to rearrange the biological map, which had far-reaching effects, in some cases devastating ones, on ecologies throughout the world.

In the eighteenth century, this was understood as a progressive and philanthropic experiment. When Cook planted vegetables in New Zealand, he anticipated that they would be as useful to locals as they would to future mariners. This is why he performs a translation exercise for Teiratu, telling him that the potato is a form of 'Coumalla', of kumara or sweet potato, that the carrots are like taro, and so on. These two men, who had little in common apart from their interest in the flourishing potatoes, walked around the small plantations on an afternoon milder than a late autumn day in England. Cook might have recalled his conversations with Banks, on the affinities of climates and the subject of transplantation. In general, he had not found Banks's botanical passions contagious, but on this point the naturalist's interest had rubbed off.

This garden might have prompted Cook to recall his own farmyard childhood, in a cold and hilly part of north Yorkshire. He might have remembered the hard frosts and the solidity of the small stone cottages. But it was also symptomatic of another nostalgia, intellectual rather than personal. In the 1750s and 1760s, Europeans began to think more systematically than before about the question of progress and the longer course of human history.

Various native American, Asian and African peoples were presumed to exemplify early social conditions, the pasts of Europeans. Treatises on the 'origin of laws' and the 'history of civil society' proposed strong associations between cultivation and civilization. Peoples who were nomadic, who hunted and did not till the soil, seemed to have no property, no rules of inheritance and no legal order. Those who practised agriculture were prompted to make social arrangements that provided some security of tenure; they formed defensive alliances to repel their enemies; they created larger and more regular social unions and eventually systems of civil government. The Maori were already regarded, by observers such as Cook and Banks, as half-civilized. But they were susceptible to improvement and that improvement might follow from a more industrious approach to agriculture, from a bit of encouragement and instruction of the sort Cook offered on that May afternoon.

It would have been simpler, if Maori society had plainly been at a particular stage of development and could have been prodded towards further advancement in this way. But Maori society was varied and anomalous. In the north, horticulture was practised intensively. In the south, the tribes were essentially fishers and foragers rather than farmers, hence they might have been classified as 'savages' who had not yet made the advances of 'barbarians'. Yet many Maori also seemed to have commercial sense, in that they traded with each other and were astute and canny in their dealings with visiting mariners. The stage they were at was therefore neither one thing nor the other; it was both pre- and post-agricultural. This was not only a problem of intellectual definition, of pigeon-holing. It was also a *moral* problem. In European minds virtue and stability were associated above all with landed communities, which appeared to be endangered: the commercialization of European societies meant that rural life and the apparent certainty of landed property were becoming superseded by trade. Even those who advocated trade were ambivalent, and many believed that the 'body politic' was afflicted with a 'distemper', a taste for luxury that corrupted personality, taste, society and government.

We think of colonialism as the imposition of a European model. Cook's garden was not much of an imposition. If it anticipated a global agricultural economy, it also harked back to a model of simple and honest rural civility that already belonged to an idealized past in England. Whatever Cook was trying to implant, the Maori would not conform to anyone else's nostalgia. They had already leapt outside the supposed order of an old rural society, into the opportunities for trade that the British visit opened up. The trafficking that took place troubled people on both sides. Those Europeans who believed that commerce was a civilizing force would not have liked what they saw in Queen Charlotte Sound in 1773.

We do not know what exactly happened. Whatever it was must have been violent and shocking. Both Cook and Forster's son George write, not of a specific incident, but in general terms. Both see what has taken place not just as a particular misfortune, but as an instance of a greater wrong that they and their voyage are implicated in.

What is reported is cross-cultural sex. In itself, this is unremarkable. At Tahiti, a commerce between sailors and local women had quickly developed during the visit of Cook's predecessor, the island's European 'discoverer', Samuel Wallis. When the *Endeavour* arrived there to observe the transit of Venus, Cook, it appears, was almost alone in refraining from taking a Tahitian lover. Common seamen, the officers, Joseph Banks and others felt no compunction about forming temporary attachments. Similarly, when Cook first called at Queen Charlotte Sound, a few sailors had slept with a few women. What changed between his first and second sojourns was the interest that Maori men took in the business. They had previously been indifferent. Now, according to both Cook and Forster, they began to compel their women to prostitute themselves.

... but for the authority and menaces of their men, [the women, Forster wrote] would not have complied with the desires of a set of people who could, with unconcern, behold their tears and hear their complaints. Whether the members of a civilized society, who could act such a brutal part, or the barbarians who could force their own women to submit to such indignity, deserve the greatest abhorrence, is a question not easily to be decided. Encouraged by the lucrative nature of this infamous commerce, the New Zeelanders went through the whole vessel, offering their daughters and sisters promiscuously to every person's embraces, in exchange for our iron tools, which they knew could not be purchased at an easier rate.

Today, it is not possible to know whether this really became a pattern of behaviour or whether there were just one or two occasions when coercion was manifest. Forster and Cook were not immune from the impulse to pronounce a generality on the basis of some possibly exceptional event. But it is most unlikely that they would have written in these terms at all had not some women made it painfully clear that they hated being used sexually by strangers, by alien white men, who were probably both desperate and careless. At Tahiti, women who were not willing simply refused sailors and that was that. At the time, there was argument about how reprehensible sexual contacts at Tahiti were, and that issue can be argued today. But what happened in New Zealand was different: all we know suggests that it was marked by immediate and unmistakable violence. For Forster, this commerce exposed the joint brutality of mariners and indigenous men.

Just a few weeks after the incidents that prompted these passages, a discovery was made that 'caused us all great uneasiness'. The news was that a man on the *Adventure* had caught a venereal complaint from a Maori woman – significant and dreadful because venereal diseases were, until this time, unknown among Maori. The woman herself can only have become infected through contact with another of Cook's seamen. Cook had tried consistently but ineffectually to prevent the spread of sexually transmitted diseases by having his surgeon monitor the conditions of those who were afflicted; he tried to bar them from contact with local women, but men without visible symptoms could still infect others.

Venereal conditions were, of course, immediately painful and disagreeable; and no one who had frequented European cities or ports would have been unfamiliar with the truly disgusting bodily decay that advanced, inadequately treated sufferers might try to live with. The period saw a rash of pamphlets and treatises that offered rival diagnoses and cures; quacks and 'man-midwives' hawked remedies. England's Royal Navy for its part treated infection as a violation of discipline, and docked the pay of men who made themselves incapable of service, through carnal carelessness. This contagion was, in short, about the worst and most morally reprehensible that the eighteenth century knew: its transmission to new peoples was something that benevolent voyagers wanted desperately to prevent.

Forster seems stunned by the fact that the disease has, despite precautions, found its way into the Maori population. Anticipating that it will spread among those of all ages, sexes and ranks, he writes that 'every feeling heart must sympathize with me for the poor Natives of New Zeeland, & detest the memory of the Man, who first disseminated this venom among this brave and spirited Nation'. The theme leads him to the bizarre proposition that it would really have been better if the first native woman to have been infected had been stabbed immediately after intercourse by her temporary lover. 'He would certainly deserve to be detested & abhorred as a most consummate villain: but if we consider the fatal consequences, which must now attend his connexion with that woman, & the general devastation his communicated evil must cause, I cannot help thinking, that howsoever detestable the murder of such a poor wretch must be, it would be a real benefit to the whole community & preserve a harmless brave & numerous Nation from all the horrors of being poisoned from their very infancy' – and so on.

The sheer turmoil in Forster's reflections on the topic, the virulence of this anxious energy, suggest that more is going on here than simple condemnation of what was, after all, the habitual conduct of the lusty able seaman. Rather, this eighteenth-century intellectual is disgusted by desire as such, and surely by the arousal he has sensed in himself when the possibility of physical intimacy has arisen. We do not know how Forster responded to the sexual opportunities that certainly arose in New Zealand and elsewhere in Polynesia. He and his son were later accused of having committed the very offence that they had denounced. Cook's own observations at this time are shorter and less passionate than Forster's, but in their own way more comprehensively damning of the very enterprise that he himself led.

The Women of this Country I always looked upon to be more chaste than the generality of Indian Women, whatever favours a few of them might have granted to the crew of the Endeavour it was generally done in a private manner and without the men seeming to intrest themselves in it, but now we find the men are the chief promoters of this Vice, and for a spike nail or any other thing they value will oblige their Wives and Daughters to prostitute themselves whether they will or no and that not with the privicy decency seems to require, such are the concequences of a commerce with Europeans and what is still more to our Shame civilized Christians, we debauch their Morals already too prone to vice and we interduce among them wants and perhaps diseases which they never before knew and which serves only to disturb that happy tranquillity they and their fore Fathers had injoy'd. If any one denies the truth of this assertion let him tell me what the Natives of the whole extent of America have gained by the commerce they have had with Europeans.

Despite the baldness of his style, Cook is carried away by his own rhetoric. According to George Forster, married Maori women were not promiscuous and were not forced to make themselves available to sailors. Forster may have been in error, but if not, Cook distorted circumstances and magnified the offensiveness of Maori conduct when he stated categorically that men rented out their wives and daughters. This is to censure Maori men, fairly or unfairly, but intensifies the point that Cook makes, that women are degraded in this way only because civilized Christians have arrived. Native morality may already be prone to vice, he observes, but natives are debauched by the British, not by themselves. He generalizes further: what is shameful is not just the permanent disruption of indigenous life in the Pacific in particular, but the entire business of European expansion.

The journal that I've quoted from was the basis of Cook's published book, *A Voyage Toward the South Pole*. Cook's idiosyncrasies of spelling and grammar were tidied up by a literary churchman, Canon John Douglas, who generally followed Cook's manuscript closely. When Douglas came to this passage, however, he must have sensed a problem. Where Cook wrote, 'now we find the men are the chief promoters of this Vice', he has 'But now, I was told, they were the chief promoters of a shameful traffic', implying hearsay rather than observed fact. Those who imagined that they had Cook's journal before them did not read that men 'would oblige their wives and daughters to prostitute themselves', but only that 'the women' were thus obliged. This was to distance and to soften a disagreeable report, the sort of thing we would expect Douglas to have done, especially because sexual allusions in the published version of Cook's first voyage had proved controversial. This is petty censorship in the interests of politeness. What is more important, and what remains outrageous, is that Cook's more general reflections beginning 'such are the consequences of a commerce with Europeans and what is still more to our Shame' are omitted from the published book altogether. It moves straight from mention of the privacy required by decency to a paragraph concerning the scientific tests of Kendal's and Arnold's watches. The wider public who read the first cheaper edition of the journals a few years later got even less. The passage on sexual traffic was deleted completely, as it was in virtually all reprints and abridgements published during the nineteenth and twentieth centuries.

It is September 1986. The contents of a country house in Kilkenny, Ireland, are up for auction. No different from hundreds of sales that take place every year, marking the transformation of old wealth into ready cash; enthusiasts and dealers gossip as they inspect antiques, china, tapestries and books. David Posnett, a London art dealer, rummages through undistinguished paintings of racehorses, dogs and children, but is impressed by what looks like a portrait of a naval officer. It is a medium-sized picture; it seems an accomplished work by some second-rank artist. The catalogue estimate suggests that the painting will sell for between £350 and £450, but another dealer is interested, and Posnett is lucky to secure it for just under £30,000. Very lucky, in fact, because what he has found is a remarkable portrait of Captain James Cook, lost for over 200 years.

Lost is not quite the right word, because in a sense the painting was never known to the public, though it had been indirectly visible through a portrait frontispiece for Cook's *Voyage Toward the South Pole*, which appeared in 1777. This was the work of James Basire, a renowned engraver to whom

1. *William Hodges,* Capt. James Cook of the
Endeavour, *1775–6.*

William Blake was apprenticed, but it in no way prepares us for the canvas upon which it is based. In the frontispiece, the navigator is framed within an oval of cracked stone, which rests on an ornamented pediment; the painting discovered in Ireland lacks the paraphernalia, and is informal. Thanks to the inscription on the print, and to technical comparisons of style and canvas, we know that the original was the work of the second voyage artist, William Hodges, who probably painted it in London in the months after he and Cook had returned from the Pacific – in late 1775 or early 1776. Hodges knew his subject intimately, and his depiction of Cook is quite unlike better-known paintings.

2. *Portrait frontispiece of Cook, from James Cook,* A Voyage Toward the South Pole, *London, 1777.*

It differs, for example, from Nathaniel Dance's portrait, which was commissioned by Joseph Banks. Cook sat for Dance, as he did for Hodges, some time after he returned from his second voyage and before departing on his third. This much-reproduced painting hung above the fireplace in the library at Banks's Soho Square house from the late 1770s until Banks's death in 1820. Throughout these years Banks was president of the Royal Society, one of the wealthiest men in Britain, and the scientific powerbroker of the age. The picture that he gave pride of place was of a rather severe naval man, tapping his finger on a great chart of the southern hemisphere. Thousands and eventually hundreds of thousands of prints after it were sold and framed, or appeared as frontispieces in edition after edition of Cook's life and voyages. Today, if you visit Whitby, Greenwich, Sydney, Cooktown, Auckland, Gisborne or Honolulu and buy a Cook tea-towel, it will have a likeness derived from this portrait. Both Dance and Hodges presented Cook in his captain's uniform, but Dance made a meal of it in the same way that Gainsborough often paid as much attention to an expensive dress as to a sitter's face. The quality of Hodges's painting was not in the fancy dress, but in a mood that did not translate into the printed engraving. There is no map, there are none of the props conventionally used to signal particular branches of distinction; Cook is alone against a sombre field, into which his dark brown jacket melts.

3. *Nathaniel Dance*, Captain James Cook, R.N., *1776.*

According to a National Maritime Museum publication, this painting 'gives a vivid impression of the indomitable resolve of the explorer'. I am not sure. In *Macbeth*, Duncan says: 'There's no art to find the mind's construction in the face.' He meant that one could never be certain that a person was not masking true feelings or intentions. I am not suggesting that Cook's portrait exhibits any straightforward deception. Rather, Hodges's evasion of the usual dignifying devices leaves us with a curiously neutral image of a man neither happy nor sad, neither humble nor proud. I see a man a few years older than myself, who is not quite comfortable. I sense disquiet in the stony face. If I do not quite see Cook, I see Hodges seeing a man, a man with whom he has travelled around the world and shared the confined spaces of a compact ship for three years. The tones he chooses are muted.

In 1970 I was a ten-year-old pupil at Mona Vale Primary School in one of Sydney's northern beach suburbs. I remember three things that happened at this school. The first was that I was unable to read the blackboard. I still recall getting my eyes tested, trying on my first pair of spectacles, and breaking out into an idiotic grin, surprised and delighted by the discovery that the world was not blurry but clear, replete with coloured things that had sharp edges.

The second was the Aboriginal boy in my class, whose name was Anderson. I do not remember that he usually found the lessons difficult, but there was one occasion when the teacher, an easily irritated old man named Woods, had him out in front of the class, unable to solve some arithmetic problem on the blackboard. It is now a bad and indistinct dream and I may be being unfair, but my recollection is that he asked Anderson again and again what the sum made and hit him with a ruler again and again as he got it wrong. It was an ordinary exercise in educational persecution, but I thought that Anderson was being treated in this way because he was Aboriginal. I did not believe that he deserved to be hit, but the injustice did not seem one that could have been challenged or changed. It was instead a strangely inevitable humiliation.

The third thing I remember was the bicentenary of Cook's discovery of Australia. That's what we mostly called it, even though we knew that the Dutch and later Dampier had visited the west and north of Australia well before Cook. Their efforts did not count because they had not been to Sydney. The bicentenary was marked by a ceremony at our school which appeared, to a ten-year-old, to be an event on an unprecedented scale. I have a dim recollection of the headmaster giving a pompous speech in which he kept referring to the year as 'Nineteen hundred and seventy', and a vivid memory of what seemed an extraordinarily large and realistic model of Cook's *Endeavour*, constructed and crewed by the sixth-formers. The school captain was, of course, Cook, who strode about giving authoritative directions and waving his telescope.

Here, as for most of his posthumous life, Cook was a monument rather than a man. As children, we were introduced not to a particular person, but to a dauntingly stern navigator who exemplified the virtues of the names of his ships: the *Endeavour*, the *Resolution*, the *Discovery* and the *Adventure*. The propensity to idealize Cook has proved durable. It began late in his own lifetime. His death provoked a flood of praise and commemoration. During the nineteenth century he became one of a series of British empire heroes. In the twentieth, Cook celebrations were of special national importance in Australia and New Zealand, but the perception of him as a major historical figure was equally sustained in Britain, Canada and elsewhere. The level of interest has not diminished in recent years, despite the discredited status of the imperial ideologies with which Cook was for so long associated. A full-scale *Endeavour* replica completed in 1994 has retraced Cook's routes and called at many places in Britain, north America and the Pacific; it is visited by thousands of people, and continues to be the focus of re-enactments, television series, and commemorative events. Feasibility studies for a further replica, of the *Resolution*, are well advanced, Cook museums are renovated, Cook films and books appear steadily. The range of more particular 'Cook effects' is positively bewildering. Inspector Morse, the British television detective, goes simply by surname as a way of coping with the fact that his father, a Cook enthusiast, felt that if girls could be called Faith, Hope or Charity, his son could be called Endeavour; Mercedes-Benz markets a 'Captain Cook Sprinter', a family van supposedly appropriate to more adventurous tourists; and Cook appears on wine labels, ashtrays, tea-towels, T-shirts, banknotes, coins and innumerable stamps.

This enthusiasm is not shared by many Pacific Islanders. Hawaiian nationalists, in particular, have been categorical in their condemnation of the navigator. In Hawaii, it is widely believed that Cook personally introduced the venereal disease that later had a devastating effect on the indigenous population. Cook is accordingly described as a 'syphilitic racist' by Haunani-Kay Trask, an influential activist and one of a group of native scholars who have documented the tragedy of contact and dispossession that Cook inaugurated. In Australia, Aboriginal people are equally negative. In many parts of the country, Cook traditions evoke a ruthlessly violent figure who goes from place to place shooting indiscriminately, never asking permission to venture into people's territory, acting with peremptory cruelty with the aim of taking the land. The title of a painting by the Arnhem Land artist Paddy Wainburranga, *Too Many Captain Cooks*, sums up their attitude. This grass-roots anti-colonialism has a scholarly counterpart in recent writing that ranges from theoretical inquiry into the ways Cook took possession of places, by mapping and naming them, to more straightforward denunciation of his violence.

This reaction against Cook cannot be dismissed. On many occasions Cook and his subordinates shot at Islanders who committed minor thefts. The worst incidents took place in the heat and confusion of the moment,

4. *Paddy Fordham Wainburranga,* Too Many
Captain Cooks, *1987.*

but Cook also sometimes acted in an extreme but considered fashion, flogging, mutilating or physically humiliating Islanders. It has to be acknowledged, also, that he was in the business of dispossession: he claimed inhabited islands and lands right around the Pacific for the Crown. Yet when we damn Cook for inaugurating the business of colonization, we are in underlying agreement with traditional Cook idealizers – we are seeing the explorer above all as a founder or precursor, and judging him according to how we judge what happened afterwards. He is history's man.

This book aims to step behind the false certainties of both the heroic and anti-heroic biographies of this navigator, to deal with the messy actualities of the past. Cook's voyages were not blameless humanitarian ventures, nor were they purely invasive. What happened emerged from a mix of motivations. Encounters with indigenous peoples entailed both friendship and exploitation, reciprocity and imposition, shared understanding and misrepresentation. In much of this book, I am concerned to tease out the ambiguities and confusions of these encounters by making the most of the rich voyage journals and visual records that are our primary sources for Cook's three expeditions. These sources are not only fascinatingly detailed, especially for places such as Tahiti, New Zealand and Hawaii, which aroused the curiosity of many of the mariners – they are also replete with intriguing revisions, omissions, misunderstandings and small cover-ups. These various failures of observation or interpretation, these cases where sailors could not get their stories straight, these moments of shame and embarrassment, all attest to what was hard to understand or hard to admit.

Today, most writers dealing with cross-cultural encounters feel obliged, as they should, to attempt to represent the indigenous as well as the European experience of these events. To do justice to both sides is invariably difficult because early records are nearly exclusively European. However, a diverse range of sources makes the task less hopeless than it might appear. For many places, native recollections of early contacts were transcribed later on – by missionaries during the nineteenth century, for example. And often anthropological research conducted later provides accounts of relevant relationships, values and practices. Obviously, it is not right to assume that what was observed in 1900 or 1950 was true of 1770, but these studies are at least suggestive of the indigenous societies and cultures that existed earlier. The writings of contemporary native scholars, and oral testimony that may be obtained today, also offer many insights of direct and indirect help. What can be said about what the people on the other side of the beach thought in 1770 or 1779 is – as I will often acknowledge – inevitably speculative. At best, what is said is confident speculation. At worst, it seems preferable to air mere possibilities than pass over native pasts in silence.

It is hard to write about cultural meetings, about encounters between people of the West and people of the Pacific, without contrasting two stereotyped cultures, without inventing a coherent 'Europe' and a coherent 'Oceania' that fail to capture the real cultural, social and historical complexities of both regions. (This is just as true if one's counterpoint to Europe is a more specific, but nevertheless still misleadingly coherent, 'Tahiti', 'Hawaii' or whatever.) This is not to say that there were not fundamental differences in the ways an Englishman such as Cook and a Maori such as Teiratu under-stood the world around them. Cook's thinking was shaped by his upbringing in a northern rural community, by an informal and limited Quaker education and most notably by his experience on and around many merchant and naval ships. More broadly, he was a product of the sort of conflict-ridden, heterogeneous and inventive place that modern Britain-in-the-making was. A gentleman-scientist such as Joseph Banks, the Admiralty lords who drafted Cook's instructions, and the literary ladies who later wrote his elegies likewise belonged to this highly commercial modern society, but the experiences that made them were very different from those that had formed Cook. Teiratu's view of the world emerged from Maori cosmology and by values such as the prestige of warfare, but he was above all the offshoot of his genealogy – an ancestral biography constituted out of many lives rather than one. The particular adventures that made up that genealogy or *whakapapa* lie beyond our vision. It is easier to say what made Cook different from other Britons than it is to say what made Teiratu different from other Maori, but that does not mean that he was not different, that Maori society was not heterogeneous and dynamic in its own way. In fact, archaeological evidence suggests that Maori production systems, settlement patterns, trade and social relations were changing. This society was not 'modern' (it lacked a state, a public sphere, markets and ideas of citizenship) but it was certainly not static. It is obvious that Pacific Islanders young and old, male and female, warriors and priests met Europeans on different terms and had different interests in meeting them or avoiding them.

Finding the right metaphor for this encounter between 'cultures' that were each themselves made up of many cultures may be difficult, but there is no doubt that Cook was in the middle of it and was the single most important European protagonist, in Oceania in the eighteenth century. Hence his life is my lens, for a new look at these formative encounters that in one man's experience produced connections between the Baltic, the north of England, both the east and west coasts of north America, the Thames, Tahiti, Tierra del Fuego and many places in the Pacific. Because he has been and still often is considered the greatest maritime discoverer of all time, there have been hundreds of Cook biographies. This fact must make another seem senseless, but the number reflects the demand for repetitions of one story, rather than any notable variety in tellings of Cook's life thus far. During the nineteenth century, most Cook books were rehashes derived directly or indirectly from the first extensive biography, Andrew Kippis's *Life of Captain James Cook*, itself largely an abridgement of the narratives of the three voyages, published between 1773 and 1784, supplemented by abbreviated accounts of Cook's experience before and between the voyages. Nearly all the twentieth-century biographies were likewise derivative celebrations; quite a few were by sailing enthusiasts, and were accordingly attenuated in their grasp of the broader historical, let alone the cross cultural, dimensions of Cook's activity. The distinguished exception is J. C. Beaglehole's 1974 *Life*, which built upon a magisterial edition of Cook's journals published between 1955 and 1967. The editions and the biography are monumental both in their sheer thousands of pages and in their scholarship. But, despite its very considerable enduring value, the book is opinionated, and belongs to the tradition of Cook idealization.

We need to broaden our history's horizons more radically, moving outside the maritime history that has framed virtually all biographies to date. From this perspective, Cook's experience, the British Navy which provided vessels and men, the practical issues of ship-running, and the navigational course of the voyages themselves have been seen to contribute to a longer and greater progress – that of European exploration and map-making. There was much more that went into the voyages and much more that came out of them, however. Beaglehole was in no sense unaware of what might be called the 'anthropological' significance of the voyages, of the importance of the contacts they inaugurated between Pacific Islanders and Europeans. But for him and most other writers these human discoveries are of secondary importance – of less importance than they were to Cook himself. The voyages' ramifications for European culture – their influence on art and literature – are relegated still further, to a domain of feminine frippery that hardly stands up against the business of masculine seafaring. Cook was indeed a navigator, but also a figure in history – in the history of not just one but many societies.

Most biographies trace a course from grandfather to grave, and do so from a paradoxical time both after and during their subject's lifespan. On the one hand, you have the wisdom of hindsight. On the other, you are there all along, for whichever character's birth, infancy and adolescence, to follow his or her mature accomplishments and share the sorrow of the family that hears of his or her death. I avoid both the mystification of hindsight and the illusion of continuous presence and try, instead, to capture the sense of a particular time, with its recollection of the past, and its anticipated but unknown future. This is the time present not in Dance's but in Hodges's portrait of Cook, and for that matter in the way we make sense of our own lives. When I reflect on where I've been, what I've been lucky enough to share, and what I've succeeded and failed in doing, I do not start by witnessing my birth and proceed chronologically through childhood. I start here and now, on an overcast summer afternoon in my study in north London. I remember moments and passages in the past, erratically, sometimes with difficulty, in more or less detail, no doubt some rosily or wrongly.

In this book, I explore a past life in a fashion consistent with this reality of personal recollection. My starting-point is not Cook's ancestry or birth, but his consciousness of himself at a particular time, at the age of about thirty-nine, during a winter when he knows what his naval years have amounted to. He has a sense of himself as an accomplished surveyor, but does not know that he will take a ship to the Pacific, which has not yet been bought by the Navy, which has not yet been named the *Endeavour*. Now, the flow of his life is diverted into waters that are uncharted, in senses that he does and does not anticipate.

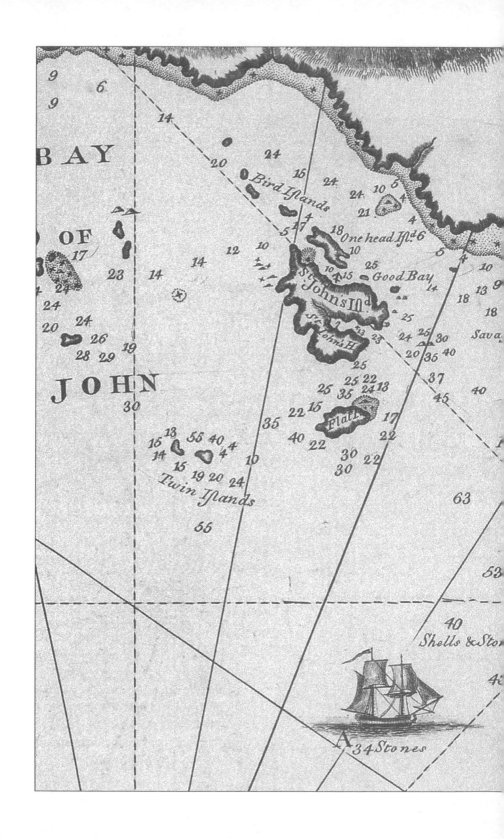

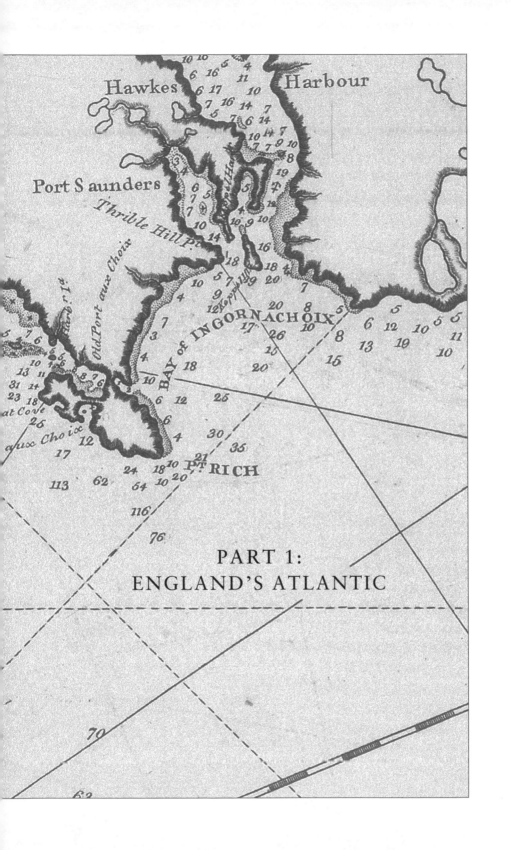

PART 1:
ENGLAND'S ATLANTIC

I

Cook's maps

Despite the cold, a good many people stand about idly in Tower Hill, a broad and open space in the middle of a congested city, a place at once grand and squalid, depending on whether you glance towards the fine buildings along its western side, or the dunghill beside the ditch. The Tower of London itself is formidable, and most of those who stand about seem to be waiting on it, as visitors do. Now, early in the afternoon, on 14 December 1767, a group of Dutch travellers, unostentatiously wealthy, gathers itself together and turns towards the gate, to pay sixpences and see the wild beasts and the jewels. They will find the lioness Dido extraordinary and the old stones dull. Others wait their turn. A couple of sharp men lean on the wooden rails before the ditch. They are there to look after visitors, if they have a chance, in their own way. Some naval officers emerge from Trinity House and walk towards the river, indifferent to the sharpers and foreigners alike. Another man comes out of the same building and walks towards the postern-gate; he has the look of someone who knows this part of the city without being of it; he is from elsewhere, but is no foreigner. He is an oddly proportioned man, tall, with a small head and a pronounced nose. He walks a little oddly too, briskly enough, while planting his feet as if the stones were liable to sway.

He enters a bookseller like others – leather-bound volumes behind the display windows, and bills headed 'TODAY IS PUBLISHED . . .' – yet in fact different to any other. The premises of Mount and Page are devoid of Latin poetry, sermons and treatises on taste. There are no political tracts, no novels, not even any pornography. Mount and Page are maritime publishers, *the* maritime publishers of the town. James Cook is comfortable, and not just because he is out of the cold. He does not own more than a dozen of these books and charts, but he has his own name on a few of them, and has at one time or another studied more than he can recall. He is in a library of his own accomplishment.

I do not know that Cook visited his printer, John Mount, on any particular day in late 1767. But I do know that he must have visited on some occasion, probably several, around this time. And when he did visit, he would surely have browsed Mount's stock, which included *The Mariner's New Kalender*, *The Seamen's Daily Assistant*, *The Principles of Mr Harrison's Time-Keeper* and a formidable number of other works. He would surely also have chatted to Mount, who was in the thick of maritime gossip, who is likely to have heard that Cook had almost lost his ship, the *Grenville*, near the Nore a few weeks earlier. If the subject came up, Cook would have been embarrassed, but would have been obliged to explain that his vessel had struck a sandbank, that he had been unable to sail her off, that the crew had secured the ship as best they could and headed for safety in her boats before venturing back the next day and refloating her. Not much had been lost, other than a canoe from Newfoundland that Cook had been asked to bring back for a gentleman naturalist, a man he did not know, one Mr Banks. Cook would no doubt have been keen to move the conversation on. Mount had published his *Directions for Navigating on Part of the South Coast of Newfoundland*; Cook has now brought his sequel, describing the island's west coast. He fishes the manuscript out of a bag. Mount – who maybe finds Cook's spare prose strangely engaging, looks forward to marking up the script, seeing it set, seeing it printed – scans the pages. As he does so, Cook recalls his words and the places that his unliterary words have laboured to describe. Cape Anguille, St George's Harbour, Long Point, Foxes Island, Foxes Tail, the river Humber, Bonne Bay, Keppell Island, Ingornachoix Bay . . . The highlands, their enveloping woods, the red and white cliffs and the salmon streams of that transatlantic summer come back to him. He remembers eating broiled cod on the beach with fishermen, fleeting moments with some Indians and the satisfying repetition of his exercises: putting out the flags, taking the angles, sounding the bottom, feeling the fine grey sand that came up off the bank. His *Directions* report the measurements rather than the meals or meetings, the passages, rocks and entrances, the bearings and distances and not the habitations and happenings.

Cook's *Directions* were adjuncts to his charts. By 1767 he had been in the Royal Navy for twelve years. The first three or four had been samples of conventional naval experience. As was often the case during the eighteenth century, Britain and France were at war and Cook, like many others, joined cruises from Plymouth and Portsmouth into the Bay of Biscay and the Atlantic, to harass French shipping. He'd spent days inspecting rope and badgering men who were supposed to be repairing sails and shifting stores, odd mornings on the warm shingle, watching seamen drinking with port women, and evenings with moronic midshipmen, who rattled dice and

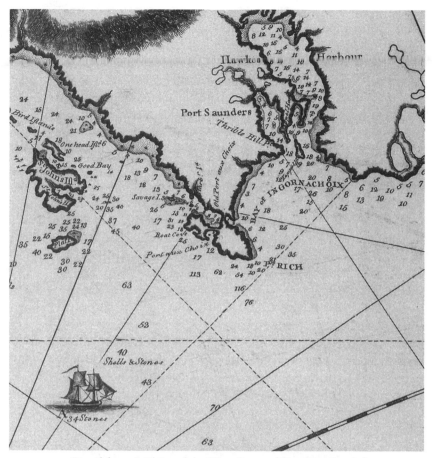

5. *Detail from* A Chart of the West Coast of Newfoundland, *by James Cook, 1768.*

recited awful poetry. In late 1757 he joined the *Pembroke* and the following year that ship formed part of the north American fleet. Cook had a bit part in the Canadian campaign that culminated in the surrender of Quebec and the deaths of both generals, Wolfe and Montcalm, in September 1759. It was along and around the coasts that made a sort of funnel into Quebec that he became less a conventional seaman and more a specialist in the arts of surveying. His chart of Gaspé harbour, the site of some French settlements on the Gulf of St Lawrence, was engraved and printed for Mount and Page; he did further work of the same sort between Quebec, Halifax and Newfoundland until the end of the summer of 1762. That October he was in England, for the first time in almost five years. He made the time to get married to one Elizabeth Batts, of Barking, whose dead father was a Wapping man. It would be a sailor's marriage: early in 1763 Cook was appointed surveyor and would be away in Newfoundland for five successive summers. He worked around the south-east from the main settlement of St John's, in the north in the Strait of Belle Isle that separates the irregular landmass from Labrador, then along the southern, and finally along the western coasts. Now, to you and I, Newfoundland perhaps seems remote and obscure. Then it belonged to a theatre of superpower contest and was the base for the richest fishery that Europeans knew. Its lands, shores and waters were disputed not only between European states, but between Beothuk and other native peoples, which Cook noticed and understood but did not report or analyse. Between voyages, he was back in London. He presented the Admiralty Lords with their charts, called periodically on the engraver Larken, on the cartographic engraver-publisher Thomas Jefferys at Charing Cross and on nautical printer-booksellers like Mount and Page.

Naval men and fishermen were not the only Europeans around Newfoundland in the 1760s. There were also a few Moravian missionaries, who were shipped about and supported by the British and who in return gave the navy reports about the so-called Eskimos and Indians. Their journals describe tense and difficult encounters between 'Fisher people' and locals. They try to prevent excesses on the part of whites and try to explain whites to natives. They are vulnerable not only because they are unarmed imperialists, but also because they don't know quite where's where.

We went to the Indians & enquired of them how they called the Bay in which they lived? answ^r: Kankerlarsoak & also the name of the great Island which lies in the middle? answ^r Kisseksakkut . . . After Dinner we went again to the Indians; When we shewed them the Chart they understood it, & directly pointed, each of them, to the place where their respective Houses stood. They told the names of the Islands &^{c}. They also shewed the place where the Ship that sometimes comes to them Anchored, & even pointed out the different anchoring Places in the Bay; We, as well as Sr Thomas who was present, were entirely convinced that Esquimaux Bay as its called in the french chart is the place of their abode.

Here, the collective journal of four of these men gives us a sense that on this September day in 1765, understanding was made out of recognition, conversation and translation. Imperfect French and English maps, probably of the same places, but with different names, were read against each other. Somehow, the Inuit immediately grasped European ways of representing places and spaces on paper. A man with an olive face and straight jet-black hair, who knows the colour and turbidity of the water in this channel and that, who knows the smell of the trees in this place and that, the soft soil full of pine needles here and the loam there, sees a flat and alien picture which, however, makes a kind of sense. He is able, even, to elucidate this European chart for Europeans. Such geographic knowledge as was made on this occasion emerged from meetings that were luckily friendly (many were not), from questions that were no doubt incompetently expressed in languages new to foreigners, and from the movements of fingers and faces.

Cook's geography did not belong to this register of uncertain human talk and gesture. It was mathematical and uncommunicative. Cartography did not proceed by consultation. Cook trusted techniques and instruments rather than people who had no particular reason to trust him. He surveyed without asking, because he had been trained to do it that way, but also because, around Newfoundland, he seemingly had no choice. The native people, the Beothuk, were few in number and kept their distance. Joseph Banks, who also visited Newfoundland in 1766, recorded their ill-treatment: 'Our people who fish in those Parts Live in a continual State of warfare with them firing at them whenever they meet with them & if they chance to find their houses or wigwams as they call them Plundering them immediately tho a Bow & arrows & what they call their Pudding is generaly the whole of their furniture.' He wrote that the Beothuk were dextrous with the bow, made birch-bark canoes, and took scalps in a different, more extreme way than those he designated 'the Canadians' – stripping their victim's whole face rather than just the top of the head. The best of Banks's remarks is his unembarrassed conclusion, 'So much for the Indians if half of what I wrote about them is true it is more than I expect.' Rarely did travellers acknowledge so readily that travellers' tales were what they told.

Cook's maps had to occupy a different ground altogether to Banks's teasing reports that offered then deprived his reader of serious notes on manners and customs. The charts start out as precise graphic documents, wonderfully big ones that are six or ten feet a side, yet intricate in their features, lines and inscriptions. In principle, we might suggest, the chart is the opposite of the traveller's tale. The latter is all event and story, and is bound up with human improbability; the former is supposedly independent of any and all stories, a simple and absolute record derived from voyages, sometimes showing a ship's track, but telling none of its transactions.

Later on, however, Cook's maps acquire a part in a story, his biography. In popular accounts of his life, and in modern scholarship, it became conventional to regard them as proofs of this surveyor's increasing ability.

They gave him deserved recognition in naval circles, and justified the inspired choice of the *Endeavour*'s commander. Equally, they can be seen as advances in a north Atlantic maritime history. They were printed, not only as individual sheets, but in compilations and portfolios such as *The North American Pilot*. The sea would always remain an uncertain domain, but these elaborately detailed printed papers gave coasts and banks and passages and rocks definite shapes and locations. Ships' masters would henceforth have a better sense of where they were, and voyages would become safer. It makes complete sense to describe Cook's maps and his navigational directions in these terms – if one is in the business of tracing destinies. This surveyor had spent the better part of his thirties engaged in exercises in measurement and applied geometry, working magic on rugged and intricate coastlines, reducing a shoreline as torn as an awful wound to points and lines on paper. Like many other eighteenth-century technicians and scientists, Cook indeed produced a new kind of accurate knowledge that suddenly showed up his predecessors' efforts for their amateurishness. He changed the way this part of the world could be dealt with; it tipped a wavering balance in favour of mariners and against the hazards of the sea and shore. It also tipped another balance, diminishing the purchase of those native peoples, and giving map-bearing Europeans a decisive advantage. Cook's findings were not merely personal. Thanks to the engraver's burin and the printing press, they could be synthesized, reproduced and sold on both sides of the north Atlantic. Subsequently, no trader or naval man was in the situation of the Moravians; he did not need to ask a native person which place was which.

In London, a fortnight after Cook had called at Mount and Page, the Poet Laureate's 'Ode to the New Year', was performed before their majesties at St James's Palace. For their sake, we can only hope that the music was a little more lively than the obsequious verses of William Whitehead.

> No more shall *George*, whose parent Breast,
> Feels every Pang his subjects know,
> Behold a faithful Land distrest,
> Or hear one sigh of real Woe.
> But grateful Mirth, whose decent Bounds,
> No riot swells, no fear confounds,
> And heart-felt Ease, whose Glow within
> Exalts Contentment's modest Mien,
> In every Face shall smile confest
> And in his People's Joy the Monarch too be blest.

The poet's expectation that 1768 would be distinguished by anything like 'heart-felt ease' on the part of the King's subjects would prove wide of the mark. No doubt the weather did not help. On the first of January, it was reported that 'a poor labouring man was found frozen to death on Harrow Would Common'. On the second, 'a poor blind man' was similarly found frozen dead in Hog-lane, St Giles; on succeeding days, so were a watchman at Wapping and 'a poor middle-aged Woman' near Bagnigge-Wells. From Portsmouth it was reported that such deep snow, and such intense frost, had 'not been known in the memory of man', while boats were upset and broken by ice in the Thames. A correspondent to the *St James Chronicle* was one of many troubled by the crisis caused by the 'dearness of provisions', since, as he put it, 'the poor must, and yet cannot live by their labour'. From its first days, the year was one not only of frigidity but of 'great Disturbances' such as those which erupted among the Spitalfields weavers. They broke 'Particular Houses Windows', presumably those of the masters who had lowered their pay, and violently opposed guards sent from the Tower to maintain order. Some people benefited from charitable gestures. Dutch ships unable to reach their home ports sold cargoes of lobsters in London, where the Lord Mayor took advantage of the overstocked market to purchase some hundreds at the rate of two shillings a score; these were distributed, mainly among prisoners. Watermen, unable to conduct their usual business of ferrying people across the river, dragged a boat through the streets, 'to excite the compassion of well-disposed persons'. But the demand for compassion was greater than the supply.

During the spring and summer of 1768, the slogan of many rioters was 'Wilkes and Liberty!' Their hero was John Wilkes, a charismatic and dissolute man, an opponent of the government, an outlaw charged with seditious libel, the subject of botched proceedings, a fugitive on the Continent and then, at the end of March 1768, decisive winner of the election to represent Middlesex. Against the wishes of the King and the parliamentary elite, he had captured the single most important seat in the country. What did Wilkes have to do with the grievances of weavers, sailors, and even Irish coal-heavers? Just about nothing. But his campaign was energized by subversive rhetoric rather than a policy programme. During the eighteenth century, Englishmen liked the idea that they were free, and liked to think that they were exceptional in their freedom. It was true that after the revolution of 1688 and the establishment of the Protestant succession, the monarch's powers were constitutionally checked. It was true that the principle of religious toleration had gradually gained ground: dissenters, at least, were free to assemble and worship. And it was true that there was less censorship in Britain than was typically the case in other European nations. Yet, as Dr Johnson observed, for the poor, liberty meant the choice of working or starving. Those who strayed were subject to a terrifyingly harsh, if inefficient and pretty arbitrary, criminal code; their superiors had freedoms accorded or denied them by a thoroughly patriarchal social order. During those first freezing days of 1768, a baronet's daughter, prevented from eloping with a black footman, poisoned herself in Northamptonshire. She and her man may have taken liberties, but evidently had little chance to enjoy them.

English liberty meant something rather than nothing, despite its manifold inconsistencies, because it enabled the men and women of a Protestant nation to oppose themselves to the French, who were seen as the mean subjects of a despotic Catholic regime. This imagining of 'us and them', founded in an uncompromising religious antipathy like that between Christianity and Islam today, and exacerbated by intermittent and longstanding war, appears to have captured the hearts and minds of aristocrats and commoners alike throughout the eighteenth century. Few of the wealthy Britons who wrote about their tours to the Continent refrained from deploring the awful effects of absolute and arbitrary 'Papist' government upon populations, manners and morals. The idea that liberty was singularly English came unstuck with the American and French revolutions of the last quarter of the eighteenth century; until then, it was a value that few were prepared to eschew, and it had the authority of patriotism. It was this legitimacy that Wilkes audaciously seized, and which the common men and women grasped at in turn, as they shouted 'Wilkes and Liberty' and made London's streets and fields often unpredictable and dangerous places, in the first half of 1768. These people were free, at least, to denounce liberty's limits.

Cook's twelve naval years had been with men who were strangely positioned, in relation to this ideal, that was central to Englishness, awkwardly vital to Britishness. That the navy was nothing if not the bulwark of British prosperity and freedom was a point rammed home by many panegyrics. If, any time after 1730, visitors to Greenwich entered the Royal Hospital for seamen, they would have encountered the elaborate pictorial argument of James Thornhill's painted ceiling, that 'Our *Trade, Commerce* and *Public Wealth* are chiefly owing to our NAVY'. Had these persons walked through the park and up the hill, they would have seen a proof of these platitudes before them: their view was of the huge shipbuilding and refitting dock at Deptford, only one of the country's formidable naval facilities. The navy amounted to the biggest branch of British government, and was perhaps the grandest and costliest of any eighteenth century 'military industrial complex'. The awesome reality fostered notions conveyed through prints, plays and popular songs, notions at once grand and simple, associating a quintessentially English tree, the vessels that were made out of it, and the solid virtues of those who served in them.

> Hearts of oak are our ships,
> Hearts of oak are our men;
> We always are ready;
> Steady, boys, steady;
> We'll fight and we'll conquer again and again

went a popular song. Yet at the heart of the navy, and of its patriotic symbolism, was an injustice and a moral contradiction that was widely recognized as such. This was, of course, the system of recruitment through the press gang. Captain John Blake, one of many authors advocating reform, referred in his *Plan for Regulating the Marine System of Great Britain* to the 'oppressive, and unconstitutional methods' used to man the navy as 'evils . . . [that] deprive those of liberty, and almost every benefit of life, who are a great means of preserving liberty to Britons'. Here, an ordinary seaman describes and reflects upon a staggeringly bloody battle to obtain men from a homeward-bound merchant ship:

we scuttled their decks with axes and fired down amongst them, while they kept firing up at us . . . After having shot one of our men through the head, and another through both his thighs, they submitted, and we got 16 brave fellows . . . Such are the methods frequently made use of to obtain seamen for service in this land of liberty. It seems shocking for the feelings of humanity, for a sailor, after he has been a long voyage, endured innumerable hardships, and is just returning to his native land with the pleasing hope of beholding a beloved wife and children, some kind relations, or respected friends, to be forced away to fight, perhaps to fall, and no more enjoy those dear connexions – it is a hardship which nothing but absolute necessity can reconcile to our boasted freedom.

The observation that seamen were unfree men defending the free was not made only by writers of earnest reforming tracts. The routine use of the term 'libertymen' for those on shore leave underscored the brutal fact that once aboard, liberty was exactly what you did not have. Sheer physical confinement might be experienced on any ship, but those on naval vessels were under additional restraints that merchant sailors were not subjected to. The barbarity of naval discipline may well have been exaggerated, but there is no doubt that the regime was rigorous, and no surprise that comparisons were often made between naval ships and prisons.

If seamen were treated not only toughly but unjustly, could they have been governed otherwise? One man who had an answer was William Falconer. His *Universal Dictionary of the Marine* consisted mainly of short explanations of vessels' parts, rigs and manoeuvres; in only one passage did Falconer enlarge on the subject of society at sea. In his entry on midshipmen, he imagined the officer-to-be entering the service, regrettably labouring under misconceptions concerning discipline, men and officers that were widely held by people outside the navy.

No character, in their opinion, is more excellent than that of the common sailor, whom they generally suppose to be treated with great severity by his officers, drawing a comparison between them not very advantageous to the latter. The midshipman usually comes aboard tinctured with these prejudices, especially if his education has been amongst the higher rank of people; and if the officers happen to answer his opinion, he conceives an early disgust to the service, from a very partial and incompetent view of its operations. Blinded by these prepossessions, he is thrown off his guard, and very soon surprized to find, amongst those honest sailors, a crew of abandoned miscreants, ripe for any mischief or villainy. Perhaps, after a little observation, many of them will appear to him equally destitute of gratitude, shame, or justice, and only deterred from the commission of any crimes by the terror of severe punishment. He will discover that the pernicious example of a few of the vilest in a ship of war are too often apt to poison the principles of the greatest number, especially if the reins of discipline are too much relaxed, so as to foster that idleness and dissipation, which engender sloth, diseases, and an utter profligacy of manners.

In May 1768, about the time Falconer composed this unforgiving assessment, a ship called the *Free Love* could have been found among the diverse and numerous vessels on the Thames. Cook had once known it well. Just over twenty years earlier, in 1747, he had been apprenticed to its owner, John Walker, of Whitby, and had twice done the sort of voyage the *Free Love* was still doing, from Whitby to the Tyne for coal and to London. This sort of ship – a 'cat', something over ninety feet long, something less than thirty broad – was on a more human scale than the wooden warriors that were under construction downriver at Deptford. Her stern was square and her bottom was flat. Between voyages, Cook had slept in the attic of Walker's house. He would have seen vessels like the *Free Love* assembled in the yards across the river.

As ships entered the river Esk during the summers, the narrow lanes of Whitby were crowded with men lugging rope, timber, sails and seamen's chests, on or off boats. On the *Free Love* Cook would at first have felt clumsy, he would maybe have been berated and beaten by a dissolute mate; but he was not slow to learn the ship's tasks, parts and motions, and become acquainted with the hazy calms and ordinary violence of the North Sea. In the intervals between trips to the Baltic and to English ports he might have sat in awe, listening to Walker's conversation with fellow-merchants and Quaker friends, which ranged over the great world of commerce and the spiritual voyages of seamen.

Twenty years later the *Free Love* had not changed, but its crew had, again and again. Cook would not have known a man aboard, though they were still in Walker's pay, and would know others of his acquaintance in Whitby. A few of those he'd sailed with perhaps remained on colliers, but many had been pressed, and others had joined Atlantic or East India ships and then been pressed, or drowned. By this time, Cook had other things to think about. Not only Yorkshire, but Newfoundland had receded into the past. He was still in London, but his mind already tried to get to grips with a new sort of voyage to a new world.

2

Banks's books

This was once the New Road, made broad and unpaved so that cattle and sheep could be taken to market without stinking and shitting their way through Westminster and the West End. Now it is Euston Road and it is the red buses and black taxis that stink their way past the British Library. This morning I walked there, past the Quaker meeting house, archive and shop, where they sell any number of books about their founder, George Fox, and have a few files relating to Yorkshire in the eighteenth century. There, last year, I learnt that Cook's Whitby employer, John Walker, had been expelled from the Society because he had supplied his ships with guns. The French privateers active in the North Sea clearly presented a more compelling argument than the Friends' principles.

Getting into the British Library is a little like joining a flight. You must check in your bag and coat, ascend staircases, traverse foyers and produce your ticket, probably twice, before entering the insulated and unreal space of Rare Books and Music. The place feels at an absolute remove from the traffic, homeless people and Irish theme pub on the street. Yet if you or I enter the library to read up on London at the time of the *Endeavour*'s departure for the Pacific, this city of books seems not so remote from the city outside. In 1768 Cook's London was nothing if not a world city, at once a place of corruption and luxury, experimental knowledge, the frippery of Francophile fashion, a new kind of public painting, pervasive prostitution, violence and poverty. Privileged Londoners had access to science, music, the theatre, and more books than had ever before been published anywhere, but considered nothing to be as extraordinary as their own opportunities to shop. 'A Man who has Money, may have at once every delicate, every dainty, and every ornamental Beauty of the four Quarters of the World. Asia, Europe, Africa and America are ransacked to indulge the Inhabitants in every Luxury,' a journalist remarked in the early 1770s. Even the 'Common Drink' of the English peasant was, he observed, made of a Chinese plant and West Indian sugar. The consumerism that London remains besotted with, like the globalization that is still a buzz word, was very much in evidence in the second half of the eighteenth century, as for that matter were some of the people who were both victims and agents of global trade. There may have been 7,000 blacks in Cook's metropolis; there were certainly many in his own maritime neighbourhoods.

Here, in Rare Books, one finds late-eighteenth-century writers remarking not only upon the stock topics of London's richness and London's immorality, but also upon the radical differences of manners and customs that separated the populations of parts of the city, one from another.

The seamen here are a generation differing from all the world. When one goes into Rotherhithe and Wapping, which places are chiefly inhabited by sailors, but that somewhat of the same language is spoken, a man could be apt to suspect himself in another country. Their manner of living, speaking, acting, dressing, and behaving, are so very peculiar to themselves.

Strangely, the foreign could be found not only across the channel but in the heart of the capital, and here, those who seemed to come from another country were simply seamen. In the abstract, these 'tars' were quintessentially British, but in the flesh, they appeared to be made not by their nation but their occupation. From the perspective of an English writer, their characters were exotic rather than exemplary. They were fish out of water; they were incomprehensible.

Europeans at this time were thinking and writing increasingly about how people, and whole populations, differed. In some cases differences were presumed to be primarily physical; in others they were manifest rather in the temper and 'genius' – meaning the singular character – of some set of people. Debate about human variety and its causes was often both speculative and practical. The most general questions of global geography, climates, manners and useful arts were discussed by authors who were not dilettantes, but the advocates or critics of particular colonial enterprises and branches of trade. The local and the remote, the familiar and the unfamiliar, the places mariners came from, and those they searched out, all entered into kinds of writing that lay behind many eighteenth-century maritime ventures, and notably behind voyages of discovery such as that of the *Endeavour*.

Here, in the British Library, several different stacks of books might gather on your desk as you collect those that shaped the *Endeavour*'s voyage. One might be made up of books of navigational method and astronomical observation, like those Cook had studied and that Mount and Page printed and sold. Another would consist of naval histories and compendia of voyages that would tell you how Cook's predecessors located islands and lost them. Still others would be made up of botanical and zoological works that, obviously enough, provided models for the gathering of information. Your pile could also include books that would seem to have nothing to do with a sea voyage, such as esoteric works on the history of law and religion, which, however, included remarks on nomadic peoples and Islanders. And many books would be between piles, somehow reconciling the most practical matters of ship management and the most rarefied of speculative anthropology.

Take, for example, these two blue-black leather volumes that have worn edges and broken covers, their pages here and there creased, unevenly stained, their folding maps torn. This copy of Charles de Brosses's *Histoire des navigations aux terres australes* – published in Paris in 1756 – has been thumbed and read, not only by many British Library readers before me, but also by Joseph Banks, who acquired the book and put his odd asymmetrical bookplate in it when he was as rakish a character as other rich young men, yet quite unlike them in being passionate about science as well as about pleasure. He probably took this book round the world in the *Endeavour* with him. This anthology of voyages to the south typifies the wonderfully undisciplined character of eighteenth-century thought, which touches on the vanity of kings in one paragraph, the physics of the world in a second and the height of Patagonians in a third. More importantly, it provides us with a plot for Cook's first (and indeed his second) voyage. For de Brosses's book was not just a history of what had been done. It was an argument for what ought to be done.

The quest for the southern continent that de Brosses advocated may not provide the most obvious context for the *Endeavour*'s voyage. It is well known that the immediate motivation for the mission was the Royal Society's interest in observing the transit of Venus. From the late seventeenth century, scientists had recognized that the precise measurement of this phenomenon, from suitably situated and dispersed stations around the world, would enable for the first time the calculation of the actual distance between the earth and the sun. Transits occur in pairs, the second eight years later than the first, the pairs more than a century apart. Observations in 1761 were inadequate, and the mathematicians of the various European scientific academies were desperate not to botch the last chance of a lifetime to make this decisive astronomical advance. The prevailing peace made international liaison easier and efforts were made to co-ordinate as large a number of expeditions as possible. If, inevitably, some scientists would travel for months and spend weeks establishing their observatories and getting dysentery all in order to see nothing but clouds, others surely would be luckier. From 1766 the matter was on the Royal Society's agendas. The King and Admiralty were lobbied to support observation from the South Sea, as the Pacific was commonly called; the earls and lords among the Society's members no doubt helped ensure that the proposals were favourably received. In short, it was agreed that a naval vessel would be provided, to carry observers to one of the islands known from earlier Spanish or Dutch voyages, from which the transit could be observed.

This act of looking was the chief purpose of Cook's voyage. It was the one set out in the instructions, the statement of directions signed by the Admiralty lords, which provided the official basis for his command. These instructions, however, stipulated that once the transit had been observed, Cook was to open a further set of supposedly secret directions – the content of which cannot have surprised him much if he indeed restrained himself from reading them until after the astronomical job had been done, in Tahiti. They indicated that the voyage had a further project, that Banks was aware of and anxious to be party to. They made the voyage a sequel to a number of earlier efforts to probe southern latitudes for land. As such, the expedition was not just a rational plan to fill spaces on a map, but also a symptom of a state of enchantment.

Charles de Brosses would have been offended by this suggestion that he was the carrier of a contagious fantasy. He saw himself as a critical analyst of the fanciful and the mystical. In 1760 he had published a treatise that had introduced the famous idea of fetishism – extrapolated from travellers' tales of west African practices – which was to prove enduringly suggestive for European thinkers from Marx to Freud and beyond. In his discourses upon southern lands, however, de Brosses exercised a mental faculty other than the reasoned scepticism that has become the hallmark of the Enlightenment. An islet discerned through mist, a rumoured cape, a bank of cloud, were all as good as landmasses. Conjoined with the theory that the northern continents required southern counterweights, the existence of the continent could be regarded as certain rather than merely probable. De Brosses was in no sense the first to engage in these wishful mappings. The *Histoire des navigations aux terres australes* is germane here because it brought an old idea up to date and articulated it in a way that captured the attention of scientists, merchants and Admiralty lords in the 1760s.

George III might have read and taken to heart de Brosses's admonition that kings ought to seek glory, not through war and the loss or ruin of their subjects' lives, but through the greater and more noble pursuit of discoveries.

In any event, soon after the peace of 1763, unusual secrecy surrounded the departure of the *Dolphin* and the *Swallow* under John Byron. The new voyage was not, as was generally broadcast, simply one to the East Indies, but one that responded directly to de Brosses's arguments that considerable lands were to be found in the south, containing unknown products and uncontacted peoples. Byron's secret instructions directed him to search the south Atlantic for these lands, and, as though this were not a task and a half, to seek out a passage from the west coast of north America to Hudson's Bay – this famous but hypothetical and elusive North-West Passage would have given Britain far more direct access to east Asian markets than routes via either India or South America permitted. Byron made only half-hearted attempts to locate either of these fabled objects; but fleeting visits to certain Polynesian atolls, which I discuss further below, suggested to him that chains of islands were perhaps linked to a larger landmass. The south Pacific rather than the south Atlantic might therefore profitably be explored further. On his return one Samuel Wallis, a veteran of General Wolfe's Quebec victory, was accordingly dispatched in that direction, again in the *Dolphin*. His instructions, like Byron's, anticipated that 'Lands or Islands of Great Extent, hitherto unvisited' might be found in the south, 'in Climates adapted to the produce of Commodities useful in Commerce'. Wallis made the notable discovery of the island of Tahiti, but otherwise his explorations were not much less half-hearted than his predecessor's. Cook was in turn instructed to make a further attempt to locate the great southern land.

De Brosses had argued that the connections between the known land-masses of America, Asia and Africa meant that essentially the same things and animals were known everywhere. The latter dispersed themselves and were adapted to different climates, but belonged in effect to known kinds. The southern continent, on the other hand, was wholly separated from other lands, and would therefore constitute a truly new world, where one would encounter 'new sorts of entirely new things, whole branches of new commerce, and marvellous physical and moral spectacles'. Or, as Joseph Banks put it, expressing less the euphoria of the theoretician than the self-deprecating confidence of a twenty-five-year-old aristocrat, 'If we proceed to make discoveries on the Terra Australis Incognita I shall probably have a finer opportunity for the Exercise of my Poor Abilities than ever man had before as there seems to be a strong Probability from the Scarce intelligible accounts of Travellers that almost Every Production of Nature is here very different from what we see at this end of the Globe.' He had, by April 1768, absorbed the theory from these battered blue-black books. The proposed voyage was just about public; the negotiations between the Royal Society and the Admiralty, and his own lobbying, had satisfactorily progressed. Hence Banks's scarcely guarded letter to his antiquarian friend Falconer. He would put the theory into practice, and indeed encounter entirely new things and creatures.

One reality of the 1760s is permanently lost to us, and this is the genuine plausibility that the southern continent possessed. Towards the end of May 1768, news arrived in London that gave credence to the most optimistic of speculations that rich and marvellous lands were to be found in the South Sea.

These reports were of decisive importance in refining plans for the voyage to observe the transit of Venus, for which preparations were well advanced. A Whitby cat, the same kind of vessel as the *Free Love*, had been chosen. The abundant space for stores was highly desirable in a voyage that would be much longer than any typical naval excursion in the north Atlantic; a strong vessel that would ride out storms well was very necessary, particularly to make the notoriously difficult passage against adverse winds around Cape Horn. And it would be highly advantageous if a ship could be beached upright, given the likely need for refitting or repair at some stage during the voyage. The *Earl of Pembroke*, the ship that was bought, had been built in 1764, in yards that Cook would have seen across the river Esk every time he looked or stepped out of the back of John Walker's house. He had probably not been back to Whitby for well over ten years, but here and there, up and down the Thames, Whitby constructions kept coming to him.

In my schoolboy sense of Cook, I always supposed that *Endeavour* was the name the captain gave the ship, a sort of emanation of the spirit that he uniquely possessed. So far as can be established, Cook had nothing to do with it; though the name was a better choice than could possibly have been anticipated, by whichever Admiralty functionary was responsible. The ship could just as easily have been called the *Racehorse* or even the *Carcass* – those were the names of the vessels which Banks's friend Phipps assumed command of, a year or so later, to explore the Arctic – names which would rather have diminished the mythic potential of Cook's voyage, one feels. In any event, the ship was selected and named just before a decision was made, early in April, to transfer Cook from the Newfoundland survey and give him the command of the expedition. During April and May the *Endeavour* was sheathed, fitted and supplied in the Deptford yards – a business that was fraught and interrupted by the riots of the sailors and coal-heavers. In early May the Royal Society agreed that the two observers of the transit should be the astronomer Charles Green and Cook himself. At a subsequent meeting remunerations were determined; whatever else Cook felt about the voyage, he must have been delighted by a decided enhancement of his finances. As master and surveyor in Newfoundland he had received £4 a month. He would now get, in addition to his pay, an honorarium of 100 guineas, as well as £120 per annum for the course of the voyage, to provide for both his own and Green's victuals.

A few days after this second meeting of the Royal Society's Council, the London newspapers announced that the *Dolphin* had just returned from her second voyage round the world. The reports of Wallis's voyage dealt exclusively with the discovery 'of a large, fertile, and extremely populous Island in the South-Seas'. They explained that the inhabitants had had no prior contact with Europeans and were initially hostile. Both these general points were true. The detail that followed was generally dubious. The Islanders' singular method of attacking the ship, it was reported, had entailed sending two separate parties, one of women who distracted the sailors 'by exposing their Beauties to their View, whilst the Men from the Canoes threw great Quantities of Stones'. The following day, efforts to collect water were resisted and a further attack was made on the *Dolphin*. The mariners were then obliged 'to have Recourse to the disagreeable Necessity of firing some of their great Guns at them, charged with Grape-Shot', while cannon-balls were also turned upon houses inland. The Islanders were said to have been awestruck by the lethal force of these weapons, and 'looked on our People, as more than human'. They sued for peace immediately, and sub-sequently engaged in an amicable trade, supplying provisions in exchange for nails and trinkets. A queen, who was not identified by name, was supposed to be the ruler of the island. On her surrender, possession was taken of what was called King George's Land, the merits of which were said to be inexpressible: ''Tis impossible to describe the beautiful Prospects we beheld in this charming Spot; the Verdure is as fine as that of England; there is great Plenty of live Stock, and it abounds with all the choicest Productions of the Earth.'

This abbreviated report omitted much detail that reached the Admiralty, which remained unpublished for some years. But the less that was said, the better. Though the show of firepower had been disagreeable, it appeared that it had had swift results. Both British superiority and friendly relations appeared to have been firmly established, and even sentimentally concluded. On the departure of the British, the queen 'expressed the most lively Sorrow . . . and the last Thing she did was to take the Crown from her own Head, and present it to Captain Wallace'. In fact, there were no 'queens' in Tahiti, though there were prominent and powerful women, of whom this one, Purea, was at the time most influential. Her temple or *marae* at Mahiatea had been recently completed, and was probably the most impressive and ritually potent edifice ever constructed on the island. Her confidant was Tupaia, a priest, a political strategist, less the stereotypic tribal elder steeped in tradition than an indigenous intellectual with experimental inclinations. In these senses and others, Purea was powerfully equipped, but was not a 'queen' and neither she nor any other Tahitian wore anything resembling a crown. In their journals, both Wallis and the *Dolphin*'s master, George Robertson, agree that she was disconsolate and distressed by the departure of the British. If this was true, it was probably because she had staked something of her reputation on an alliance with them rather than because she'd fallen in love and was missing them already. The gift of the crown can only have been a nonsense concocted somewhere between Plymouth and a London printer, by someone who felt that something was lacking, that the story of the Tahitian submission to the British was inadequate without this symbolic conclusion.

It is perhaps not surprising that the report was elaborated upon in this way. Those who look back from the early twenty-first century upon the whole history of global imperialism must have the sense that lands were routinely taken and people regularly subdued without compunction. The proponents of exploration in the late eighteenth century went, however, to considerable pains to define liberal commerce as something utterly different to the Iberian conquest of America – which they dismissed as a vicious looting operation. It was anticipated – in de Brosses's theory of colonization, and the Admiralty instructions to Byron, Wallis, and Cook – that what were called 'convenient situations' might be purchased with the consent of a country's inhabitants, which would provide bases for a mutually beneficial commerce. The potential of the model to produce a more humane colonization may be judged by de Brosses's unfortunate choice of a south African illustration in support of his thesis. He believed that the Dutch at the Cape of Good Hope had 'never distressed' the so-called Hottentots, and that the latter had in return made themselves useful to the settlers. Social conditions at the Cape were actually well known in Europe, and this port that demanded land and produce and yet was supposed to have left natives undisturbed was a fiction of wishful ignorance. Yet the rhetoric could not acknowledge the inevitable consequences of imperial expansion, and official directions included what amounted to ethical guidelines: invasive actions were implicitly prohibited, and all efforts had to be made to establish and sustain good relations with local inhabitants.

The claim, of course, was that the ship had been stoned and that the *Dolphin*'s cannonade was hence defensive and legitimate. But the stoning was maybe itself an equally legitimate and defensive Tahitian response to the aggression of the ship's arrival. Irrespective of how the Tahitians understood the action, the murkiness of the conflict could readily have been inferred by an English reader, who might also have thought that the bombardment was out of proportion to the Tahitian threat. It was a sensitive point. An engraving, printed some years later, represented the conflict as rather a splendid affair. Presumably the artist, who had nothing but a written description to go on, borrowed the visual formula of the naval battle scene and hence depicted the Tahitians being subjected to the sort of crushing defeat that was routinely inflicted, to the satisfaction of the patriotic viewer, on the French or Spaniards. But the Tahitians were not continental Catholic enemies. Rather, they were people who reasonably enough resisted an intrusion upon their own land. The print was described by the geographer Alexander Dalrymple as 'Disgraceful to an English book'. He admittedly bore the navy a grudge – he had wanted to command the *Endeavour* – but he was by no means alone in believing that the British conduct raised questions of justice and morality.

Cook probably saw both the newspaper report and the fuller documents in due course. In some form, the latter must have been made available to him, because it was decided very soon after Wallis's return that 'King George's Land' was the place from which the transit would be observed. Tahiti's longitude had been carefully established. It could not only be readily found, it was a well-provisioned and now pacified British possession.

Cook no doubt talked to Wallis, or at any rate some of his men. He might have been disturbed, as he learned more of the violence that had marked the first contacts between the British and these Polynesians. The newspaper had implied that the use of guns had resulted very promptly in a Tahitian surrender. In fact, skirmishes in which the mariners killed Tahitians continued intermittently for a week. The battle referred to in the report had extended over a full day. A further major confrontation was actually initiated by the British, who fired pre-emptively on canoes that they thought were preparing to attack. It is now impossible to establish how many were killed or injured in these shows of force. Cannonballs discharged in the general direction of scattered houses can only have produced random victims, but grapeshot aimed in calm conditions into crowded canoes within stone-throwing distance of the *Dolphin* must have caused many deaths. Yet the published claim that the Tahitians were awestruck and regarded the British as gods was plainly nonsense. Even after the lethal effects of firearms were

6. *The* Dolphin's *assault on the Tahitians at Matavai Bay, June 1767.*
Engraving from John Hawkesworth, An Account of the Voyages
Undertaken by order of his present Majesty for Making Discoveries
in the Southern Hemisphere, *London, 1773.*

well understood, they sustained their resistance. Hostilities seem to have
been brought to an end not by any Tahitian action that amounted to a
surrender, but by gifts that produced a truce, at first an uneasy one, but one
that made further exchanges possible. Both sides were anxious to put an
end to violence, the British because they desperately needed fresh water and
provisions, the Tahitians because they knew that they could best resist these
people by accommodating them.

By the beginning of June 1768, Cook knew that he would spend some
weeks on this island, and knew that he would have to live with people who
would not have forgotten their last encounters with men on British ships.
The drama of this bloody, then supposedly happy and finally sentimental,
first encounter between a 'new people' and European power must have
brought to mind what Cook already knew of conflicts with native peoples.
We have no report that he personally had been caught up in violent encounters in Canada, but over his years around uneasily colonized Newfoundland
coasts he must have been struck, as Banks had been, by the relentless
intrusion that made the Beothuk refugees in their own land. He might have
gathered that questions of sovereignty and rights to resources tended to be

resolved neither swiftly nor definitively. He should have suspected that the Tahitian 'surrender' was a provisional way of managing British superiority, not a permanent acceptance of it. But it seems (from what he says later on) that he was not yet sceptical. He took Wallis's report more or less at face value. He thought that a show of force had solved a problem, and would presume that it might do so again.

A further piece of information that came back with Wallis featured in no public report. This was the sighting of mountains to the south, as Tahiti was approached. 'We was now fully persuaded that this was a part of the southern continent,' George Robertson had written on 20 June 1767; but on the departure from the island, Wallis was preoccupied with his own sickness and that of other men, and made no attempt to confirm that land existed, instead sailing east for a faster voyage home. The apparent sighting seems to have been kept secret to diminish the possibility that rival expeditions might take prior possession or be the first to open up trade with the new land. Cook's additional instructions resembled Byron's and Wallis's in directing him to seek 'a Continent or Land of great extent', but now there was a difference. For the first time, this land had a definite location, and – if Tahiti was taken to be representative – it was indeed a place of superabundance.

An enduring stereotype of eighteenth-century naval life imagines a deep division between officers and common seamen. In fact, even though many ships carried representatives of the very wealthy as well as the very poor, none exhibited a clean class divide. The hierarchies of naval vessels were manifold. 'Able' or experienced seamen had different roles and entitlements to 'ordinary' men and to newly recruited 'landmen'; ratings, warrant officers such as mates and masters, and commissioned officers such as lieutenants all occupied intermediate situations between captains and common seamen. Occupations, especially on larger vessels, were highly differentiated: there were gunners, coopers, carpenters, barbers, cooks, chaplains and surgeons; many of these, as well as officers, had 'servants' who were often deputies rather than personal attendants. There were status differences that arose from age and experience as well as rank and role. And there was, in any case, no typical ship. The social dynamics of the very large warships, which might carry 800 or more men, were quite different to those of small vessels, in which tasks were inevitably shared and ranks less differentiated.

The *Endeavour* and her crew were different again – made more or less out of naval ingredients, but amounting to something fundamentally different. In general, naval ships were made to fight, or at any rate to support and supply fighting fleets. Their designs differed from merchant ships because they were built around cannons rather than cargo. However infrequently battle actually took place, their personnel were organized around imperatives to sail, manoeuvre and maintain fire. In a social and economic sense they were also, at least during wartime, driven by the aspiration to capture prizes, the values of which were divided among commanders, officers and ordinary seamen, from time to time bringing spectacular reward. The *Endeavour* carried guns but was not a fighting ship. It was instead an adapted trading vessel crammed with a singular and specialized human cargo, and with the provisions and equipment that that cargo required. Its voyage would be considerably longer than any normal naval cruise. Its crew were excluded from the prospect of obtaining prizes; and in many cases their experience would not have prepared them for the opportunity. It is true that Cook's first naval years gave him fairly standard wartime experience. But from as early as 1758 he was beginning to be a surveyor, and, as we have seen, he became a professional. The *Grenville* was a navy ship but one dedicated to capturing coastlines, not French merchant ships. The gear that the ship carried, the kinds of manoeuvres it made, its day-to-day business, all revolved around navigational observation and map-making rather than actions which were either immediately aggressive or defensive, or connected with the servicing of fleets.

When he was given the command of the *Endeavour*, Cook followed conventional practice and took men from the *Grenville* with him. William Howson and Thomas Hardman had sailed with him only a year, John Charlton had been with him three years and Peter Flower had been with him five years. If these four had some experience of surveying operations, Isaac Smith, Elizabeth Cook's cousin, apparently had positive aptitude, and was something of a draughtsman himself. It is not surprising, given the decision to return to the place that Wallis had presumed to call King George's Land, that the *Dolphin*'s crew should also have been drawn upon. One man, lieutenant John Gore, had in fact been around the world twice in that ship, with Byron on his voyage from 1764 to 1766 and with Wallis from 1766 to 1768. Both Francis Haite and Charles Clerke had been on the first voyage but not the second; three others had sailed with Wallis but not Byron. By the standards of the time, or by any standards, these men had already led rather extraordinary lives. Though the Pacific had been crossed by Magellan more than 200 years earlier, it was still an unknown ocean of enlarged distances. From the perspectives of its Polynesian inhabitants *te moana*, the sea, was nothing like this: it was no fluid emptiness, but a place of marine paths suspended beneath a stellar map. From Micronesia in the north-west to Hawaii in the east and New Zealand in the far south, Islanders knew currents, constellations, routes and the places and people at the end

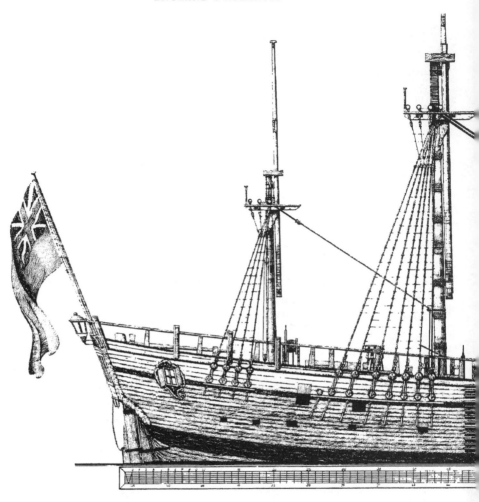

A RECONSTRUCTION BASED ON ADMIRALTY DRAUGHTS 3814; PARKINSON DRAWINGS 1769 ; DEPTFORD YARD OFFICERS REPORT
TACKLES ; BOWER ANCHOR BEING FISHED;MAIN & MIZEN TOPMASTS HUNG ON MAST-ROP

7. H.M. Bark Endeavour, *profile drawing by Ray Parkin.*

of them as well as any Baltic trader knew his passages. The Islanders were, as de Brosses guessed, in communication with each other, but over greater distances than he would have thought possible.

Those who had been on the *Dolphin*'s first voyage had experienced the daunting storms of Cape Horn. They learned the 'strange dejection of spirits' and the relentless erosion of bodily well-being brought about by scurvy – then regarded as an almost magical disease for the diversity of its awful

*PMAN 1768; FALCONER 1780; STEEL 1794; REES 1819, &c.: SHEWING LOWER MASTS, BOWSPRIT & RIGGING; FORE & MAIN HATCH
:ED.*

manifestations. They had also glimpsed Pacific islands and Islanders. Byron deftly missed all the larger Polynesian archipelagos, but passed a few of the dozens of Tuamotu atolls that form a long scatter of reefs and low islets to the north-east of Tahiti. Approaching one of these, called Tepoto, in June 1765, he sighted 'Savages' who appeared to make signal fires, but was frustrated by the lack of any harbour:

the whole Island was surrounded with a steep Coral Rock. That news was great grief to us, for had I found a place to anchor the Ships, I intended to have landed my Sick here, & have remained till they recover'd, as this little beautiful Spot seemed to promise all the Refreshments necessary for Scorbutick People [i.e., those stricken with scurvy]. We saw abundance of Cocoa Trees, & I make no doubt but there are Limes, Bananas &cᵃ common to most places between the Tropics.

This romantic response to a fairly arid atoll tells us just how desperate a long sea passage made mariners for land and fruit, even though the inhabitants brandished spears and appeared intent on resisting any landing. A further island, which appeared 'vastly pleasant', was likewise devoid of any safe anchorage. Here Byron fired nine-pound shot to disperse those who shouted threats from the beach, a pointless aggression since he had in any case to sail on, naming the group the Islands of Disappointment. A further long low island, Takaroa, was sighted. Once again, this looked 'extremely pleasant full of Coco Nut trees &c'. Here Islanders came off in canoes, and stole or tried to steal articles of clothing. After trying unsuccessfully to procure refreshments from the adjacent atoll of Takapoto – where stone-throwing Islanders were again fired upon and '5 or 6', according to Byron, killed – cannon were used to frighten the inhabitants of Takaroa away from an inlet that served as a landing place. While the *Dolphin* stood off, parties went ashore and appropriated several boatloads of coconuts. They were delighted also to find much 'scurvy grass'; the people of the island remained hidden while the British poked around among their houses and belongings.

The following day, back at Takapoto, 'a very stout venerable looking old Man, with a long white Beard, who seemed to be their King' addressed 'a long Song' to the visitors and waded out into the water to present them with a green bough. When this was accepted, he in turn accepted a few trinkets they threw towards him and further gifts were exchanged, but the mariners (who had discovered pearl oyster shells) were unable to make their keenness to trade for pearls understood. The lack of an anchorage deprived Byron of any opportunity to try further, though he was confident that they would soon have been able to communicate and perhaps obtain pearls in exchange for hatchets and iron. He sailed on, pausing to reflect a day or two later that the presence of people on these atolls could not be accounted for unless a chain of islands reached all the way to a continent.

Byron formed no real impression of the people themselves, but was struck by the ingenuity manifest in their artefacts, notably two canoes which the British had appropriated: 'the Plank is extremely well worked & carved in many places. It is sewed together, & over every Seam is a strip of Tortoise Shell to keep the water out. Their Cordage is as good & well laid as any I ever saw tho' made out of the rind of Coco Nutt.' For more than twenty years, looking at boats and assessing the quality of rope had been part of Byron's job. Small wonder that what we might call his anthropological observations began with Polynesian canoes, the planks of which were in fact sewn together with coconut fibre cord, ingeniously through diagonal holes that were all on the boat's inside. He went on, however, to record the 'great veneration' for the dead manifest in carefully tended graves, 'something like our Tombs in Country Church Yards'. He remarked on the cloth made by women, and on the houses, which he thought were mean and low. These were literally 'observations', in the sense that they were statements of things seen, and not of meanings communicated. Byron had seen people from a distance, and inspected their houses and ritual sites in their absence. His show of force had made his undisturbed inspection possible, and made it inevitable that it would be a tour without a guide. No one could try to explain, even by sign language or gesture, why turtle heads and bones were hung from the boughs of trees over graves. No one could tell him who lived here or owned that canoe.

Over a few days in June 1765, Gore, Clerke and Haite had met, or rather sighted, their first Polynesians. We do not know what roles they played in these hurried and tense visits. Were they among the men who remained on the ship and had merely glimpsed 'savages' with spears shouting from a beach? Or had they ventured into the village with Byron? Was Gore, who was often later the first to venture ashore, the man who plunged into the surf and made a gift of his waistcoat?

Wallis's Tahitian discovery, marked as it had been by exchanges of stones and cannon fire, was a replay on a grander and bloodier scale of Byron's Tuamotuan encounters; the actuality of the experience, as opposed to the report, could only have reinforced a sense that the people were immediately intractable, though perhaps subsequently manageable. The presence of these populations hinted at, but hardly disclosed, the reality of a southern land; their behaviour did not suggest that it would be easy to secure the 'convenient situations' which the Admiralty wanted purchased; and the mutually benevolent commerce, which these trading stations were supposed to enable, must have seemed as enchanted a notion as that of the southern continent itself.

I have no idea what proportion of fantasy and scepticism occupied the mind of Gore or Clerke, or Haite. The records leave us with a paradoxical sense of the quality of observations made on Byron's voyage. On the one hand what is said of the Tuamotuan peoples is plausible, so far as it goes. The characterizations of canoes, cloth and implements are right; the description of the mortuary place is consistent with later and more detailed accounts of such precincts on many other Polynesian islands. It is, for that matter, consistent with the look of sites that can still be visited today. All this would lend support to a sense that these voyagers were empirically minded, even floating agents of Enlightenment reason. But, on the other hand, Byron not only reported the natural riches of tiny islands in fantastic terms, he also 'confirmed' an old report that the inhabitants of Patagonia were giants. Accounts of astonishingly large people in the southern extremities of the American continent went back to Magellan's circumnavigation and had been rejected and revived by various subsequent navigators. It is not surprising that the announcement, on Byron's return, that most Patagonians were around nine feet high met with some scepticism. It is more remarkable that the Royal Society, the pre-eminent vehicle of English rational inquiry, not only listened to but published a paper by none other than Charles Clerke, who was to sail with Cook. This communication advised that, out of a crowd of some 500 Patagonians, 'there was hardly a man less than eight feet' tall, while the women ranged 'from 7½ to 8'. There is something impressive about the fact that Clerke, a mere midshipman, a farmer's son, might impose such a story on the most distinguished astronomers, physicians and natural historians of his time, many of whom were wealthy and politically influential men. He did so in a tongue-in-cheek fashion, hoping that his eminent audience would find them 'amusing or agreeable', apologizing for his lack of literary qualification and trusting that they would have the 'goodness to excuse a tar's dialect' – which dialect, needless to say, was in no way evident in his respectable prose.

The eleven men who joined the *Endeavour* from the *Grenville* and the *Dolphin* brought experience of geographic investigations, of first contacts with indigenous peoples and of the myth-making and contention that often surrounded the publication of discoveries. No doubt much other remarkable experience joined the new voyage through the ship's company, but we know very little of the lives of the other sixty-five seamen and twelve marines. Not all were British: they included Antonio Punto and John Dozey, from Venice and somewhere in Brazil respectively. Isaac George Manley, the master's servant, who was twelve, seems to have been the youngest; the oldest was probably the sailmaker John Ravenhill, at forty-nine ten years older than Cook. Most others were in their twenties. This age range, and the presence of a couple of foreigners, was nothing unusual. One of the younger men, however, represented a group which made the voyage wholly different from any previous British maritime venture.

In addition to the seamen and marines (who were generally looked down upon by sailors) the *Endeavour* carried supernumeraries. Joseph Banks, together with Constantine Phipps, had already travelled on a naval vessel in this capacity to Newfoundland. There was nothing odd about super-numeraries as such, though they were usually pilots, survivors of wrecks or members of an Admiral's retinue, and not gentlemen scientists. Banks, however, had an ambitious sense of the possibilities of the voyage. Today, the notion that researchers work in teams under the direction of a senior scientist is wholly familiar; in the eighteenth century, anyone with the leisure to pursue experiments would have had servants and assistants, but Banks's vigorous mobilization of a support staff designed to broaden the reach and efficacy of a natural history expedition was unprecedented. Opportunities to observe, describe and collect in the course of the *Endeavour* voyage would not be missed simply because he personally was unwell, as he had been during his Newfoundland stay. The mere inclusion of scientists on such expeditions was still unusual. Small wonder that Banks's novel pro-posals had been resisted by the Admiralty. Some must have felt that a vessel with such a large civilian party ceased to be manageable in the customary naval manner. Influence and diplomacy, however, paid off, and it was agreed that Banks would be accompanied by two naturalists, two artists, two footmen and two black servants. (The astronomer Charles Green was another supernumerary, though he was one of the Royal Society's two nominated observers of the transit – the other being Cook himself – rather than a member of Banks's party.) The perception among scientists at the time was that no expense was spared in the equipment of this team.

They have got a fine library of Natural History; they have all sorts of machines for catching and preserving insects; all kinds of nets, trawls, drags and hooks for coral fishing; they have even a curious contrivance of a telescope, by which, put into the water, you can see the bottom to a great depth, where it is clear. They have many cases of bottles with ground stoppers, of several sizes, to preserve animals in spirits. They have the several sorts of salt to surround the seeds; and wax, both beeswax and the *Myrica*; besides there are many people whose sole business it is to attend them for this very purpose.

If you went to school in Australia you would have learned as I did that Banks was a botanist. This would not have been inaccurate, in the sense that botany was indeed his particular passion, but it left you with an impoverished sense of the scope of his interests, which in fact embraced an extraordinary range of animate and inanimate things, and were not even limited, as the list of his team's equipment may suggest, to the observation of natural phenomena. In this period natural history was truly capacious, and trespassed into just about every field of history and human activity. We have some sense of the reach of Banks's curiosity from what he recorded in the course of short journeys within Britain – journeys that anticipated, on a domestic scale, the more ambitious voyages that he hoped to undertake. He would notice herbs, pick flowers, take ladies to visit docks, describe cathedrals and call on a country gentleman to see his stuffed hawk. It is not hard to see why natural history was regarded as foolishly eclectic, and even immoral: Linnaeus's sexual system for classifying plants was considered a sort of veiled pornography. But Banks was not in fact totally indiscriminate in his interests. He was fascinated by the productive nexus between natural life and human activity, and though he could be diverted by any oddity at all, he would return to more serious inquiry into extractive processes, into the utility of minerals, plants and materials, and into the techniques of operations such as brewing. He would look at anything, but his mind was often on how some branch of industry might be increased and improved.

It is Friday, 15 August 1768. The *Endeavour* under Cook's command has already left Deptford, for Plymouth. A young Swiss aristocrat, Horace Benedict de Saussure, goes to the opera in London.

Saw for the first time Miss Harriet Blosset, with Mr Banks, her betrothed. Returned on foot from the opera with them and supped together. The eldest daughter, tall, decided, agreeable, a great musician, splendid voice, fond of society, polished. The second Miss Harriet, desperately in love with Mr Banks, from whom she was to part next day – hitherto a prudent coquette, but now only intent on pleasing her lover, and resolved to spend in the country all the time he is away. The youngest, a Methodist devote, delighted to pass two or three years in the country with her sister and live out of the world. The mother, a good-natured little woman, talking politics. As Banks cannot speak a word of French, I could not judge of his abilities. He seems to have a prodigious zest for natural history. I supped there with him and Dr Solander, who is also starting with him for Isle St George. They will work on natural history. They have an astronomer for the passage of Venus, a draughtsman, all the instruments, books and appliances possible; after observing the passage they will endeavour to make discoveries in the Southern Ocean and return by the East Indies. Miss Blosset, not knowing that he was to start next day, was quite gay. Banks drank freely to hide his feelings.

Saturday, 6 August, had been Cook's last night at home. Had he, too, drunk freely to hide his feelings? No book, no manuscript, in the British Library or anywhere else, will tell. The coasts and contours of his familial life are not so much smudges as blanks on the maps in the archive.

PART 2:
TO THE SOUTH SEA

3

Punished Henry Stephens Seaman

As they travelled south, Banks found the ship a slow sailor, though this suited him: fish could be caught, nets lowered and odd sea insects collected. He could note that the sea was almost covered in tiny agile crabs, 'as if the surface of the water and not the bottom was their Proper station'. Within days of departing Plymouth, new creatures and new phenomena were noted. A few sooty brown birds flew erratically about the *Endeavour*, gliding, darting, diving in turns. Occasionally one seemed to merely pat the water's surface, taking food with the precision of an instrument. The sailors called the petrels Mother Carey's chickens and said they were sent to warn them of a storm; Mother Carey was possibly the Virgin, possibly a New York witch. 'As indeed it provd,' Banks wrote; as night fell the gale hit. He, and no doubt the other landmen, relapsed into the seasickness they had just about shrugged off. The seamen were reassured by the soundness of their portent. Cook's measurements and judgements of positions and winds were not the only system of reason that informed the handling of a ship.

Soon afterwards the *Endeavour* passed the north-west coast of Spain, within six to ten leagues of Cape Finisterre. In these waters, the vessel moved between points that were not only geographically but historically known. The name of Finisterre would not have meant much to Banks's fellow-naturalist Solander, who was a Swede, a pupil of Linnaeus, and it probably meant little to Banks himself. But most of those on board had grown up or started to grow old in the navy, and the history that was passed down in naval conversation made much of Lord Anson's carefully plotted assault on a French fleet, around here somewhere, in May 1747. The accomplishment lay less in the defeat of ships named *l'Invincible* and *La Gloire*, given that Anson's force was a great deal stronger than that of his opponents, and more in the seizure of Indiamen and other prizes worth £300,000. This was, in a way, an ocean of history, not just an expanse of water but a space of mythic glory. Yet if old land battlefields admit and even nurture memory – a stream or escarpment, the site of some turning-point in the action, can still be seen and walked – seascapes leave history without purchase. The ocean presents both infinite variety and bleak uniformity, but no constant, characteristic or recognizable peculiarity. Its only features are things that cannot properly be said to belong to it, things like the rocks and lands that pierce and indent it, that define its edges. If this fluidity meant that Finisterre was less a place than a name, this sea-site or sea-lane nevertheless meant something to British sailors. It was a space in which their near antecedents had triumphed over national enemies, a space in which a few of them had made a spectacular amount of money. The Pacific would not be this kind of ocean: its known and story-bearing spaces would be few and far between.

Maderia was known too, not as a site of any notable British exploit, but as an old Portuguese settlement and a familiar port for provisioning. On 13 September 1768 Cook found another British naval ship and several merchant vessels in what was called Funchal Road. He had not anchored here before, but those who had sailed on the *Dolphin*, and no doubt some of the others, had. An English visitor approaching the island a few years earlier had thought that 'it made a very hideous appearance, occasioned by several vast mountains, the lower parts of which seemed of a red gravelly colour and quite barren, and the summits a dirty dark green'. Banks wrote that 'When you first approach it from the seaward it has a very beautiful appearance', which indicates that Europeans responding to unfamiliar places had, at this time, little to go on, nothing like an aesthetic checklist that guided them towards a consistent judgement.

Soon after the ship's arrival, the first fatality of the voyage occurred: 'in heaving the Anchor out of the Boat Mr Weir Masters mate was carried over board by the Buoy-rope and to the bottom with the anchor,' Cook wrote, as though the event was unremarkable. Only Banks's Quaker draughtsman, Sydney Parkinson, who was not a sailor, was moved to express regret in his journal, to record that the unlucky mate had been 'a very honest worthy man, and one of our best seamen'. A few days later another man fell into the hold while provisions were being loaded and was 'dangerously bruis'd' – such were ordinary occupational hazards.

During the preceding month, Cook had been learning how a ship carrying almost 100 men might be managed: his previous experience on the *Grenville*, commanding eighteen to twenty, would have seemed, in comparison, to have been on a familial scale. Although the *Endeavour* was smaller than many naval vessels, the difference of scale deprived its captain of intimate acquaintance with the crew. The *Endeavour* was large enough to contain distinct strata and subcultures that were at mutual remove even when cramped together. The marines and Banks's party were, for example, self-consciously apart. In handling this larger ship and her people, Cook was in fact less experienced than some of his officers, such as John Gore, who had been to the Pacific twice, on both the *Dolphin*'s voyages. It was later recorded that 'Cook was jealous of him, conscious of not having that thorough stile in naval affairs, nor that courage'; there is no way of knowing whether there is any real substance behind this but it is probable that his relationships with Gore and others were in fact awkward, at least initially. Under other circumstances, Cook took offence when forms and hierarchies were not respected. He would have wanted his rank explicitly acknowledged, and it is not hard to imagine that he would have resented ambiguities of status and experience.

If he had a problem, one of his solutions was to make his command visible. He made discipline tangible by flogging men. The report is pretty bald: on the fourth day at Funchal, 'Punished Hen^ry Stephens Seaman and Thos Dunster Marine with 12 lashes each for refusing to take their allowance of fresh Beef'. It is puzzling why the men should have refused fresh beef, which had probably only just been shipped on board and, one would have thought, would have been considerably more palatable than the usual rations. Presumably what was shipped was of mixed quality, and these men objected to their portions; Gore records that they were flogged simply for 'mutiny', which suggests that irrespective of the specific issue around the food, Cook felt that this was an instance of insolence which he could not tolerate. This question – of what could or should be tolerated and what not – would arise just about every day over the course of the voyage. It would arise in more complex and difficult ways when the *Endeavour* was not self-contained at sea, but half-displaced, as it were, on to beaches and islands. There its finely tuned society was disrupted by crowds of Islanders, by sexual possibilities, and by the interplay between naval and native hierarchies. Madeira was a known port, not a Polynesian island. The visit was brief, and most men were pretty busy, getting wine and water into boats on the steep shingle beach through the broken water, and out to the ship. But it is not surprising that the first rupture of authority that had to be resolved through sanctioned violence occurred here in port, where the space of the captain's government was not the only space that there was.

While Cook worried about what he paid for a live bullock, sweetmeats, fruit and onions, Joseph Banks and Daniel Solander collected specimens and compiled a flora of Madeira, of some 300 items. Over the same few days they were entertained by the Portuguese governor. In turn they entertained him with an electricity machine – one of Banks's gadgets – brought ashore from the *Endeavour*, so that his excellency could be shocked 'full as much as he chose'. If not exactly science, this diplomacy created good feeling and helped assure that permission was given to make the purchases that Cook required.

Banks passed his time at Madeira much as he passed it in the course of his excursions within Britain. If botany was his chief passion, he would take time also to look at buildings, to socialize and to report on agricultural technologies. Madeira was, of course, an outpost of a Catholic nation and Funchal's townscape was therefore dominated by substantial monasteries and convents, institutions typically described in censorious terms by British travellers because the seclusion of men and women was seen to suppress population growth and depress society, though nunneries were also thought to possess secret entrances and function as brothels. Banks does not exactly trot out the stereotypes of the day. He makes fun of the naïvety of the nuns, who expect that because he is a philosopher he ought to be able to divine a water source within their walls. He is kinder to the friars who promise his party a roast turkey on a Friday, even though it is their fast day, 'which does great credit to their civility, and at the same time shews that they are not bigots to their religion'. He approves of the efficient organization of the sick-room in a Franciscan house. He finds the chapel built out of human bones curious and is struck especially by a skull in the wall featuring a partially fused jaw; the unfortunate person had evidently been fed through a hole smashed through the teeth, on one side of the face.

All of these are miscellaneous observations, unconnected facts of the kind that promiscuously inquisitive eighteenth-century natural historians thought there was a point to accumulating. But here as in England, Banks's inquiries were not without focus. He describes the system of wine-making and expresses surprise at the 'simple and unimprovd' methods, which entailed servants getting into a box and squashing grapes with their feet and elbows. He remarks facetiously that this was probably the way Noah made his wine, 'tho it is not impossible that he might have used a better, if he rememberd the ways he had seen us'd before the flood'. The people of Madeira, in other words, were 'as idle, or rather uninformed a set as I ever yet saw'. This typifies an intellectual inclination to make an assessment of productive techniques and in turn of the 'set' of people who exhibited a lack, or some degree, of improvement. This was not racism. But it was an overtly judgemental system of thought that ranked some peoples higher than others; it was a system that could be applied to aspects of subsistence or production among any people anywhere, and could thus potentially rank all peoples on a scale of progress. Whether that potential to distil an invidious hierarchy out of disparate observations would be realized remained still to be seen; Banks was noticing things, and not yet ordering them.

Cook, Banks and Solander dine with an English doctor, Thomas Heberden, who is in his sixties, his health seemingly failing. He is a philosopher. His head is full of meteorology and measurements. He writes for the proceedings of the Royal Society. He has heard by letter that the ship on Royal Society business will call at Funchal. It is as though all his rewards have come at once and he talks incessantly, seeming unsure which of his guests is the man to address about temperatures and the heights of mountains. Banks has brought up his apparatus, and Heberden too enjoys an electric shock. His servants bring dried figs, preserved pears, boiled eggs, salads, rock fish and Newfoundland cod. He is pompous but congenial. He is just about the last Englishman they will meet for two years.

At sea again, sharks are caught, which some sailors do not want to eat. Banks infers that their reluctance derives from an idea that the sharks have fed on human flesh; he imputes a daft fear of becoming a cannibal at one remove. Cook has little to say about what sailors think or do, outside his records of day-to-day work around the ship ('Exercised the People at Great Guns and sm'arms'; 'The Caulkers Emp'd in Cauking the Decks'). Seamen's ideas and habits he takes for granted and had no reason to report; their odd charades and games are beneath the official notice of his journal. We are indebted to the naval doctor Charles Fletcher, who later met Cook at Saint Helena, for accounts of a few such diversions, and might wonder whether one of those many members of the *Endeavour*'s crew about whom we know just about nothing, such as John Gathrey, had, like a Webb of Fletcher's acquaintance, 'fitted himself out in *Monmouth-street* with a *three tailed* wig of an enormous size; when thus equipped, he had the art of assuming an uncommon solemnity of countenance, which added to the remainder of his appearance as a sailor, rendered him truly ridiculous and consequently a subject of great mirth'. Or whether a sort of sketch, which was supposedly commonly played, was exhibited, perhaps in the course of the passage between Madeira and Tenerife:

The *Miller of Mansfield*, another of their sports, argues likewise their taste for low comedy . . . One of the sailors, habited like an old miller and powdered with flour, appears grinding at his mill, which consists of a large wooden bowl, with a shot in it: he is singing the while – some sailors in the mean time mounted on each others backs, represent horses loaded with corn to be ground. He is amused with various pleasantries 'till those above, on the forecastle or gangway are prepared to drown him, together with the sacks of corn, &c. which before they can make their escape, is sometimes nearly effected, by large buckets of water thrown over them, and which is termed *sluicing*: and herein, and in the circumstance of their pitching upon persons unacquainted with the tendency of the sport, consists its jocularity.

The more famous seamen's ritual which both Cook and Banks did report marked the crossing of the Equator. Here this ship hove to, and those who could not prove that they had crossed the line before either had to pay a fine in alcohol, or suffer a triple ducking in the sea from the main yard. A list was made, apparently of every living creature, including dogs and cats, on the ship. All then gathered on the quarterdeck and were each examined by a lieutenant who had crossed – in all likelihood Gore, who would surely have relished the role – and who marked off every name

either to be ducked or let off according as their qualifications directed. Captn Cooke and Doctor Solander were on the Black list, as were my self [Banks wrote] my servants and doggs, which I was oblig'd to compound for by giving the Duckers a certain quantity of Brandy for which they willingly excusd us the Ceremony. Many of the Men however chose to be ducked rather than give up 4 days allowance of wine which was the price fixd upon, and as for the boys they are always duckd of course; so that about 21 underwent the ceremony . . . sufficiently diverting it certainly was to see the different faces that were made on this occasion, some grinning and exulting in their hardiness whilst others were almost suffocated . . .

The line-crossing ceremony suspended the most fundamental social distinctions, allowing everyone to gather on the quarterdeck – otherwise strictly reserved for officers (and, on the *Endeavour*, gentlemen such as Solander and Banks). The usual bases of rank were not dissolved or reversed, but briefly replaced by a sort of republic governed by those seamen of experience who had already crossed the line, who could call everyone including Cook to account and who inflicted a fine or an initiation rite upon all. The fact that the ceremony was fully and elaborately indulged in – it occupied a whole afternoon and evening – tells us something that can be set against the flogging of Stephens and Dunster. Cook understood that discipline had to accommodate itself to custom. There was an ebb and flow in punishment and liberality. How the *Endeavour*'s seamen and officers regarded their captain at this particular time is something that can only be guessed at. The very sparse indications and the lack of any suggestion in the various logs that the commander was harsh or overbearing make it seem that if Cook was a literal man, and one legally obliged to be an autocrat, he saw the need to be a benign one.

The grand notion of a sea voyage pits a frail vessel against a great ocean. The idea commonly implies that explorers may have a few old and inadequate charts that provide them with no real guide to the shoals and shores they encounter. If this is romantic, it is not entirely wrong for Cook's first voyage. As the *Endeavour* moved further south into the Atlantic, and most particularly as the ship moved into the Pacific, the guidance provided by older charts and narratives would prove unreliable and generally irrelevant. But the voyage was nevertheless more than simply an encounter between men at sea and new spaces. Those men were not simply searching and seeing, but also *reading*. Voyaging was, for officers and scientists, a surprisingly bookish business. Off duty, if one could read, there was not much else to do, and lieutenants and midshipmen passed around copies of books like *Tom Jones*. Joseph Banks's reading was far more various. In the course of writing his journal of the passage south, from England to Madeira, past Tenerife and to Rio, he cites a veritable library. A rare fish is known from Sir Hans Sloane's *Voyage to Jamaica*; a bonito carries a parasite depicted in the Dutch scholar Baster's *Opuscula Subseciva*; he 'shot the black toed gull of *Penn. Zool.*', that of his acquaintance Thomas Pennant's *British Zoology*, published two years earlier. For one reason or another, he alludes to Willem Piso's *Historia Naturalis Brasilae*, William Dampier's *Discourse on Winds*, Edward's *Natural History of Birds* and Brisson's *Ornithologie*. For his part Cook consulted manuscript copies of the logs of Byron and Wallis and works such as Anson's *Voyage Round the World*. The authors of this narrative happened to recommend Rio as a place for refreshment: 'any quantity of hogs and poultry may be procured', and Cook very likely had this advice in mind when he chose to call there before negotiating the notoriously difficult passage around the bottom tip of South America.

This was to trust in a guidebook more than twenty years out of date. The viceroy of Brazil, Dom António Rolim de Moura, had been directed to regard British vessels and visitors with suspicion. Permission was granted to purchase provisions, but the movements of the ship's company were strictly constrained. All purchases had to be made through an agent appointed by the viceroy. No one apart from Cook and those directly engaged in taking off boatloads of beef, greens, rum and water could venture ashore; soldiers were placed in the boats; and Cook himself had to be accompanied by a guard wherever he went. Cook was infuriated by what he saw as offences to the British flag, and remonstrated with the viceroy in person and through a series of letters. De Moura, unmoved, repeatedly accused the *Endeavour*'s crew of smuggling, evidently believing that the purpose of the voyage was spying with a view to subverting the Portuguese trading monopolies. 'He certainly did not believe a word about our being bound to the Southward to Observe the transit of Venus but look'd upon it only as an invented story to cover some other design we must be upon.' In the case of the *Endeavour*, there were legitimate grounds for suspicion, given that the ship did not look like a British naval one and was in fact essentially a cargo vessel. Given also the obscure and dilettantish status that natural history possessed in Europe at the time, it is not at all surprising that Cook's account of the voyage's rationale met with some scepticism. As Gore reported, Banks and Solander were presumed to be 'Supercargoes and Engineers and not naturalists for the Business of such being so very abstruse and unprofitable That They cannot believe Gentlemen would come so far as Brazil on that Account only'.

One of the ironies was that Banks and Solander did understand botany and natural history as profitable endeavours, albeit only in the longer term. Discoveries of useful plants would create new possibilities for trade; certain species might be transplanted to Europe or to other colonies, hence industry generally would be improved. They resented de Moura's refusal to let them spend time ashore during the stay. Several times they gave his sentries the slip in the dead of night, or on another account bribed them, and rowed to unfrequented parts of the shore that were explored once it became light. The upshot was a list of some 300 Brazilian plants. The governor's regulations were flouted also by a number of people who gained access to the town. A journal believed to have been written by the American midshipman James Magra described houses, observed that the city was unlike those of Europe, in being devoid of beggars, and scurrilously claimed that 'the genteeler prostitutes here make their assignations at church'.

What happened at Madeira happened here too. On 19 November, Cook 'Punished John Thurman Seaman with 12 lashes for refusing to assist the sailmaker'. On the 30th, as the ship prepared to depart, he flogged three men: Robert Anderson for attempting to desert, William Judge for abusing an officer, and the boatswain's mate, John Readon or Reading, 'for not doing his duty in punishing the above two men'. And, as the *Endeavour* made way out of the harbour, Cook's former servant from the Newfoundland surveys, Peter Flower, fell overboard and drowned. 'In his room we got a Portuguese.' No doubt Cook was saddened by the loss of a man he had regarded as a good sailor, whom he had known more than five years. But we do not know that from log- and journal-keeping, which at this early stage is conventionally naval, abbreviated, to the point and unimaginative: many of the entries for days at sea are less than 100 words and report little more than position, weather and variation of the compass. To the entry for 7 December, however, Cook appended 'A Description of the Bay or River of Rio de Janeira' which is much longer than anything he has written before. It describes the navigation of the port and the forts, batteries and troops which defend the bay, from the perspective, as one would expect, of an attacking force: 'They lay low and Ships may come so near as to have them intirely within the reach of their guns, but it would require five or Six sail of the Line to insure Success.' To these explicitly tactical directions – which remind us that, for all its singularity, the *Endeavour* remained a naval vessel – Cook added a thumbnail description of the city, but said little about the people, beyond reporting an estimate of population of some 100,000, of whom nineteen out of twenty were black, 'many of whom are free and seem to live in tolerable circumstances'. He went on to say much more about the availability of water and the sorts and qualities of provisions.

Here, Cook was more or less the same writer who prepared Newfoundland directions. The scope of his journal was, however, soon to become distended, to spill outside the obviously practical concerns of ships. He would find himself increasingly in the muddy water of human circumstance, tolerable or not.

From Rio, the *Endeavour* travelled south towards Cape Horn. It became colder. No one could have been complacent about the passage through to the Pacific. Whether the treacherous zigzag of the Strait of Magellan or the route much further south around Cape Horn was chosen, the passage in frigid weather into adverse winds and heavy seas was notoriously slow and difficult.

With the exceptions of the still unpublished voyages of Byron and Wallis, Anson's *Voyage*, written up by Richard Walter and Benjamin Robins, was the most substantial and relatively recent British report of a voyage to the South Sea. In the mid eighteenth century it had been tremendously popular, and one of its most gripping and harrowing sections recounted the struggle of Anson's squadron to make their way around the Cape. Most of those who were literate aboard the *Endeavour* would have read the book and the copy or copies aboard were no doubt examined again as Tierra del Fuego was approached. Benjamin and Robins had described a horrific series of storms that repeatedly blew the ships back to the east, and drew the passage out by many weeks:

We had a continual succession of such tempestuous weather, as surprized the oldest and most experienced Mariners on board, and obliged them to confess, that what they had hitherto called storms were inconsiderable gales, compared with the violence of these winds, which raised such short, and at the same time such mountainous waves, as greatly surpassed in danger all seas known in any other part of the globe: And it was not without great reason, that this unusual appearance filled us with continual terror; for had any one of these waves broke fairly over us, it must, in all probability, have sent us to the bottom. Nor did we escape with terror only; for the ship rolling incessantly gunwale to, gave us such quick and violent motions, that the men were in perpetual danger of being dashed to pieces against the decks, or sides of the ship. And though we were extremely careful to secure ourselves from these shocks, by grasping some fixed body, yet many of our people were forced from their hold, some of whom were killed, and others greatly injured; in particular, one of our best seamen was canted over-board and drowned, another dislocated his neck, a third was thrown into the main-hold and broke his thigh, and one of our Boat-swain's Mates broke his collar-bone twice; not to mention many other accidents of the same kind. These tempests . . . were yet rendered more mischievous to us by their inequality, and the deceitful intervals they sometimes afforded . . . the weather proving more tolerable, would perhaps encourage us to set our top-sails; after which, the wind, without any previous notice, would return upon us with redoubled force, and would in an instant tear our sails from the yards. And that no circumstance might be wanting which could aggrandize our distress, these blasts generally brought with them a great quantity of snow and sleet . . . adding great difficulty and labour to the working of the ship, benumbing the limbs of our people, and making them incapable of exerting themselves with their usual activity, and even disabling many of them, by mortifying their toes and fingers. It were indeed endless to enumerate the various disasters of different kinds which befel us . . .

To this succession of dreadful ordeals was added an acutely poignant detail: the report that the man lost overboard had been sighted swimming strongly by his fellow sailors, at once helpless to assist him but appalled that 'he might continue sensible for a considerable time longer, of the horror attending his irretrievable situation'. The odd anonymity of the man was to make the passage a sort of literary tomb to an unknown seaman; the awful idea of the sailor's certain awareness of his impending death, lost to his ship and thousands of miles from home, would make this one of the most enduring passages in maritime literature: right at the end of the eighteenth century, it motivated William Cowper's poem 'The Castaway': 'Yet bitter felt it still to die / Deserted, and his friends so nigh.' Many readers before the poet certainly dwelt on the incident; my sense is that one of them might have been Banks's sentimental draughtsman, Sydney Parkinson, who lacked the bulky body of a seaman and found the cold hard in the passage south, who maybe doubted that his own survival was part of Providence's great scheme, who might well have shuddered, envisaging himself clutching at nothing, alone on the face of a great wave, as the *Endeavour*'s squat stern slid out of view.

4

As miserable a set of People as are this day upon Earth

If, in the 1890s, a Haush or Selk'nam woman told her child about how it had once been, she would have said that each people had occupied its 'earth', its *haruwen*. Within those territories, big families or little bands had moved, hunting guanaco, foxes, birds and other creatures, collecting shellfish, catching fish, sometimes killing seals and gathering plants. Guanaco, foxes, tucotuco and cururo were killed for fur as well as food, fur for clothes and shelters. In the winters people had stayed mostly at the coast, where it was milder. In the summers they had chased guanaco through the hills. Usually they moved in small groups, but when a whale was beached, smoke signals told everyone to come, and they would camp and feast until it was eaten, trading, playing and performing. Other times too, if there were plenty of food, everyone gathered, people would give feasts, shamans would show their powers and outdo each other, wrestlers would fight and rare things like arrowheads, body paint, flints, fox fur capes and mushrooms would be bartered.

All this had emerged from a primal struggle: women had at first kept men in subjection. Then men discovered the tricks behind the women's frightful magic and rose up – the myth related – and killed them all. From then on, men managed ceremonies and business, hunting, trading and marriage. That is, until the societies that lived out this intimate antagonism witnessed a new massacre, not of women but of everyone, not at the hands of local men but of foreigners – soldiers, hired killers, sheep-farmers and gold-seekers, determined to usurp the place they called Tierra del Fuego. By the 1890s, this woman would have known that the lands her ancestors had known, hunted over and lived and died on were theirs no longer. A way of life that her mother had taken for granted, that had been both rich and hard, she could only remember.

In January 1769, neither awesome rites nor quotidian hunting had to be recalled nostalgically. These activities were alive in the habits and reflections of a group of men and women who occupied a cluster of huts made from low walls, branches and the skins of guanaco, not far from the shore of a broad spectacularly blue bay. Among them were renowned women and beaten women, old men who mumbled songs that no one else understood, proud hunters and uninitiated boys. There were men who made arrows for different game from a dozen sorts of bushes, and thought nothing of it. They saw birds such as the ibis and a hundred others, knew which men they had once been and when and how they could be caught. They were painted, sometimes just red, sometimes with red and white streaks and spots, to represent spirits and ancestors such as dolphins and sea-lions.

The name that a set of voyagers gave the triangular island occupied by Selk'nam and Haush had nothing to do with these people or what they called it. In 1520, Ferdinand Magellan sailed past its northern coast and through the strait that was given his name. He saw no one. For all he knew, the inhabitants might have had scales for skin, they might have been black, white or red. He knew nothing of their lives, but he did see fires which, it was later supposed, were lit by the native people to draw attention to the unprecedented spectacle of Magellan's ships. In fact, the Selk'nam and Haush had many reasons for lighting fires. They may not have noticed Magellan's vessels. If they did, they were not necessarily startled by them or interested in them. Their history did not begin or end at that moment. But the smoke he could see, here and there, did prompt Magellan to call the place the 'land of fire', Tierra del Fuego.

Two hundred and fifty years later, a good many ships had been past. Some Europeans 'knew' the fact that Charles Clerke had 'confirmed' for the Royal Society: that hereabouts, on the neighbouring Patagonian mainland, the people were giants. What the Haush 'knew' for their part about whites is anybody's guess. The set of people around the place that Europeans called the Bay of Good Success had not themselves sighted or smelt Europeans. They had heard of them, though, and perhaps had heard that they were like cormorants, who stopped for a little while on a rock and then flew away. The Haush were not much bothered when a ship rather slowly and awkwardly made its way into their bay.

Cook too had seen several fires; Banks thought them 'made probably by the natives as a signal to us'. He was excited, not by the prospect of meeting the people, but by the opportunity to examine the flowers and plants of 'a country so intirely new'. On successive days several attempts had to be made to bring the ship into the Strait of Le Maire. Banks, unable to contain himself, prevailed on Cook to ply about a bay while he and Solander ventured ashore, 'and found many plants, about 100, tho we were not ashore above 4 hours; of these I may say every one was new and intirely different from what either of us had before seen'. The hopes that Banks had entertained of encountering an absolutely novel natural world, the sort of world of unprecedented things that de Brosses had envisaged, began to seem real. The voyage was on its cusp, between the known Atlantic and the unknown Pacific. Cook went about his business uninfected by Banks's enthusiasm. 'At 9 they return'd on board bringing with them several Plants Flowers &c^a most of them unknown in Europe and,' he noted drily, 'in that alone consisted their whole value.'

On 15 January 1769, the *Endeavour* came to anchor in the Bay of Good Success. Cook, Banks and Solander went ashore directly 'to look for a Watering place and to speak with the Natives who were assembled on the beach'. In Newfoundland, Cook had spoken to 'natives' from time to time, though he wrote little about such meetings; they were not significant to his surveying. Here, not at the top but the bottom of the world, his mission was different. For the first time, he was trying to orchestrate some sort of sociable interaction. Here, and elsewhere, he might have presumed that indigenous people saw him as an intruder, and in most cases he would have been right. Cook would want to dislodge this sense; hoping that those on the beach and half-concealed in the trees might instead see himself and his people as friends, and the encounter as a mutually beneficial one. But they, the people on the beach, here and elsewhere, did not make the assumptions that lay behind the voyage. They did not understand commerce as a great thing like the tide that would bring them new things and improvements. This abstract idea of progress hardly made itself visible, in the small things – beads, beef, alcohol – that Cook introduced some few Haush to, on this occasion. For the Haush, these things were just what they were: not tokens of a global future that would be good for them.

No encounter was shaped by Cook's orchestration alone. He had to deal with the predispositions and sometimes hasty acts of other members of the ship's company, and – more importantly – he could not anticipate how indigenous people felt and how they might act on their feelings. Here, it was not Cook but Banks and Solander – according to Banks's account – who followed a group that had 'retreated'. Two Haush men, closer than the rest, sat down, and threw aside sticks that they held as Banks and Solander approached. Banks presumed that this meant peace, though it is not clear whether the men discarded actual weapons, or mimicked that action. In either case, and despite the otherwise limited character of mutual understanding, the presumption was evidently right. The two Haush walked back towards the rest of their party, indicating that the naturalists should follow. When they did so, and joined the group, they were received with what Banks called 'many uncouth signs of friendship'. Cook reported that the people were not at all afraid or surprised, and that three without hesitation came on board the ship. Beyond implying that they were unconcerned, he says little of their disposition and little about their behaviour on board the *Endeavour*. What he does do is write a journal entry a day or so later that distils what he and others have noticed of these people. This is Cook's first essay in anthropology:

They are something above the Middle size of a dark copper Colour with long black hair, they paint their bodies in Streakes mostly Red and Black, their cloathing consists wholy of a Guanacoes skin or that of a Seal, in the same form as it came from the Animals back, the Women wear a peice of skin over their privey parts but the men observe no such decency. Their Hutts are made like a behive and open on one side where they have their fire, they are made of small Sticks and cover'd with branches of trees, long grass &c^a in such a manner that they are neither proff against wind, Hail, rain, or snow, a sufficient proff that these People must be a very hardy race; they live chiefly on shell fish such as Muscles which they gather from off the rocks along the sea-shore and this seems to be the work of the Women; their arms are Bows and Arrows neatly made, their arrows are bearded some with glass and others with fine flint, several pieces of the former we saw amongst them with other European things such as Rings, Buttons, Cloth, Canvas &c^a which I think proves that they must sometimes travel to the Northward, as we know of no ship that has been in those parts for many years, besides they were not at all surprised at our fire arms on the contrary seem'd to know the use of them by making signs to us to fire at Seals or Birds that might come in the way. They have no boats that we saw, or anything to go upon the water with. Their number doth not exceed 50 to 60 young and old and there are fewer Women then Men. They are extreeamly fond of any Red thing and seemed to set more Value on Beeds than any thing we could give them: in this consists their whole pride, few either men or Women are without a necklace or string of Beeds made of small Shells or bones about their necks. They would not taste any strong Liquor, neither did they seem fond of our provisions. We could not discover that they had any head or chief, or form of Government, neither have they any usefull or necessary Utentials except it be a Bagg or Basket to gather their Muscles into: in a Word they are perhaps as miserable a set of People as are this day upon Earth.

Is it too obvious to say that this is the result of observation, not communication? There is a fundamental difference between seeing people and hearing from them. Cook's contacts with indigenous peoples over the course of the first voyage would involve both these ways of knowing. Some encounters would proceed through much rich if often muddled dialogue. Voyagers would go away with a sense – often a limited or scrambled one – of what mattered to a people and how they saw their world. Nothing like this took place on this occasion. There was no shared language and Cook knew nothing of the social distinctions and forces that filled the Haush world with energy. He had no sense that, for the groups he caught sight of, the sun and moon were anything other than heavenly bodies. He had no sense that these people understood the origins of their way of life in a cosmic struggle between Sun and Moon, between husband and wife, a struggle that was bloody and unresolved and ceremonially re-enacted, which was there every day between man and woman. He could see 'Streakes' of paint but he could not see the ibis, the sea-lion, or the other creatures that painted people personified.

So far as appearances went, perhaps he could not reasonably have been expected to grasp much more than he did. He was right that they ate mussels, but wrong to extrapolate from what they were eating at this particular time to the proposition that they subsisted 'chiefly' on shellfish. He did not consider that they might move seasonally, that they might in fact eat a great variety of plants, birds and animals at different times. He saw them almost as wretched scavengers and imagined that their menu would be limited.

Cook was right that the Haush did not use canoes. Although it was cold, the environment was rich; fish were readily caught from the shore. He was hence probably wrong that they had travelled or were in the habit of travelling to the north. Only rarely, and with particular permission, did people move beyond their 'earth'. It is more likely that European objects and information about mariners reached the group through a succession of local exchanges. Cook's interest in this point probably derived from the larger issue of commerce, the larger question that de Brosses and others had broached. There were resources here that might – that soon would – tempt traders, and the question of whether the 'natives' already trafficked and were thus predisposed to trade was important.

On this point, Cook's findings are mixed. He observes, on the one hand, that the Haush know something of Europeans. Notably, they know that they possess guns, though they're not afraid. Rather, they hope that the mariners will save them some trouble by shooting a few birds and a seal or two. On the other hand, beads are all they want, though their utensils are so poor that Cook takes them to be the most miserable people in the world. Needless to say, the Haush do not tell Cook that they are miserable; he does not say that they look miserable. Rather, he imputes misery, on the basis of their limited material possessions.

Over these few days in January 1769, Joseph Banks is likewise the author of a description of these people. Words come more easily to him than they do to Cook. Yet for him too the exercise is novel: he has on no previous occasion tried to give an account of people who were essentially new to observant Europeans.

For all the mariners grasped of Haush ideas, concerns and feelings, the natives might have been standing behind a paper screen, through which only the haziest outlines of their actions, and their indistinct silhouettes, were visible. But there were just a few perforations in that screen. Banks glimpses through one when he notes that one of the three men who came on board the ship 'seemed to be a Preist or conjuror or at least we thought him to be one by the noises he made, possibly exorcising every part of the ship he came into, for when any thing new caught his attention he shouted as loud as he could for some minutes without directing his speech either to us or to any one of his countreymen'. Modern knowledge of the varied activities of the several kinds of Haush shamans is limited; but it is entirely possible that ritual formulae were being pronounced, and that some pollution or spiritual threat was being dispelled. Banks registers, however superficially and hesitantly, something that was real and dynamic in an indigenous cosmology.

Horizontal lines, too, could be seen through a tear in the screen between Haush and Englishmen. These lines were those they generally painted on their faces, varied so that no people were painted in quite the same way, 'whether as marks of distinction or mere ornaments I could not at all make out'. The most obvious sense behind these lines, then, was either that they were badges of office, or mere finery. Yet:

They seem also to paint themselves with something like a mixture of grease and soot for particular occasions, as when we went to their town there came two out to meet us who were dawb'd with black lines all manner of ways so as to form the most diabolical countenance imaginable, and these two seemed to exorcise us or at least made a loud and long harangue which did not seem to be address'd either to us or any of their countreymen.

Here we see Banks writing hastily, excited by the plethora of entirely new things and scenes he has met with; the same phrases spill out, repeating themselves in the space of a few pages. Again, it is speech addressed neither to friends nor strangers, but to something or someone else present, that puts this observer in mind of ritual; he mentions it because it may help explain the face paint, and particularly a disturbing form of it. Banks does understand that there is something that he does not understand. He tries to cut through the screen that blocks his insight, with blunt notions like rank and decoration and priestcraft, while knowing that they do not serve him well.

This puzzlement of Banks before Haush 'countenances' has no counterpart in an interest in their physical distinctiveness. He mentions their 'reddish' colour, without making it clear whether he refers to a natural skin colour or (probably rather) one produced with ochre and fat. He says nothing about the forms or angles of their faces, nor does he discourse on their racial characters. He has no stake in assigning them to this race or that. He says that their language is guttural. He tells how women fish. He makes the same remarks as Cook about their prior contacts with Europeans. He notes that some wear shoes and the fact that women cover their genitals while men do not. He acknowledges what 'is merely conjectural' and does not try to stitch his disparate observations into any coherent portrait of a people. To the contrary, what he says suggests a negative judgement at one moment and a neutral or almost positive one at another. Banks considers their houses 'the most miserable ones imaginable' but reasons that they are appropriately so: if the people are nomads, reasonably enough their dwellings 'seem intirely built to stand but for a short time'. He finds their bows 'neatly enough made', their arrows 'neater than any I have seen', but says also that these were their only neat things. On a more fundamental point, he wrote that 'Of Civil government I saw no signs, no one seemd to be more respected than another', implying a condition of pretty complete savagery, and the absence of distinctions of rank that he was personally committed to – but added 'nor did I ever see the least appearance of Quarreling or words between any two of them'. This is barely idealizing, but suggests a peaceful and harmonious life, and thus ameliorates what is said before, or is at least at odds with it.

This was about as affirmative as it got. Though Alexander Buchan, Banks's second artist, an epileptic who is almost unknown to us, made 'ORNAMENTS used by the People of TERRA DEL FUEGO' the subject of three delicate watercolours. In these illustrations, small things become big and somehow wonderful as they fill his page. The only caption that incorporates any sort of assessment told Banks, and those of his scientific acquaintances and friends who would see the picture, that Fig. II depicted a necklace 'of small Shells beautifully polished'. It would not be the last time that a native people would be denigrated, while their arts were appreciated.

*

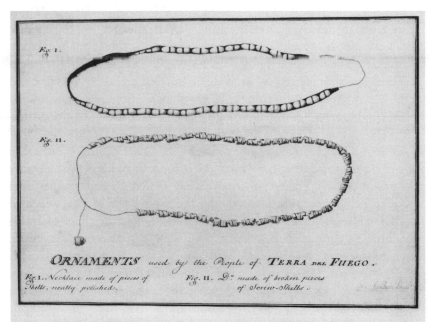

ORNAMENTS used by the People of TERRA DEL FUEGO.

Fig. I.—Necklace made of pieces of
Shells, neatly polished.

Fig. II. D.º made of broken pieces
of Screw-Shells.

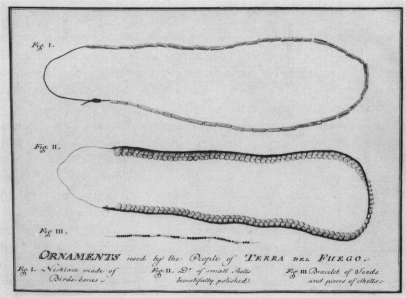

ORNAMENTS used by the People of TERRA DEL FUEGO.

Fig. I.—Necklace made of
Birds-bones.

Fig. II. D.º of small Shells
beautifully polished.

Fig. III. Bracelet of Seeds
and pieces of Shells.

8. *Alexander Buchan,* Ornaments used by the People of
Terra Del Fuego, *1769.*

Early on 16 January Banks's party picked a route into the woods just westward of the watering place. He took Solander, Buchan, the astronomer Green, the surgeon Monkhouse, several seamen and probably all four of his servants, two of whom happened to be black. The plan was to 'try to penetrate into the countrey as far as we could, and if possible gain the tops of the hills' where there appeared to be grasslands. They spent a good many hours climbing and pressing through thickets and around three in the afternoon reached a point where they had a nearer view of the hills they hoped to reach. The going became much harder: what had from a distance looked like open country turned out to be dense, waist-high brush on boggy ground. 'No traveling could possibly be worse than this which seemd to last about a mile.' Beyond this, Banks thought he could see bare rock, which he was 'infinitely eager to arrive at expecting there to find the alpine plants of a countrey so curious'. It was warm, the people 'tho rather fatigued were yet in good spirits' and all seemed satisfactory – until Buchan fell into a fit. A fire was prepared to warm him, and at this point the party divided. Those who were tired remained with Buchan, while Banks, Solander, Green and Monkhouse pressed on, and were soon gratified to find, 'according to expectation plants which answerd to those we had found before as alpine ones in Europe do to those which we find in the plains'. He means, presumably, that more stunted varieties were found at the higher altitude.

Here, however, it was bitterly cold and the afternoon was well advanced. Banks had given up any thought of returning to the ship that night, but hoped that they would be able to reach the 'thick of the wood' and make a fire. Green and Monkhouse returned to collect the others, the plan being to rendezvous at a hill where Banks proposed to 'build our wigwam'. The high summer meant that there was plenty of light, even at eight, but it began to snow. Suddenly, as they were again struggling through the field of waist-high brush, 'the cold seemd,' Banks wrote, 'to have an effect infinitely beyond what I have ever experienced'. The accounts of what then happened do not agree. According to Banks, Solander, who understood that it might be fatal to stop and rest, nevertheless announced that he was unable to carry on and lay down in the snow, in the face of Banks's remonstrance. Richmond, one of the black servants, 'also began to lag'. At this point Banks says he sent five forward. Buchan, who was recovered and stronger than anyone expected, would try to make a fire. Those with him must have been Monkhouse, Green and two seamen. The others – Banks says 'myself and 4 more', which must mean the second black servant, George Dorlton, and other seamen – remained to try to move Solander and Richmond on. 'With much persuasion and intreaty', he wrote, they got through most of the brush,

which had seemed virtually impenetrable even in the warmth of the afternoon, but then 'both gave out'. Richmond, told that he would freeze to
death if he did not move, could only say that 'there he would lay and dye'.
Solander for his part said he had to sleep, and in fact did so for a quarter of
an hour. At this point the news reached the group that a fire had been lit a
quarter of a mile ahead, and Banks split the party again, leaving two with
Richmond, while he, presumably with one other, carried Solander to the
fire. Here they rested, and once two – we do not know who – were warmed,
they were sent back to try to bring the other three. They looked and shouted
and called through the steady snowfall for around half an hour, but got,
according to Banks, no answer. 'We now guess'd the cause of the mischeif,'
he wrote, 'a bottle of rum the whole of our stock was missing, and we soon
concluded that it was in one of their Knapsacks and that the two who were
left in health had drank immoderately of it and slept like the other.'

At about midnight, however, shouting was heard, and Banks 'and 4 more'
went out and encountered the seaman in an exhausted state.

Him I sent back to the fire and proceeded by his direction to find the other two,
Richmond was upon his leggs but not able to walk the other lay on the ground as
insensible as a stone. We immediately calld all hands from the fire and attempted by
all the means we could contrive to bring them down but finding it absolutely
impossible, the road was so bad and the night so dark that we could scarcely ourselves
get on nor did we without many Falls. We would then have lit a fire upon the spot
but the snow on the ground as well as that which continually fell renderd that as
impracticable as the other, and to bring fire from the other place was also impossible
from the quantity of snow which fell every moment from the branches of the trees;
so we were forc'd to content ourselves with laying out our unfortunate companions
upon a bed of boughs and covering them over with boughs also as thick as we were
able, and thus we left them hopeless of ever seeing them alive again which indeed we
never did.

All this had taken something like an hour and a half. Another of Banks's
servants, Peter Briscoe, was just about dead from cold, but managed to
return to the fire with the rest of the party. The gales and snow showers
continued in the dark. They had scarcely any food. Banks thought that
Buchan would lapse into fits, and that Briscoe would die. In short, the
situation was desperate. Even as it became light, the snow squalls continued
and gave little hope. At six, the sun appeared and three went back to see
what had become of Richmond and Dorlton, 'but soon returnd with the
melancholy news of their being both dead'. Around eight in the morning,

the sun was stronger, a breeze sprang up and the sky cleared a little. Briscoe 'continued very ill but said he thought himself able to walk'. Buchan was better than Banks expected, 'so we agreed', he wrote, implying that in the crisis rank was put aside and decisions made jointly, 'to dress our vulture and prepare ourselves to set out for the ship'. The bird, which had been shot the day before, ceased to be a specimen and became a meal; it was carefully cut into ten equal portions, each cooked by each who had 'about 3 mouth-fulls of hot meat'. The thaw progressed and the party set out around ten, luckily finding easier paths and reaching the beach by the ship without further incident around the middle of the day. For all the detail of Banks's account, he concluded his story of the day by emphasizing that the horror of the situation was indescribable: 'no one can tell who has not been in such circumstances' are the last words of his journal entry for 17 January.

Most of those who kept logs on the *Endeavour* made some mention of this tragic excursion. Only Parkinson describes it in detail. What he says is in part consistent with, and in part different from, the account in Banks's journal. He records that while the naturalists ventured up to the highest ground, the 'two negroes and a sailor' who had been left in charge of the provisions drank the spirits and were thus unable to keep up with the rest of the party, as they became lost in the course of a desperate effort to reach the ship before dark. 'But time, that waits for no man, brought on the night.' All were afraid, fatigued, dispirited and numb with cold. Solander had to be carried for two hours; 'they held a consultation' and chose not to proceed, but to make a fire, which they were happily able to do. The three men who were left behind slept where they stopped. The sailor, who luckily woke, tried to rouse Richmond and Dorlton, but failed, and ran shouting, he hoped towards the rest, who at length heard him and responded. He eventually reached the fire – Parkinson does not say that the others went out to bring him to it – and told the company of the sorry condition of his companions. 'They were disposed to have yielded them assistance, but, it being almost dark, there was not any probability of finding them, and the attempt would have been attended with the risque of their own lives; they therefore declined it.' Early the following morning, this seaman was sent back to where he had left the two servants; he there found them frozen to death, though survived by a dog – elsewhere described as Banks's dog – 'sitting close by his master's corpse, who seemed reluctant to leave it'.

Parkinson had remained on the *Endeavour* and was not of the party. His information might have come from anyone and everyone – the business was no doubt the talk of the ship for at least a day or two. In any event, in his account the descent from the mountain appears to have been rushed and panicky; Banks may by mid afternoon have countenanced the prospect of spending the night in the forest with equanimity, but others got lost in their haste to avoid doing so. If this report is believed, Banks did not, as he claimed, take up the rear. They did not venture back to urge the three stragglers on (who were drunk already, not subsequently). Nor, when the sailor appeared, did they go back to Richmond and Dorlton, and try to shift them the last quarter mile to the fire. Banks tells us that the critical and unsuccessful effort to move the men, or induce them to move themselves, occurred between midnight and half past one; Parkinson says the attempt was declined because it was 'almost dark', surely meaning, even if it was cloudy and stormy, no later than about nine or nine thirty.

Banks's account is a first-hand one, and is plausibly specific. But it has to be said that it presents its author in a positive light. It places him at the centre of a vigorous effort to preserve the lives of the whole party. This does not mean that he fabricated any specifics and it is entirely possible that Parkinson simply got particular points wrong. But Parkinson contradicts Banks's claim that an effort was made to rescue Richmond and Dorlton. Parkinson's version is not implausible and cannot be discounted. It is not hard to imagine that nine cold and frightened men might have preferred to remain by a fire rather than risk their lives to preserve those of a sailor and two servants; and it is not hard to imagine that, had this occurred, the group's leader might have felt ashamed and written that a rescue had been attempted.

The question is unresolvable but important. Banks and, for that matter, Cook were embodiments of Enlightenment inquiry. They were empirical travellers who would replace confusion with precision and obscurity with information in matters geographical and natural-historical. They would not take the Royal Society for a ride, with tales of Patagonian giants. The meaning of the mission hinged absolutely on the creditworthiness of its reports, but voyagers were renowned for retailing the incredible. Cook, Banks, Parkinson and others did not report everything. Some of them record facts that others do not. In some cases it is plain that Cook does not mention circumstances and events that reflect poorly upon him. We know, also, that confusing circumstances are experienced differently, depending on the positions and perspectives of different people who see what happens, or who later make history out of them. Neither the ordinary sin of omission, nor the dependence of any 'truth' upon a particular perspective, concerns me right now. Here, we encounter another kind of problem: the possibility that the most literate intellectual on the ship, the man who wrote most extensively about the human contact that occurred over the course of the expedition, our star witness if you like, has not simply left out events, or told a story in a way that ennobled his own role, but instead actually lied.

It is vital that we are nagged by this doubt. But it is also important that we do not blow it out of proportion and dismiss a document – Banks's journal – that is rich and ragged if not absolutely reliable. Remember that at Newfoundland Banks repeated some hearsay about the Beothuk, and added that if half of it was true, that was more than he expected. Remember that just here, in making observations on the Haush, he is at pains to remind himself and his readers that an opinion is 'merely conjectural'. Pretend that you know already that he later writes frankly about acts of violence that he perpetrates and regrets. Instead of asking whether we are ever to trust Banks, we might instead work on the assumption that his truths, half-truths and lies circulate in a kind of economy. Most of the time, he appears, so far as we can establish, to write empirically, cautiously, and with qualification; sometimes, he is self-deprecating; sometimes he is ruthlessly honest, to his own cost; at other times, the price of telling the truth may have been just too high.

Cook's mind, I imagine, tacked back and forth between the realities of grey water before him and the abstractions of lines and numbers on charts. The exercises that punctuated his every day were measurements of position, direction, variation, temperature, tide, sounding and bearing. His business – which he carried out almost automatically – was to know precisely where he was in the world. He recorded this information, as a matter of course, in log and journal entries every day, and saw it incorporated in charts and views of coasts and landmasses, as he proceeded. In the Bay of Good Success, the *Endeavour* lay around 54° 44' south. Cook was born in Marton, Yorkshire, which happens to be situated around 54° 35' north. His ideas and ambitions were cartographic. He might have put himself to sleep with the thought that he had turned a world upside down.

Just as Cook had no idea who the Haush really were, the men and women who watched this odd man watching them, his head too small for his height, his nose pronounced, his dark eyes piercing, had no sense that his thoughts and feelings were not quite there, but with wife, children and kin at Mile End, where it would be dark, and at Marton, where it would be darker and colder still. For the Haush, the world, the land, living beings and daily life were made out of the hostility between Sun and Moon, out of uncertain balance, fear, love and mutual dependence between man and woman. They might have seemed incurious, but they were probably utterly perplexed by a boatload of men without land, without head-dresses, without paint or ornament, without women. If these white men felt that the Haush were scarcely human, there is a good chance that the Haush felt the same way about them.

5

As favourable to our purpose as we could wish

The clouds were heavy, and the *Endeavour* ran well before a strong breeze. On 26 March 1769 a 'quiet & industrious' marine named William Greenslade committed suicide by jumping overboard. Or so it was presumed: he'd been caught pilfering and his fellow-marines harangued him with having dishonoured their corps. The offence had been trivial, but the persecution went so far that the young man, who had maybe been bullied since the voyage began, found his situation insupportable. Cook noted the 'rash action', stressing that he knew nothing of the supposed crime until after the man had disappeared. His implication was that his own response would have been moderate, that it would not have pushed Greenslade to such an extremity. Banks lamented the young man's death at greater length. He was astonished and dismayed. He thought he knew sailors, but was still discovering the petulant savagery that confinement nurtured.

Just over a fortnight later Tahiti was sighted and on 13 April the ship anchored in Matavai Bay. This was to resume the place that Wallis's *Dolphin* had occupied two years earlier, where cannon and grapeshot had splintered canoes and bodies. The bay was largely sheltered and the water calm. The visitors faced black sand beaches and a shimmering mass of coconut palms. Here and there appeared thatched houses. The smoke of cooking fires suggested others. Ridges and valleys rose abruptly towards higher mountains obscured by mist. For Parkinson, 'the land appeared as uneven as a piece of crumpled paper', but he thought it beautifully green. A party went ashore and encountered people who brought banana or plantain leaves. Cook, Banks and others presumed these were emblems of peace, which indeed seems to have been the case. They themselves took leaves and carried them forward until the people with them stopped, and all threw their leaves upon the ground. In Banks's understanding, 'thus peace was concluded'. They walked further, accompanied by the Tahitians, making gifts of beads as they proceeded; Banks was delighted by the groves of shady breadfruit trees and the houses scattered amongst them. 'In short the scene we saw was the truest picture of an arcadia of which we were going to be kings that the imagination can form.'

The identification of Tahiti as a paradise was not yet cliché, but it would be remarkably quickly. Banks's idea that this was moreover a paradise in which Europeans were kings suggests that he took Wallis's account of the 'surrender' of the island at face value, or at any rate presumed that the status and authority he enjoyed at home would be acknowledged here. But those aboard the *Endeavour* who had participated in the *Dolphin*'s voyage and witnessed that supposed surrender were disturbed rather than delighted. Wilkinson wrote that they had proceeded to 'the Queens House but Could Not find it Likewise we found all the Principle Houses had been Demolishd; we observe that they have amongst them an Inveterate Ich or yaws & on Account of this we imagine the Principle People have Abandon'd the Place and also the hogs fowls & other Articles which we found in such great Plenty last Voyage are now scarce to be seen'. Gore likewise was struck by changes that he could not immediately understand: 'allmost everything was alter'd for the worse since I was here in the Dolphin'. Cook's journal indicates that the transformation was discussed, and put down to a political upheaval: 'a very great revolution must have happen'd' in the two years since the visit of the *Dolphin*'. Later, he would have a good deal to say about venereal disease, but unlike Wilkinson he did not presume that it was this that had caused the depopulation of the area. The Tahiti that Cook and Banks discovered was no true Arcadia or Eden, but a place with a turbulent history, and a place that itched.

The barest outlines of the latest phase of that history were soon established. The 'queen' Purea and her husband Amo, whose base was in any case not Matavai but Papara on the southern side of the island, had been defeated in war by Tutaha, among others. The particulars were more fully recorded only long afterwards. The massive *marae* of Mahaiatea, and the unprecedented political claim it represented, offended those in other districts. They at first challenged their cousin Purea, who did not back down and distribute the foods that had been protected by *rahui*, by prohibitions, but instead insisted that they be preserved for the rite when her son would be inaugurated with sacred feather sashes, and declared a great chief, an *ari'i rahi*. It was this failure to accede – as was customary – to pressure from relatives to scale down a politically assertive ceremony that led to an outbreak of hostilities. War was catastrophic for Purea and her friend and adviser Tupaia.

Cook and Charles Green had things on their mind other than the successes and failures of a Tahitian dynasty. They were immediately anxious to locate a suitable site from which the transit could be observed. If you ever walk the shores of Matavai, you will not be surprised that they chose the point at the great bay's eastern end. It became Point Venus, a famous historical site. No doubt when you or I take in the view from its black sand, of the glittering bay and the ridges that rise away from it, your or my perception is distorted by hindsight: there is nothing naturally 'historical' here. But this slightly curling, flat peninsula is a meeting-space between land and sea. It does seem the most obvious of stages for a cross-cultural drama, the place for arrivals, departures, beginnings and turning-points. Prosaically, also, it is and was somewhere that commanded a view, its anchorage was at this season safe and easy, and fresh water was nearby. This was just the sort of strategic and 'Convenient Situation' that Cook was encouraged to take possession of with the inhabitants' consent. Two days after arrival, he had an area of sandy ground just behind the beach marked out. He did not presume that, because of Wallis's action, British visitors could use the land without negotiation, nor was he interested in possessing it in perpetuity. He did make an effort to explain to a couple of men of authority that he wanted the use of the land for 'such a number of nights' and that he and his men would then depart. He was not sure, but had the impression that the proposal troubled no one. Men got to work, constructing a ditch, a bank, and defences around what would be a British fort.

People were troubled, though, by what happened immediately afterwards, late in the day on 15 April. From the first moments of contact Tahitians had snatched and stolen things, and while Cook and Banks were away from the new camp on a walk one man, more assertive than others, pushed over a sentry and grabbed his musket. The officer present – Jonathan Monkhouse – ordered the others to fire and the man was shot dead. Everyone fled in consternation, taking the musket with them. According to Parkinson, the marines had fired 'with the greatest glee imaginable, as if they had been shooting at wild ducks'. In addition to the man killed, 'many others' were wounded. It was, he remonstrated, 'a pity, that such brutality should be exercised by civilized people upon unarmed ignorant Indians!' Banks confirms what Cook does not mention, that 'several', if not many, were wounded, and likewise censured the violence. He, rather than Cook, went off to find some of the people who had run away and induced a few of them back to the tent, where an attempt was made to explain to them that the Europeans meant to be friends, but

that the man who sufferd was guilty of a crime deserving of death (for so we were forcd to make it) we retird to the ship not well pleasd with the days expedition, guilty no doubt in some measure of the death of a man who the most severe laws of equity would not have condemnd to so severe a punishment.

The following day the beach was deserted. Banks was preoccupied not with the poor state of relations with the Tahitians, but by the deteriorating health of his artist, Alexander Buchan, who suffered another epileptic fit and lapsed into a coma. He died the next morning and his body became almost immediately fetid. 'It would not be practicable to keep him even till night' was how Banks expressed it. Because nothing was known of how the dead were dealt with locally, it was thought best to bury him at sea. On occasions like this, compassion was not uppermost in Banks's mind. 'His loss to me is irretrevable,' he wrote, 'my airy dreams of entertaining my freinds in England with the scenes that I am to see here are vanished . . . had providence spared him a month longer what an advantage would it have been to my undertaking.'

During the first days of the Tahitian sojourn, Cook exhibited something new – new at least to the reader of his journal – namely a heightened curiosity concerning local custom. The astronomer and surgeon, out on a walk, had sighted the body 'of the Man we had Shot'. Its unusual treatment 'surprized us all very much', Banks wrote, and on the following day Cook and others went to see it. Near the man's house was found a sort of 'shade' or shed some fifteen feet long and ten to twelve broad, within which the corpse rested upon a bier, with a fighting club, a stone axe, a considerable number of coconuts, some bags containing cooked breadfruit and a dish of water. The visitors speculated as to whether all dead, or only those of high rank, were dealt with in this fashion, whether Tahitians believed in a supreme being, and whether the foodstuffs were offerings to a god or were for the use of the deceased in another world. 'If it is a Religious ceremoney we may not be able to understand it, for the Misteries of most Religions are very dark and not easily understud even by those who profess them,' Cook observed. His point – that religious ideas are typically obscure, and all the more difficult for outsiders to grasp – is less significant than his assumption that in this remote part of the world he encountered a sort of 'religion'. He was not an anthropologist – anthropology was anyway still a branch of natural history, and not yet named, at this time – but his way of thinking was proto-anthropological. He took the human species as a unity, and he assumed that every particular people had its own variations on broader human institutions.

*

Some Tahitians remembered the *Dolphin* too well. They anticipated violence and were afraid. A priest prophesied that 'after 4 Days we should fire great guns from the Ship', Cook understood. Given that one man had already been killed and others shot, it is not surprising that some believed this and evacuated the vicinity, though others were friendly and unconcerned. On 28 April Purea appeared, received a variety of gifts, and was delighted by a doll which Cook told her was a representation of his wife. This playfulness is not characteristic. It suggests that Cook could, at least occasionally, suspend seriousness of purpose and enjoy the humour and the surprises of a cross-cultural meeting.

From the beginning of the encounter, commoner women were 'very Kind In all Respects' as Wilkinson put it, meaning that they willingly engaged in sexual traffic – as they had during the visit of the *Dolphin*. Other kinds of barter proceeded. Tutaha visited on several occasions, bringing welcome gifts of pigs and other foods, taking cloth and iron in return. Sometimes barter failed. The ship's butcher, Henry Jeffs, violently threatened a woman called Tomio or Tamaio, a relative by marriage of Purea's, after she refused to give him a stone axe for a nail. Her husband complained to Banks. Banks promised that the man would be flogged, as he indeed was, on Cook's instruction on 29 April, before the offended people. The Tahitians were horrified by the procedure – Jeffs was stripped, bound to the rigging and then lashed – and interceded for the man, as soon as it had begun. But Cook insisted on completing the punishment. It was not his style to do things by halves.

Time passed. The dealings between mariners and natives were marked by mutual generosity at one moment and tension or antagonism at another. On 1 May, Tutaha visited the *Endeavour* and spent some time looking 'into every Chest and Drawer' in Cook's cabin. He was offered various things and collected them together to take away, but then saw a singular Euro-Polynesian object that we know of only from Cook's reference on this occasion – an iron 'Adze I had from Mᴿ Stephens that was made in immitation of one of their Stone Adzes or axes' – presumably cast from, or on the pattern of a Tahitian one brought back by Wallis. Tutaha preferred to leave all the other things and take this, which 'he was well pleased with'. It is symptomatic that what he valued above all else was not an exotic object, but an improved version of a familiar one. He and Cook appear to have parted on good terms, but the next morning Green and Banks, who were about to set up the astronomical quadrant, discovered that this bulky and essential piece of equipment had been stolen. Banks quickly established who had taken it and set off in pursuit with Tepau, Purea's brother, who had already acted as a helpful go-between. Cook seems to have resolved initially to impound all canoes and take Purea, Tutaha and other chiefly people hostage against the return of the instrument, but it became apparent that none of them were implicated and he dropped the idea. As he followed Banks with a party of marines, a double canoe nevertheless was seized and Tutaha was detained until they returned, much later that night, with nearly all the various components of what had been taken. It is difficult to recover any sense of the emotions of the moment since Cook only witnessed and described what was, from his perspective, the happy resolution of the crisis. Tuteha had been convinced that the British intended to put him to death, perhaps because a guard made a joking threat along these lines. 'No man Ever suffered More from Apprehension', wrote Wilkinson; many Tahitians, waiting anxiously in the vicinity of the fort, also anticipated the worst. They were tremendously relieved when the chief appeared unharmed and could depart. Before doing so, he insisted on leaving a gift of two pigs. This puzzled Cook, 'for it is very certain that the treatment he had met with from us did not merit such a reward'; Tutaha, probably, was insisting that sociality was re-established, that there was no excuse or reason for any further outrage on the European side. The next day, it became known that the chief had quit the area, and was unlikely to return for some time.

The supply of provisions dried up and it became obvious to Cook and Banks that they had to go out of their way to make amends, to regain Tutaha's confidence. They sent word that they would visit him, bearing an axe and a shirt that he had requested in return for his pigs. On 5 May, a few of his people arrived to summon the Europeans, who took the pinnace to Tutaha's principal home at Pare, where an enormous mass of people awaited, 'calling out *Tyo Tootaha*, that is Tootaha was our friend'. This acclamation was subtly misread. In fact, the crowd was almost certainly hailing Cook, addressing him as '*taio Tuteha*', Tutaha's *taio*. The word meant something stronger and more specific than 'friend'. It referred to a personal alliance or partnership between equals and was marked normally by an exchange of names. Cook had perhaps already been identified as Tutaha's *taio* – appropriate because they were each perceived as the pre-eminent men within their groups – but the relationship was now being reaffirmed and insisted upon. Ashore the Europeans were led to the chief, who was seated with a party of senior men. Surrounded by an 'immense throng', Cook and Banks handed over gifts and were then led to a nearby enclosure to be entertained by a show of wrestling. They later described the manner in which the sport was conducted – which they took to be vigorous but good-natured – in considerable detail. This hospitality was part of another tussle, which they were experiencing without fully understanding: Tutaha was not simply 'reconciled' nor did he simply want to be 'friends', he was demanding a deeper reciprocity. It was this claim and his superior status as host that he exhibited to the crowds of his followers and dependants. The thoughts of the ordinary people who made up those crowds are beyond the reach of any historian, but my guess is that they were there in such numbers, in such a state of evident excitement, because there was something astonishing about this diplomacy. By now, they'd all seen white men before: they'd encountered not only the *Dolphin*'s crew, but that of Louis Antoine de Bougainville, who had visited Tahiti in the *Boudouse* and *Etoile*. What fascinated, on this great day, was not the sight of Europeans, but the spectacle of them being hospitably, but unambiguously, put in their place.

Banks traded from a boat by the fort at Point Venus. Some Tahitians alerted him to the arrival of a double canoe bringing several women and one man. By the time he was on the beach, this group was within ten yards of him, and others formed a sort of lane between the two parties. There was a pause, then the man advanced towards Banks and presented him with plantain and other branches, which were received on Banks's behalf by Tupaia – who was spending more and more time with the visitors. A second man then brought forward a large bundle of barkcloth. He spread at first three sheets on to the ground, and then the woman who appeared to lead the group, who seems to have been called Uratua, came forward, stepped on to the cloth and quickly unveiled 'all her charms', giving Banks what he called 'a most convenient opportunity for admiring them by turning herself gradualy round'. This performance was repeated. Further sheets of tapa were spread out, the woman stepped on to them and lifted or removed her own clothing. She did this a third time, then the cloth was gathered and presented to Banks. He took her and another woman to his tent, 'to both of them I made presents but could not prevail upon them to stay more than an hour'.

Banks was plainly delighted by this occasion, which seemed symptomatic of voluptuous Tahiti. What had been central, it seemed, was an act of sexual exhibitionism, but the behaviour obviously amounted to something other than an exotic strip-show. In fact it initiated a sort of trading partnership. From what Banks says, it is clear that the ceremony began with a formal greeting and that the presentation of cloth was its consummation. From information about Tahitian beliefs gathered later, we can be confident that when Uratua uncovered her lower body, she was revealing not her genitals but her tattoos and this is why she turned around, to demonstrate that her pudenda and buttocks were covered with the standard series of arched motifs. These designs were not decorations, but the results of a painful and protracted but essential ritual operation performed on male or female Tahitians around puberty, and understood to dispel the dangerous and contagious sacredness that every human body was charged with at birth. This sacredness, this *tapu*, was the life-force and the energy the child brought from the primal other world, but it was also threatening. It could contaminate objects, places, actions and people, causing illness, infertility, misfortune, deformity, even death. Tattooing 'sealed up' the person and made him or her safe, from others and for others. The ritual that Banks witnessed was a revelation of this status, an assurance that the woman was a mature social actor and an appropriate person to barter with. It was not a sexual invitation, but it is unsurprising and understandable that the male visitor took it as such, and as a further sign that he had arrived somewhere utterly unusual, a place of luxuriant sensuality.

The Europeans could think like this about Tahiti as long as they put political and practical matters out of their minds. Tutaha was pressing his point: it became evident to the mariners that they depended absolutely upon his goodwill for supplies of provisions. On 8 May Green and Molyneux took the pinnace some twenty miles to the east along Tahiti's north coast, and attempted at many places to trade for turtles and pigs. Everywhere people said that they all belonged to Tutaha and that they could not dispose of them without his permission. This is unlikely to have been true. Tutaha was an unusually powerful man of rank, but he was not 'the' chief, and certainly not the chief of this region, which was well away from his *marae* of Atehuru and his home district to the west. Yet he had nevertheless effectively persuaded people not to sell. He did this, perhaps, because he did not trust the Europeans, and maybe hoped they would not remain long. He was cautious, but he cultivated a guarded friendship and manipulated the visitors so that their dealings were principally with him, rather than with other high chiefs, such as Vehiatua – whose base was on Tahiti's eastern peninsula. Yet he avoided at any time ingratiating himself, and was generous and unforthcoming, attentive and cavalier in turn. He invited Cook, Banks and others to visit him a second time at Atehuru, and promised that if they did so they would receive pigs. On their arrival, he was amiable, but produced only one pig in return for some fine cloth, and that night, as they slept, he either encouraged or tolerated the theft of some of their clothes. The following day he could not be persuaded either to give them more pigs or to make any effort to have their garments recovered, which in Banks's case included a 'white jacket and waistcoat, with silver frogs'.

There was nothing the mariners could do but return sheepishly and almost empty-handed to Matavai. Their curiosity, at least, was compensated during the return trip by the sight of a 'truly surprizing' form of local amusement. In a high surf that, Banks judged, no European would have survived, a dozen Tahitians were swimming, and some riding the breaking waves on an old plank broken off a canoe. The 'incredible swiftness' with which they were rushed in was fantastic. 'We stood admiring this very wonderful scene for full half an hour,' Banks wrote, reporting the first European encounter with the Polynesian art of surfing.

On 3 June Cook wrote that 'This day prov'd as favourable to our purpose as we could wish, not a Clowd was to be seen the whole day and the Air was perfectly clear, so that we had every advantage we could desire in Observing the whole of the passage of the Planet Venus over the Suns disk.' Banks and others wrote in equally glowing terms of the perfection of the conditions, as though the great purpose of the voyage had been successfully accomplished. Cook acknowledged, however, that 'an Atmosphere or dusky shade round the body of the Planet . . . very much disturbed the times of the Contacts particularly the two internal ones. Dr Solander observed as well as Mr Green and my self, and we differ'd from one another in observing the times of the Contacts much more than could be expected.' In short – though no one quite said so at the time – the exercise failed. At this time, Cook could not know that it failed more comprehensively. The observations made in other parts of the world were no more adequate than those from Tahiti, and though it was many years before the data were fully analysed, it was apparent soon after the various observers returned that the results would not help determine the distance between the earth and the sun.

How did Cook feel? Was he devastated? Did he see his chances of future recognition and promotion scotched, or did he already have a sense that these observations were not necessarily central to the voyage's accomplishment? Had his attention already shifted towards the exploration of the South Pacific? Cook's terse journal entry leaves us with no idea. Whether troubled or not, the business was over and his agenda was different. His aim was no longer to reach a known place by a particular time, and see a certain operation performed. It would now be to search for places that were unknown over a time frame that was indefinite.

*

Before any of that, things remained to be done at Tahiti. There were disciplinary problems to be dealt with. While most officers were preoccupied with the transit, Archibald Wolf, a Scottish able seaman, had stolen a large quantity of spike nails from the stores, which he and others urgently required to buy the sexual attention of Tahitian women. Cook, who remained anxious to control trade and secure the ship's supply of food, punished him with twice the usual number of lashes. A week later he flogged two other men who were so desperate to acquire local curiosities that they stole bows, arrows and a *tamau* – a sacred head-dress made out of more than a mile of braided human hair.

Banks, whose position was generally one of privilege rather than responsibility, made the most of the opportunity to witness, enjoy and participate in Tahitian life. An old woman of rank had recently died. He expressed an interest in the funeral ceremony and on 10 June was allowed to take part. Naked apart from a narrow strip of cloth, blackened with charcoal, he joined the mourning party who visited the European fort and otherwise ranged around the countryside, chasing, threatening and frightening every person encountered. Banks was fascinated by the costume that the 'chief mourner' wore. He wrote that it was 'most Fantastical tho not unbecoming', but described it no further, referring his reader to 'the figure annexd' for explanation as though the outfit itself was so weirdly exotic as to be indescribable. And it is indeed a hard ensemble to characterize. Its lower portion consisted of a sort of tapa skirt bound around the waist, upon which were hung coconut shell and cowrie shell discs. Above this was mounted a shimmering board made of more than 1,000 intricately cut strips of mother-of-pearl shell that rose from the bearer's waist to chest, and above this a series of whole pearl shells, backed on to a thin board, rising at each side, those on the ends decorated with blue and green feathers. A mask and head-dress were made out of further pearl and other shells. The long tail-feathers of what was called the 'tropic bird' radiated out and up from the head-piece. This is the baldest of descriptions of a spectacular and intricate construction that included many particular and distinctively coloured shells, feathers and tufts of dogs' fur, the whole thing firmly but flexibly sewn together, worn by someone moving energetically, shaking shell clappers, brandishing a heavy sharktooth-tipped staff, used to threaten all and sundry, even to wound those who failed to make their escape.

Conversion to Christianity in the nineteenth century saw the end of this awesome and dramatic rite, which therefore remains obscure today, though elements of the costume have associations with genealogy and high rank and can be seen to memorialize the deceased. All the rampaging, clapping

9. Tahitian chief mourner's costume.

and chasing away may also, or may rather, have been intended to ensure that the dangerous spirit of a person of high status actually did quit the vicinity of their home and undertook its proper journey via the sea to the afterworld. Banks's own interpretation was that the performance provided a vent for the sorrow and anger of the bereaved – who took out their grief by threatening and occasionally harming those who remained among the living. But the accent of his account is not upon explication. He supposed, quite rightly, that his grasp of the Tahitian language simply did not enable the kinds of inquiries that would fully explain the rites. He does not so much regret as celebrate the inexplicable peculiarity of the wildly ingenious chief mourner's costume, which he desperately but unsuccessfully attempted to purchase. When the ship finally left this group of islands some months later, and Banks wrote more systematically about the culture of the Society Islands, he repeated himself, writing that the chief mourner wore 'a dress so extraordinary that I question whether words can give a tolerable Idea of it'. Perhaps this was all a way of saying that he had travelled not just to the opposite end of the world, but to somewhere beyond the reach of the English language.

Cook's attitude to theft vacillated. At Atehuru, as Tutaha's guest, he felt it was better to overlook than make an issue of the loss of clothes. But on 14 June an iron rake that had been leant up against the inside of the fort's wall was deftly pulled over that wall by a man who waited until the guards' backs were turned. Cook wrote:

I resolved to recover it by some means or other and accordingly went and took possession of all the Canoes of any Value I could meet with . . . to the number of 22, and told the Natives then present . . . that unless the Principal things they had stolen from us were restored, I would burn them every one, not that I ever intend to put this in execution, and yet I was very much displeased with them as they were daily either committing or attempting to commit one theft or other . . .

The rake was returned the same day, but Cook thought it worth holding the canoes against other things that had been taken, though it was doubtful that any of the vessels' owners were either implicated in any theft or had the power to retrieve any of the stolen things from other people. The following Tuesday, almost a week later, Cook acknowledged that he had no hope of recovering further property 'and therefore intend to give them up their Canoes when ever they apply for them'. But at this time only four were returned, and the remainder held for a further ten days. From the start, Banks doubted both the justice and the strategy of the step and reports problems that Cook does not: the canoes that had been seized were full of food, including freshly caught fish, which quickly spoiled, and which the owners were not allowed to take away. Further tension arose a few days later when seamen collecting ballast began taking stones from a *marae*, which locals protested – the place, of course, was sacred. Trade almost ceased with the people of the district, though Purea and visitors of rank from elsewhere continued to make and receive occasional gifts. They seem to have been unconcerned by the plight of the local fishermen, just as Tuteha appeared untroubled by the fatal shooting that took place just after the *Endeavour* arrived. Had the interests of Tahitians not been varied and conflicting, the first incidents of violence and the subsequent seizure of valued property would have provoked much deeper crises. Cook, ironically, only got away with his anti-theft aggression because he was targeting people less powerful than the real thieves.

In the last week of June 1769, Cook and Banks made a circuit of the island, in part by boat and in part on foot. Early on the second day they reached the narrow neck that separated the body of the island, Tahiti Nui, from the peninsula of Taiarapu or Tahiti Iti. Here they inquired into matters of government, and gathered that the isthmus divided 'the Island into two districts or Kingdoms'. Cook's grasp of the topic was flawed, as European understandings of Oceanic political systems often would be. The tendency on this occasion, and in general, was to reduce fluid relationships to fixed ones. In Polynesia, chiefly titles, rank, prestige, power, property and authority were associated but never wholly aligned. Often, high rank did not carry political power. This was true in Tahiti for many reasons, not least because chiefly children were considered more sacred than their parents, and therefore outranked them from birth. Subtleties aside, Cook made a basic error in presuming that Tahiti Nui, the larger part of the island, was a single district 'Subject to Tootaha', when Tutaha was in fact pre-eminent within his district of Atehuru, influential but certainly not sovereign outside it.

Cook and Banks proceeded further, impressed by canoes much larger and more elaborately carved than those they had seen before, by the fine and intensively cultivated landscape and by the great number of *marae*, 'all ornamented with carved work, some with the images of men standing on each others head'. They had by now gleaned that these were temples, where offerings of pigs or vegetables would often be seen, but would have been bewildered by the various types, some particular to families, others serving whole districts, others associated with particular chiefs and their cults. They stopped a night, then proceeded by boat. At one place they entered a house where the jawbones of dead warriors were suspended. At another they 'met with a very extraordinary curiosity call'd Mahuwe', a representation or maybe an incarnation of the god Maui, a trickster who was thought to have drawn Tahiti and many other islands up from the sea's bottom, while fishing from his canoe. The huge wickerwork figure was covered in white and black feathers, the latter representing Maui's hair and tattoos. Cook gathered that

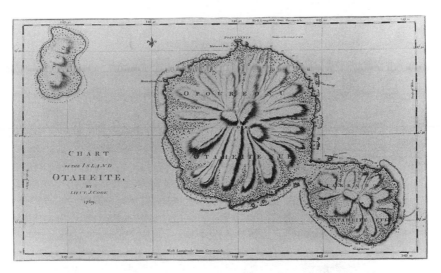

10. *Cook's chart of Tahiti, surveyed during his tour of June 1769.*

it was paraded somehow in their *heiva* 'or publick entertainments'. They proceeded further around the island's south coast, reached Purea's home at Papara, and were astonished there by the spectacle of the *marae* Mahaiatea – completed just a year earlier. Cook thought it 'a wonderfull peice of Indian Architecture and far exceeds every thing of its kind upon the whole Island'; he described its stepped, pyramidical structure, its regular proportions, its fine combination of worked coral and red stone, its expansive walled pre-cinct, and its many altars and sacrifices. Banks thought it 'almost beyond beleif that Indians could raise so large a structure without the assistance of Iron tools' and noted that though there were certain imperfections – elements of the structure had apparently subsided – the standard of workmanship was excellent. 'The stones are also polishd and as well and truly as stones of the kind could be by the best workman in Europe.'

There is a pencil sketch of this *marae* that is at first sight schematic and unimpressive. Yet this modest representation reflects a development that was in its way more truly extraordinary than the architectural wonder that was depicted. For the drawing was the work not of one of Banks's draughtsmen, but of Tupaia – who had proved himself as avidly curious about European arts and technologies as the Europeans were about those of their Polynesian hosts. We do not know exactly when Tupaia began to draw and paint, but over May and June 1769 he spent an increasing amount of time with Banks and Banks's artists. Both Parkinson and Herman

11. *Tupaia,* The Marae Mahaiatea, *1769.*

Diedrich Spöring produced many studies of people, artifacts and scenes, and of course paid particular attention to things that fascinated Banks, such as the costume of the chief mourner. It was perhaps at this point that Tupaia joined them, and painted musicians, a young woman dancing, canoes before a village, a chief mourner and two views of *marae*, including this representation of Mahaiatea. From the vantage point of his own culture, this was radically innovative. Not because pictorial representation was unknown in Tahitian art: drawn figures sometimes appeared in tattoos and rock engravings. But Polynesian art was never descriptive. It invoked deities, it expressed rank, it marked genealogy and sovereignty: it was about presence and power. The idea that a place or activity might be represented, just because it was typical, or that the purpose of a drawing might be to show what a drum, a costume or a canoe looked like, can only have been alien and wholly novel. But this was a time of novelty, and just as many Tahitian men and women took iron and ran with it, Tupaia made a new sort of art his own.

Soon afterwards, Cook and Banks were back at Point Venus, preparing for departure. The fort was dismantled. There were further thefts, further gifts of pork from Purea and further scuffles between undisciplined common seamen and locals. On 9 July two marines, Samuel Gibson and Clement Webb, deserted. Word came that they had retreated to the interior, taken wives, and proposed to remain on the island. What is remarkable about this is not that they should have wanted to remain with the women they had met, but that they anticipated feeling secure and comfortable among an alien people they were only just getting to know. Cook took drastic action. Purea and eight other chiefly people, then within the camp, were told that they would not be permitted to leave until the men returned. Cook believed that the seizure of Tutaha 'would have more weight with the Natives then all these put together' and sent Lieutenant Hicks to decoy him to the ship, which Hicks succeeded in doing. Purea and the rest were by now in a state of consternation, and though they had apparently wanted the two to remain on the island, they became anxious for their swift return. A Tahitian party was sent out with the midshipman Monkhouse and Edgcumbe, the serjeant of marines. Cook expected that they would return quickly with his men, but day turned to night and they failed to reappear. He removed some of the hostages, including Purea, to the ship; 'in going into the boat they expressd much fear and shed many tears,' Banks reported. Around nine that night some Tahitians returned, but with only one of the marines, as well as the alarming news that the midshipman and serjeant had been taken counter-hostages, and would be held until Tutaha was released. Cook dispatched an armed boat with one of the chiefs and Tupaia, described on this occasion as 'our voluntary prisoner'. The 'women cryd a little' overnight, Banks noted, and in the morning the crowd near the fort were uneasy and angry.

Fortunately the conflict was defused: those holding the Europeans had debated strategy and come close to blows among themselves, but resolved to give their hostages up. They did so without opposition, to Lieutenant Hicks, who found them some time before dawn. They returned safe, but Cook insisted on holding the chiefs until Monkhouse's and Edgcumbe's weapons, which had been taken from them, were brought back, which took a further half hour. Only then were people freed, to the great joy of the local crowd. The master's mate, Robert Molyneux, who for the most part wrote blandly, without exaggeration or dramatization, said that the hostage taking 'struck a general Terror through the Island & the Prisoners ('tho very well Treated) was inconsoleable'. Banks, who had remained on shore, also reports a level of tension that Cook omitted to record: 'I met them from the boat but no sign of forgiveness could I see in their faces, they lookd sulky and affronted' – as well they might have done, given that they had been held captive because of the offences of people they had no relationship with and no control over. Only one man had been killed, but to seize and threaten Tahitian chiefs was however to disturb the people as a whole, far more than they would have been by the actual killing of one or two commoners. It was to induce a worse terror and trauma than any of the Europeans could possibly have anticipated. Cook himself lamented the injustice, and that 'the folly of two of our own people' meant that they would leave the Tahitians 'in disgust with our behaviour towards them'. But he remained certain that had he not taken the hostages, the men would never have been recovered and their recovery was a necessity. If Cook's men thought they could remain on the island rather than on the ship, he might have lost the lot.

The *Endeavour* had remained at Tahiti for almost three months. It was an unprecedented encounter, not only for this sheer duration, but for the nature of interaction and for the growth of mutual knowledge. Virtually all previous visits had been fleeting and inconsequential, so far as mutual understanding was concerned.

Language was at once vital to the emergence of familiarity and a mark of it. Vocabularies of some hundreds of basic terms for body parts, numbers, foods, objects, plants, planetary bodies, actions and so forth were recorded. No European acquired fluency or sophistication in Tahitian, but it appears most were able to communicate in a rudimentary way. There was evidently some more complex conversation that touched upon the detail and the purposes of practices, and the reasons for events having occurred. And the mariners made the most of their Tahitian. Just as they relished the local pork, deliciously cool coconuts and sweet breadfruit, those who wrote journals embraced the smattering of the language they had acquired, noting that they passed 'morais', saw 'heivas', witnessed sacrifices to 'eatuas' and so on.

One of the Tahitian words that ceases to be Tahitian, in these writings that cease to be purely English, is *tatau*. *Tatau* was the onomatopoeic name for the Polynesian body art that sailors were quite literally struck by. Ta-tau was, roughly, the sound made when a sharp instrument with a row of fine teeth was repeatedly hammered, puncturing the skin and marking it indelibly. Though this sort of body decoration had been widely practised in classical and medieval Europe, its use had become rare and idiosyncratic by

12. The first European image of Oceanic tattoos: drawing by Sydney Parkinson, Tahiti, 1769.

the modern period. Those on the *Endeavour* encountered it as something entirely new. They referred to it by its local name, and wrote a good deal about what they called 'tattowing'. They were intrigued by its effect and by the sheer endurance that the process demanded. As Banks wrote:

This morn I saw the operation of *Tattowing* the buttocks performd upon a girl of about 12 years old, it provd as I have always suspected a most painfull one. It was done with a large instrument about 2 inches long containing about 30 teeth, every stroke of this hundreds of which were made in a minute drew blood. The patient bore this for about ¼ of an hour with most stoical resolution; by that time however the pain began to operate too stron[g]ly to be peacably endurd, she began to complain and soon burst out into loud lamentations . . . The arches upon the loins upon which they value themselves much were not yet done, the doing of which they told causd more pain than what I had seen.

And Parkinson wrote, remarkably casually, 'Mr Stainsby, myself, and some others of our company underwent the operation, and had our arms marked.' At this moment, the bodies of sailors were altered forever. Parkinson had no idea that tattooing would catch on, that by the end of the eighteenth century men who had never been to the Pacific would be tattooing each other, that tattoos would swiftly become the proverbial mark of the mariner. For the Polynesians, *tatau* was vital to diminish the dangerous sacredness of the body. This would have made no sense at all to the seamen, for some of whom 'tattows' were probably rather the sign of a special fraternity, a brotherhood that had travelled the world together. But the motivations of Joseph Banks – who was among those tattooed, though with what marks we do not know – must have been different. He would not have placed himself in a club with common men, but perhaps did not mind enduring a little pain for the most exotic of possible souvenirs.

There is another word that entered the journals of Cook, Banks and others, but that never caught on and entered language at home, as *tatau* did. It is *matau*. During the journey around Tahiti, Cook writes that during one night it was necessary to chase a thief to recover a cloak; afterwards 'we return'd to our lodgings where all hands were mattow'd, that is frighten'd, and fled'. 'Mattow' is used just a few times, of this sort of circumstance: Banks wrote that at Atehuru it had seemed politic 'rather to put up with our losses than to mattow or frighten the Indians'. In one copy of the manuscript to his journal, a note reads 'Mattow in their Language signifies to frighten, or affront. Indeed the general consequence of frightening them, was their being affronted.' The word – or this understanding of its dual meaning – captured one of the most conspicuous patterns of the relationship between Europeans and Tahitians during this visit. Repeatedly, the response to theft had been violence, hostage-taking, or the seizure of local valuables: these actions had on each occasion alarmed prominent individuals and intimidated the population as a whole, who made it plain that they had been offended and affronted. It was not only a word, but the pattern of behaviour that the word signified, that had become on the one hand almost habitual, on the European side, and unfortunately predictable, from the Polynesian one. In hindsight, we are surprised not that Tuteha was wary, but that he was ever as generous as he was.

Yet the qualities of the *Endeavour*'s sojourn here were reflected in tattowing as well as mattowing. The visit, or intrusion, was nothing if not paradoxical: at one moment it was marked by gift-giving, mutual admiration, and real affection; at another, Tahitians were subjected to a sort of terrorism. The encounter had a friendly as well as a dangerous side; hence the *Endeavour* would take away two people who had not arrived upon her. On 12 July, Banks wrote that

Tupia came on board, he had renewd his resolves of going with us to England, a circumstance which gives me much satisfaction. He is certainly a most proper man, well born, chief *Tahowa* or preist of this Island, consequently skilld in the mysteries of their religion; but what makes him more than any thing else desirable is his experience in the navigation of these people and knowledge of the Islands in these seas; he has told us the names of above 70, the most of which he has himself been at. The Cap^m refuses to take him on his own account, in my opinion sensibly enough, the government will never in all human probability take any notice of him; I therefore have resolvd to take him. Thank heaven I have a sufficiency and I do not know why I may not keep him as a curiosity, as well as some of my neighbours do lions and tygers at a larger expence than he will probably ever put me to; the amusement I shall have in his future conversation and the benefit he will be of to this ship, as well as what he may if another should be sent into these seas, will I think fully repay me.

Banks's characterization of Tupaia as 'a curiosity' in the same class as a tiger has rightly become notorious. If the future president of the Royal Society did not regard the world as his oyster, and value other people in so far as they afforded him amusement, he had an unfortunate habit of writing as though he saw things that way. Yet his attitude was entirely unlike that of nineteenth-century imperial entrepreneurs who really did collect indigenous people, really did keep them in zoo-like conditions, and really did exhibit them in precisely the way they exhibited animals. Banks saw Tupaia as a collectible, but also as a companion, and he was not someone who would use the expression 'a most proper man' lightly. He goes on to make it clear that what he means is that Tupaia is a man of rank and social eminence. Banks would never have described any of the common seamen in these terms, and no doubt saw Tupaia as a fitter person to conduct a conversation with than any of them. In any case, Tupaia was not 'collected' by anyone on the *Endeavour*. He made a decision to voyage (and he took a boy, usually described as his servant, with him). We can guess that his decision owed something to the awkwardness of his situation in the wake of Purea's defeat. He had, after all, been the chief architect and priest of her *marae* Mahaiatea, which was finally regarded not as a splendid, but as an excessive and maybe even obscene assertion of pre-eminence and power. But Tupaia did not join the *Endeavour* simply to make an escape. He was above all a navigator. He was thought to have visited some seventy islands. He was ready to discover new paths, new *taio*, and new temples.

As Tahiti shrank on the eastern horizon behind the *Endeavour*, Cook set out his observations on the place he still called King George's Island. More than 8,000 words, the tone of this long discussion is utterly different to that of his account of the Haush; he seems to have felt that describing them was an unpleasant necessity; the less said the better. Off Tahiti, his prose is excited. There has been so much that has been new, rich, singular, curious and wonderful. His description positions the island, characterizes its great mountains, its harbours, its wood, its topography, its pattern of human settlement and its delicious and diverse vegetable productions. Breadfruit, coconuts, bananas, plantains, 'a fruit like an apple', sweet potatoes, yams, sugar cane, pineapples and other edible nuts, fruit and leaves: 'All these articles the Earth almost spontaneously produces or at least they are rais'd with very little labour, in this article of food these people may almost be said to be exempt from the curse of our fore fathers; scarcely can it be said that they earn their bread with the sweat of their brow.' He went on to talk of their fish, shellfish, crabs, and lobsters, their domestic animals, their modes of preparing and preserving food, their meals, their physique, their skin colour and hair, their use of scented oils, their tattooing, their clothing and matting, their ornaments, their diversions, their music, performances and indecent dances. He described houses and canoes, noting that the larger vessels were managed 'very dextrusly and I beleive perform long and distant Voyages'. He detailed the making of cloth, the division of the island into kingdoms, and broached the subject of their religion, 'a thing I have learnt so little of that I hardly dare touch upon it'.

Cook had long known how to make geographic observations; he had recently learned a great deal from Banks, about the observation of matters economic, social, behavioural, and political, and about the writing out of observations; but he had by now grasped these skills and made them his own. Though he obviously read, and sometimes copied wording from Banks's journal, the borrowing on this occasion was the other way around. Banks only composed his own account of the 'Manners & customs of S. Sea Islands' a month later, after the neighbouring islands of Huahine and Raiatea had been visited, and though he then wrote more than twice as much as Cook, he drew closely on Cook's descriptions of tattooing among other practices.

Only a few days later, the ship arrived at Fare harbour, a place to which the vessel is likely to have been directed by Tupaia – who took charge of their arrival there. As soon as they landed he stripped to the waist, a customary expression of deference, and required Monkhouse the lieutenant to do the same. He asked the bulk of the party to remain behind and then advanced addressing 'a long speach or prayer' to the people gathered to receive them.

. . . in the Course of this speach [he] presented to the people two handkerchiefs, a black silk neckcloth, some beads and two very small bunches of feathers, these things he had before provided for this purpose, at the same time two Chiefs spoke on the other side in answer to Tupia as I suppose on behalf of the people and presented us with some young Plantain Plants and two small bunches of feathers. These were by Tupia order'd to be carried on board the Ship, after the Peace was thus concluded and ratified every one was at liberty to go where he pleased and the first thing Tupia did was go and pay his oblations at one of the Maries.

Perhaps because due formalities had been observed, the short visit here was free of trouble: the people seemed notably less inclined to steal than they had been at Tahiti. They proceeded to the neighbouring island of Raiatea, 'the first thing done was the performing of Tupia's ceremony in all respects as at Huaheine. I then,' Cook wrote, 'hoisted an English Jack and took posession of the Island & those adjacent for the Use of His Brit^k Majestys, calling them by the same names as the Natives do.' He must have felt this wording was not quite right, and changed it to read 'took posession of the Island & those adjacent in the name of' His Majesty. The amendment does not look simply stylistic. Cook was instructed to take possession of places newly discovered with the consent of the inhabitants. He had taken no steps to obtain such consent at Raiatea, and had just been welcomed there, through the diplomacy of another Polynesian. We do not know what Tupaia said, but we can be pretty sure that he did not tell his relatives that their lands were about to become the property of a distant European king. Cook's chief concern was to forestall claims on the part of French or Spanish explorers: perhaps he therefore felt there was no reason or sense in raising the issue with the inhabitants. Yet his deletion of the words 'for the Use of' does imply a degree of discomfort with what he had done. By omitting them, he was perhaps reassuring himself that this ceremony added something to an English map: no 'use' would be made of these lands, no Islanders' rights would be taken away. I am not sure what Tupaia would have made of this.

6

In order to seize upon the people

The *Endeavour* was neither the first nor the second nor the last great boat to sail from the Society Islands to New Zealand. Such voyages had begun centuries earlier. They were motivated by Polynesian passion. They had many beginnings and many endings – made out of lust, conquest and loss. Some people descended from Society Islands chiefs travelled in the Tokomaru and Arawa canoes to the land they later called Te Ika a Maui, the fish of Maui. They lived on Great Mercury Island but left there after fighting about who owned a plantation. Paoa, grandson of the priest of the Arawa canoe, built the Horouta canoe and took his people south. They carried seven calabashes containing seven gods and five sacred adzes, and sailed to the Bay of Plenty to find the entrance to the Ohiwa estuary, where the Horouta struck and capsized. One woman drowned, others reached the shore and had to dive later for parts of the canoe that had sunk. Here, the party split up. Hinekauirangi took the women and children inland. Her brother Paoa and his warriors, joined by some Ohiwa people, followed. Kiwa took the damaged canoe further south with as many skilled sailors as it could hold. At the Awatere River they stopped, planted sweet potato and trees, named the garden, the trees and a patch of black sand, and proceeded. They landed next at Te Muriwai; Kiwa ventured across the bay, found a broad and sandy river that snaked inland, flanked by flat land, surrounded by a great circle of cloudy hills that were like the rim of an open basket. This place, he decided, would be right for the three parties' rendezvous. He named it – the land, the streams and the sea – Turanganui-a-Kiwa, 'the meeting place chosen by Kiwa'.

Paoa's group followed streams, took short cuts through inland hills and came across to the east coast. They named places after the spots where Hinekauirangi spread her clothes to dry, they named rocks after the calabashes they resembled and called a beautiful pool of clear water in the Whakamarie stream Te Mimi o Paoa, 'the piss of Paoa'. Their travels were difficult. They searched beaches for the Horouta and returned inland to obtain food. The party, who divided and re-formed, included Kahutore, who carried a two-pronged roasting spit; Koneke and Whioroa, who each had short spears; Tangitoronga, who netted birds and fish; Kura with his eelpot; Te Paki, who owned a dog; Irakaiputahi, who had a parakeet, and Mahaututea, who brought a long bird spear, with which he jabbed fat wood-pigeons. Kiwa's messenger, Rongokako, who had been supposed to tell Paoa where the Horouta had finally landed, went off without bothering to do his duty, but the group eventually reached Turanganui. Paoa's sister had already made the first kumara garden to the south, she found a source of drinking water and named it Umurau, and she had a house constructed for her, called Paapaatewhai. At Turanganui, a village was built called Heipipi. The streams flowing into the Turanganui River were variously named Waikanae, 'mullet water', Waimata, 'obsidian or dark water', and Taruhera, after a bank of scented moss. This was a landscape and seascape marked by founding women and men who had planted crops and given names. No place would be without genealogy and history. None would be given up without a fight.

In mid August 1769, after passing Rurutu, Cook embraced the letter of his secret instructions and stood 'directly to the Southward in search of the Continent'. The seven weeks which followed were weeks of anticipation. The *Endeavour* sailed at first due south to about 40°. Nothing happened, except that one John Reading, aged about twenty-five, drank himself to death. Everyone looked out for land birds, but sighted nothing apart from albatrosses and other sorts, 'All . . . generaly seen at a great dist^ce from land'. In increasingly heavy weather Cook turned back north, then west towards New Zealand, which was known from Abel Tasman's visit of almost 130 years earlier. In 1642, Maori hostility had discouraged Tasman from landing and he had no sense of whether he had found a continent or merely a large island.

It must have been frustrating, as uncertain signs of the southern continent appeared and disappeared. On 1 October, a day after Cook had promised a gallon of rum to the first man who sighted land, a seal was observed. He wrote that although it was usually supposed that seals never ventured into deep water, 'the few we have seen in this sea is certainly an exception to that rule'. Weeds were encountered, which meant nothing, despite the hypotheses that they evidently gave rise to. A piece of wood was picked out of the water, which as Banks wrote 'must have been a long time at Sea yet more hopes are drawn from this than the sea weed, as we now have in our possession a part of the produce of the Land of Promise'. A few days later,

'Our old enemy Cape fly away entertaind us for three hours this morn all which time there were many opinions in the ship, some said it was land and others Clouds which at last however plainly appeared.' Finally, early in the afternoon on 7 October, the boy on the masthead, Nick Young, saw high land in the distance, which was visible from the ship's deck by dusk. Over the next day and a half, the *Endeavour* approached and tacked into the coastal amphitheatre that would soon be called Poverty Bay. It was not until the afternoon of Monday the 9th that the ship was anchored in about ten fathoms just off the entrance to the Turanganui River. With the wind coming from the south-east, the harbour was not sheltered but was safe enough. The bottom consisted of fine sand. The land appeared fertile and peopled. In short, this was a good-looking place. Though Cook's first observations on the hilly and green face of the country are characteristically matter-of-fact, the excitement on board must have been intense. Most if not all supposed that this was the southern continent: the riches it had for so long promised would soon be seen, sampled and enjoyed.

As soon as the Europeans landed, however, it became evident that nothing, not even access to the shore, was here simply for the taking. Cook, Banks, Solander and a party landed first on the eastern side of the river, but saw that some Maori were on the other bank, at the end of the long beach that runs right around the bay. Cook wanted to make contact and ordered the yawl, the smallest of the *Endeavour*'s three boats, to take the group across. The people – he calls them 'the Indians' – vanished, so the mariners walked a few hundred yards inland to some Maori dwellings, looking for water and leaving four boys to look after the yawl. The surviving fragment of the journal kept by the surgeon, William Monkhouse, which covers only the *Endeavour*'s first fortnight in New Zealand, tells us a great deal more about this brief excursion than does Cook or anyone else. Houses, a net, a garment, some fish-pots, an earth oven and 'a piece of white pumice Stone formed into a very rude resemblance of a human figure' were noticed. Huts were ventured into and judged. The figure was examined, presumed to be of religious significance, and carefully replaced, adorned with a few beads. Meanwhile, however, a few men had appeared from the trees on the other side of the river and were approaching the boys in the yawl with what were presumed to be hostile intentions. They

would certainly have cut her off, had not the people in the pinnace discover'd them and called to her to drop down the stream which they did being closely pursued by the Indians; the Coxswain of the pinnace who had the charge of the Boats, seeing this fire'd two musquets over their heads, the first made them stop and look round them, but the 2ᵈ they took no notice of upon which a third was fired and killed one of them upon the spot just as he was going to dart his spear at the boat; at this the other three stood motionless for a minute or two, seemingly quite surprised wondering no doubt what it was that had thus killed their commorade: but as soon as they recover'd themselves they made off draging the dead body a little way then left it.

Those who had walked inland were alarmed by the shots. Gathered together, they made their way back to the beach – and then followed a trail of blood to discover and inspect the dead man's body. He – Banks notes, Cook does not – 'was a middle sizd man tattowd in the face on one cheek only in spiral lines very regularly formd; he was covered with a fine cloth of a manufacture totally new to us'. Monkhouse not only described the marks but made a stab at their purpose: 'he had three arched tattaous over his left eye drawn from the root of his nose towards the temple; each arch about four lines broad – the interval between each about a line broad; this was an exceeding new and singular appearance and seem[ed] meant to give fierceness to the Visage'. No one is clear about times, but it sounds as though all of this happened within an hour or so of Cook's first landing. Within that hour, a man had been killed and the rudimentary properties of the first sustained encounter between Maori and Europeans had emerged: Europeans would meet, fairly consistently, with Maori hostility; and they would admire Maori. They would be favourably impressed by cloth and by utensils; they would be struck by the involuted spirals of Maori facial tattoos or *moko*; they would be awed by other arts of Maori warriorhood.

There was another aspect of this moment that was profoundly significant. Neither Cook, Banks nor Monkhouse immediately remarked on the point in their journals, but the identification of the dead man's *moko* as a tattoo had extraordinary implications. Remember that the word was still a Tahitian one, and was only just entering the English language. Banks and Monkhouse used it because what they saw was akin to Tahitian puncturing and staining, if also different from it – Tahitian tattoos were normally on the buttocks and chest, not the face. The affinity, as well as the physical similarities between New Zealanders and Tahitians, and the point that they too evidently cooked in earth ovens, raised the remarkable likelihood that these peoples were related, despite being separated by thousands of miles of open ocean, and had somehow travelled in one direction or the other.

Accordingly, when Cook landed again with Banks and Solander, cautiously positioning themselves across the river from gathering Maori, they called out greetings in Tahitian. The response was described by Gore, who must have been watching from a boat:

About an hundred of the Natives all Arm'd came down on the opposite side of the Salt River, drew themselves up in lines. Then with a Regular Jump from Left to Right and the Reverse, They brandish'd Their Weapons, distort'd their Mouths, Lolling out their Tongues, and Turn'd up the Whites of their Eyes Accompanied with a strong hoarse song, Calculated in my opinion to Chear Each Other and Intimidate their Enemies, and may be call'd perhaps with propriety A Dancing War Song.

Cook does appear to have been intimidated, or at any rate felt that it was prudent to retreat until his marines landed, at which point he and a few others, including Tupaia, returned to the river bank. Tupaia addressed the Maori and all were agreeably surprised, as Cook put it, 'to find that they perfectly understood him'. After some conversation, one swam across, and then twenty to thirty more. As Tupaia warned that the Maori were not friends, Cook made them all presents, but found his efforts to inaugurate some sort of sociability were failing. The Maori took the gifts, but wanted more, especially the Europeans' weapons. The astronomer, Green, was momentarily inattentive and one snatched his hanger – a type of short sword – prompting others to be more 'insolent', as Cook put it.

'Insolence' is a loaded word, but one that was less specific in the eighteenth century than it has become. Then, it could refer to the arrogance and contemptuousness of the powerful, as well as the impertinence of inferiors and subordinates. Cook and his men were supposed to acknowledge that the Maori were 'the natural, and in the strictest sense of the word, the legal possessors' of the land they inhabited. They had to be treated with civilly, but they had also to be convinced of the 'superiority' of Europeans. That morning, on the sandy edge of the Turanganui River, it must have seemed unlikely that the Maori who daunted Cook would ever acknowledge European superiority. Their 'insolence' was the arrogance of the powerful.

In a draft of this journal entry, Cook provided detail that he chose to omit from the official record. He says that he 'got Tobia to tell them that we was their friends and only come to get water and to trade with them and that if they offer'd to insult us we could with ease kill them all'. Cook may have considered this a judicious combination of greeting and threat. It can only have struck Maori men, who made and exhibited their identities through warrior performance, as provocation. Yet they did not respond immediately with counter-threats. Monkhouse alone tells us that 'A long conversation ensued, which seem[d] to consist on their part of inquirys from whence we came, of complainings that we had killed one of their people, and of many expressions of doubt of our friendship.' Tupaia prevailed on one man to swim across to a rock in midstream. Cook left aside his musket and ventured out to join him. They touched noses, and Cook presented a few trinkets, which delighted the man, who was quickly joined by others, 'the ice was broke', according to Monkhouse. Cook noted that those Maori who now came across the stream 'would willingly have exchanged their arms for ours but would not part with them on any other condition'. Part of the problem, in other words, was that he was attempting to impose terms of trade that stipulated that a bead or nail was worth a club or spear. The Maori saw that Cook and his kind carried swords and guns – the latter approximately resembled their own longer clubs, even if their use was not yet fully grasped. They wanted to exchange like for like, and only when this barter was refused did they snatch at the mariners' weapons. Trade broke down before it had really begun, not because the Maori were committed to attacking the intruders, but (at least in part) because Cook was unwilling to start handing over swords and muskets. If this is not surprising, neither is it so that the Maori valued their own weapons as highly as he valued his.

Jubilant Maori were at once dancing and feinting to catch at whatever they could. Monkhouse found himself 'engaged with three of these young active heroes' and gathered that he had 'to play the counterpart in these curious gesticulations' – that is, he had to dance and to parry and play a game, which for the Maori was perhaps no longer about trying to steal, but about amusing themselves by frustrating the mariners' efforts to stop them stealing. One cannot imagine that Cook felt prepared for this or that a surgeon's training had prepared Monkhouse for it. Though he, more than Cook, comes across as a willing improviser and a deft performer. A moment later Green's hanger was snatched. The man 'set up a cry of exultation, and waving it round his head, retreated gently', Banks wrote. Cook's draft reads:

and one of them at last Tore Mr Greens hanger from his side and was making off with it when I orderd him to be fired upon. Mr Banks first fired with only small shot which the fellow did not seem to mind but turnd about and flowrished the hanger about I then order Dr Munkhouse whose piece was load with a ball to fire at him and the man fell upon this some of the others who had retreated to the rock before mentioned return'd and attem[pte]d to seize the hanger and actily made themselves master of the mans own arms, and this Mr Munkhouse who was close by could not prevent unless he had run his Bagnet [that is, bayonet] into them upon the men return from the rock I fire'd so did Mr Green and Tobia we all three being load with small shot, yet three more was wounded, but got a Cross the River and lead off by the others. The man who I thought at first was dead recovered so far as talk to Tobia – yet their was great probability of the wound being Mortal.

In his account, Banks wrote that once the man had made off with the hanger, 'it appeard nescessary for our safeties that so daring an act should be instantly punishd'. It was no doubt a reasonable enough presumption, for five men exposed among more than twenty Maori, that their lives were at risk – we do not know what the marines, whom Cook had ordered to take up a formation some 200 yards to the rear, were doing at this time. On the other hand, it appears notable that Maori aggression was directed solely at obtaining the mariners' weapons. There is no suggestion that any warrior at any point during the encounter struck or struck at Cook, Banks, Green, Monkhouse or Tupaia. Had the man who grabbed Green's hanger wanted instead to club him, it is hard to see why he should not have done so; as it is notable that the men who ventured back to the rock were concerned not to attack Monkhouse, who was alone and vulnerable, but to recover their friend's greenstone *patu*, which was a treasure and an heirloom as well as a weapon. Others presumed that they were trying also to retake the hanger that he had dropped as he fell. Pickersgill, watching, has this definite impression. Monkhouse, who was there and should know, gathered that they wanted nothing but the *patu* and did not prevent them taking it. He indicates, more clearly than Cook, that 'Matters were now in great confusion – the natives retiring across the river with the utmost precipitation, and some of our party unacquainted with the true state of things begun to fire upon them by which two or three were wounded – but this was put a stop to as soon as possible.' In other words, some Europeans seem to have continued firing on the retreating Maori.

There are details of this exchange that cannot be disentangled. Those who wounded two or three were, on Cook's account, himself, Green and Tupaia; yet they cannot have been so far away as to have been 'unacquainted with the true state of things'. If they were 'acquainted', they thought it appropriate to keep shooting at men seeking to recover either the dead warrior's *patu* or Green's hanger or both. Monkhouse's imputation is that since he saw that they wanted the former and not the latter, he should leave off attacking them. It is tempting to rely on Monkhouse's record, which has almost the character of an exposé, in making it clear that the encounter entailed a more confusing succession of aggression, greetings, and gifts. But the surgeon himself was prone to omit information: the hanger thief, hit by small shot, 'continued to make his escape till a musket ball dropt him', he wrote, passing over the fact that that ball came from his own gun.

One of the things that I would like to know about what happened around this river entrance on 9 October 1769 is at what point it became inevitable that people would be injured and killed. The previous evening's incident suggests that the Maori were disposed to resist and repel the intruders, so Cook's commitment to landing and making contact perhaps made some clash unavoidable. Yet there is no indication in Maori behaviour on the morning of the 9th, before the shooting started, that they had planned any massacre or even intended physical harm. They were defiant, and once they saw what the visitors had, they were eager to obtain it from them in whatever way they could. Perhaps there was no retreat, no way of defusing this, once Green's hanger was taken. The Europeans fired because they would not submit to being stripped of their property, and because of what they feared, with or without justification. They started shooting to prove that this sort of encounter was susceptible to their control, but they convinced neither the Maori nor themselves.

No contact at Tahiti had gone as badly wrong as this. Cook decided immediately to try another approach at the other end of the bay, and without going back to the ship rowed in that direction to obtain water and 'if possible to surprise some of the natives and to take them on board and by good treatment and presents endeavour to gain their friendship'. This, the mate Molyneux considered, 'was certainly a generous christianlike Plan'. The surf proved too heavy to permit a beach landing. Otherwise Cook would have found himself at Muriwai, the site settled by Paoa's sister, Hinekaui-rangi. But two canoes approached from the sea and Cook rowed towards one 'in order to seize upon the people' whom Tupaia called alongside. The occupants immediately tried to paddle away, but Cook's boat was between them and the shore. He ordered a gun fired over their heads, hoping to induce their surrender; but they then began throwing paddles, and whatever else they could. This 'attack', Cook calls it, 'obliged us to fire upon them and unfortunatly either two or three were kill'd' – Banks says four. The remaining three jumped overboard and at length were picked up by the boat. One swam and dived a considerable distance, and had to be repeatedly assured that he would not be killed before he consented to be taken aboard.

The three were said, however, to become unexpectedly cheerful once they had been brought on to the *Endeavour*, presented with clothes and fed. Banks wrote that they enjoyed their dinner, especially the pork, ate a good deal of bread and seemed content going to sleep. 'After dark,' he added, 'loud voices were heard ashore as last night. Thus ended the most disagreable day My life has yet seen, black be the mark for it and heaven send that such may never return to embitter future reflection.' Does Banks mean that the violence of the whole day had been appalling and regrettable or is he only referring to the transactions of the afternoon? Cook likewise records that what happened should not have happened, but it is clear that his misgivings emerge specifically from the massacre of the people in the canoe:

I am aware that most humane men who have not experienced things of this nature will cencure my conduct in fireing upon the people in this boat nor do I my self think that the reason I had for seizing upon her will att all justify me, and had I thought that they would have made the least resistance I would not have come near them, as they did I was not to stand still and suffer either my self or those that were with me to be knocked on the head.

Troubled as this passage is, it hardly represents a full or candid account. It might be suggested that the encounters with the Maori the previous day and that morning might have given Cook a sense that these 'insolent' people were not likely to give themselves up just because they were asked to do so. And the fact that only one stone was thrown suggests that there was no great risk to Cook and the others in the pinnace; no European was even slightly hurt. The other missiles were paddles and whatever else the Maori had to hand. This sounds less like a counter-attack than a desperate attempt to forestall kidnapping.

The last two lines of the journal entry I've just quoted replace a more elaborate statement in Cook's rough draft: 'but when we was once a long side of them we must either have stud to be knockd on the head or else retire and let them gone off in triumph and this last they would of Course have attributed to their own bravery and our timorousness'. Here Cook acknowledges that it was not a choice of killing or being killed. Withdrawal was also an option, but not one that he would countenance. Though he did not, he says, anticipate that these Maori would resist seizure, he now knows them well enough to be sure that they would interpret his retreat as a sign of weakness. Here is a sign that in dealing with Pacific Islanders, he was Captain Wallis's pupil rather than that of the President of the Royal Society. The President, the Earl of Morton, was the sort of humane man, probably *the* humane man who had not experienced things of this nature and whose censure Cook feared. Cook believed that if European mariners were challenged or threatened, the prompt use of force – if need be lethal force – would demonstrate that resistance was futile. This is not to say that he would not always try to exchange gifts and greetings and exhibit friendship first. But when it came to ambiguity and disorder, he preferred a swift resolution, even a violent one, to an uncertain or unpredictable situation. That was his approach, which he felt made sense. Yet it was an approach inconsistent with the spirit of his instructions, and one explicitly disapproved of by his Royal Society sponsors. So it is not surprising that he thought it prudent to edit the rationalization of the Poverty Bay violence that appeared in his official journal. He frankly acknowledged his fault, but did not acknowledge its motivation.

Strangely, though, the plan that he thought had failed, the cause of his self-castigation, that of gaining 'the friendship' of these captives through good treatment, appeared to be realized before him. The three young men, as Banks too would report, were unexpectedly merry, given the circumstances. Cook proposed to spend a further day around Turanganui to see what the effect might be upon other Maori. The immediate complication was that the three were most unwilling to be landed at this place, rather than the southern part of the bay from which they came. They asserted that the people at the river mouth were their enemies 'who would kill and eat them'. The group landed, some cut wood, and others walked a mile or so inland, but Maori began to appear, all armed. The mariners became anxious and retreated back to what had become their usual landing place.

Banks 'despaird of making peace with men who were not to be frightned with our small arms', and says that Cook resolved to re-embark. At this point, one of the boys 'calld out that the people there were their freinds and desird us to stay and talk with them'. One Maori man cautiously crossed the same stream that had divided the parties the day before. Accepting a few gifts, both from the mariners and from the three young Maori, he spoke with Tupaia. He carried a green bough, which Banks thought was an 'emblem of peace'. He was with them only briefly, and on his return Cook thought it advisable 'to prevent any more quarrels' that he and the *Endeavour*'s company return to the ship. As they were leaving, the man walked up to the body of the man killed the day before, 'with great ceremony' and in a curious sideways fashion, and threw a second bough towards it. Later, other men carried this corpse away. Cook thought that this 'was probably a ratification of our peace' and had Tupaia take the three boys ashore a second time. They were still reluctant to be left, going so far as to plead and wade into the water after the departing boat. Banks implies that they were then forced to remain, only because Cook's orders had been so emphatic. Cook says that he wanted the boys left ashore because he had Tupaia aboard and that other Islanders would be superfluous, which is not convincing because these people could have provided local guidance which Tupaia could not. His real reason was perhaps that like Banks he was discomposed by the bloody mess of these first meetings. He wanted them over, and they were not over while the boys remained with him. Whether their imposed repatriation concluded the injustice was not quite clear. Later, they were seen joining an apparently friendly group and walking along the beach, leaving Banks hopeful but evidently still concerned that harm might come to them.

Expressing frustration and disappointment, Cook called the place Poverty Bay 'because it afforded us no one thing that we wanted'. The name is superficially one of his dull descriptive appellations like Cloudy Bay or Dusky Sound, but in this case strangely distorts the qualities of the place, which 'afforded' the mariners neither water nor provisions not because it was impoverished or drought-stricken. On the contrary, it clearly supported a considerable population. Today the plain is manifestly fertile. The confluence of river, estuary and bay has surely always been rich in fish and shellfish. The ancestor Kiwa knew what he was doing when he picked Turanganui as a suitable place for the people of the Horouta canoe to settle. His descendants and the descendants of Paoa and Hinekauirangi had guarded their precious wells, waters and gardens jealously and fought off more incursions than they bothered remembering. Cook's visit was only another, though it became different in hindsight. He obtained 'no one thing' that he wanted, not because the place was poor, but because it was rich.

7

He was laughed at by the Indians

Over late 1769 and early 1770, Sydney Parkinson, working obsessively, made some fifty sketches of people, scenes and objects in New Zealand (as well as dozens more of plants, birds and fish). Herman Diedrich Spöring likewise made the most of the long light of the antipodean summer and produced about forty painstakingly detailed drawings. In depicting canoes, Parkinson was extending a series that he had started in the Society Islands. Banks, increasingly excited by everything Polynesian, had no doubt told him that he wanted the character and construction of the Polynesian vessels illustrated. The drawings now look a little contrived. Composed of people and things observed at different times, packaged together in something vaguely reminiscent of a European port painting, common folk and their children fish and consort in the foreground, their canoes positioned before a fine mountainous island: the scene is as much an amiable sample of local life as a study of nautical technology.

Parkinson's views of New Zealand boats are different. They register something other than the complacent interest of a natural historian. They show a 'New Zealand War Canoe bidding defiance to the Ship', as the ink caption has it. Spöring too sketches a canoe, 'The Crew bidding defiance to the Ships Company'. These drawings reflect sustained Maori hostility. Though not every meeting was violent, and a few were positively friendly, 'defiance' was the dominant characteristic of Maori performance before the mariners. At first, on 12 October, Cook might have thought that his show of force at Turanganui had succeeded in convincing people of the benefits of friendliness. The next day, however, as the *Endeavour* coasted south, a few canoes came off and kept behind the stern 'threating us all the while'. Cook, thinking he might need to send boats ahead to sound, was concerned and ordered a musket and then a four-pound cannon fired near them. These did not particularly frighten the people, who shook spears and paddles but then withdrew, perhaps because the ship was moving out of or away from the sea space they considered their own. The next day, 14 October, canoes

13. Sydney Parkinson, Vessels of the Island of Otaha *(Taha'a), 1769.*

came off and 'seem'd fully bent on attacking' the ship, prompting Cook to fire a cannon loaded with grapeshot 'a little wide of them'. On 15 October, fishing canoes came off and sold some 'stinking' (probably preserved) fish. Cook did not find it appealing but wrote that he was 'glad to enter into traffick with them upon any terms'. Then, however, another canoe full of warriors appeared. Cook presented a few pieces of cloth, and tried to obtain a black cloak 'something like a bear skin', more it seems because he wanted to establish what animal the fur came from than because he was especially interested in the garment. The bearer took a piece of red cloth from him, but then pushed off without handing over the cape, probably a valuable dogskin. After a little while his canoe and others returned, and as more fish was being traded, Tupaia's boy Tiata was grabbed. 'This obliged us to fire upon them which gave the Boy an oppertunity to jump over board'. He was recovered, but two or three more Maori were killed. Cook named the place Cape Kidnappers and must have despaired of establishing any sort of amicable dealings here.

The next day he decided to turn the ship around and follow the coast north into warmer climates with, perhaps, 'more valuable discoveries', as Banks put it. On 19 October, as the ship again passed Poverty Bay, a canoe came off with five men who willingly came on board, accepted gifts and food, and insisted, rather to Cook's disquiet, on remaining on the ship overnight.

14. *A Maori canoe: 'The Crew bidding defiance to the Ships Company,' wrote Herman Diedrich Spöring on the bottom of his sketch, 1769.*

These people and those encountered the next day were friendly, and on 21 October, at Anaura, Cook was encouraged enough to land again for the first time in ten days. Banks indicates that the people were at first cautious. They 'sat by our people but did not intermix with them' and sought Tahitian cloth rather than European commodities in trade. They had their own barkcloth in limited quantities – tiny strips used in ear ornaments – because the appropriate trees scarcely grew in this climate, which was considerably colder than Tahiti's. Cook's seamen, eager to obtain clubs and paddles, were unwittingly bringing Maori into contact again with the material culture of their place of origin.

Here, for the first time, the mariners were able to spend time with Maori women. Banks noted that their red face paint was 'easily transferrable to the noses of anyone who should attempt to kiss them' and they seemed not to object to such familiarity 'as the noses of several of our people evidently shewed'. Though it sounds as if a joke was made of these transfers of face-paint, these men may merely have been greeted by women with the *hongi*, that is by pressing noses. Another source indicates, however, that sex took place. If so, these must have been hasty and strange intimacies. Men who had been repeatedly daunted by the 'defiance' of Maori warriors, who might have expected those warriors to be jealous of their women, can only have been afraid as well as aroused. The women were no doubt curious and scared but for all we know were aroused too.

William Monkhouse, the surgeon, is alone in reporting an unusual incident that similarly exhibits an odd combination of unfamiliarity and intimacy. One house on its own up a hill was occupied by a family of some status, who kept a couple of slaves or servants. The man was pleased to give a few of the Europeans a sort of tour, showing them the jawbone of a large fish, his paddles, his tools and his weapons. He was reluctant to allow the strangers into his house, but did let them satisfy their curiosity, and then 'brought out a child which was in a dried state'. If he was understood correctly, it had been his wife's, born alive but deformed, and had died soon afterwards. Given that Polynesians took birth – which marked the passage from the other world to this – as an intensely *tapu* and dangerous process, and that gods were often thought to enter the world as miscarried foetuses, the corpse of this child was probably considered a singularly sacred thing. He or she would not have been embalmed, unless regarded as precious. It is astonishing, then, that Monkhouse reports that 'he readily bartered it for a trifle'. An obvious but facile explanation might be that the Europeans were thought to be divine beings and therefore appropriate recipients of sacred gifts, but the Maori did not otherwise treat the mariners as gods, either in this place or generally. The event is one that can only remain enigmatic, sadly so, because this was the first occasion when Maori human remains – here not those of some disparaged enemy, but apparently of this man's own child – were acquired by a European.

The sexual contacts that may have taken place and this strange transaction marked the fact that here, at last, a relationship had been established. Cook must have been relieved, but the difficulty of getting water casks out through heavy surf meant that the place could not deliver what the *Endeavour* needed. So they moved on, but after the ship had been pushed south again by adverse winds, the Maori guided the vessel into a nearby bay called Uawa, the name of which was somehow scrambled into Tolaga, where people were again friendly. Water and wood were easily obtained and 'celery' – edible grass, an antidote to scurvy – was collected in quantity. People bartered a little, especially for barkcloth and glass bottles, but did not bring the quantities of food Cook hoped to see. For Banks, the high point of the visit was the discovery of a natural arch, through which the waters of the bay could be seen, 'the most magnificent surprize I have ever met with, so much is pure nature superior to art in these cases', he wrote, and had Spöring draw it immediately.

Cook does not mention this but was profoundly impressed with the place's natural abundance, and collected specimens of twenty different sorts of wood. He also began to make more dedicated observations of Maori life, composing a series of rough notes that touch upon religion and gods, cannibalism (about which more below) and artifacts ('Thier carving good'). He noted that 'they have a god of war, of husbandry &cᵃ but there is one supreme god whom the call   he made the world and all that therein is – by Copolation'. This is a poor rendering of the Maori account of the origin of the world in the ecstatic union of Rangi and Papa, sky father and earth mother, who had to be forced apart by their sons to make space for living things. Tupaia spent a good deal of time in conversation with men, no doubt including priests, and must have been the source of what Cook wrote. Local culture and local religion, scarcely grasped in even the most oblique or superficial way at Tierra del Fuego, began to be recognized here. With the help of a go-between, a man who was neither Maori nor European, but both a Polynesian and a mariner, a new kind of knowledge began to take shape. It was initially muddled and insecure, but it was made out of shared discussion rather than blank looks.

After Tolaga, the *Endeavour* followed the coast of the North Island past the places Cook named East Cape and the Bay of Plenty. Meetings with Maori tended to be fraught. On 31 October, grape and round shot were fired to warn off five canoes full of men 'all Arm'd with Pikes &cᵃ'. On 1 November canoes were fired upon more directly, after people took things without reciprocating; on 2 November a double canoe was sighted. The occupants engaged in some dialogue, and then pulled away 'but not before they had thrown a few stones'. The next morning this same canoe reappeared, and the ship was pelted again. On 4 November, a number of canoes appeared, and manoeuvred, seemingly with a view to attacking the ship, but dispersed after warning shots, including one that smashed the hull of a canoe. On the 5th, some people were met who conducted a little trade in a friendly manner. This was lucky because a transit of Mercury was to take place on 9 November, and 'If we should be so fortunate as to Obtain this Observation the Longitude of this place and Country will thereby be very accurately determined,' Cook wrote. The observations were made, the ship was brought on to a sandbank and scrubbed and a good deal of fish was obtained through exchange. The tensions underlying much of this barter were exposed, however, when Gore did what Cook had done before. He tried to secure a man's cloak in return for a piece of cloth. As happened earlier, the man, whose name is believed to have been Otireonui, took the cloth without handing over the cloak, at which point Gore shot him dead.

The cannon – the four-pounder – was then fired to disperse the group. Cook, who was not present, wrote that 'I must own it did not meet with my approbation because I thought the punishment a little too severe for the Crime, and we had now been long enough acquainted with these People to know how to chastise trifling faults like this without taking away their lives.'

Local tradition records that a council took place afterwards to consider whether or not the man's death should be avenged. The judgement, apparently, was that it should not because he had committed an offence. His death had been *utu* – recompense – for that offence. The pattern, however, continued as it had begun: Europeans were pilfered from or threatened, while Maori were frequently wounded. In the space of a month between nine and thirteen were killed.

From Cook's perspective, Otireonui's death appeared to have no repercussions. He would not have known whether this was because the Maori were convinced of European superiority, or because there was a local logic that favoured revenge in some cases and restraint in others. If Tupaia discussed the question with the Maori, Cook might have begun to learn about that local logic.

At other places Cook continued to use musket and cannon fire to ward people off. Some on board would have preferred a more vigorous deployment of force. On 22 November, when Cook was off on an excursion and a good many Maori were aboard trading, Lieutenant Hicks apprehended a man attempting to steal a half-hour glass, a vital if not highly valuable piece of equipment that timed the two- and four-hour watches that made up the ship's day. Hicks forced the man to the gangway and subjected him to twelve lashes. The Maori present were said at first to be astonished and indignant, but to acquiesce once the reason for the punishment was explained. Who knows now how they really felt?

Cook wrote that this treatment 'might have had some good effect had we been going to stay any time in this place, but as we were going away it might as well have been let alone'. He then deleted the passage, in order to leave negative comment on Hicks out of the record, but what he said nevertheless marked one of the limits of his mission. He had been told to take possession of lands, and in this sense he was a colonizer, but Cook's colonial interventions in Maori life were tentative and tactical. He was not authorized to make the Maori subject to European law, and he well understood that he was in no position to do so. He tried to cultivate 'friendship', meaning trade, and would deploy force if friendship, or trade, failed, but he tried to do no more than manage the meeting. He presumed that the Maori governed their own lives and would continue to do so. He did not see himself creating a society or civilization that was wanting. Hence Hicks's show of punishment seemed pointless.

When Cook had jotted down 'Their carving good' he was expressing, characteristically curtly, an awe and excitement that many others avowed. The mariners' interest in Maori art was manifest in the pieces they collected and in the sketchbooks of Parkinson and Spöring, who produced intricate drawings of a variety of artifacts, notably the prows and sterns of canoes. They did not do a bad job in representing the powerfully complex carvings made up of interlocking sinuous forms and thrusting humanlike and hybrid beings.

These Europeans found Maori *moko* similarly arresting. They had, of course, been intrigued by Tahitian tattoos, and turned on by the tattooed buttocks of Tahitian women, but the effect of the Maori version of the art was entirely different. In New Zealand, the challenging spiral forms were on the face as well as on the back and buttocks. They gave Maori warriors an exoticism that was shocking rather than pleasing or teasing. Yet *moko* were not said to be disgusting. Rather, those who wrote about them acknowledged that they were awe-inspiring, and this quality comes through in two of Parkinson's portraits that were to be published, widely reprinted, and to become more or less icons of Pacific culture.

The values and meanings of Maori culture were largely obscure to those who visited fleetingly in the *Endeavour*. Worldviews were basically different, and the communication that did take place, facilitated mainly by Tupaia, was never as sustained as it had been in Tahiti. Hence, though Europeans might guess that carvings represented gods, they had almost no idea who Maori gods were. Nor did they realize that local ancestors, rather than gods, were often the most consequential figures. It was people such as Paoa and Kiwa whose travels had brought them to places such as Turanganui. They had named and claimed land that continued to give life to their descendants. In all likelihood they were the ones embodied in the houses that mariners thought were ingeniously carved. Those outsiders who passed by had no grasp of the presence that these ancestors had among the people that they tussled with and were intrigued by. In these respects and others, their sense of what they saw was indeed superficial.

Yet when Banks writes of one carving style that it was 'in a much more wild taste and I may truly say was like nothing but itself', he was acknowledging that the art form was captivating – precisely its intent. Though Maori carvings and tattoos have meanings – that usually, for knowledgeable viewers, signalled details of ancestral histories – it would be

15. *Sydney Parkinson,* Portrait of a New Zeland
Man, *1769.*

a fundamental mistake to suppose that these art forms existed in order to
convey these meanings. Rather, the daunting carvings on canoes, the powerful embodiments of ancestors carved into houses and palisades and the
frightening designs on warriors' faces were there to project power, to captivate and awe visitors, strangers and enemies. An elaborately decorated
canoe was not a symbol of a tribe's pride but an instrument of it. It thrilled
and invigorated the warriors who cut through the surf in it, startling and
shocking those who might be fishing or just paddling along when a canoe

16. Patu paraoa, *whalebone club.*

full of chanting fighters appeared from nowhere. While the modern museum may regard the paddle or the canoe as a piece of tribal art, the actuality was that the carved canoes, flashing paddles, feather streamers, glistening bodies, tattooed faces, gyrating weapons and insolent oratory were not separate things – boats, tools, weapons, words. They worked together, to create an intimidating performance. The mariners took these performances for exactly what was intended. They were impressed, captivated and alarmed, and exhibited their own aggression in return, as Maori probably anticipated.

During November and December Cook was on this metaphorical voyage into waters he was not quite prepared for. Literally, he followed the intricate coast of the North Island of New Zealand towards what he prosaically called the North Cape. Fewer people made contact, and once the *Endeavour* rounded the cape and turned south, the prevailing seas were a great deal heavier – as anyone knows who has looked at, or played in, the dangerous white water of west Auckland beaches such as Piha and Kerikeri. It was therefore advisable to shadow the coastline from further offshore and there was no contact with the Maori again until mid January, when the ship entered what Cook at first presumed to be a great bay. He turned out of this bay into a long inlet, looking for a place to careen the ship '(she being very foul), to repair some few defects, recrute our stock of Wood, water, &cᵃ'. As it happened, in addition to these essentials, he would 'recruit' some disturbing facts here.

On 16 January, a 'very snug cove' was found with a safe anchorage, 'a fine stream of excellent water, and as to Wood the land here is one intire forest'. Seemingly ideal, though the people encountered were at first 'inclineable to quarrel' rather than trade. They became more friendly the following morning. While most of the crew were occupied painting the careened ship with protective oils and resins, Cook and a few others took the pinnace and visited the next bay to the north. *En route* they saw the floating corpse of a woman and when they arrived they found that the people had just been 'regailing themselves upon human flesh'. Some fight had taken place with enemies in a canoe, the woman sighted had been drowned and others had been killed and cooked. Cook 'got from one of them the bone of the fore arm of a Man or a Woman which was quite fresh and the flesh had been but lately pick'd off which they told us they had eat'.

This moment was the culmination of an obsessive inquiry that had begun months earlier, just after the *Endeavour* had arrived at Poverty Bay. You may not be surprised to learn that the mariners had become preoccupied with cannibalism. It has been well established that many western travellers, especially during the nineteenth century, labelled people from all over the world cannibals in the absence of any credible evidence for the incidence of the practice. Hence a recent commentator on Cook has argued that 'cannibalism is what the English reading public wanted to hear. It was their definition of the Savage.'

But this happens to be badly wrong for these early responses to Maori practices. During the 1760s, before Cook's first voyage, the 'English reading public' probably had no 'definition' of Pacific people at all. The one account of the South Seas that they would have known was Anson's, whose expedition made scarcely any contact with Oceanic peoples. No one expected Pacific Islanders to be cannibals, and Cook, Banks and the ship's company seem to have been genuinely unprepared for this discovery.

The possibility that the Maori might eat people was first mentioned when the boys kidnapped from the canoe in Poverty Bay expressed their reluctance to be landed at Turanganui. As Cook wrote, 'they were very unwilling to leave us pretending that they should fall into the hands of their enemies who would kill and eat them'. Others agreed that the boys' fear was a pretence, or as Pickersgill put it, 'a Stratigem' to get the Europeans to land them back at their own end of the bay. No mariner seems initially to have supposed that cannibalism might be an actuality. Banks noted their concern in passing but made no further reference to the topic until six weeks later, when he wrote:

It is now a long time since I have mentiond their Custom of Eating human flesh, as I was loth a long time to beleive that any human beings could have among them so brutal a custom. I am now however convincd and shall here give a short account of what we have heard from the Indians concerning it. At *Taoneroa* the first place we landed in on the Continent the boys who we had on board mentiond it of their own accords, asking whether the meat they eat was not human flesh, as they had no Idea of any animal but a man so large till they saw our sheep [Maori ate dog but had no larger quadrupeds]: they however seemd ashamd of the custom, saying that the tribe to which they belongd did not use it but that another very near did. Since that we have never faild wherever we went ashore and often when we convers'd with canoes to ask the question; we have without one exception been answerd in the affirmative, and several times as at Tolaga and today the people have put themselves into a heat by defending the Custom, which Tubia who had never before heard of such a thing takes every Occasion to speak ill of, exhorting them often to leave it off.

This indicates retrospectively that the suggestion arose first not from the boys' fear of the neighbouring people, but from their assumption that the mariners were man-eaters. It also makes it clear that many on board the *Endeavour* then became preoccupied with the issue, though Cook confirms that the most vigorous questioning of the Maori came not from Europeans but from Tupaia. He himself had come back to the topic a couple of weeks before Banks, noting in his journal on 15 November that the people of Mercury Bay 'confirm the custom of eating their enimies so that this is a thing no longer to be doubted'. Earlier still, on 22 October, Pickersgill had stated that 'they eat their enimies which they kill in Battle'.

Until mid-January, the Europeans had, however, done no more than ask after and *hear* of this practice. Banks gave a fuller account than Cook of their first encounter with direct evidence for it. In the bay to the north of Ship Cove, a family preparing food had, near their earth oven, many 'provision baskets'.

Looking carelessly upon one of these we by accident observd 2 bones, pretty clean pick'd, which as appeard upon examination were undoubtedly human bones. Tho we had from the first of our arrival upon the coast constantly heard the Indians acknowledge the custom of eating their enemies we had never before had a proof of it, this amounted almost to demonstration: the bones were clearly human, upon them were evident marks of their having been dressd [i.e., cooked] on the fire, the meat was not intirely pickd off from them and on the grisly ends which were gnawd were evident marks of teeth, and these were accidentaly found in a provision basket. On asking the people what bones were these? they answerd, The bones of a man. – And have you eat the flesh? – Yes. – Have you none of it left? – No. – Why did you not eat the woman who we saw today in the water? – She was our relation. – Who then is it that you do eat? – Those who are killd in war. – And who was the man whose bones these are? – 5 days ago a boat of our enemies came into this bay and of them we killd 7, of whoom the owner of these bones was one. – The horrour that appeard in the countenances of the seamen on hearing this discourse which was immediately translated for the good of the company is better conceivd than describd. For ourselves and myself in particular we were before too well convincd of the existence of such a custom to be surprizd, tho we were pleasd at having so strong a proof of a custom which human nature holds in too great abhorrence to give easy credit to.

Banks goes to uncharacteristic trouble to detail the circumstances of these observations and this conversation. This, in fact, is almost the only passage in his entire journal where he goes as far as to transcribe (or rather recall) an interview in order to document a circumstance. He also notes not once but twice that the bones were sighted accidentally, as if to forestall a sceptical claim that they had been produced in response to European interrogation. He had noticed that the Maori saw that the foreigners were disturbed, fascinated and frightened by the practice. Banks would not have gone into so much detail, had he not been aware that some sort of invention was possible and had to be ruled out, if this was to constitute the secure 'proof' that he was after.

Tupaia's interest was different to that of Banks and others. His interrogation sought not only to confirm or disconfirm, but to censure the practice, and this he did frequently and vigorously, in the course of conversations between the ship and Maori in canoes, as well as with people on shore at the many places where they called. We can only assume that like the British he brought his own ethnocentrism to the Maori. Tahitians and Raiateans, like the Maori, were often at war, but war was far less central to life in the Society Islands and it took place in order to secure political gain that was sought and claimed in a variety of ways – through cult ceremony, diplomacy and marriage – apart from war. For the Maori, on the other hand, the pursuit of *utu* – revenge – appears to have been one of the governing preoccupations of male identity. We have no way now of getting inside

Tupaia's head, but he probably found the resolute bravery of the Maori brutal. He was, in any case, repelled by cannibalism. The Maori in turn found his arguments singularly unconvincing, and resented his presumption. Their affirmation of cannibalism was not simply an acknowledgement of something they did, it was an assertion that they lived their lives as they chose.

The European responses to the 'proof' of the practice were varied. Parkinson seems to have been dismayed. Wilkinson is shocked, but finds the relentless conflict that seemed to characterize Maori life pitiful; 'These poor Wretches are at war even with their Next Door Nabours.' Pickersgill expressed none of this empathy, but opined that 'I belive these are the only People who kill their fellow creatuers Puerly for the meat which we are well Assured they do by their laying in wait one for another as a sportsman would for his game . . .' This is to suggest that the Maori were an irretrievably cruel people, and were alone in (supposedly) killing in order to eat. Cook's response, and that of Banks, was quite different. Both emphasize that the practice was a 'custom'. In his rough notes, Cook explicitly presents this as an excuse, for what might otherwise be an expression of savagery. 'They eat their enimies Slane in Battell – this seems to come from custom and not from a Savage disposission this they cannot be charged with – they appear to have but few Vices –'. Banks adds that 'They however as universaly agree that they eat none but the bodies of those of their enemies who are killd in war.' Pickersgill has no 'however': his implication is that Maori practice makes the Maori despicable. Banks's qualification sets the observation in a social frame rather than a moral one. He sees it as brutal, but softens the point by finding that its usage is specific. Cook is more categorical. So far from taking cannibalism to *define* savagery, he uses the 'customary' character of cannibalism to *exempt* the Maori from savagery. His overall judgement of them is shaped not by the practice but by the fact that, after initial hostilities, the various Maori who were encountered 'were ever after our very good friends'.

The Maori were consistently strong-willed, but their will did not always prevail and they were not always happy with the conduct of commerce. It was part of the sequel to the scene of cannibalism that the mariners became aware that the Maori preserved some people's heads. Perhaps because Cook and Banks were pressing for every possible confirmation of the account that they had been given, Tupaia demanded of an old man named Topaa whether heads were eaten or if not, what was done with them. Some days later, Topaa brought four heads by way of further demonstration that a battle had taken place and that men had been killed. Banks was evidently intrigued by these trophies, 'somehow preserved so as not to stink at all'. At this time, he is perhaps embarrassed and makes no mention in his journal of the fact that Cook noted, that he 'bought or rather forced them to sell' one only, which was damaged by a club-blow, 'for they parted with it with the utmost reluctancy and afterwards would not so much as let us see one more for anything we could offer them'. Banks later acknowledged that the purchase had been

much against the inclinations of its owner, for tho he likd the price I offerd he hesitated much to send it up, yet having taken the price I insisted either to have that returnd or the head given, but could not prevail untill I enforc'd my threats by shewing Him a musket on which he chose to part with the head rather than the price he had got, which was a pair of old Drawers of very white linnen.

We have seen already – in the hills of Tierra del Fuego – that Banks would put the business of natural history ahead of other considerations, even his own safety, that of his servants and here of the feelings of a local man he elsewhere described as a 'friend'. His commitment to his collection was such that he would use his gun to insist on a transaction, even though he was otherwise guilty and troubled by the work that guns had done in dealings between mariners and Maori. And after all this, he did not know what to make of the head – he was no physiologist – but he did know that he wanted it.

Reservations were expressed, too, about the barter in provisions that Cook was vigorously engaged in while carpenters and ironworkers repaired various components of the ship. Few gardens were seen around Motuara, but the fishing grounds were evidently rich, and in one island *pa* Cook found 'split & hanging up to dry a prodigious quantity of various sorts of small fish', some portion of which he purchased on 26 January. A week later he went back to the same place and bought a good deal more, but evidently pushed the opportunity too far: 'at last the Old men fairly told him that he must go away or he would leave them without provisions, which they enforced by some threats'. Even this brief visit tested local resources, raising the question in the minds of the men who managed these communities of whether the costs of contact were greater than any reward.

Another sort of traffic was evidently under way. On the same day that Cook was warned off his barter, 'One of our gentlemen', Banks reports, probably meaning one of the lieutenants, returned to the ship fulminating against the Maori, who he said were 'given to the detestable Vice of Sodomy'.

His grounds for this accusation were that he had met a family and paid, he thought, to spend time with a young woman, but the young person who 'willingly retird' with him turned out to be a boy. When he complained, a second was sent who was also male. Complaining again, 'he could get no redress but was laught at by the Indians'. Banks was unconvinced by the charge against the whole nation: 'in my humble opinion this story proves no more than that our gentlemen was fairly trickd out of his cloth, which none of the young ladies chose to accept of on his terms, and the master of the family did not chuse to part with'. The common thread behind all these transactions or failed transactions, in heads, cloth, fish, beads, trinkets and sex was that the Maori keenly wanted what Europeans had to offer, but rather doubted that it was worth what Europeans demanded. Exchange was therefore energetic, but unstable and replete with misgivings. The Maori impulse, not only here in Totaranui, but during the whole period of the *Endeavour*'s circumnavigation of New Zealand, was to take without giving, not because the Maori did not understand barter but because they did and too often thought they were getting a bad deal.

The Maori were nevertheless generous, not least with information. Cook climbed hills and made forays into bays on a number of occasions, aiming to confirm his growing (and correct) supposition that the waters around them formed not a bay but a strait that passed through into what he was calling the 'eastern sea'. Topaa explained that the surrounding lands consisted of two large lands 'that might be circumnavigated in a few days'. One of these was called 'Tovy-poenammu' as Cook transcribed it, more accurately Te Wai Pounamu, though he did grasp the sense of the name 'which signfies green Talk or stone such as they Make their tools on, oramints &cª' – the main sources of pounamu, which was traded throughout New Zealand, were in the mountains of the South Island, and the whole place appears to have been named after this sacred resource. Cook would later inscribe this name on the sculpted body of land that would find form on his chart. He would write Teerawitte on the southern protuberance of what is now most commonly known as the North Island, and give that whole landmass what he understood was its native name, Eaheino Mouwe, in all likelihood a confused rendering of Te Ika a Maui – the fish of Maui, who pulled up the land from the bottom of the ocean while fishing from his canoe.

In recording and reproducing these place names he was acknowledging that these were Maori lands. Yet before departing from the waters of Totaranui to circumnavigate the South Island – which he did without making contact with southern Maori at all – he would repeat the ritual he had performed at Raiatea. Reading his journal entry for 31 January, it sounds at first as though his intention is simply to leave unambiguous marks that will be known by future navigators. These marks take the form of posts, 'seting forth the Ships name month and year', one of which was placed with a flag in Ship Cove, and the other taken over to Motuara. Here, Cook had Tupaia explain to Topaa and a number of other men present that he wanted to set up a mark 'in order to shew to any ship that might put into this place that we had been here before'. He is pleased to note that they 'not only gave their free consent to set it up, but promise'd never to pull it down'. Cook then made gifts to everyone, 'silver threepenny peices dated 1763 and spike nails with the Kings broad Arrow cut deep in them'. The post was then carried up through the brush to the island's flattish summit. It was there erected, and as Cook explains, 'after fixing it fast in the ground hoisted thereon the Union flag and I dignified this Inlet with the name of *Queen Charlottes Sound* and took formal posession of it and the adjacent lands in the name and for the use of his Majesty, we then drank Her Majestys hilth in a bottle of wine and gave the empty bottle to the old man (who had attended us up the hill) with which he was highly pleased'. He did not have the second thoughts he'd had in the Society Islands, and did not later cut out the words, 'for the use of'.

Cook is clear that he negotiates one thing and proceeds to do another. Though here again the declaration was strictly for European consumption. It was not about the reality of Motuara, or of the lands 'adjacent', by which he may have meant the whole of Te Ika a Maui, including places such as Turanganui, which George III would have made 'use of' at his peril. It was about lines on maps that would be studied by geographers and shown to kings; it was done because it might forestall French and Spanish claims; it was not a statement for the Maori, who got on with their lives as though it had never been uttered or inscribed. But this was to make this January afternoon on Motuara still odder. On the one hand, Cook, Banks, Pickersgill, Gore and others were beginning to become accustomed to these great islands, that were still perhaps offshoots of a continent. They were used to the ponga tree ferns and the red flowers and convolutions of the pohutukawa trees, they recognized birds, and plants and fish, and started to speak the language; they'd eaten Maori food; they'd got beyond stone-throwing and shooting and could greet some Maori by name; neither Cook nor Banks nor Parkinson but probably a good few others had spent time too in Maori huts with Maori women, caressing and laughing and mis-communicating. They were becoming people who knew this place; yet, in another sense, they were not there at all.

8

An alarming and I may say terrible Circumstance

Thanks to a bright moon, the *Endeavour* had sailed through the night, and from nine in the morning was running parallel to a long beach. Through glasses, those on board could see about twenty Aboriginal people, each carrying a bundle of leaves or grass. The group remained in sight for over an hour, until they took a path that led them inland over a low hill and out of sight. The puzzling feature of the occasion was this:

Not one was once observd to stop and look towards the ship; they pursued their way in all appearance intirely unmovd by the neighbourhood of so remarkable an object as a ship must necessarily be to people who have never seen one.

This was characteristic of Cook's passage up the eastern Australian coast. Contacts with people were starkly limited. Though the voyage was later seen to mark the real beginning of Australian history, these first meetings between British mariners and indigenous Australians could not have been said to have inaugurated much. In this case, there seems scarcely to have been mutual observation, let alone any meaningful meeting. Cook and his men had experienced a variety of tense and pleasurable encounters in Tahiti and around New Zealand and were ready to be resisted or greeted, but not at all prepared to be ignored. They were bewildered by the indifference of people who ought to have been awed and astonished by the unprecedented spectacle of a British ship.

By this time, Cook had been following this coast for just under a month. On Wednesday, 18 April, the birds encountered had included Port Egmont Hens, 'certain signs of the nearness of land', which were sighted the following day just south of a point that Cook named Cape Howe. Over the next few days, smoke was observed, 'a certain sign that the Country is inhabited'. On the 22nd a gentle breeze carried the ship near the shore, and some inhabitants were seen 'of a very dark or black Colour but whether this was the real colour of their skins or the C[l]othes they might have on I know not', Cook noted. He hoped to find a harbour but was deterred by the heavy sea that rolled on to the coast from the south-east. Adverse winds discouraged him from investigating potential ports further north. On the 28th, people were seen carrying a canoe along a beach; Cook supposed that they might be about to launch it to visit the ship. When they did not, he, Banks, Solander and Tupaia approached the beach in the ship's yawl, but the Aboriginal people disappeared into the bush as soon as they saw the mariners, who felt unable, in any case, to risk the surf. The following morning, a bay, apparently well-sheltered, was discerned. After sending the master ahead to sound the channel, Cook took the *Endeavour* into it, and anchored 'under the South shore'.

Botany Bay is still beautiful, despite the oil refineries massed around this 'South shore', the airport runways that stab into its waters from the north-west, and diverse other excrescences of suburban and industrial Sydney. There are places behind the dune where all this can be imagined away, where the shallow waters are stained yellow-brown from bracken and wattle blown or washed into the water, where sandbars have become crab ghettoes, where flathead and mullet are motionless in the hot still water at the top of the tide.

Around here it is the stone that makes the landscape. It is an orange sandstone that weathers and hollows into grey. It forms rock platforms that bask like whales between brush and shore; their surfaces are not jagged but gentle and corporeal; their holes hold clean clear water after rain; their shelves and steps provide fireplaces and places to sit, to sleep and to swim from. At dawn and dusk, as the low sun picks out the pocks and lines in this stone, you discover – and can still discover – old rock engravings, etched tracks and weird figures as well as naturalistic wallabies and whales. This stone is not just natural, these are not just animals, but mythic beings, dreamtime ancestors of this land. There is not just a zoology but a cosmology inscribed here, a series of stories around this shoreline.

As the *Endeavour* entered the bay, Aboriginal people were fishing, 'totaly engag'd in what they were about: the ship passd within a quarter of a mile of them and yet they scarce lifted their eyes,' Banks wrote. After the ship came to anchor a woman with a couple of children nearby on the shore looked at the ship 'but expressd neither surprize nor concern'. Later, some people who had been out in canoes arrived and began to cook, 'to all appearance totaly unmovd at us'. Only when the mariners approached the shore did these Eora people pay them any attention at all. Two men came to the water's edge, brandished spears and shouted in a guttural language that not even Tupaia could understand: the voyage had passed out of the islands in which he counted as a go-between. Though decidedly out-numbered, these two remained defiant, even after being fired at twice with small shot, at which point one went to fetch a shield. When some of the Europeans landed, the two men threw spears, were fired upon again and then retreated, 'but not in such haste but what we might have taken one,' Cook wrote, which is to imply that, despite the disaster of the Poverty Bay massacre, he still felt that there was a place for taking captives in the good management of cross-cultural relations. Banks advised against doing so, not because he thought the attempt might go as badly wrong as it had in New Zealand, nor because it might have been thought unjust or inhumane, but because he believed (erroneously, as it happened) that the spears might be poisoned. The two men were permitted their retreat, and the European party proceeded to explore a cluster of huts, where the children sighted earlier were hiding beneath a bark shelter. These they left alone, but placed ribbons and trinkets on the hut, and 'thought it no improper measure' to remove all the spears they were able to find, which numbered some forty or fifty. Over succeeding days, at several places, Aboriginal groups were sighted. On two or three occasions they followed or approached the mariners but then withdrew. 'Mr Hicks who was the officer ashore did all in his power to entice them to him by offering them presents &c^a but it was to no purpose, all they seem'd to want was for us to be gone.' Cook saw another indigenous group, who fled. He landed at places people had just left. He, Solander and Tupaia tried to follow others, but they kept walking away. Still others were sighted 'who made off as soon as they saw us'. One officer met with a couple of old people and two children. He tried to give them a bird that he had shot, which they refused. On returning to the shelters that they had first visited, the mariners found, moreover, that the ribbons and trinkets left on or by the bark hut had not been touched.

It is clear what the Aboriginal attitude was: they wanted absolutely nothing to do with these intruders and would have none of their gifts. They did not want to make war upon them, but they did want them out of their lives. As Cook acknowledged, 'we could know but very little of their customs as we never were able to form any connections with them'. What was said of Eora was purely observational: they painted their bodies and faces, they clearly subsisted by gathering shellfish and spearing fish and they went naked. Their canoes, made from a single sheet of bark, sewn together at its ends and held apart by two or three sticks, were 'the worst I think I ever saw', Cook wrote.

From someone who made a lot of use of boats, this was damning. Yet it was a particular proposition, not a comment on a race, and Cook's first impressions of indigenous Australians were very different to those of his predecessor William Dampier. Both Cook and Banks were concerned to correct Dampier's claim that the people of New Holland were 'negroes'. Cook said they were 'of a very dark brown colour but not black' and Banks described them as 'blacker than any we have seen in the Voyage tho by no means negroes'. The distinction turned in part upon hair which was not woolly or frizzled but as Cook put it 'black and lank much like ours'. The issues were fundamental, because the claim commonly made in the second half of the eighteenth century by apologists for slavery was that 'negroes' were not members of the human species: their skins were not simply darker but were distinctively black, and they were supposed not to have hair like other people but 'wool'. Banks would have been more acquainted with these debates than Cook, but the comment in both journals makes it clear that the issue was discussed and – irrespective of what was thought of the nasty theories relating to so-called 'negroes' – both felt that Dampier's categorization had to be corrected. Aboriginal people were, Cook considered, intractably incommunicable but nevertheless unambiguously human. If only in one respect, they were 'much like' himself.

The whales, people, and other beings drawn on the rocks around this basin passed unnoticed. Indigenous life was observed here, as it had been at Tierra del Fuego, through a screen. Cook, who had now acquired a taste for the description of people's manners, was frustrated. It was not quite compensation, but Banks gathered a staggering range of plants – more here, more quickly and more that were new than he and Solander had found anywhere else. He discovered one that he thought extravagantly wonderful and that would be named after him. He was so busy collecting, arranging, drying and preserving things that he did not even mention *Banksia serrata* in his journal, but I can hear him telling Parkinson that he is vastly pleased by it, and that he must draw these fibrillous flowers, jagged leaves, and broken fruity genitals. This banksia would, much later, become nothing if not an icon of the Australian bush. As yet, there was no nation for it to represent; it was just another specimen, but a wonderfully idiosyncratic antipodean one. Banks's harvest here was such that the place, at first called Stingray Bay after the creatures caught and consumed, was named Botany Bay. It is not surprising that the science it commemorated dealt with plants rather than people. What name could have expressed the failure of communication that took place here?

*

The passage up the eastern Australian coast was for some time uneventful. Smoke was often sighted, distinctive hills were named. Indeed the names of prominent landmarks right up the side of this huge landmass are nearly all Cook's. Port Jackson, Broken Bay, Port Stephens, Three Brothers, Smoky Cape, Mount Warning, Morton Bay: you pass all these places today as you drive up the long coastal highway from Sydney to Brisbane, though most drivers will not know who Jackson, Stephens, Morton, Cleveland, Hawke and Sandwich were. Cook's concern to honour English gentlemen, mainly Admiralty gentlemen, along this coast is lost now; the places seem simply themselves. Further north, at what was called Bustard Bay, some time was spent ashore; a native turkey was shot and proved good eating. Cooking fires were found but no people, and Cook thought the country 'vissibly worse than at the last place we were at', the soil dry and sandy. Just after this, on 25 May, the tropic of Capricorn was crossed. On 4 June a couple of Aboriginal people were sighted on an islet with an outrigger canoe 'both larger and differently built' to those observed before, but once again they were seen without being spoken to.

Cook did not know it, but he was well inside the Great Barrier Reef – in effect, in a potentially fatal maze. As it approached 11 p.m. on the evening of Monday, 11 June, the ship was moving slowly through water that seemed to be nearly twenty fathoms deep, and the man responsible for sounding was about to cast his lead and line again, when the *Endeavour* struck and stuck fast. Banks was just getting warm in his bed when he heard the news – implying that he had not felt it, that the initial impact cannot have been palpable, though moments later he was convinced, he says, by the ship 'beating very violently against the rocks'. The situation was terrifying, because, as Banks correctly presumed, 'we were upon sunken coral rocks, the most dreadfull of all others on account of their sharp points and grinding quality which cut through a ships bottom almost immediately'. What made matters worse was that they had been sailing away from the shore for some hours: were the ship lost, reaching the land in small boats would take many hours longer. It was dark, though not so dark that boards broken away from the hull could not be seen, floating thick around the ship, which was repeatedly lifted and dropped and smashed against the reef. Banks found it hard to keep his footing on the quarterdeck, and was in a state of great alarm, thinking not just of the ship breaking up, of water in his lungs and death by drowning, but of the bloody loss – the loss of his specimens and curiosities, of a greater haul of new plants, birds, fish and Indian things than any other mortal had had a chance to acquire. He might have thought too of the loss to Europe of Tahiti as a place and culture known a lot better than Wallis had known it; of the loss of tattooing, no longer simply a Polynesian but now also a European body art; of the loss of Tupaia and his map; of the loss of measurements of the transit of Venus; of the loss of cannibalism's discovery; and the loss of lists of Maori words and drawings of Maori canoes. If men worked now to save their lives, a great deal more than men would have gone down with the *Endeavour*. A set of findings would have been unfound. A set of histories, that for better or worse were just beginning, would have come to a premature conclusion.

Sails were taken in. The long boat was put out, soundings were made, and it was established that the ship was on the south-eastern edge of a reef, rock just a few feet below the surface in some places, and somewhat deeper in others. Anchors were carried out, and an effort made to heave the ship off, which met with no success as the *Endeavour* was evidently now jammed or pinned on to the reef. Regrettably, too, this had taken place just at the top of the tide. She could be floated off not by waiting for higher water but only by being lightened considerably. Water casks were opened, and all through the night and morning things were thrown overboard: cannons, iron and stone ballast, casks, hoops, staves, oil jars, stores Cook says were 'decay'd' and which formed a sea of rubbish, floating around what some must have felt was a doomed ship. Their pessimism can only have been compounded around eleven in the morning, when the tide was high again, and Cook was shocked to find that the ship would not move. Every possible effort was made to lighten it further, and the only hope now lay in a piece of sailor's folklore, that high tides at night were higher than those during the day. This is not generally true, but sometimes and in some places is, and the 100-odd men aboard the *Endeavour* were very lucky indeed that it was true off north Queensland at this time of the year.

Getting the ship off the reef was, however, no guarantee of survival. The coral had not only smashed a hole or holes through the hull but stopped them up. To refloat was to unstop, perhaps to allow the sea to flood into a broken body whose wounds could not be properly detected or diagnosed. The ship was already leaking fast; sailors were working like dogs at the pumps. Banks privately gave up, packed a few things – I wish I knew what, at this moment, he thought he ought to pack – and prepared himself for the worst. His grim reasoning, he explained later in his journal:

if (as was probable) she should make more water when hauld off she must sink and we well knew that our boats were not capable of carrying us all ashore, so that some, probably the most of us, must be drownd: a better fate maybe than those would have who should get ashore without arms to defend themselves from the Indians or provide themselves with food, on a countrey where we had not the least to hope for subsistance had they even every convenence to take it as netts &c, so barren had we always found it; and had they even met with good usage from the natives and food to support them, debarrd from a hope of ever again seing their native countrey or conversing with any but the most uncivilizd savages perhaps in the world.

At no time can Banks have felt further from Burlington Gardens than now as he faced permanent severance from his sister, his library, his claret, his collections and his philosophers. The prospect of conversation with savages does not arouse his curiosity, he anticipates social as well as physical starvation. No one else spelt out their reflections and anxieties, but we can be pretty sure that every other man on board, even as he laboured desperately to pump water or heave things overboard, conjured with the short brutal course his life seemed now set to take. The sand, dryness, heat and vastness of the place so inappropriately called New Holland (there were no old towns or tulip farms) was no longer simply something to be observed and recorded; it was now a source of fear for those who even thought they might reach land, eternally separated from the women and kids they drank and ate and laughed and slept with in Plymouth or Shadwell or Southampton.

It became dark, the tide rose. At nine o'clock the ship righted and in Cook's words, 'the leak gaind upon the Pumps considerably. This was an alarming and I may say terrible Circumstance'; Banks wrote, 'the anziety in every bodys countenance was visible enough . . . fear of Death now stard us in the face; hopes we had none but of being able to keep the ship afloat till we could run her ashore on some part of the main where out of her materials we might build a vessel large enough to carry us to the East Indies'. At ten in the evening, after twenty-three hours on the coral, the ship floated off, and there was at first a moment of relief as the leak seemed to gain no more on the pumps than it had before. Then, however, the man who ventured below to check the water level came up to say that it had very quickly become sixteen to eighteen inches deeper. The crew, up until this point composed and purposeful, now panicked, the news causing 'fear to operate upon every man in the Ship'.

Shipwrecks are marked by moments when disciplined efforts to preserve a vessel, or effect an orderly evacuation, break down suddenly and irretrievably, as men reject their superiors, abandon their friends, and seize whatever means to unlikely survival are at hand. Cook must have felt himself face to face with this moment and with the end of his expedition and command. But, just before alarm turned to anarchy, somehow someone realized that a mistake had been made and the depth of water mismeasured. No sooner was this cleared up than the mood was altered as if by a charm. The men were now full of hope. The exhausting work of pumping continued. By morning a considerable gain on the leak was observed. The situation was further improved by a technique called fothering, which the surgeon's brother, Jonathan Monkhouse, knew from experience on a merchant ship that had survived a leaky voyage across the Atlantic. Cook accordingly gave him 'the deriction of this', which entailed spreading ockam and wool and sheeps' dung 'or other filth' over a sail which was then hauled under the ship's bottom, and sucked into any hole. This done, the leak's flow again decreased, it was necessary only to man one pump. Morale improved still further. No longer would it be necessary to run the *Endeavour* ashore and build a new vessel, rather 'the feild of every mans hopes inlarged so that we now thought of nothing but rainging along shore in search of a harbour where we could repair the damages we had susstained'.

This took a few days, which must have been anxious days, as the master proceeded ahead of the ship in one of the boats, sounding carefully, and Cook felt that he personally needed to mark out an opening through a reef with buoys, as heavy seas made it advisable to keep the crippled vessel at anchor rather than try the passage. Finally, on Sunday, 17 June, six days after the crisis had commenced, the *Endeavour* was run into a river entrance where she promptly struck a sandbank. But this, as Cook put it, 'was of no concequence any farther then giving us a little trouble'. In the middle of the next day the tide was high again. The ship was refloated, towed into the harbour and moored alongside a steep beach. Work began immediately. Anchors, cables, ropes, and other goods were shifted ashore. Tents were set

17. A view of the Endeavour River . . . where the ship was laid on shore, in order to repair the damage which she received on the rock, *an engraving after Parkinson.*

up for the sick and for provisions. A stage was built to constitute a sort of bridge between ship and shore, and efforts were made to catch fish.

On 19 June 1770, Cook climbed the grassy hill behind the ship. He had 'a perfect View' of the river and adjacent country, 'which afforded but a very indifferent prospect, the low lands near the River is all over run with mangroves among which the salt water flowes every tide and the high land appear'd to be barren'. I suppose he was consciously or unconsciously comparing what he saw with stone-fenced fields around Great Ayton and the Esk valley's frosty gardens. There have been other ways of seeing the country around the present town of Cooktown. One of them was available to an Aboriginal man named Tulo Gordon, an artist and storyteller who died, just over seventy, in 1989.

There was a blackbird, called Dyirimadhi, who wanted to marry the daughter of old Mungurru, the Scrub Python. But that old Mungurru wouldn't give his daughter to Blackbird. He didn't want them to get married.

So Blackbird got cross with that old Scrub Python.

One day Scrub Python went out to sun himself. He lay down and stretched himself out in the heat of the day. Soon he fell asleep.

Dyirimadhi, the blackbird, had been out hunting. He was just on his way back to camp, when he heard some little birds laughing at something.

'What are these little birds laughing at,' he said. 'Let me just go and have a look.'

He went over quietly and saw that old Python sunning himself. The little birds were laughing at him, asleep in the sun.

'Ohh,' said Dyirimadhi, 'that's my old father-in-law. That's the fellow who didn't give me his daughter.'

So he went off quietly again, and he looked all around. He looked and he looked and he looked until he found a big, heavy stone. He took that big stone, and he flew way up high into the clouds with it. He flew around and then he looked down to see where that old Mungurru was lying. When he was right above him, he let go of the big stone.

The big stone went down, down, and landed right where old Python's head was. And you know, whenever you see a Scrub Python nowadays, he's got a flat head, from where the rock hit him.

When that rock landed on his head, that old Mungurru started to thrash about. He rolled this way, then he rolled over that way. He didn't know what to do with all the pain.

Then the thought of the sea came into his mind. He headed off to the East, running towards the sea. He went straight down and came upon the sea right at Gan.garr, where Cooktown is today. He left deep tracks behind him, and that's where the Endeavour River is now. Before that old Scrub Python travelled down to the sea there was no river there.

Tulo Gordon's telling is not the creation myth that would have been known, in several sacred and secular versions, by Guugu Yimidhirr people at the time of Cook's visit. His version, rather, is a modern recollection, the expression of a twentieth-century Aboriginal culture that had seen its own past largely destroyed, most notably by prospectors and miners who entered the area during the gold rush of the 1870s, and ruthlessly assaulted and dispossessed indigenous people. Yet this story nevertheless preserves a sample of another sense of this land, seeing the acts of ancestral beings in the shape of the country today. Other tales of Tulo's, and others recorded from both this region and elsewhere in Aboriginal Australia, typically dwell upon acts of transgression and retribution that often revolve around marriage and rights over resources, and that result in hills, lakes, dunes, caves, waterholes and cliffs. Places were always animated; cosmology, nature, history, and present lives and rights to this tree or that fish were not things that occupied separate spheres but were like the waters of this shallow river, flowing one into the other, caught in the current, inhabited in innumerable ways.

None of this was evident to Cook in 1770. For some weeks, the area appeared scarcely occupied. Though cooking fires that were still burning were found on 29 June, those who had lit them had evidently chosen to avoid the Europeans, as people in the area continued to do. Then, on 10 July, a group of seven or eight was sighted walking along the north shore. As soon as Cook ventured towards them in a boat they ran off, but a few reappeared the next morning and began fishing from a canoe. 'Some were for going over in a boat to them but this I would not suffer,' Cook wrote, thinking – for the first time – that it might be best to let people alone, to leave the questions of whether and when a meeting might take place to them. Eventually two men came close to the *Endeavour* in their canoe, close enough to be thrown a few petty gifts. They then went away and brought back their two companions, and came closer to the ship this time, to receive further trifles before going ashore with their spears. Tupaia followed them and addressed them, presumably more through gestures than words. They laid down their spears and the group, including a few more of the mariners, sat together for some time. Cook tried to induce them to come and share their midday meal, but they did not want to come aboard the ship and went away in their canoe. He observed that they were about five and a half feet high, that their skins were the colour of dark chocolate, that their teeth were not knocked out (as Dampier had claimed of the people he had seen), and that they wore various sorts of body paint. 'The Voices were soft and tunable and they could easily repeat many words after us, but neither us nor Tupia could understand one word they said.'

The next day three of these men came back with one other. If introductions were understood, one was called Yaparico. This was the first occasion when any European learned the name of any Aboriginal person. Banks and Cook note also that one man had a bone through his nose. They were able to inspect the other men's noses and establish that theirs too were pierced. If this sounds intrusive, there is no indication in the record that it bothered these Guugu Yimidhirr men. They were troubled, however, when some officers were, as Banks put it, 'rather too curious in examining their canoe', and departed without further ado. Some of the same men, and others, visited again the next day, and allowed themselves to be measured; Banks may have wanted to do this because some among the Europeans could not make up their minds whether the Aborigines were short or tall. He thought them 'a very small people or' – correcting, qualifying his statement – 'at least this tribe consisted of very small people', even though, 'I do not know by what deception,' he wrote, 'we were to a man of opinion, when we saw them run on the sand about ¼ of a mile from us, that they were taller and larger than we were.' When the simplest physical facts were unclear, it is small wonder that description failed to capture less tangible traits of Aboriginal humanity.

Over the next week, 'Indians' continued to visit the ship and became seemingly friendlier, but on 19 July it became clear that their chief interest was in obtaining turtle, which men from the *Endeavour* had been moderately successful in fishing. When Cook refused to let them drop two over the side, 'they grew a little troublesome and were for throwing every thing over they could lay their hands upon'. They were further offended rather than mollified when Cook offered them bread and went ashore, where one immediately lit a handful of dry grass: 'before we well know'd what he was going about he made a large circuit round about us and set fire to the grass in his way and in an Instant the whole place was in flames'. The occasional use of fire against later European explorers suggests that this was a conventional tactic of military harassment in the region; on this occasion, further fires were lit in places where nets and washing were spread out to dry. The Aboriginal men only desisted when Cook fired a musket loaded with small shot at a man he described as one of the 'ringleaders' – a word implying trouble-making rather than any sort of legitimate opposition or reaction to his actions.

But among the Guugu Yimidhirr, fish and animals were often appropriated from those who captured them, to be eaten by others, because of complex rights and totemic relations with species as well as more obvious questions of property. For whatever reasons of this kind, these men probably thought they had cause to claim the turtles, while Cook assumed that they were his to keep or give away. He might have recalled something that in England he had known as well as he'd known his own shoes: that trout, hare, pheasant, deer and other game were wild but not just there for the taking. He did not reflect that what was true in north Yorkshire was true here too: the matter of who could catch and keep creatures was a serious one.

It is understandable that Cook felt that the immediate dietary needs of his crew were more important than making better friends of these people. Perhaps Cook did not recognize anything like the beginning of a commerce. Perhaps he had already decided that they had too little interest in taking from, and nothing to give, the Europeans. Perhaps he felt that, for all their emergent friendliness, they were a people beyond the reach of his instructions, that plotted dealings with peoples as potential trading partners. Among the mangroves here, those schemes to enlarge the commerce of Great Britain must have seemed at an unreal remove from the realities of the southern hemisphere.

The expression of Aboriginal 'obstinacy' was short-lived. After the man had been shot and only slightly wounded – it was inferred from 'a few drops of blood on some of the linnen he had gone over' – the people retreated, but were heard in the bush not long afterward. Banks, Cook and a few others went in search of them, hoping to accomplish I know not what, and met a group carrying spears, some of which the Europeans seized, alarming the Guugu Yimidhirr who ran off but then stopped. 'Some unintelligible conversation' took place, which somehow impressed each side with the willingness of the other to be friendly, and the spears were returned, 'which reconciled every thing', Cook thought. These people accompanied the mariners part way back to their ship, but – even though the *Endeavour* remained in the river a further two weeks – neither these people nor any other Aboriginals ventured near the vessel again.

Had the *Endeavour* not struck the reef and not spent time here, the voyage's most famous natural-historical discovery would not have been made. On 23 June, a curious beast was sighted. At first described as 'something less than a grey hound, it was of a Mouse Colour very slender made and swift of foot'. Two days later Cook himself saw one of these animals, which he said was 'the full size of a grey hound and shaped in every respect like one,

18. *The first European image of a kangaroo: drawing by Sydney Parkinson, Endeavour River, 1770.*

with a long tail which it carried like a grey hound, in short I should have taken it for a wild dog, but for its walking or runing in which it jumped like a Hare or dear'. Banks was excited to see 'the beast so much talkd of' which he too compared with a greyhound, adding, however, 'what to liken him to I could not tell, nothing certainly that I have seen at all resembles him'. He did not get a good look at one until 7 July when he went for a long walk 'and saw 4 of the animals'. He was struck by their ability to outrun his greyhound, who was slowed by thick grass 'while they at every bound leapd over the tops of it'. He was surprised that they did not go on all fours but instead 'only upon two legs, making vast bounds just as the Jerbua [an African rodent] does'. On 14 July, finally, John Gore lived up to his nickname, Master Hunter, and shot the animal that, as Banks put it, 'had so long been the subject of our speculations'. Under the running manuscript heading, 'Kill Kanguru', he wrote

To compare it to any European animal would be impossible as it has not the least resemblance of any one I have seen. Its fore legs are extreemly short and of no use to it in walking, its hind again are as disproportionaly long; with these it hops 7 or 8 feet at each hop in the same manner as the Gerbua to which animal indeed it bears much resemblance except in size, this being in weight 38 lb and the Gerbua no larger than a common rat.

Despite what we might call the educated quality of their eyes, the observational abilities that we know both possessed, neither Cook nor Banks were quite able to see what was there in the grass and brush in front of them. Both describe a heavy, upright quadruped, with massive rear legs and a thick tail as though it were the slenderest of dogs, that leapt rather than ran. They screwed up their eyes and squinted and made it look – at first – like something more familiar. Parkinson, too, in his first kangaroo drawings, struggled to get proportions right. The animal Gore shot – which was cooked and found good eating – appears to have been male. In any case, Banks was not lucky enough to see a female with a joey, and hence did not understand that this extraordinary creature was not only physically entirely different to anything known in Europe, but moreover belonged, like the American opossum, to the marsupial family – distinguished by their practice of nurturing young in a pouch. Yet he must have felt all his hopes for the voyage being realized. New Holland was not the southern continent that had been sought, but it was a land replete with entirely new things. It appeared arid but was, for an emerging discipline obsessed with novelty, nevertheless a paradise.

This absolutely un-European animal would receive an absolutely un-European name. Just a few days earlier, and most probably on the occasion when Banks or Cook or both together had inspected the noses of a few Aboriginal men, a list of words was obtained, that included 'kangaroo'. It has long been widely believed, both inside and outside Australia, that this was not in fact the name of the animal. Rather, it is suggested that when an Aboriginal man was asked what it was called, he responded, '*Kangaroo*', meaning something like 'I don't understand' or 'What did you say?' This would indicate that the name of what became a national symbol thus arose from nonsensical miscommunication. Nor is this just a particular nonsense; by implication it is a larger one that suggests that Cook's communicative abilities were pathetically limited, that his scientific findings were howlers, that the act of naming prefigured the profound and tragic misunderstanding of Aboriginal meaning on the part of Europeans. The etymological anecdote could therefore be seen to have a postcolonial moral. The real irony is that the story is apocryphal. Not only is 'kangaroo' in fact a close transcription of the Guugu Yimidhirr word, but the *Endeavour* voyage wordlist, of some sixty terms, is regarded by the most expert contemporary scholar as generally accurate. Cook's and Banks's ears even appear to have been more sensitive than those of the ethnologists and linguists who worked at the end of the nineteenth century and as recently as the 1960s, though the mariners did make predictable mistakes, confusing words for pubic hair and penis among other body parts, when it was no doubt unclear what exactly they were pointing to.

I am not sure what alternative moral this yields. It has to be said that no one on the *Endeavour* obtained the least sense of how Aboriginal society was organized, no one had the least inkling of the significance of local myth, no one had any idea that there were elaborate taboos and rights in food that, perhaps, motivated the claim upon the turtles. In these respects, Cook and his companions made the most superficial of observations of both Eora and Guugu Yimidhirr culture. This superficiality was not, however, the result of their own incompetence – otherwise their grasp of Tahitian language, society and culture would have been equally slight. It resulted, rather, from the stance that Aboriginal people adopted towards them. Had Aboriginal people conceived of strangers more as the Tahitians did – as people who might be productively manipulated – the European experience of Botany Bay and the coast further north would have been entirely different. They might have stayed longer, given and taken more, and perhaps had a worse impact sooner. But the Aboriginal attitude was profoundly cautious. When their cautiousness and evasiveness were relaxed for just a few days, Cook and Banks began to learn, and they did get a set of words right. They did not learn, and were perhaps not willing to understand, how important two or three turtle might have been. What Guugu Yimidhirr gathered for their part was, evidently, that evasion remained the best policy. Such was the basis on which this first contact ended.

Cook did not stop thinking about Aboriginal people as the repaired *Endeavour* made way out of the river, north past Cape Bedford, but he was preoccupied by difficulties that seemed just about insurmountable. The number of coral reefs and shoals was extraordinary. Heavy broken surf was visible right around the south, south-east and out to sea. Cook wrote that the sailing was 'dangerous to the highest degree' and though he climbed the mast himself repeatedly to try to spy out safe routes, he was at a loss as to which course to follow. They landed on a hilly island – called Lizard Island after its scaly inhabitants – which Cook climbed for the view. To his mortification he saw only further reefs and shoals. After much discussion, he decided that it was best to attempt to escape the reef, into deeper offshore waters, and a passage near Lizard Island was successfully negotiated to this end. Within two days, however, the situation was again highly dangerous: a strong sea carried the ship back towards the reef, and the lack of wind made it impossible for her to sail away from it. For those who read his journal, who were perhaps familiar with north Atlantic seas or no seas at all, Cook felt the need to explain exactly what hazard it was that great waves were thrusting the ship towards.

All the dangers we had escaped were little in comparison of being thrown upon this Reef where the ship must be dashed to peices in a Moment. A Reef such as is here spoke of is scarcely known in Europe, it is a wall of Coral Rock rising all most perpendicular out of the unfathomable Ocean, always overflown at high-water generally 7 or 8 feet and dry in places at low-water; the large waves of the vast Ocean meeting with so sudden a resistance make a most terrible surf breaking mountains high especially as in our case when the general trade wind blowes directly upon it.

At around six in the evening, the situation was critical. The *Endeavour* was only eighty to a hundred metres from the breaking water, only 'a dismal Vally the breadth of one wave' from wreck. In this place and under these circumstances no one at all would have escaped. Suddenly a gentle breeze, that would scarcely have been noticed at any other time, nudged the ship just a little further out to sea. It lasted only ten minutes or so before lapsing into a calm 'when our fears were again renewed for we as yet were not above 200 yards from the breakers'. The breeze rose again, and a gap in the reef was sighted and a boat sent to inspect it. Though it appeared perilously narrow, it offered the best prospect of saving the ship, which was towed towards it. When they reached the passage, however, it became apparent that the ebb tide was rushing out through it, with the result that once the ship entered this stream it was carried back out to sea. The *Endeavour* was now clear of the reef, but only temporarily so. Once the tide turned, with adverse or no winds, they would be in the same position as before. A further break in the reef was sighted which Hicks went to inspect. The tide began to rise. The ship was carried back towards the reef, despite being towed away from it by the boats 'some times gaining and at other times looseing'. Hicks thought that the passage could be attempted and it was resolved that it should be. Soon afterwards the ship entered a narrow opening between the great coral reefs and was rushed through it 'by a rappid tide like a Mill race'. Once within, the *Endeavour* anchored over coral, in safety again. While all efforts, just a few days before, had been directed at getting outside what is now known as the Great Barrier Reef, over 16 and 17 August equally desperate efforts had been made to get back inside it, 'such are the Vicissitudes attending this kind of service', Cook wrote. The passage up the remainder of the Australian coast would follow the shore closely, a course that despite its hazards suited Cook better: it made it possible to resolve one of the questions that vexed him, which was whether or not New Guinea was joined to the Australian mainland. In 1607 the Spanish navigator Torres had in fact sailed through the strait that now bears his name, but reports of his voyage had been suppressed, even though the rumoured passage appeared on charts such as those appended to de Brosses's *Histoire des navigations aux Terres Australes*.

Less than a week after the *Endeavour* re-entered the waters within the reef, the issue was resolved, as the Australian mainland gave way to islands. The island continent's northern promontory was rounded, and by the following day Cook was pretty confident of 'the great Probability of a Passage' 'into the Indian seas'. He reasoned that

on the Western side I can make no new discovery the honour of which belongs to the Dutch navigators *and as such they may lay Claim to it as their Property* but the Eastern Coast from the Latitude of 38° South down to this place I am confident was never seen or viseted by any European before *and therefore by the same rule belongs to great Britton* and Notwithstand I had in the Name of His Majesty taken posession of several places upon this coast, I now once more hoisted English Coulers and in the Name of His Majesty King George the Third took posession of the whole Eastern Coast from the above Latitude down to this place by the name of *New South Wales*, together with all the Bays, Harbours Rivers and Islands situate upon the said coast, after which we fired three Volleys of small Arms which were Answerd by the like number from the Ship.

The two phrases printed here in italics were scored through, presumably because Cook was uncertain about the 'same rule'. As well he might have been, because his secret instructions empowered him to take possession of lands, but 'with the Consent of the Natives' that he had at no time sought. The Earl of Morton's 'Hints' – which, as has been noted, were really a supplementary set of quasi-instructions from the voyage's official sponsor, the Royal Society – did not touch on which territories might be taken possession of under what circumstances, but made categorical statements about the standing of native peoples: 'They are the natural, and in the strictest sense of the word, the legal possessors of the several Regions they inhabit.' Morton's chief concern – which in all likelihood stemmed from some repugnance to the reports of Wallis's conduct in Tahiti – was to emphasize that indigenous peoples might be legitimately hostile to visiting voyagers, who should for their part use every 'gentle method' and avoid the use of firearms.

Cook presumed to equate 'first discoverers' with 'first European discoverers', but neither the Admiralty nor the Royal Society made any such identification. He was, in other words, deviating from his instructions, as he had in New Zealand where he'd pretended for the benefit of the Maori to do no more than erect a mark and in fact proceeded to claim the islands in the name of the Crown. His revision of his journal at the place he appropriately called Possession Island is significant, because it no doubt occurred to him that the justification that his act demanded was more complex.

Despite the impulsive imperialism of this declaration of possession, Cook's excursus upon the coast and environment of Australia and on the people of the land, which he composed soon after the visit to Possession Island, shows us just how far this seaman had come since Tierra del Fuego, where his remarks on the Haush amounted to less than 400 words. Here, his descriptive reflections were much longer. They ranged over physique, hair, ornament, body paint and piercing, canoes, subsistence and houses. He provided the wordlist that I've already discussed, and proceeded to make a set of remarks that were not published at the time, but became famous much later:

From what I have said of the Natives of New-Holland they may appear to some to be the most wretched people upon Earth, but in reality they are far more happy than we Europeans; being wholy unacquainted not only with the superfluous but the necessary Conveniencies so much sought after in Europe, they are happy in not knowing the use of them. They live in a Tranquillity which is not disturb'd by the Inequality of Condition: The Earth and sea of their own accord furnishes them with all things necessary for life, they covet not Magnificent Houses, Houshold-stuff &cᵃ, they live in a warm and fine Climate and enjoy a very wholsome Air, so that they have very little need of Clothing and this they seem to be fully sencible of, for many to whome we gave Cloth &cᵃ to, left it carlessly upon the Sea beach and in the woods as a thing they had no manner of use for. In short they seem'd to set no value on any thing we gave them, nor would they ever part with any thing of their own for any one article we could offer them; this in my opinion argues that they think themselves provided with all the necessarys of Life and that they have no superfluities.

This passage offended Cook's biographer, J. C. Beaglehole, who thought it was unlike the navigator to write as though he'd been reading Rousseau. Cook must, he suggests, have 'been listening to some oration of Banks' or been reading 'the Banks version of the fashionable intellectual indiscretions'; he is thoroughly relieved when the journal returns to commonsense navigational matters. It is true that there is no other passage in Cook quite like this, and true that he had plainly been talking through the state of nature with Banks, who included related reflections in his own journal:

Thus live these I had almost said happy people, content with little nay almost nothing. Far enough removd from the anxieties attending upon riches, or even the possession of what we Europeans call common necessaries: anxieties intended maybe by Providence to counterbalance the pleasure arising from the Posession of wishd for attainments, consequently increasing with increasing wealth, and in some measure keeping up the balance of happiness between the rich and the poor. From them appear how small are the real wants of human nature, which we Europeans have increasd to an excess which would certainly appear incredible to these people could they be told it.

But Cook's statement is not Banks's. Banks airs the anxieties of an aristocrat, and speculates about a providential principle; Cook, in contrast, exercises his characteristically empirical intelligence and makes a particular point, which is closely connected with his mission. At every opportunity, he has tried to do what he was told, 'to cultivate a Friendship and Alliance with' Aboriginal people, to make them presents, to invite 'them to Traffick'. But they were generally indifferent to the mariners' gifts, they never brought a thing to sell and at no point engaged in any barter. Aboriginal behaviour was not only puzzling but problematic, because it blocked what Cook saw as his mission. He dwelt upon it, he talked about it, he resolved it in these terms in his mind. Banks's comment on Aboriginal happiness is emptily philosophical. Cook notices not just an absence of want, but details what is unnecessary, given the climate; local sufficiency and material happiness explain what he needs explained, and why these people place themselves outside the sphere of commerce.

Banks's acknowledgement of Aboriginal happiness is qualified and grudging, but Cook goes so far as to say that it is superior to happiness at home. He perhaps does so because he is put off by ways of life that he, unlike Banks, has always been a stranger to. Cook's attitudes towards one of the wealthiest and most sharply divided societies in the world are not easily discerned. He came from people without wealth, and never disowned them. His master Walker, a modestly affluent merchant, had been a mentor, almost a second father. We do not know his politics, but it is very likely that he, like other Whitby traders, like Quakers and dissenters, like the new middle classes generally, would have disapproved of the opulence of London's dissipated aristocracy. Cook saw a good deal of those who inhabited and coveted 'Magnificent Houses, Houshold-stuff &c*' but he lived only inter mittently on the edge of the richest city in the world. For most of his adult life his home was at sea and luxury never became simply familiar. We might guess that a little Quaker censoriousness rubbed off on him, and that he did not just notice but approved of people with a paucity of possessions.

9

The Calamitous Situation we are at present in

On 17 August 1770 the *Endeavour* had been rushed on the tide back within the Great Barrier Reef. Pickersgill called it 'the narrowest escape we ever had'. Cook named the passage Providential Channel, yet the thoughts he committed to his journal concerned not religion but risk and reputation. 'Were it not for the pleasure which naturly results to a Man from being the first discoverer, even were it nothing more than sands and Shoals, this service would be insuportable,' he wrote, acknowledging the stress and discomfort of exploration in 'far distant parts'. Equally 'insuportable', however, was the calculation performed by public opinion.

The world will hardly admit of an excuse for a man leaving a Coast unexplored he has once discover'd, if dangers are his excuse he is than charged with *Timorousness* and want of Perseverance and at once pronounced the unfitest man in the world to be employ'd as a discoverer; if on the other hand he boldly incounters all the dangers and obstacles he meets and is unfortunate enough not to succeed he is than charged with *Temerity* and want of conduct. The former of these aspersins cannot with Justice be laid to my charge and if I am fortunate enough to surmount all the dangers we may meet the latter will never be brought into question.

It was two years since he had left England. He might have estimated that it would take a full further year to return, but he was already pleading his case. He admitted that he had 'ingaged more among the Islands and shoals upon this coast' than was strictly prudent, but gambled on survival, and justified his gamble by citing the sort of knowledge he would bring home. That the land was arid and the produce sparse to an Englishman's eye did not matter. What mattered to Cook was that he had 'ingaged' closely enough to observe; his observations were precise; he might evade the censure of the public.

Two weeks later, having taken possession of this same coast and passed through Torres Strait, Cook sailed west and north through shallow water, at times as muddy as the river Thames, Banks thought. Early in the morning of 1 September 'a very Fragrant smell came off the land' – the coast of south-west New Guinea – that diminished as the day progressed. It became intolerably hot. Banks and Solander were anxious to inspect the country. Cook was keener to quit it, worried that the monsoon might delay their westward passage, but a landing was made, a hut was found and the voices of people heard. Best not to enter the bush, the visitors thought, but rather to walk along the beach. They got no more than 200 yards before a few men appeared and threatened them. They were fired upon and retreated. Cook judged that it was impossible to examine the place 'with any degree of safety' and took his people back to their boat. As they withdrew, more men emerged from the forest, who shouted aggressively and appeared to discharge fire-sticks of some sort, but let the Europeans depart. Once afloat, they let the oars rest; 'we now had time to View them Attentively,' Cook wrote, though he was unable to report much beyond their superficial similarity to the Australians. The fact that some were painted made it difficult to establish their skin colour.

Cook remarked that some people here – it sounds as though he meant Banks and Solander – had craved the refreshment of coconuts, and been so frustrated by the inability of anyone to climb the palms that they recommended sending a party ashore to cut some down. This proposal, Cook considered immoral:

for as the Natives had attack'd us for meer landing without takeing away any one thing, certainly they would have made a vigorous effort to have defended their property, in which case many of them must have been kill'd and perhaps some of our own people too – and all this for 2 or 300 green Cocoa-nutts which when we had got them would have done us little service, besides nothing but the utmost necessity would have oblige'd me to have taken this Method to come at refreshments.

The bulk of the ship's company was however delighted when they made sail and steered away from the coast. The *Endeavour* was approaching the known waters of the East Indies. The trials of exploration were all but at an end. 'The greatest part of them,' Banks wrote of the crew, 'were now pretty far gone with the longing for home which the Physicians have gone so far as to esteem a disease under the name of Nostalgia.' He thought that of the whole company, only Cook, Solander and himself, whose minds were constantly occupied, were really 'clear of its effects'.

Cook could not place their track on the old and inadequate charts he carried. He lamented the record-keeping of his predecessors, and censured the compilers and publishers who would peddle a rough sketch as 'a *Survey Plan*', an accurate and entirely distinct thing in Cook's mind. Yet in due course he was confident that he lay between Timor and Roti, and on 18 September the island of Savu was reached, where Gore – once again in the vanguard – landed and learned of a likely anchorage. They found a local rajah and a representative of the Dutch East India Company. They were promised buffalo and much else in the way of provisions, but were disappointed that little was in fact brought for sale, at what were considered exorbitant prices. Parkinson got the company agent alarmed by taking an interest in cloves and spices; for both parties, the visit looked like more trouble than it was worth, and Cook took his ship away just three days later. He described the place, pretty cursorily; he was once again within the known world, and his curiosity was receding.

At the beginning of October they reached the coast of Java; Dutch ships were sighted and visited by Hicks, who brought back some European news: that (as Banks put it) 'the government in England were in the utmost disorder', which suggested that nothing much had changed. Cook noted that the Dutch went through the form of examining him, as to his ship's origin, route and findings, but were not much bothered when he refused to answer. On 9 October they anchored in Batavia Road, and were called on by an officer. 'Both himself and his people were almost as Spectres,' Banks wrote, 'no good omen of the healthyness of the countrey we were arrived at.' Cook had his carpenter survey the leaky ship. It was evident that the hull had suffered a good deal of damage. He therefore obtained permission from the authorities to have the *Endeavour* heaved over and repaired here. This was no doubt unavoidable, but unfortunate: Banks had read his 'omen' right. But almost the only unwell people on board were Tupaia and Taieto, who were at first delighted and uplifted by the novelty of a European settlement. Batavia was an extensive colonial town with some thousands of houses, a few public buildings, a grand domed church, and many virulently stagnant canals. Tupaia was astonished to see the 'Houses, carriages, streets' that he had been told about 'but never well understood'. 'He danc'd about the streets examining every thing to the best of his abilities.' He was struck by the diversity of costume. When he gathered that each different 'nation' here – there were Chinese, Malays, Europeans and few indigenous Javanese – dressed in its own way, he was concerned to do likewise and had some tapa brought from the ship so that he could represent Raiatea appropriately.

Sadly, however, his 'broken constitution' was the first to be afflicted by the diseases endemic in the humid, mosquito-ridden place. Almost all the *Endeavour*'s company contracted malaria, dysentery, both, or something else. Tupaia asked to be taken from town to the ship, where the air was better. 'The Seamen now fell sick fast so that the tents ashore were always full of sick.' Banks's servants were as ill as himself. Solander was worse. The surgeon Monkhouse was in bed with an increasingly violent fever. Cook had at first been put out that the Dutch insisted on taking on the repair of his ship, but in the event only a fraction of his crew were well enough to watch as the vessel was heaved over. Its hull was examined; the breakage and worm damage was much worse than anyone thought: 'it was a Matter of Surprise to every one who saw her bottom how we had kept her above water,' wrote Cook with a certain degree of satisfaction, yet by the time he did so, he might have been more alarmed by the longer stay that the repairs would require. Monkhouse had been the first to die, on 5 November, Taieto died on 17 December. Tupaia was profoundly distressed by his loss, and died himself on 20 December. In addition, three seamen, and the astronomer Green's servant, were lost. Over this whole period, Banks was sick himself. He put aside his journal. He resumed it. He wrote up this period, muddling dates. He did no more than mention the passing of the 'most proper' Polynesian man whose future conversation, he had once imagined, would provide him with much 'amusement'. It was left to Cook to compose an obituary of sorts:

Tupia's death indeed cannot be said to be owing wholly to the unwholsom air of Batavia, the long want of a Vegetable diat which he had all his life before been use'd to had brought upon him all the disorders attending a sea life. He was a Shrewd Sensible, Ingenious Man, but proud and obstinate which often made his situation on board both disagreable to himself and those about him, and tended much to promote the deceases which put a period to his life.

This is a back-handed appreciation, if ever there was one. It is intriguing and frustrating to hear, only now, that Tupaia has made himself unpopular, in some consistent way, by counting himself smarter or better than European seamen. We might guess that Cook's comment registers a sense in which Tupaia perhaps irked him by taking charge of his ship, by seeming to command it, as the Maori certainly presumed he did. Or maybe Tupaia thought he knew more geography than Cook did, and that got to Cook, who respected native navigational knowledge but who always imagined that he outdistanced his European rivals, and did not quite know how to reconcile himself to an Islander better informed than he. Cook was himself proud, if discreetly so, and as obstinate as his sense of his mission required. Like may have grated against like. If this is speculative, there can be no doubt that Cook uses these personality traits to suggest that Tupaia's 'disagreeable' situation worsened his disease, that in other words the man's death was his own fault.

On 25 December, they were finally ready to depart. Banks remarked. 'There was not I beleive a man in the ship but gave his utmost aid to getting up the Anchor, so compleatly tird was every one of the unwholesome air of this place.' In general, the crew were on their way to recovery; but the respite was false. On 24 January, eight days after departing Princes Island, where wood and water had been obtained, Jonathon Truslove, the corporal of marines, died. 'Many of our people,' Cook wrote, 'at this time lay danger-ously ill of Fevers and fluxes.' The breezes were at best light. Often the air was still, the heat unforgiving, fetid. The next day the weather was 'Sultry'. 'Departed this life Mr Sporing a gentleman belonging to Mr Banks retinue.' The day after, Cook recorded that the ship was cleaned between decks and 'wash'd with Vinegar'. As matters got worse, he wrote less, and his journal entries for these weeks are among the shortest he ever wrote for any phase of any voyage. On Sunday the 27th 'Departed this life Mr Sidney Parkinson, Natural History Painter to Mr Banks, and soon after Jno Ravenhill, Sail-maker, a Man much advanced in years'. Seven men had died over six weeks at Batavia, now four had died in four days. On Tuesday the 29th:

Died Mr Charles Green who was sent out by the Royal Society to Observe the Transit of Venus; he had long been in a bad state of hilth, which he took no care to repair but on the contrary lived in such a manner as greatly promoted the disorders he had had long upon him, this brought on the Flux which put a period to his life.

Cook often resorted to the same wording when he had the same idea in mind. Green, like Tupaia, was blamed for his own death. Cook takes the trouble to say so because Green had status, he was a Royal Society appointee, not a common seaman. He resumes his bald reporting the following day, when two further men, Francis Haite, who had sailed with Byron, and one Samuel Moody of Worcester, 'Died of the Flux'. On 31 January four more men died, the ship's cook, the carpenter's mate and two seamen, the latter as it happens both Scottish. Cook's approach to his command had always placed him at some distance from his men, but he now adds a single sentence that admits both grief and desperation. 'A Melancholly proff of the Calamitous Situation we are at present in, having hardly well men enough to tend the Sails and look after the Sick, many of the latter are so ill that we have not the least hopes of their recovery.' 'Melancholy' was not a word he used often or lightly.

On 1 February the decks were again cleaned and washed with vinegar. The onset of a fresh wind – the south-east trade – refreshed those on board. Yet many were already 'so far gone and brought so very low' by disease that there was little hope of their recovery. On the second of the month, Daniel Roberts died. On the third, John Thurman died. On the fourth, so did both John Bootie and John Gathrey. On the sixth, Jonathan Monkhouse, the surgeon's brother, succumbed. On 12, 14, 15 and 21 February further seamen died. On 21 February, also, Thomas Rossiter was flogged 'for geting drunk, grossly Assaulting the Officer of the Watch and beating some of the Sick'. Rossiter was venting anger, maybe, because he was in better shape and had to do the invalids' work. On 26 February, Henry Jeffs, Peter Morgan and Manoel Pereira, recruited at Rio, all died, but only after having been very sick for some time. Others were generally recovering, 'so that the death of these three men in one day did not in the least alarm us,' Cook wrote.

It is what is not said rather than what is that resonates in these emaciated journal entries, in their way as spectral as the dying men Banks had encountered in Batavia. Just as no one explicitly acknowledged that the Endeavour's observation of the transit of Venus had failed, no one now acknowledged that another of the voyage's experiments – to preserve the lives of seamen – had failed even more calamitously. The experience had not been on the truly catastrophic scale of that of Cook's great predecessor, Anson – who lost four ships and well over 1,000 men – but almost a third of the company had nevertheless lost their lives. If Cook could not reasonably be faulted, since he had done nothing contrary to his instructions and could hardly have avoided Batavia, he would nevertheless have been uncomfortable. He might indeed bring back good maps, but his accomplishment would otherwise lack the perfection of a 'survey plan'.

In early January, before men began to die like flies, Banks occupied himself, before he himself became ill again, by analysing the linguistic affinities that jumped off Tahitian, Javanese and Malay wordlists at him. They were too numerous and too unambiguous to miss. In all these languages, *mate* meant to kill or strike, *manu* meant a bird, and *i'a* or *ika* meant a fish. The words for numbers – in all cases cognate with *tahi, rua, tolu, va* and *lima* for one, two, three, four and five – were even more obviously variants. Banks was bewildered because the words from Madagascar – which he 'had from a Negro slave' born there, at Batavia on an English ship – were also 'vastly similar to those of Otahite'. This constituted a 'strange problem' specifically because he understood that the tongue was spoken by 'the Black inhabitants of Madagascar'. Had he in fact encountered Malagasy people, he might have realized that they were not black but light-skinned like Malays and Polynesians. His expectation that language and race would coincide would not have been contradicted, though it was in fact wrong. 'I should have venturd to conjecture much did not Madagascar interfere,' he wrote. He had been on the point of grasping that what was long called Malayo-Polynesian, known now as the Austronesian language family, embraced islands around three-quarters of the southern hemisphere. But he could not imagine migration or communication between Java and Madagascar, still less could he do so if that meant that 'Brown long haird people' shared a language with a 'Black wooly headed people'. As would so often occur in the sub-sequent history of inquiries of this sort, a racial premise led him to entertain ridiculous speculation, that perhaps the 'Egyptian learning' had run in two courses, one via Africa and the other via Asia, somehow resulting in common words for numbers among people who had nothing to do with each other. He admitted that his 'depth of knowledge in Antiquities' was too slight to enable him to understand the problem, but in fact he knew too much – too much about race – rather than too little.

On 5 March the Natal coast was sighted. On 12 March Cape Agulhas, the southernmost point of the African continent, was rounded. On 14 March Table Bay, the site of Cape Town, was entered. Cook for the first and last time enlarged upon the effect that disease had had upon morale on board. The 'despondency' among those ill was such that 'a man was no sooner taken with it than he look'd upon himself as dead'. But if the ineffectivity of medicine made their despair understandable, irrational panic did much to make matters worse:

I shall mention what effect only the imagery [imaginary] approach of this disorder had upon one man. He had long tended upon the Sick and injoy'd a tolerable good state of hilth: one morning coming upon deck he found himself a little griped and immidiatly began to stamp with his feet and exclaim I have got the Gripes, I have got the Gripes, I shall die, I shall die! – in this manner he continued until he threw himself into a fit and was carried off the deck in a manner dead, however he soon recover'd and did very well.

The Cape can only have impressed Cook as a far more salubrious place for refitting and refreshment. Arrangements were made to lodge those who were still sick ashore, fresh meat and greens were obtained for those who remained on board, sails and rigging were repaired and Cook sent letters to the Admiralty and Royal Society via fast East India ships. He learned that another Indiaman, the *Holton*, had lost 'between 30 and 40 men' and others that had been away from England for less than a year had also suffered. But he complained

Yet their sufferings will hardly if atall be mentioned or known in England when on the other hand those of the Endeavour, because the Voyage is uncommon, will very probably be mentioned in every News paper, and what is not unlikely with many additional hardships we never experienced; for such are the dispossission of men in general in these Voyages that they are seldom content with the hardships and dangers which will naturaly occur, but they must add others which hardly ever had existence but in their imaginations . . .

He was not only worried, he was sure the voyage's accomplishments would be distorted by his own men, who would, he expected, fuel the sensationalism of publishers. And they would be, though not exactly in the way he anticipated. On 15 April, the *Endeavour* shaped a course out of the bay. The passage back to England was uneventful, though just after leaving Cape Town, the master, Robert Molyneux, died. He 'had unfortunately given himself up to extravecancy and intemperance which brought on disorders that put a pirod to his life'. Him too.

10

My intentions certainly were not criminal

Cook had returned to London half a dozen times after seasons surveying in Newfoundland. He had returned still more often to Whitby. He was used to homecoming, even though his homes, like those of all seamen, were not places of habitual abode, but places he was habitually away from. But his return, in July 1771, was different to his homecomings after shorter voyages, different even to his return from nearly five years in north America, in 1762. This time, Cook had not passed his time away in colonial towns and well-frequented ports. For the bulk of the three years he had been in places of all sorts, ranging from the luxuriant to the inhospitable, that had little in common other than their absolute distance from Europe. In one sense he had been everywhere, in another sense he'd been nowhere but on his ship, which he and every other man aboard now felt intuitively. His feet knew every worn step, his fingers every bleached rail, his ears every sort of crying bird, every flapping canvas. Cook's body was poised against the roll of the deck. His mind and temper were balanced against his men.

To be home was to be disconcerted. Society was suddenly no longer exclusively masculine. It was no longer confined. It was no longer something one was responsible for; I can only surmise that being back in London was strange for Cook in these sorts of ways. He arrived somewhere that was much the same, yet no longer familiar. The town appeared as it would to a resident who suddenly acquired spectacles. What they or you would ordinarily not see, what would belong only to background and blur, was abruptly in focus and oddly noticeable. The paving stones under one's feet, the crowds and the aroma of coffee in the Strand, the cod and the barrels of Colchester oysters in Billingsgate market, the rattle of coachwheels on cobbles, briefly all presented themselves as particular and unusual sensations. Then feelings, tastes, smells, sights and sounds re-established themselves. There was a moment when a great chestnut tree looked as curious as a coconut palm. The moment passed.

*

The papers reported that the *Endeavour* had returned safely, having observed the transit of Venus and touching 'at every coast and island' 'to collect every species of plants and other rare productions of nature'. One story announced the discovery of 'a Southern Continent' where the people, among whom Mr Banks passed some months, 'were hospitable, ingenious, and civil', though without any kind of religious worship. The deaths of Green and of two natives at Batavia were lamented and noted respectively. Several brief notices emphasized the botanical accomplishments of Banks and Solander and do not mention Cook. It was not until 29 August that any better account was published, though what was again supposed to be an officer's letter moved freely between the accurate and the outlandish. It was noted, on the one hand, that Banks's black servants died at Tierra del Fuego, and that he and Solander had likewise almost been lost. It was claimed, on the other, that at the island of Savu they met with provisions in abundance and also 'the first miracle of this world – a country well inhabited, where *fornication* was never known'. Mention was made of Tahitian fruit, of the near wreck upon the Endeavour reef and of the kangaroo. The warriors of Borabora were said habitually to cut off the lower jaws of their war captives, 'and leave the wretches to linger and die'. It was hardly the scientific aspect of the voyage that was brought to the fore, in this unashamed account:

[At Tahiti] We married with their women, and enjoyed a felicity amongst them peculiar to the salubrity of so sweet a clime. As for my part, I never relinquished a situation with so much grief and dissatisfaction . . . Monsieur Bougainville had been before us with two sail of ships, and brough the French disease among the poor people . . . We sailed from Utahitee to Hou a Hanie, which is the isle of handsome women . . . but our crew being injured by the villainy of Bougainville's people, the Captain would not suffer them to go on shore . . . I vow, with the greatest sincerity, that it justly deserves the name; for I never beheld such a beautiful race of women, so elegantly limbed, and so divinely featured . . . [At Savu, supposedly fornication-free] This chastity not entirely agreeing with our desires, we soon abdicated the virtuous Indians, for the sumptuous city of BATAVIA . . .

Another letter published at about the same time introduced Tupaia by name and included more precise descriptions of agricultural produce and implements, but was equally ecstatic about Tahitian sexuality, laced here with allusions to a stereotypic Asiatic sensuality:

The women are extremely lascivious . . . A virgin is to be purchased here, with the unanimous consent of the parents, for three nails and a knife. I own I was a buyer of such commodities – and after some little time married one of my nut-brown sultans – and then became so habituated to their manners and a hut, that I even left my lady and the island with reluctance . . . They are not very decent in their amours, having little regard to either place or person: this is not general among them – though it is often seen and done . . . the women dance in the most indecent manner, performing a thousand obscene gesticulations, like the Indostan dancing girls.

One of the people who read or heard of these reports was Elizabeth Cook. How did she feel, to know that her husband's voyage was being talked of as a tour of tropical bordellos? How confident could she be that Cook had no part in this? How confident was she that she still even knew the man who had been not only away but beyond the reach of all correspondence for so long, whose ship had been rumoured lost more than once, whose existence had become almost hypothetical?

When Cook's marriage is described, which is admittedly rarely, it is said to have been distinguished by mutual devotion and fidelity; 'of the depth and strength of this relationship there can be no doubt,' writes, for example, Ray Parkin. But in fact there is no good evidence for either depth or shallowness, either strength or weakness. The evidence we have does not go much beyond the warm, even idealizing things that Elizabeth Cook had to say about her husband many years after his death. But a spouse is surely likely to speak fondly and proudly of a late husband or wife, unless their marriage was notably bad. I do not say that there is a case *for* an unhappy relationship, or for infidelity on either side. But were there either unhappiness or infidelity, neither fact would have been recorded. The historical record is all but devoid of observation of any sort, affirmative or otherwise, upon Cook's domesticity, on Mrs Cook, or on the Cooks together. So, I can give you no sense of this couple's reunion, no sense of what may indeed have been a happy renewal of intimacy, or an awkward failure.

Less obscurity surrounds Joseph Banks's affairs. Before his departure from England, it was widely understood that he was betrothed to Harriet Blosset, but the idea of marriage made him acutely anxious. He thought it too much like a gamble. If one knew the 'mental Qualifications' of a future partner, he feared that one could only be 'in the dark' about 'her bodily ones'. The prospect of being tied to someone 'unfit for sensual Enjoyment' utterly horrified him; he was evidently confident that he was fit for sensual enjoyment and that there was no risk of disappointment on his wife's side. Whatever doubts he had before the voyage were compounded by absence, to such an extent that he nowhere mentions his fiancée in his journal and was too occupied with visits to other friends on his return to London to contact her. She was placed in the unenviable position of having to write to him. He replied, declaring that he loved her, 'but that he found he was of too volatile a temper to marry'. On receipt of this letter, Harriet Blosset was devastated. A meeting was arranged. Banks and Blosset talked – or perhaps more likely cried and argued – from ten one night until ten the next morning. At some point during this discussion, Banks said he would after all marry her straight away, but she was cautious enough to tell him to go away for a fortnight, and that she'd accept an offer renewed then. I doubt she was surprised to hear from him a few days later 'desiring to be off'. People talked about Banks's 'infidelity', and he must himself have considered his behaviour shoddy, or he would not have compensated Miss Blosset financially.

But he was probably too busy to feel terribly guilty. He and Solander were presented twice to the King. They gave him resumés of the voyages. They presented him with what was described in the newspaper as 'a coronet of gold, set around with feathers' supposedly from Chile, probably in fact a Tahitian pearl-shell and feather gorget. They had one dinner with Boswell and Dr Johnson, another with Benjamin Franklin at the house of the president of the Royal Society. They went to Oxford and received honorary doctorates. There were innumerable cases of specimens to be unpacked. There were plans for opulent and extensive publications. There was a steady stream of society visitors to New Burlington Street, and there was already talk of another voyage. Cook was no celebrity, and there is nothing in the newspapers that suggests that he was sought out or in any way lionized. But within Admiralty circles, the navigational rather than the botanical findings of the voyage were noticed. Sandwich, the first Lord of the Admiralty, presented Cook too to the King – who promoted him to commander, looked over his charts and heard his own account of the voyage. The honour of an audience with His Majesty would have been unanticipated and unthinkable for a lieutenant engaged in a thorough but unromantic Newfoundland survey a few years earlier. The approbation he received was, Cook admitted, 'extremely pleasing'.

Just after this, in mid August 1771, he wrote hastily to John Walker of Whitby, beginning and promising an account of his voyage, which he continued in a longer second letter a month later. This communication distilled Cook's feelings about the peoples he encountered and it is the only extant expression of such feelings that was written for a friend rather than for the Admiralty. What he says to Walker is in no sense at odds with his official records, but is more sentimental. His Tahitian 'Terrestrial Paridises' are wonderful not for the women, whom he does not mention, but for natural benevolence, for happy people 'exempted from the curse of our fore fathers, scarce can it be said that they earn thier bread with the sweat of thier brows'. His New Zealanders are 'a brave warlike people with sentiments voide of treachery' who 'when once Peace was settled . . . ever after were our very good friends'. Aboriginal Australians, he still felt, were 'in reality . . . far more happier than . . . we Europeans'. He had a copy of his journal in front of him and repeated and enlarged upon the positive but not the negative remarks he made there. The people were undisturbed 'by the inequality of condition' and 'happy in not knowing the use' of the various necessary and superfluous luxuries that Europeans yearned for. 'They sleep as sound in a small hovel or even in the open as the King in his Pallace on a Bed of down.'

Perhaps because he was writing to Walker, Cook also placed Aboriginal people, as he had the Tahitians, in a particularly Christian paradise. 'Men women and children go wholy naked, it is said of our first Parents that after they had eat of the forbidden fruit they saw themselves naked and were ashamed; these people are Naked and are not ashame'd.' Though derived from complete misunderstanding of Aboriginal ideas of clothing and nudity, this was to value rather than devalue the mode of life of these nomadic hunter-gatherers, who lived on what the land produced naturally, without cultivating 'one foot of it'. From the perspective of a secular natural history, people who fished, collected and hunted without keeping herds or cultivating the ground were barely removed from animality. But for Cook, at any rate at this moment, their disengagement from productive labour associated them not with brutes, but with Adam and Eve before sin.

Cook's references to religion in his journals and such other personal letters as we have are conspicuous for their infrequency, and these reflections are religiously framed primarily because he was writing to a man whose religious household he had inhabited. His contrary use of nakedness to elevate Aboriginal people tells us both that he thought sometimes in Christian terms – which is after all no more than we would expect – and that his Christianity was loose. There was no space in any orthodox theology for either Australian or Tahitian Edens, and no space, after the fall, for people without shame.

By the time Cook wrote this second letter to Walker, a second voyage had been determined upon. Public interest was aroused by the likelihood that Banks would undertake a new expedition, but the Admiralty's commitment was driven rather by a proposal that Cook had ventured to put forward. In a postscript to his *Endeavour* journal, drafted at the Cape and provoked by conversations with French officers who refused to accept that Tahiti had been first discovered for Europeans by Wallis (a point they continued to contest for at least sixty years), Cook reported that new French and Spanish voyages were in progress, or planned, in the Pacific. They raised the threat of competing schemes of colonization. The fact that Wallis's voyage, and his own, were not 'published by Authority to fix the prior right of discovery behind dispute' left room for contention wide open, he noted, before suggesting that the 'most feasable Method' for making further discoveries in the south Pacific would be via the Cape and New Zealand, where refreshment, wood and water could be obtained at Queen Charlotte Sound.

... takeing care to be ready to leave that place by the latter end of Sepember or beginning of October at farthest, when you would have the whole summer before you ... with the prevailing Westerly winds, [you could] run to the Eastward in as high a Latitude as you please and, if you met with no lands, would have time enough to get round Cape Horne before the summer was too far spent, but if after meeting with no Continent & you had other Objects in View, than haul to the northward and after visiting some of the Islands already discover'd, after which proceed with the trade winds back to the Westward in search of those before Mintioned [i.e. the islands Tupaia had told of], thus the discoveries in the South Sea would be compleat.

It was perhaps the first set of Cook's remarks, rather than the second, that particularly captured the attention of Sandwich, and probably of George III. The scheme for the discovery of any southern continent was elegantly simple, but it was the need to forestall European rivals, rather than the sheer attractiveness of the project, that made the Admiralty act so precipitately. Cook had been home for less than ten weeks when the Navy Board was instructed to buy two ships of the same sort as the *Endeavour* for the anticipated voyage. Elizabeth Cook may have been dismayed, since it was assumed that Cook would be in command. He was intimately involved in the choice of vessels, which were again Whitby colliers, built like the *Endeavour* by Thomas Fishburn, in a yard just across the river Esk from Walker's house. The one was considerably larger than the *Endeavour*, the other slightly smaller. The Admiralty at first called them the *Drake* and the *Raleigh*, but it was thought that these names would be offensive to the Spanish, whose hospitality or assistance the voyagers might at some point need, and they were changed in December 1771 to *Resolution* and *Adventure* – names Cook considered more appropriate. Cook would command the *Resolution* and the voyage. Tobias Furneaux, who had been to the

Pacific with Wallis in the *Dolphin*, was to be captain of the *Adventure*. No doubt a capable sailor, he appears to have been a disastrously dull man. His encounters with new lands and peoples may occasionally have excited him, but you would not know it from his journal. Cook's first lieutenant would be Robert Palliser Cooper – a relative of his patron, Hugh Palliser – he had sailed on the *Niger* with Banks to Newfoundland in 1766 but, like Furneaux, appears to have been a stranger to imagination. Several officers from the *Endeavour* volunteered for the new voyage. Charles Clerke, who had been around the world with Byron, who had reported upon the Patagonian giants for the edification of the Royal Society, who had something of Banks's playful humour, who had become his friend during the first voyage, was now thirty-eight, but still something of a boy – still someone out for a good time. He became the *Resolution*'s second lieutenant, and Richard Pickersgill, attracted to the idea of revisiting Tahiti, its third. Isaac Smith, Elizabeth Cook's nephew, would be master's mate, and some eleven others from the *Endeavour*, including Edgcumbe, in charge of the marines, were transferred to the *Resolution*. John Gore, so far as we know, had no desire to be under Cook's command again.

Many years later John Elliott, the first midshipman entered in the muster book, composed a memoir for the amusement of his children, which dealt primarily with his experience of Cook's second voyage, and was prefaced by succinct portraits of his fellow-mariners. Pickersgill was 'A good officer and astronomer but liking ye Grog'. One John Whitehouse was a 'Jesuitical, sensible but an insinuating litigious mischief making fellow'. Thomas Willis was 'Wild and drinking'. Most other men were either 'Steady and good', 'Steady and clever', or 'Steady and sober'. Elliott's manuscript moreover gives us a sense of himself, and what a midshipman might have been. Like Cook, he was born in Yorkshire. His family was respectable but lived beyond their income. To relieve financial strain, he was dispatched first to his grandmother and then to an uncle in London, a wealthy merchant with shipping interests. While accommodated there he met his cousin Sibbela. Their growing affection 'bid fair to have ended in a connection for life' but was thwarted by the villainous intrigue of another branch of her family. He was placed at a nautical academy run by one James Ferguson, near the Tower of London. Though this was evidently a sort of prep school for officers who entered the East India Company's service or the Navy, the event that impressed itself on Elliott's memory had nothing to do with learning to make observations or read charts. He wrote that 'Many people have heard of the Conjuror and his black Cock, but here we underwent the ceremony', and proceeded to describe a ritual of divination that followed the theft of a half-guinea, which he found 'awful' and 'imposing'. All those present had to take their turn to enter a darkened room,

the floor covered with circles, figures, signs of the Zodiac and so on, in chalk. One of the Men took me by the hand and led me into the Circle, and told me to walk round them all, and then go into the corner of the room where there was a Basket, and in that Basket, was a Cock; that I was to stroke the Cock's back three times, and if I had got the half-guinea, the Cock would crow, but if I was innocent the Cock would be silent. I did most strictly as I was bid, and tho perfectly innocent, yet I could not help having a great dread of the Cock's crowing. Upon leaving, the man looked at my hand, which to my great surprise was black as coal. This ceremony was gone through by all fairly, except by a teacher of the name of Green, who appeared to have a clean hand, and whom the wise Men declared in their opinion had got the half-guinea.

Elliott's evidently varied education at this institution was interrupted late in 1770 when he sailed with 'another young gentleman', both on their first voyage, to St Kitts in the West Indies. Crossing the Bay of Biscay, 'that Grave of many thousands of Brave Men, and Fine Ships', they met a horrific gale. Elliott was able to congratulate himself on having 'stood composed and fearless on the Quarter deck' while his young companion cried 'and called out Oh, my Mammy, Oh my Mammy, most lamentable'. On the passage home they called at Madeira, where he saw, 'for the first time those seclusions of Female beauty, Nunnerys' and where the kindness of women – whose devotion to faith he does not quite seem to have understood – embarrassed him. Returning from this voyage, Elliott had 'no great relish' to undertake another, but found his destiny sealed. He undertook further studies at Ferguson's Academy. He travelled to Russia's Mediterranean ports, where he saw sailors dying by the score of a plague. He came home via Italy, where they suffered quarantine – all this before his thirteenth birthday in January 1772, by which time he was committed to the *Resolution*.

Elliott recalled the divination rite, because it terrified him, and probably because it was exceptional, but it gives us some sense of the kind of folk-belief that figured, even only occasionally, in the lives of officers as well as seamen. It suggests that when these men went on to witness Oceanic rites, they were not on one side of a gulf that separated reason from superstition. Despite the 'enlightened' nature of the mission, despite the persons and instruments of enlightenment science aboard, their perspective was not exactly that of rationality nor that of orthodox Christianity. Some, if not all, of these Europeans inhabited a world full of signs and omens.

On the *Adventure*, no one other than the captain had Pacific experience. The naval records as usual give us the barest details of the lives of men, many Irish, Scottish or Welsh as well as English. The man we do know something about is James Burney, brother of the novelist Fanny and son of the eminent musical historian Charles. The Burney household being what it was, James could not only play and read music, but transcribe it, and he would be the first European with a trained ear to describe and respond to Oceanic songs. That Banks and Solander would voyage again was presumed. As early as September Banks was engaged in correspondence with seamen, scientists, artists and assistants, prospective members of a party twice the size of that he had taken on the *Endeavour*. After the deaths of Richmond, Dorlton, Buchan and Parkinson, he was concerned, reasonably enough, that work could be carried on if a draughtsman or two were unlucky enough to be frozen or lost to fever. He was also concerned to voyage in style. His troop of servants would include two horn-players, maybe intended to entertain Islanders as well as relieve the tedium of long passages at sea. He recruited the distinguished society painter Johann Zoffany, and the Edinburgh physician James Lind, and would take several artists, who at this time, to judge from their surviving output, were working day and night at New Burlington Street, drawing Maori *patu*, Tahitian ornaments, fish-hooks, weapons, carvings and natural specimens of all kinds.

Banks did not enlist the services of William Wales or William Bayly. The astronomers of the *Resolution* and *Adventure* respectively were appointed by Nevil Maskelyne, the Astronomer Royal. Wales, like Cook, Elliott, Pickersgill and others, was from Yorkshire. Unlike them, he was properly educated. He knew when to see a resemblance to Homer's warriors, and when lines from James Thomson's *Seasons* were apt. He had also voyaged before, he had observed the Transit of Venus in 1769 from Hudson's Bay and he knew the risk that a voyager ran. He was married to the sister of Charles Green, who cannot have liked the thought that her brother would die on one voyage, and her husband fail to return from its successor. Wales was not narrow-minded, but did tend to be precise, sceptical and severe. I can see him teaching mathematics, which he did later. I suspect he would not have entertained his wife's anxieties.

Towards the end of 1771, Banks was painted by Benjamin West, whose *Death of General Wolfe* had been the sensation of the Royal Academy's annual exhibition. West's rejection of the usual classical treatment of grand and tragic subjects, his preference for contemporary military uniforms, his claim to produce a heroic but nevertheless specifically accurate image, were seen at the time as revolutionary. Banks would have appreciated the modernity of West's approach, and West's singular portrait fully exploited Banks's own modernity. Though it incorporated a classical column and drapery, its subject was not some latter-day Cicero but a traveller of an unprecedented kind. The display included a Maori *taiaha*, a tapa beater, and an adze. The volume of drawings at Banks's feet was open at the representation of the New Zealand flax, which was also the material that, in the processed form of a Maori cloak, he held and pointed out. The painting does more than declare that this naturalist's accomplishments and curiosities are novel and remarkable, it conveys Banks's understanding of his own public worth, by insisting on the usefulness of his findings.

To provide the public with more of the same was what Joseph Banks aspired to do. The obstacle that he ran up against was the size of the *Resolution*. Though the ship was larger than the *Endeavour* – the length of the lower deck was 110 feet, thirteen longer than that of the *Endeavour* – the question of how the larger scientific party could be accommodated was problematic. The naval architects got to work. The vessel, which had in any case to be sheathed to protect the hull and otherwise adapted, was given an extra upper deck. Banks would have the great rear cabin normally reserved for the captain and Cook would be accommodated in a round house on the upper deck (which would, I imagine, have been miserably exposed to storms, had he in fact made the voyage in it). These works were completed, but when the ship was sailed down the Thames to the Nore, it proved dangerously top-heavy. Clerke wrote to Banks that, 'By God', he would go to sea 'in a grog-tub if required, or in the Resolution as soon as you please, but must say I think her the most unsafe ship I ever saw or heard of'. The vessel was removed to Sheerness where what had been added was vigorously demolished. Banks, when he saw this, was infuriated, and was supposed to have 'swore and stamp'd upon the Warfe, like a Mad Man'. He had his servants and effects promptly removed from the ship. He disputed the appropriateness of the vessel and the work, and even tried to use his parliamentary friends Edmund Burke and Constantine Phipps to intercede. He thought he was sacrificing his youth, his energies, a great deal of money, perhaps even his life, in the interests of science and the public; was he really expected to sacrifice any sort of comfort, also? Sandwich had been Banks's friend, and must have found the dispute embarrassing, but he shared Cook's view that the success of the *Endeavour*'s voyage owed a good deal to the

19. Joseph Banks, *mezzotint after Benjamin West,*
c. 1772.

type of ship that had been chosen, which had never been employed in
exploration before. He and other Admiralty men were irked by Banks's
meddling in matters marine. In his contribution to a correspondence war,
Sir Hugh Palliser restated the advantages of the Whitby colliers. They were

spacious for their size, their hulls were relatively shallow, and their bodies would 'bear to take the Ground', that is, they could be brought to rest upright in shallows, as the *Endeavour* had been in the Endeavour River. Cook, it appears, avoided any direct altercation with Banks, but must have been satisfied by the outcome, which retained the collier that he had chosen and restored it essentially to its original form. He had a profound faith in the ships he'd seen built and learned to sail in. He liked, I think, the wooden bridge they made between his past and his future, between an old home and the most remote of possible places.

The withdrawal of Banks in May 1772 was the withdrawal of his whole party. The ships' departure had been much delayed by the business of construction and reconstruction and at this late stage the expedition was abruptly without either a naturalist or an artist. The choice of William Hodges, a twenty-eight-year-old 'landskip painter' of humble origins, was fortuitous. Hodges had been a pupil of Richard Wilson's and had acquired conventional classical training, but was also a remarkably deft and adaptable artist, and an open-minded and genuinely curious young man. Hodges would try to reconcile unprecedented subject-matter with the conventions of high art. Sometimes he succeeded, sometimes he failed, but his voyage took British painting to places it had never been before.

Daines Barrington was a wealthy but eccentric antiquarian with interests ranging from polar exploration to the fate of the Cornish language. In May or June he was in touch with Sandwich. He knew of Banks's withdrawal and had a replacement in mind. The fact that the man he knew became the senior natural historian on the second voyage was as fortuitous as Hodges's appointment, though the choice was often lamented, and occasionally cursed. Johann Reinhold Forster was born near Danzig in 1729 and educated in Berlin and Halle, where he completed theological studies. He briefly became an apprentice pastor, while reading widely in languages and natural history. He sought employment nearer these passions and obtained a Russian commission to report on the new Volga colonies – this is what he had been doing, with his son and favourite assistant George, in the mid 1760s, while Cook was surveying Newfoundland. His investigations dealt with natural resources but also focused upon living conditions among the new settlers; Forster frankly and fully described a plethora of bureaucratic abuses and other problems that made their lives difficult. This was an early expression of a propensity, perhaps commendable but certainly unfortunate, to represent things as he saw them – without regard for the patrons and superiors he offended. Catherine the Great and her minister were appalled to receive a document that denounced their colonial programme. Forster senior and junior left Russia without payment. They travelled to London and then to Warrington, where Forster became a teacher of natural history at a famous dissenters' academy. He made contacts, joined societies, delivered lectures and impressed people. His astonishing range of interests embraced medical history, human social development, comparative linguistics and political economy as well as botany and zoology; he had written an *Introduction to Mineralogy* (1768), and, with George, translated a host of books, including many by the scientific travellers inspired by Linnaeus. When Cook read Bougainville, he would do so in the Forsters' translation, which appeared in January 1772; he would read not only Bougainville's text, but also the footnotes that Forster liked to add, which freely corrected and occasionally even ridiculed the writers whose works were relayed to the public. Johann Forster knew the value of his own opinions and was rarely backward in expressing them; he was nothing if not an 'original', as an extraordinary character was called in the eighteenth century; and his son George, who would join the *Resolution* with him, was likewise an imaginative radical intellectual, though one lucky to lack his father's consistent tactlessness.

Among Johann Forster's distinctions is having aroused the antipathy of J. C. Beaglehole. Cook's editor and biographer complained that when the midshipman John Elliott described him as 'a clever, but a litigious quarelsom fellow', he stopped 'far too short'. Beaglehole thought it important to add, 'Dogmatic, humourless, suspicious, pretentious, contentious, censorious, demanding, rheumatic, he was a problem from any angle.' But if Forster's voyage journal is indeed replete with his crankiness, it is full also of rich and varied descriptions of natural phenomena and indigenous peoples and efforts to remould scientific hypotheses around new findings. This journal reveals a racing mind, and as much about the second voyage as Banks's does about the first. It tells us rather more about custom and contention among the ship's company. It tells us a good deal about Cook that we would not otherwise know. The prospect of participation was, it seems, first broached with Forster on 26 May 1772. On 13 July, the ships were at sea. 'Farewell to old England,' wrote Richard Pickersgill, with awkward ornament.

If a new voyage was the first consequence of Cook's report, a book would be the second. Sandwich took his point, that discoveries made were not discoveries recognized unless they were published. Such was the proliferation of untrustworthy travellers' tales, they had to be published by authority. It was not, in other words, a question of encouraging Wallis to make some private arrangement with a printer, supposing even that he had the time or ability to do that. What was needed quickly was rather an official account of the several British voyages that had been undertaken with the blessing of George III. It was natural to assume that the work would be written by someone other than Cook, whose absence on the new voyage was already anticipated. Cook could not, in any case, be expected to prepare Byron's, Carteret's or Wallis's journals for publication. Sandwich knew little about literature and asked friends such as David Garrick and Charles Burney for advice. Both appear to have suggested John Hawkesworth. In his early fifties, he had written essays, criticism, poetry and Oriental tales. Almost twenty years earlier, he'd been Dr Johnson's collaborator on the well-known periodical *The Adventurer*. He no doubt appeared a respectable choice. As early as mid September 1771, Hawkesworth and Sandwich had met and concluded an agreement which provided Hawkesworth with his materials – in the form of the voyage journals – and left him free to strike whatever deal he could with a printer.

The excitement was such that the best publishers scrambled for the book, offering sums for the copyright beyond the dreams of the most successful essayists, novelists and historians of the day. After conducting something like an auction, Hawkesworth obtained the astonishing sum of £6,000 from Strahan and Cadell – equivalent to millions today. The book would be lavishly illustrated with plates derived from Parkinson, or otherwise concocted (there had been no artist with Byron or Wallis, so no sketches to work from). It was eagerly anticipated.

Hawkesworth opted to use the first person. By writing 'in the person of the Commanders', he thought he might excite the reader's interest more effectively than if 'a stranger' intervened between 'the Adventurer and the Reader'. But he also thought that if the account were not to lapse into meaningless particularity, he had to intersperse 'sentiments' that would make diverse and remarkable incidents intelligible to a European readership. And, while Cook's journals contained 'a very minute description' of the places visited, Banks had naturally been less focused upon navigational matters and the management of the voyage. His records were therefore 'much more full and particular' than the captain's. Hawkesworth's narrative of the *Endeavour*'s voyage was therefore ostensibly Cook's, but it used Cook's journal selectively. It added material from Banks as well as Hawkesworth's own reflections. Hawkesworth claimed that the commanders had approved his text. Cook later disputed this. The book, *An Account of the Voyages Undertaken by the Order of his Present Majesty for Making Discoveries in the Southern Hemisphere*, was published in June

1773. In one sense, it was a success. According to lending library statistics, it was one of ten most popular books borrowed in the last quarter of the eighteenth century. But, if commentators were representative, it failed disastrously to please the bulk of these readers. Hawkesworth's book was not only subjected to immediate and intense criticism but has been vilified ever since. Early controversy focused on Hawkesworth's supposed immorality and impiety. In their turn, twentieth-century scholars took up where Cook himself left off, censuring alterations to the original journals. Most recently I have myself listened, at a gathering of Cook scholars and enthusiasts, to an enthusiastically venomous speaker detailing Hawkesworth's errors in descriptions of Atlantic islands.

Hawkesworth did indeed distort his sources. He omitted the good things Cook had to say about Aboriginal Australians and instead reinforced the racism that was emerging in accounts of them. But his *Account* arguably dealt honestly with a problem that scarcely any other voyage writer would even acknowledge. He responded to the anguish in Cook's and Banks's reflections upon the Poverty Bay massacre with a considered acknowledgement of the injustice of this violence. Cook had admitted that 'most humane men who have not experienced things of this nature will cencure my conduct' but proceeded to embed an explanation for the event in the experience that he, and not those 'humane men', had. He conceded that his expectation that the people in the canoe would not resist capture had been wrong, that the effort to take the people had been imprudent and unjustified, but that once his effort had begun, and once it had been resisted, he 'was not to stand still' and suffer assault. Hawkesworth, assuming Cook's voice, enlarged upon this:

I am conscious that the feeling of every reader of humanity will censure me for having fired upon these unhappy people, and it is impossible that, upon a calm review, I should approve it myself. They certainly did not deserve death for not chusing to confide in my promises; or not consenting to come aboard my boat, even if they had apprehended no danger; but the nature of my service required me to obtain a knowledge of their country, which I could no otherwise effect than by forcing my way into it in a hostile manner, or gaining admission through the confidence and good-will of the people. I had already tried the power of presents without effect; and I was now prompted, by my desire to avoid further hostilities, to get some of them on board, as the only method left of convincing them that we intended no harm, and had it in our power to contribute to their gratification and convenience. Thus far my intentions certainly were not criminal; and though in

the contest, which I had not the least reason to expect, our victory might have
been complete without so great an expense of life; yet in such situations, when
the command to fire had been given, no man can restrain its excess, or prescribe
its effect.

This passage translated Cook's regret into more general and morally
pressing register. The problem was not one of misjudgement. It lay in what
a voyage required and made inevitable. The inspection of lands visited was
an essential part of Cook's mission. Yet description depended on contact
that the inhabitants of newly found places might decline or resist. The
necessary negotiation or suppression of their resistance might lead to shooting, and Hawkesworth surely grasps the essentially unpredictable quality
of any armed violence, when he insists that once shooting starts, no one
'can restrain its excess, or prescribe its effect'. This was a bald, but an
appalling admission. British scientists and seamen, members of a mission
justified by the promise of commerce, mutual improvement and the enhancement of civilization, would somewhere be drawn to commit acts of savagery
that could barely be comprehended by humane readers in Europe. Cook's
excuse was, in effect, that you had to be there to see why this occurred.
Hawkesworth extracted a larger, perhaps a dangerous conclusion: what
happened on these remote beaches could simply not be accounted or
answered for, at the remove of home; which was to beg the questions of
whether civilized men were only civilized in civilized places, and whether
their travels took them into situations beyond the scope of ethical and moral
principles that were surely supposed to apply universally.

Hawkesworth's consideration of this issue was followed immediately by his
most contentious passage. He did not attribute 'any of the critical escapes
from danger that I have recorded, to the particular interposition of Providence'. His view was that it made no sense to suppose that when the wind
lapsed while the *Endeavour* was on the reef on the northern Australian
coast, Providence intervened, to prevent the ship being beaten to pieces. If
this was a natural event, he suggested, it made as much sense to say that
'providentially the sun rose in the morning'. If it was not, why had Providence placed the ship at risk in the first place? This was theologically
unorthodox. It threatened ideas of divine preference and patriotism. It was
denounced unusually harshly: a correspondent to the *Public Advertiser*
advised Hawkesworth, 'You are *lawful game*, and ought to be *hunted*,
by every Friend of Virtue.' The author's immorality on this point was
compounded by a frankness unwelcome to some readers on sexual subjects,

where a few passages did much to turn the South Seas sensuality already cited in newspaper reports into an enduring image. The most arresting of these derived from Cook's report of an incident that had taken place at Point Venus on 14 May 1769. It was a Sunday, divine service was held and a few Tahitians attended who seemed to respect the seriousness of the occasion. Later in the day, however, what Cook called an 'odd Scene' took place at the gate of the British fort,

where a young fellow above 6 feet high lay with a little Girl about 10 or 12 years of age publickly before several of our people and a number of the Natives. What makes me mention this, is because, it appear'd to be done more from Custom than Lewdness, for there were several women present particularly Obarea and several others of the better sort and these were so far from shewing the least disaprobation that they instructed the girl how she should act her part, who young as she was, did not seem to want it.

Hawkesworth's treatment of the incident appears to follow Cook's text closely, but introduces definite rhetorical effect. In the journal, the event occurs well after the service and there is no indication that it is more than a coincidence that it takes place on the same day. Hawkesworth juxtaposes the rites, describing the Christian ceremony and then observing 'Such were our Matins; our Indians thought fit to perform Vespers of a very different kind.' He inserted the word 'great' before Cook's 'number of the natives', stressing just how public the act was, and states emphatically that intercourse took place 'without the least sense of its being indecent or improper, but, as it appeared, in perfect conformity to the custom of the place'. The scene, he hastened to add, was 'not mentioned as an object of idle curiosity' but because it shed light on the question of whether the shame associated with sex was 'implanted in Nature or superinduced by custom'. This amounted to an early rehearsal for the debates about nature versus nurture that were to dominate much twentieth-century thought about human behaviour, and sex in particular. Hawkesworth expressed himself equivocally – that was one of the devices of the polite Georgian essayist – but his implication was that shame was artificial. If it were natural, he pointed out, one would have to know how it had somehow been suppressed or erased in the Tahitian case.

Hawkesworth's book travelled quickly across the channel and one of those interested in the passage was Voltaire, who referred on two occasions to the wonderful Tahitian 'divine service', which he thought reflected their preservation of 'the oldest religion of the earth'. Another of the most influential French Enlightenment thinkers, Denis Diderot, was equally enchanted by what he took to be the custom of public lovemaking and its most significant feature, a lack of shame. It is not surprising that other readers responded very differently. John Wesley, the founder of Methodism, wrote that he had sat down to read Cook's voyages with 'huge expectation' but found the book full of incredible, impossible things, as much a fiction as *Robinson Crusoe*. 'Men and women coupling together in the face of the sun, and in the sight of scores of people! Hume or Voltaire might believe this, but I cannot.' Some in England castigated Hawkesworth for adding fuel to what were already bonfires of lasciviousness and immorality. Others thought that the 'odd scene' demanded emulation. *Nocturnal Revels*, a salacious review of London's sex trade, reported that Charlotte Hayes, one of the most notorious high society brothel-keepers, 'certainly consulted these pages' in Hawkesworth's *Account*

with uncommon attention, and she concluded, that shame upon similar occasions 'was only superinduced by custom;' and being so much of a Natural Philosopher as to have surmounted all prejudices, she resolved not only to teach her Nuns all the Rites of VENUS as practised at *Otaheite*, but to improve upon them.

Mrs Hayes therefore sent announcements to her most distinguished clients, advising them that the rites of Venus, Tahitian style, would take place at her establishment, presided over by 'Queen Oberea', a role taken by Mrs Hayes herself. Her audience consisted 'chiefly of the first Nobility'. Her performers included Royal Academy models, and her ceremony got under way as each presented his partner 'with a Nail at least twelve inches in length, in imitation of the presents received by the Ladies of *Otaheite*'. The champagne flowed, and in due course spectators became participants.

This live show was probably a one-off event, but Tahitian practices interested other pornographic periodicals. The idea that the South Sea was a place of easy fornication seized many European imaginations. Joseph Banks's participation became a focus of satirical commentary that represented natural science less as a virtuous inquiry than a cover for promiscuity. An engraving of Banks inviting so-called 'Indians' to look at Venus through a thick telescope exemplifies the sort of innuendo that was much circulated. It was only because of Hawkesworth's apparently subtle revisions of Cook that the Point Venus event could fuel these imaginings. The navigator's reference to an 'odd Scene' was omitted, which was to remove the imputation that the event was unusual, within the mariners' Tahitian experience; behaviour that they did not in fact witness repeatedly was evoked as though it was typical. When Cook wrote that the act was 'done more from Custom than Lewdness' he was making an either/or statement. He indicated that intercourse took place, not because the young man and woman desired each other, but because a sexual performance was required by a custom or ritual of some sort. In Hawkesworth's wording, this inference disappears, and 'custom' is no longer the cause of the act. Instead, it is the public expression of 'lewdness' that is said to be 'in perfect conformity' with custom, in other words there was nothing out of the ordinary about it. The revision was made because he wanted to challenge the natural status of shame, but it altered absolutely the point of Cook's remark.

This would be nit-picking if the stereotype of Tahiti was founded in fact, and public lovemaking in fact routine. But the behaviour that Cook described is mysterious, and nothing quite like it is ever reported again. Though certain Tahitian ceremonies did have erotic elements, no later visitor sees anything like this public act. The silence on this point does not reflect any wider lack of information. Many Europeans visited this part of Polynesia during the late eighteenth and early nineteenth centuries. Some, such as the *Bounty* mutineer James Morrison, were there for extended periods, knew the language well, and acquired nuanced understandings of Tahitian culture. Later, missionaries wrote at great length about Tahitian behaviour, society, and religion. Their evangelical prejudices did not stop them describing many customs that they censured. Their archives, and those of ethnologists who came later, are extensive. Yet in none of these sources is there a description of anything like the scene that Cook witnessed that was supposed by Hawkesworth and so many of his readers to represent a Tahitian 'custom'. What kind of customary act takes place only once?

Clues to what really happened in May 1769 emerge from a short work published nearly ten years later by the astronomer William Wales. His pamphlet was an angry response to George Forster's narrative of the second voyage, but he went out of his way to agree with Forster on just one point, that the characters of Tahitian women had been traduced. The fact that at one time or another Wales, Forster and Cook all said much the same thing suggests that it was something that the *Resolution*'s officers and scientists talked about from time to time at sea. Wales, like them, wrote that prostitution could be found in most places, and that the broader pattern of Tahitian behaviour was no better or worse than that at home. His comment is relevant here because he mentions the 'brutal indecency' described by Hawkesworth, and stresses that neither he nor his companions on the second voyage saw anything like it. Still more interesting is his elucidation of the role of Purea, who, according to Cook, was present, and verbally directed and encouraged the couple; Wales goes further and says he had 'not the least doubt, that the whole scene was her contrivance, and that the island was ransacked to find out two actors'. He adds this suggestive footnote:

Since the above was written, I have been informed from the authority of a gentleman who was in the Endeavour, and saw the transaction here alluded to, that it is very imperfectly, and in some measure erroneously, related by Dr. Hawkesworth. Oberea *obliged* the two persons to *attempt* what is there said to have been done, but they were exceedingly terrified, and by no means able to perform it. The same authority adds, that most of the natives reprobated Oberea in very severe terms for the part which she had in it.

Although this adds a good deal to Cook's initial report, it is consistent with it. Indeed, Cook's understanding that the act was some kind of custom, rather than an expression of 'lewdness', was a response to something and most probably to an observation that the actors did not exhibit normal desire. Their performance was awkward, unwilling, perhaps incomplete.

We know that Islanders frequently performed theatricals of one sort or another, which often included dramatization of contact with the Europeans or satire upon them. We know also that when seamen began to have sex with Tahitian women during Wallis's visit, the first such act took place completely in the open, the young Irishman concerned being in great haste to have the 'Honour' of inaugurating such relations. This singular behaviour can only have impressed itself upon the Tahitians, among whom, at this time, Purea was prominent. It appears to have been repeated by other seamen, who were likewise desperate to get on with the act, perhaps not troubled by privacy, perhaps titillated and delighted by the notion that they had discovered a whole society of prostitutes, an island of rampant and open voluptuousness. This was false and nonsensical, but even without contact with women, scurvy-infected sailors were inclined to regard islands as utopias, and it is not difficult to understand their investment in the fantasy. Nor is it surprising that they did their best to turn fantasy into reality, by acting out the idea that in this enchanted place, everyone made love everywhere.

The event made notorious by Hawkesworth took place directly outside the British fort, obviously the site on the island most associated with the visitors and the place that Tahitians would have chosen, had they wanted to show them something. If we can never finally be certain why this 'odd Scene' took place, it does seem most likely that it was not merely Purea's contrivance, as Wales asserted, but that it contrived a parody of the mariners' behaviour. It was their custom, not that of the Tahitians, to fuck in public. Purea – who comes across as an astute woman with a sense of humour – was improvising a little performance that drew attention to this gross behaviour. Her send-up was hardly unjust. In London, the brazen character of commercial sex was always being lamented. Polite people were unwilling to visit many city parks because they could encounter women and their clients. Such behaviour was even acknowledged by participants such as James Boswell, who mentions enjoying the view of the river whilst at it beside the then-new Westminster Bridge. The Enlightenment sophisticates who thought that they were being clever when they used a Tahitian custom to question European morals did not realize that they had been beaten to the game. They could credit Tahitians with innocence, happiness and sensuality, but not with critical intelligence. They had no idea that mere savages might be satirists too.

PART 3:
TOWARDS THE SOUTH POLE

11

The Inhospitable parts I am going to

To voyage is to die. Not certainly, not literally, but in a host of ways that troubled the imaginations of mariners long before Cook. Some years before the explorer first went to sea, a philosophically inclined merchant departing England reflected upon the situation of the Scilly Isles, which he supposed had been part of the mainland before some horrific earthquake or inundation.

. . . the Rocks seem now with terrible accent to lament the separation. Who knows but we likewise are severing eternally from our Friends! It is a voyage that we shall at some time or other make; and those solitary Rocks that bound the last sight of our Homes and Countries, naturally bring to my mind some reflections . . .

And pretty gloomy reflections they were. 'Our personal Identity must be destroyed in the first Transmigration,' John Atkins wrote, before meandering towards the Bay of Biscay and questions of faith. James Cook was less disposed to either geological or theological speculation, but the questions of whether and when he might see friends again were nevertheless on his mind in November 1772. He wrote to John Walker:

Having nothing new to communicate I should hardly have troubled you with a letter was it not customary for Men to take leave of their friends before they go out of the World, for I can hardly think my self in it so long as I am deprived from having any Connections with the civilized part of it, and this will soon be my case for two years at least. When I think of the Inhospitable parts I am going to, I think the Voyage dangerous, I however enter upon it with great cheerfullness, providence has been very kind to me on many occasions, and I trust in the continuation of the divine protection; I have two good Ships well provided and well Man'd . . . Please to make my best respects to all Friends at Whitby.

Cook wrote in these terms, not on passing out of sight of Britain, but on the day he was leaving Cape Town, which was to mark the difference between his sense of the world and Atkins's. For the merchant, the seas were the domain of danger and uncertainty. For Cook, the Atlantic was now familiar. More than four months after the departure of the *Resolution* and the *Adventure* from Plymouth, the voyage into regions that lay almost beyond life had scarcely begun.

The passage south had been uneventful, but the expedition nevertheless already had exceptional qualities that had been manifest in unusual kinds and quantities of provisions, in the rituals of science and in the sorts of attention that ports and people received. The two ships were laboratories of mariners' health, and there were abundant stocks of experimental foods that, it was hoped, would prevent scurvy more effectively. They included malt, sauerkraut, salted cabbage, soups, lemon and orange concentrate, carrot marmalade and the 'inspissated juice of wort' – a sort of base for beer. The voyage would also provide the toughest and most prolonged test of the new clocks that sought to resolve the longstanding problem of how longitude might be precisely determined at sea.

On the 10th of July, the watches were set a-going in the presence of the two astronomers, Captain Furneaux, the first lieutenants of the ships, and myself, and put on board. The two on board the Adventure were made by Mr. Arnold, and also one of those on board the Resolution; but the other was made by Mr. Kendal, upon the same principle, in every respect, as Mr. Harrison's time-piece. The commander, first lieutenant, and astronomer, on board each of the ships, kept, each of them, keys of the boxes which contained the watches, and were always to be present at the winding them up, and comparing the one with the other; or some other officer, if at any time through indisposition, or absence upon any other necessary duties, any of them could not conveniently attend.

This triple-locking and joint time-telling was intended to forestall debate about whether these clocks performed adequately or not. The measures might be thought over-scrupulous, but as it happened this voyage would have a remarkable capacity to engender dispute that would outrun these and many other regulations. This was not yet evident as the ships moved from the northern to the southern summers of 1772. At Madeira, Heberden was dead, but Cook and others were entertained by one Loughnans, an English merchant. Monasteries and convents were visited, the usual provisions were obtained. The only thing out of the ordinary here was the report that a 'Mr Dutton', a natural historian, had been awaiting the arrival of Joseph Banks for some three months. This person, pretending to be a man, was universally said to have been a woman, and anticipated recruitment to the voyage at the time the ship passed by. Cook must have been amused to gather that Banks's preparations for the expedition had been even more elaborate than had been apparent in London. It is assumed that Banks was simply providing himself with a sexual companion, but his motivations probably also included an unwillingness to be outdone by any French naturalist: Philibert Commerson, on Bougainville's voyage of 1766–9, had been accompanied by Jeanne Baret, a lover passing herself off as his male assistant, now believed to have been the first woman to have travelled around the world. Though Baret's circumspection around dress and bodily functions had aroused some suspicions, these had been allayed by her indefatigable energy. She had lugged Commerson's guns, provisions and specimen books up and down the icy hills of Tierra del Fuego and otherwise worked as hard as anyone else on the voyage. The Tahitians, however, did not assume that a strong woman could not be a woman and recognized her instantly for what she was. It is characteristic of Banks that he would go to some lengths and presumably considerable expense to smuggle a disguised woman into his scientific team, but the lady in fact spent her time at Funchal collecting specimens. She probably had her own reasons for risking the expedition, which involved, as Cook had reflected, nothing less than relinquishing the world. If she was someone such as Sarah Primatt, who had earlier written to Banks from Oporto, overflowing with passion for plants, she would have been a stimulating co-investigator rather than just a companion, and a writer who could well have left a journal of this voyage more engaging than many of those we possess. It was not to be, and whoever 'Mr Dutton' was had given up and quit Madeira a few days before the *Resolution*'s arrival.

At Cape Town, the Dutch governor was all hospitality. Provisions were easily obtained. Cook and his crews, however, encountered a grim reminder of the hazards of sea voyages. Just a few days after their arrival, two Dutch ships appeared, having taken more than four months to travel from Holland, and having between them lost nearly 200 men to scurvy. Those not already dead were taken to an overcrowded hospital 'in very dreadful circumstances'. On 22 November, Cook wrote the letter I have quoted, and the ships sailed during the afternoon. By eight the next morning they had lost sight of the Cape, and were heading into waters unknown.

They had left behind one lieutenant in poor health and gained a third naturalist. The Forsters had met up with Anders Sparrman, a young and energetic pupil of Linnaeus, who had already travelled to China and extensively within southern Africa. Johann fully expected that a southern continent would be discovered and that he and his son would be over-whelmed by the range of new things to collect, draw and describe. Thinking he would benefit from further assistance, he therefore offered Sparrman employment for the duration of the voyage. The young Swede hesitated. His grasp of English was poor and he was concerned about the 'disposition of the people' with whom he would spend so many months at sea. The prospect of savage British sailors, it appears, bothered him rather more than the dangers of the southern oceans or the potential violence of previously unknown peoples. Yet he felt in the end it was an opportunity that he had to embrace. Forster was able to persuade the reluctant Cook to accept a further supernumerary.

Not only Sparrman and the Forsters, but all the more seasoned seamen appear to have been shocked by how swiftly the temperature dropped as the ships moved south towards 'Cape Circumcision' – named after the feast day. This apparent promontory, sighted by the French navigator de Lozier Bouvet in 1739, was firmly believed by him to be part of the southern continent. Gales pushed the ships well to the east of the supposed position of this cape – which had been misplaced by Bouvet, and was in any case a small island, one of the most remote and isolated in the world – and caused havoc as most of the sheep, pigs, and geese on board were washed overboard or killed by frigid waves and storms. Cook wrote that 'every man in the ship' felt the effects of the 'sudden transition' from the warm weather of the Cape to freezing conditions. He augmented allowances of spirits and gave men 'a dram whenever I thought it necessary'. Worse was to come. By the second week of December, the weather was 'thick and hazy'. There were frequent sleet and snow storms. Icebergs, or rather 'ice islands' miles in diameter, began to surround the ship. Some members of the crew would have seen ice in the north Atlantic, but no one had seen such prodigious ice masses, which were, from a detached perspective, curious and impressive. As Cook put it, they 'exhibited a view which for a few moments was pleasing to the eye; but when we reflected on the danger, the mind was filled with horror'. The great swells broke upon them as relentlessly as they broke upon any reef, and scarcely anywhere else could the outcome of shipwreck be so certainly fatal.

In mid December, the ships were in the right latitude to encounter any land that might extend eastward from Bouvet's cape. Some on board, including Cook himself, believed they saw land between or beyond the ice. The discovery of the southern continent was keenly anticipated, but days went by and nothing but more ice, whales, penguins and occasional seals and birds were sighted. Yet some were encouraged because it was widely believed that sea water could not freeze, and that the 'ice islands' could therefore only form from rivers and coasts; 'under this supposition we were led to believe that land was not far distant'. Cook thought that he might well be able to sail a little further east and then south behind the ice shelf to put the matter beyond doubt.

On Christmas Day, 1772, the *Resolution* and *Adventure* were around 57° south. Here, in midsummer, the temperature was just over freezing, probably no warmer than it was in these mariners' various British, German and Scandinavian home towns. Both officers and common seamen made the best of circumstances by drinking punch, porter, port, Madeira, Bordeaux and South African wine steadily from the midday meal throughout the afternoon and night. Sparrman, still regarding the sailors as an exotic species, described their 'Christmas entertainment', 'fighting in the English fashion, which is called boxing' for his genteel Swedish readers, naturally ignorant of such barbarities. Though fights often took place standing up, he explained that on this occasion, probably because the men were so drunk, they fought seated astride their trunks, stripped to the waist, vigorously punching each other's stomachs and bloody faces, aiming particularly for the eyes and jaws at a rate that the spectator's eye could barely follow. Some fought in order to revenge insults. Others who were merely watching became ambitious to match themselves against champions. Sparrman believed that in this case and that of dancing, those spectators 'whose natures are not sufficiently controlled by reflection and good sense' were easily prompted to participate.

The tricky business of government at sea was at issue here. Cook told Sparrman that on larger ships boxing was banned, but that on a long voyage, it was advisable to take a more relaxed view. 'It was better that the crew should settle their disputes and disagreements . . . thereby establishing a certain peace aboard the ship, than to quarrel for the duration of the voyage.' Surely Cook understood that more was at issue than the resolution of differences. Even in the most confined spaces, duty and discipline could not be all-encompassing. Society at sea had to allow time and space for entertainment – and even a sense of accomplishment that arose from violence – that was not ratified by official hierarchies. If this was his approach, it paid off. He tracked back to the west to be sure that there could be no land in the region of Cape Circumcision, then moved east and south again; the weather was a little warmer, but there was still much snow and sleet that froze in the rigging, sails and blocks, so 'as to make them exceedingly bad to handle'. But, he reported, the people dealt with these hardships 'with a steady perseverance, and withstood this intense cold much better than I expected'.

The ships continued to travel east across the farthest southern part of the Indian ocean. On 17 January the *Resolution* crossed the Antarctic circle and was just a few miles to the south of it around noon. There was no land to be seen, but Cook was confident, and so far as anyone knows justly so, that his was the 'first and only Ship that ever cross'd that line'. On 8 February, further north again, the vessels were separated in fog. Cook cruised around the vicinity for three days firing cannon, but then gave up and resumed an eastward course, presuming to meet the *Adventure* again at an agreed rendezvous in New Zealand. Some days later, different sorts of smaller penguins were seen, leading some to believe that land might be near. Cook was less inclined to watch these creatures than the water itself. Like the Polynesian navigators who closely observed currents, colour and waves, he studied the swell, and felt that its huge hollow roll here, and its trend, at first from the west and then from south and south-east, made it unlikely that they were near any land in those directions. On 15 February he noted in passing that there had lately been incidents of petty theft aboard. He accordingly made a thorough search, 'and punished those in whose custody' missing objects were found.

In late February he resolved to venture south of the Antarctic circle again, but was deterred by high seas and vast numbers of ice islands. They struck him as aesthetically remarkable objects, when they were not simply alarming. He expanded on his earlier remarks, noting that the apprehension they caused was 'in some measure compencated by the very curious and romantick Views many of these Islands exhibit and which are greatly heightned by the foaming and dashing of the waves against them and into the several holes and caverns which are formed in the most of them, in short the whole exhibits a View which can only be discribed by the pencle of an able painter'. The able painter was, of course, William Hodges, who was in the process of producing the first visual images of the Antarctic. His ink and wash drawings capture the chaotic architecture of the ice islands, the vulnerability of suddenly diminutive ships on high seas in their vicinity and the crazy vigour of sailors hacking and hauling at loose and broken ice to be got aboard and melted for washing and drinking water. If seamen were always in the wrong element, at an uncomfortable remove from the normal ground of human existence, these mariners were surely doubly displaced, since this harshly frigid and semi-solid ocean was like no other – as removed from the usual temperate sea-lanes as the sea itself was from land.

It was not until mid March – after fully four months of these extraordinary conditions, and by which time Cook had sailed right across the waters to the south of Australia – that course was altered toward the north-east, towards New Zealand. By this time many on board were suffering from scurvy. The success of efforts, dietary and otherwise, to suppress this notoriously awful, capricious and debilitating condition was something of a point of honour on the voyage, and Cook acknowledged its incidence only implicitly. George Forster was less evasive: 'several of our people had now strong symptoms of the sea-scurvy, such as bad gums, difficult breathing, livid blotches, eruptions, contracted limbs, and greenish greasy filaments in the urine'. Scurvy was known to accentuate the longing for land, and heighten the joy of those who reached it again. The seamen became 'exhilarated' as they approached the far south-west of New Zealand, by sightings of floating trunks and weeds; on 26 March 1773 they entered Dusky Sound, a place that would seem not just pleasant, but a sort of utopia.

Dusky Sound is less a straight fiord than an infinitely ramified series of branches, inlets and islets. Its broad entry is protected by the broken peninsula Cook called Five Fingers point. Some way within this, depending on prevailing seas, the oceanic swell gives way to placid and protected waters. Here, in the early autumn, the breeze was light, the temperature benign and the water birds abundant. The *Resolution* anchored, lines were thrown out, and for the first time in months fish were immediately caught, 'which heightened the raptures we had already felt', Forster wrote. The forests, streams, and rugged scenery, he maintained, suggested the paintings of Salvator Rosa, and 'altogether conspired to complete our joy . . . so apt is mankind, after a long absence from land, to be prejudiced in favour of the wildest shore, that we looked upon the country at that time, as one of the most beautiful which nature unassisted by art could produce'. The situation was made still more convenient by the discovery of a small but deep cove, within which the ship could be moored directly beside the shore and where a horizontal tree provided a natural gangplank. Even Cook was effusive: 'every place abounded with excellent fish and the shores and Woods we found not destitute of wild fowl, so that we expected to injoy with ease what in our situation might be call'd the luxuries of life'.

The sense that the place was a paradise was somewhat diminished when seamen began clearing the slope and low hill immediately beside this mooring, to set up a forge, make space for sail-makers' repairs and create a vantage point for astronomical observation. The forest possessed primeval density. Huge moss-covered trunks lay everywhere, rotten ground collapsed underfoot, and creepers and vines seemed placed to snare every movement. Yet the expectation that the place was one of plenitude was sustained. Fish such as blue cod were caught every day and there were plenty of delicious

20. *William Hodges,* View in Pickersgill Harbour, *1773.*

crayfish. Seamen and officers alike revelled in the diet of fresh seafood, which was boiled, broiled, fried, roasted and turned into soups and pasties. It was discovered that a sort of myrtle made a palatable tea. Cook used a spruce, together with the wort base he had brought, to brew what was regarded as a wholesome beer. Ducks, shags and seals could be shot, and though the creatures killed appear all to have been consumed, the gentlemen clearly treated their hunting recreationally. One seal, which weighed over 200 pounds, gave Cook 'much sport'. The Forsters were delighted by the botanical as well as the marine environment, disappointed only because the season meant that most plants bore neither flowers nor seeds.

Though the area was at first thought to be uninhabited, canoes were soon sighted. Their occupants kept their distance. Perhaps because wood, water and provisions could evidently be obtained without local negotiation, perhaps because he'd decided that it was the best policy, Cook did not chase after the native people in order to initiate contact. But on the afternoon of 6 April, one local man was standing on something very much like a natural pedestal on a rocky point at one end of a small island not far from the *Resolution*'s mooring. This man saw a small boat, containing some eight to ten men, making its way back towards the ship and chose this moment to confront, to meet, to know these strangers.

The men in the boat included Cook, Hodges, Sparrman and the Forsters. They say they heard a 'loud hallooing'. They saw the man, who had a substantial club, and two women with spears in the brush behind him. They brought the boat up to the foot of the rock and greeted him in Tahitian, but he remained where he was, delivering an extended oration, some of it vehement, some of it punctuated by gestures with his weapon. This appears to have been of the *taiaha* type, possessed of a powerful but not quite human face, and bright *paua*-shell eyes, which flashed at these Europeans as they caught the sun. What he said was not understood and cannot now be reconstructed. He may well have demanded of the mariners who they and their fathers were, and from whence they came. He would not have been much impressed, had he gathered that Cook's progenitors were labourers without land, which was to say contemptible slaves, from a Maori perspective. He might have thought they brought pollution, and was reciting formulae that would dispel their threat. Cook entreated him from the bow of the vessel, and threw his and other handkerchiefs on to the rock, objects which were ignored. It was now nearly two years since he'd last tried to coax contact, then with Aboriginal people around the Endeavour River, but he had a sense that this man was not fundamentally hostile, that he indeed wanted to initiate interaction. Cook got out of the boat, scrambled up the rock towards the man, and presented him with a few sheets of white paper, which he probably appropriated from Hodges's sketchbook. The man trembled visibly, not knowing whether Cook was voyager, ancestor or killer, but he took the paper and accepted Cook's greeting. Forster supposed that it was the *hongi*, the nose-touching ritual, that relieved his apprehensions, yet the paper too probably played a part. It would have seemed a form of cloth to this man. For all Oceanic people, cloth was and is a substance of sociality, a wrapping that protects bodies spiritually as well as practically, a valuable, a sort of currency, a gift. Admittedly these sheets were not substantial. They were not the feather or dogskin capes that were real treasures to native New Zealanders, but they betokened something promising rather than threatening.

At this point people almost relaxed. The women came forward and 'a short conversation ensued' which was mutually unintelligible but was, the older Forster thought, 'at least as edifying as great many which are usual in the politer circles of civilized nations, & which here at least passed with a great deal more sincerity and cordiality on both sides'. The mariners had immediate regard for the man, who was distinguished by a 'very pleasing and open countenance'. The older woman was disfigured by some kind of huge growth on her upper lip, but the younger, George Forster wrote unpleasantly, 'was not wholly so disagreeable as one might have expected in New Zealand'. Hodges quickly sketched the man and younger woman. Although his two-dimensional drawing was unlike any form of traditional Maori art or representation, they saw what he was doing, and were amused. They called him, or what he was doing, *toetoe*, which refers to marking or painting. Maori used a kind of red ochre in body painting, and it was fortuitously precisely this medium – red chalk – that Hodges was now employing to depict them. Despite the fact that the genealogies, languages and life-experiences of the people gathered on this rock had been worlds apart, there was thus, suddenly and accidentally, a point of mutual pleasure and recognition.

The Europeans tried to give the Maori some fish and fowl, which were not accepted. The man observed them gravely, while the younger woman talked volubly. It was getting dark and the visitors took their leave, but returned the next morning, equipped with the usual trinkets, which the man paid little attention to. However, he immediately wanted the iron hatchets and nails that were patently useful. On this occasion he introduced what was presumed to be his whole family: two women, the girl encountered the day before, a boy of about fourteen and three younger children. Their huts were toured. They produced ornaments and weapons by way of return gifts. The man came to the water's edge to see them off, and gave Cook more things, seeking in exchange a heavy cloak that Cook felt he could not spare. On the third day of this intercourse the mariners visited again to find the family elaborately dressed up, all with ornaments and their hair carefully combed and tied. They 'received us standing, with marks of friendship and great courtesy'. Cook this time was wearing a red baize cloak, which he removed from his shoulders to present to the man, who was plainly gratified. He promptly gave Cook his whalebone *patu*, probably an heirloom rather than simply a weapon. Efforts were made to conduct a conversation, but Gibson, who had been supposed to have some facility in Tahitian, could understand no more than anyone else.

A couple of days later the man and some others of the group cautiously approached the ship, which they refused to board. Cook tried to entertain them by having the fife and bagpipe played. These they totally disregarded and were only slightly attentive to a drum, but they did seem to enjoy conversation with a few officers and seamen who ventured ashore to talk, again I suppose unintelligibly, to them. The girl encountered before seemed particularly attracted to a young seaman 'and from her gestures' – what gestures I do not know – 'it was supposed she took him for one of her own sex', though she would have nothing more to do with him, once she understood her error. The people were not seen again for some days, but just over a week later the man and the younger woman visited the ship again. Before coming on board, they presented Cook and Johann Forster each with new flax cloaks. He broke a green branch from a tree, with which he struck various parts of the ship's side, repeating 'a kind of speech or prayer, which seemed to have regular cadences, and to be metrically arranged as a poem; his eyes were fixed upon the place he had touched, his voice was raised, and his whole behaviour grave and solemn'. Somehow, the dignity of this man's conduct impressed itself on European Christians, who did not interrupt or ignore it, who did not record that some silly superstition had been practised, but who instead were prompted to write about a *tapu*-lifting ritual in a way that makes immediate sense to anyone who has themselves witnessed this sort of Maori ceremony.

Once aboard, the man and woman paid curious attention to all sorts of things. They liked a cat 'but they always stroked it the wrong way, so as to make the hair stand up-right, though we showed them to do it in a contrary direction; probably they admired the richness of the furr'. The man was particularly impressed by the ship's construction. In due course both went below decks, gave and received further presents, and wanted to know where people slept. The man tried to oil Cook's hair, which the navigator resisted; perhaps unfortunately, because the head was for the Maori the most sacred part of the body, and this can only have been a peculiarly intimate and affirming gesture. The young woman, who seemed to have warmed to Hodges when he sketched her, would not suffer opposition and insisted he wear a tuft of oiled feathers. What puzzled Forster and others was that after this visit, and despite all the gifts and expressions of friendship, the man and his family simply disappeared and were at no point seen again though the *Resolution* remained at its mooring for a further ten days. Other Maori were heard and sighted. A naturalist meditated on a perfectly still, hidden lake, on 'the silence of this sacred wood'. Hills were climbed, waterfalls were discovered and painted. More fish were caught, more plants collected, more coves surveyed and ducks shot. I can imagine these were idyllic weeks, even though some were, as you still tend to be, tortured by sandflies. Cook, however, had a rendezvous with the *Adventure*. Over 11 and 12 May, the ship followed a new passage out of the sound to the north.

The series of meetings with the Maori had here been more genuinely and consistently amicable than any during the course of Cook's first voyage. It is possible that one of the preconditions for this was the mode of life of these Maori – who probably belonged to the Ngati Mamoe tribe, which at this time occupied the bulk of the south island. The *Endeavour* had mainly visited people of the densely populated north who were sedentary, who occupied highly productive areas and who made claims to particular tracts of land and coastline that they were accustomed to defend. In the far south, there was little horticulture, people collected and processed fern-root, caught birds and fished. Nomadic, they ranged over intimately known territories, but they were probably less jealous of particular places and landings. Perhaps, with this relationship to what was indeed a sparsely occupied environment, they never feared that Cook was there to invade or dispossess, but rather assumed that he was there to visit and depart.

For their part, the mariners responded positively to the group, perhaps because they were few. In other places, Cook's ships were confronted by mobs of people, who were at once unpredictable and liable to be identified generically as samples of an 'Indian', an 'Otaheitian' or a 'New Zealand' population. Here, a few individuals were immediately recognizable as such.

This makes it all the more surprising that the liberal George Forster should conclude his account of the period in Dusky Sound with a memorable image that effaced the dignity, the civility and the personalities of these Ngati Mamoe. This was written some three years later, but was based on an entry in his father's journal that was composed as the *Resolution* departed from the convenient cove, and from the tiny settlement on what was called Astronomer's Point.

The superiority of a state of civilization over that of barbarism could not be more clearly stated, than by the alterations and improvements we had made in this place. In the course of a few days, a small part of us had cleared away the woods from a surface of more than an acre, which fifty New Zealanders, with their tools of stone, could not have performed in three months. This spot, where immense numbers of plants left to themselves lived and decayed by turns, in one confused inanimated heap; this spot, we had converted into an active scene, where a hundred and twenty men pursued various branches of employment with unremitted ardour . . . We felled tall timber-trees, which, but for ourselves, had crumbled to dust with age; our sawyers cut them into planks, or we split them into billets for fuel. By the side of a murmuring rivulet, whose passage into the sea we facilitated, a long range of casks, which had been prepared by our coopers for that purpose, stood ready to be filled with water. Here ascended the steam of a large cauldron, in which we brewed, from neglected indigenous plants, a salutary and palatable potion, for the use of our labourers. In the offing, one of our crew appeared providing a meal of delicious fish for the refreshment of their fellows. Our caulkers and riggers were stationed on the sides and masts of the vessel, and their occupations gave life to the scene, and struck the ear with various noises, whilst the anvil on the hill resounded with the strokes of the weighty hammer. Already the polite arts began to flourish in this new settlement; the various tribes of animals and vegetables, which dwelt in the unfrequented woods, were imitated by an artist in his noviciate; and the romantic prospects of this shaggy country, lived on the canvas in the glowing tints of nature, who was amazed to see herself so closely copied. Nor had science disdained to visit us in this solitary spot: an observatory arose in the centre of our works, filled with the most accurate instruments, where the attentive eye of the astronomer contemplated the motions of the celestial bodies. The plants which clothed the ground, and the wonders of the animal creation, both in the forests and seas, likewise attracted the notice of philosophers, whose time was devoted to mark their differences and uses. In a word, all around us we perceived the rise of arts, and the dawn of science, in a country which had hitherto lain plunged in one long night of ignorance and barbarism!

This evocation of the arrival of civilization in a non-European land is not only lyrical but also almost comprehensive: the strictly masculine business of voyaging precludes reference to the emergence of any sweet domesticity in this remote part of Te Wai Pounamu, but Forster otherwise imagines the brief visit inaugurating not only various branches of industry but sociability, science and art. Barbarism is marked not by savage or debased custom, but simply by its failure to use or clear forest, which is equated with ignorance and darkness. All the empathy present in Forster's account of the liveliness and intelligence of the man and young woman are gone, as their race is dismissed and consigned to the past for its association with a primeval wilderness.

Yet Forster did not imagine that the 'ignorance' that supposedly characterized the Maori association with this land was about to vanish before a proliferation of settlements and a Europeanization of New Zealand. That did in fact take place over the middle decades of the subsequent century. The act of tree-felling that he so approved of would prefigure the devastation of forests on an extraordinary scale. This might just have been imaginable, but would have appeared no more probable in 1773 than shopping malls on Mars seem at the beginning of the twenty-first century. Forster's overblown elaboration of the meanings of the tiny camp was a poignant romance, rather than a prediction of triumph. He went on to observe that 'this pleasing picture of improvement was not to last, and like a meteor, vanished as suddenly as it was formed . . . it is obvious that the shoots of the surrounding weeds will shortly stifle every salutary and useful plant, and that in a few years our abode no longer discernible, must return to its original chaotic state'.

George Forster would later write more about the Maori in general. His father would discourse on their society at some length in his remarkable, anthropologically minded book of *Observations Made During a Voyage Round the World*. But neither the natural historians nor Cook produced any synoptic account of the Maori of Dusky Sound in the aftermath of this visit, which was a little unusual. There was something fundamentally confusing about the small group of Ngati Mamoe the voyagers had encountered. In this period, the capacious subjects of family, kinship and sexual relations that were later to form anthropology's field of study were beginning to be systematically reflected upon, as non-Europeans were regarded increasingly by intellectuals as representatives of early stages of European society. Forms of marriage and the status of women were, in the second half of the eighteenth century, absolutely central to assessments of the 'stage' that particular peoples had reached. The notion that the original condition of humanity had been a primitive promiscuity was already subscribed to. Polygamy was presumed to characterize barbaric life, and monogamy civilization. Among barbarians, women were supposed to be brutally enslaved by their men. Their increasing status was correlated closely with the growth of civilization, and moreover with a morally worrying feminine trend in the most advanced commercial nations, which were distinguished by fashion, luxury and the corrosion of public spirit. These values were implicit in many observations about many societies, ranging from the noble and vigorous ancient Germans (barbaric but masculine) to the modern French and Italians (civilized but effeminate). The Forsters were conversant with the most recent and sophisticated essays in 'the history of civil society', which provided them with tools for the interpretation of Maori life.

But what conjugal forms and what relations between men and women had they witnessed? Unfortunately, they suffered basic confusion about who was who, in the 'family' that they had met. On the occasion of the first meeting, the Europeans had sighted a man and two women, both of whom carried spears. Cook among others made the assumption that these were for fighting rather than hunting, and that women as well as men were therefore warriors. The older of the two, who was disfigured, was thought to be the man's wife, and the younger his daughter. Yet Cook later added a note to his journal, that stated categorically that 'We learnt afterwards that this young Woman was not his Daughter' – quite why is not explained. On the second day, when the 'family' was introduced, it was said to consist of two older women in addition to this younger one. These two were 'supposed' to be the man's wives, though in fact it was not evident whether he had one wife, two, or three. The puzzle of the relationships among these people was compounded when an altercation was witnessed, just before the man and younger woman finally ventured aboard the ship on 19 April.

In the mean while they had a quarrel among themselves, the man beat the two women who were supposed to be his wives; the young girl in return struck him, and then began to weep. What the cause of this disagreement was, we cannot determine; but if the young woman was really the man's daughter, which we could never clearly understand, it should seem that the filial duties are strangely confounded among them; or which is more probable, that this secluded family acted in every respect, not according to the customs and regulations of a civil society, but from the impulses of nature, which speak aloud against every degree of oppression.

The best explanation, in other words, that can be offered for this anomalous treatment of the father by the supposed daughter is that the family truly inhabited a domain outside any society, outside custom or regulation – a notion which Forster cannot seriously have entertained since he saw that these people conducted rituals, had artifacts, canoes, tools and habitations and clearly lived in close proximity, if not necessarily amicably, to other Maori sighted elsewhere around the sound.

The confusion of the European responses to the group was captured most succinctly by William Hodges. An engraving based on his voyage sketches and paintings claimed to depict precisely the 'Family in Dusky Bay' that was so difficult to identify and define. In this image, the younger of the two wives may be conflated with the girl supposed to be the daughter. But what is more interesting is the fact that the two women represent two radically different models of savage womanhood – one noble, the other degraded. One wife, a little like the classical figure of liberty, holds a spear and seems to share the proud and independent warriorhood of her husband. The other, carrying a baby and perhaps a load, is clearly submissive. Oddly – and this is a departure from Hodges's original drawings – this contrast is also given racial expression. The subordinate woman has distinctively frizzy hair, which would have been associated by the eighteenth-century viewer with the 'wool' allegedly characteristic of 'negroes'. The standing woman's hair is merely wavy, and suggests no racial distinctness or inferiority.

While the connotations of both figures are clear, the sense of the image

21. Family in Dusky Bay, *engraving after Hodges, from Cook,* A
Voyage Toward the South Pole, *1777.*

as a whole is utterly contradictory. On the one hand, the man may be a
nasty savage who treats his degraded wife as a beast of burden. On the
other, he may be a noble savage whose companion shares his aggressive
liberty. Eighteenth-century thinkers had no notion of a type of society in
which these very different relations might exist together. They used these
very relations to define the difference between mean savagery on one side
and vigorous barbarism on the other. (Needless to say, neither model bore
any relation to the realities of Maori forms of marriage or women's power,
but that is another issue.) It is perhaps therefore not surprising that this
image – published first with Cook's *Voyage Toward the South Pole,* the
official account of the expedition – was adapted fairly drastically in the
plates that accompanied various abridgements, adaptations and translations
of the voyages. A slightly later 'Family in Dusk [*sic*] Bay' lays the spears on
the ground and relegates the women to the background. An Italian print
retained the title but accompanies a completely different image. A widely
read nineteenth-century French survey of Oceanic peoples changed one
woman – the warrior – into a man, and the other into a conventionally
voluptuous maiden. What was perplexing about these people was thus
revealed to viewers of the pictures *first* published in Europe, but very soon
afterwards was displaced by more stereotypic images. These all suppressed
in different ways the challenging woman warrior.

*

*22. Stumps of trees presumed to have been cut down
by Cook's crew in 1773, Astronomer's Point, Dusky
Sound: photo by Mark Adams, 1995.*

Dusky Sound remains a remote wilderness that feels at the world's end, where the wind and water change fast, where sunlight glints somewhere high as melting snow slides over wet stone, as mist abruptly clears, as a seal splashes. But, if this is far from the only incommunicably beautiful part of the south Pacific, it is probably the only place where you can see and touch material traces of any visit of Cook's. There is an irregular rock platform around the spot where the horizontal tree provided a bridge across to the *Resolution* (there is still a horizontal tree, for that matter, but it's not thick enough to be the same one). With the watering stream to your left, you can zigzag up the slope, probably through the space where the sail-makers worked and the spruce beer was brewed.

George Forster supposed that the low hill of Astronomer's Point would quickly revert to a primeval jungle, but he was wrong. This is a temperate rainforest, in which great trees not only grow slowly but decay more slowly than you might imagine. On this hill-top, frequented by the wrens and tits that delighted the naturalists, and the fat pigeons that the Maori hunted, the stumps of the trees cut by Cook's men in 1773 are still there, and the area that was cleared remains entirely distinct from the forest around it. Today you see a tangle of secondary growth crowded with saplings that are clearly centuries younger than the great hardwoods of nearby hills and slopes. The stumps are weird things, nondescript but strangely impressive lumps of rotten wood, heavily covered with dark kidney ferns, of the sort Forster collected here and took back for the botanical collections that ended up in Kew. They put one in mind of eroded gravestones or natural monuments, but they bear no inscriptions. They do not tell you who to honour or who to mourn. In fact, they're pretty useless, if you want help with history, if you want judgement.

12

Mingling my tears with hers

On 16 May, 1773, on their way to Queen Charlotte Sound, the crew of the *Resolution* met liquid tornadoes, at once scientifically curious and quite horrifying. They saw them at first some way away, dancing across the water, 'bent or incurvated', proceeding in different directions that seemed undetermined by the wind. They then became distended and exploded or collapsed. Nearer the ship, however, the waves suddenly became shorter and more broken, 'the wind continually veered all round the compass, without fixing in any point'. Then, some 400 yards away, this broken water gathered itself together in a broad vaporous column and was carried up into the clouds, 'hurled upwards with the greatest violence in a spiral'. Everyone was alarmed and topsails were drawn in, though most expected this to have little effect, if the ship were 'drawn into the vortex'. Some thought that a cannon fired into the waterspout would break it and Cook wanted to test the theory, but the spout abruptly collapsed before a gun could be made ready. For all their dangerous instability, these phenomena would be easier to observe and make sense of than the people whom the mariners proceeded to encounter, around the parts of Queen Charlotte Sound that Cook had already visited and surveyed.

The Maori around Totaranui never formed settled communities. Even before European contact, this had been a place like a market, where people who had little in common arrived, confronted each other, settled for a time, and moved on. Sometimes they traded and feasted. Other times they fought.

None of the Maori here in 1773 had been there when Cook had visited before, but they all knew that a famous man had arrived in a great and unusual *waka*, and that he had brought remarkable sorts of gifts. When Tobias Furneaux and the *Adventure* arrived at Motuara, six weeks before Cook, the Maori assumed that this man had returned. The first thing that they asked the visitors was: where was Tupaia? Cook joined them, and other Maori appeared. They all wanted to know what had become of the renowned voyager. 'When I told them he was dead,' Cook wrote, 'one or two of them express'd their sorrow by a kind of lamentation, which appear'd to me to be merely formal.' If these people were disappointed to have to deal with men who were probably just Tupaia's subordinates, who communicated ineptly and who could tell them no histories, they were nevertheless ready to do so. Forster found the first Maori he met here – a group of about five men – 'familiar and unconcerned'. There was none of the wonder or trepidation that had been encountered in Dusky Sound. They sold some fish, came aboard the *Resolution* without hesitation, ate some food, relished sugared water and coveted iron and glass bottles – which they called *taha*, or gourds – while ignoring gifts of beads, ribbons and white paper. They could, in other words, tell the difference between a tool and a trinket. The next day they returned with women and children and their names – probably Te Wahanga, Ko Tuka, Ko Koa, Koa, Ko Raki and Te Weherua – were learned. Cook, away from the ship investigating a bay, encountered another group in a double canoe. Several further canoes appeared a couple of days later, as did a separate Maori party on 1 June. On 4 June, while the family whom the mariners had met first and got to know best were aboard, a larger double canoe with another set of people approached. The Maori already on the ship warned the mariners that these were enemies. 'Towahanga, the head of the family jumped on the arm chest, which was placed on our quarter deck, and taking hold of a stick, made a number of warlike motions with it, and soon after spoke to them very violently, but with some degree of solemnity, at the same time brandishing, as it seemed in defiance, a large hatchet of green nephritic stone, which he had never shewn us before.' One man among the new arrivals, wearing a chequered cloak, was standing in the canoe, holding a green plant. Another, also standing, delivered a speech; 'he appeared by turns to question, to boast, to threaten, to challenge, and to persuade us'. When he had finished, Cook invited him on to the ship. Though suspicious at first, the man did venture aboard, as did his companions, who greeted the Maori already there in the customary manner, 'as our sailors expressed it, they nosed each other, and paid every one of us upon the quarter-deck the same compliment'.

These people seemed healthier, bigger and richer than those already encountered. Their ornaments and weapons were of different sorts and they had fine, elegantly patterned cloaks, well lined with dogskin, that 'might have passed for the work of a much more polished nation', George Forster thought. Not only the natural historians, but the common seamen were impressed by these people and what they had to barter. The sailors avidly gave up things Cook thought they needed for objects that he did not rate.

'A trade soon commenced between our people and these, it was not possible to hinder the former from giving their clothes from of their backs for the merest trifles, things that were neither usefull nor curious, such was the prevailing passion for curiosities and caused me to dismiss these strangers sooner than I would have done.' In the course of the first voyage, discipline had broken down and men had been flogged when the *Endeavour* had entered port and the ship's social regimes ceased to be self-contained. Here, this happened again, when the vessel was briefly a marketplace, inhabited by new actors and new things. Cook could presumably have suppressed the trade, had he really wanted to, as at other places he did subject barter to rigorous regulation, in order to sustain the supply of provisions. That was not at issue at this time, and if the captain was irritated by the sailors' indiscriminate 'passion', he evidently thought it was better indulged than frustrated.

Cook himself bought 'an Ear ornament made of glass very well form'd and polished'. This piece interested him because it could only have been made from a bottle trafficked at some point during his previous visit, though he did not know the man he bought it from. But did he therefore value it because it manifested the versatility of Maori craftsmanship? Cook had already noticed that artifacts such as *patu* were made in the same form out of a range of materials – jade, basalt and whalebone – and had acquired one of the first of many objects, in which a traditional form was replicated out of imported, novel material. Why were the Maori axes, *tiki*, combs or clubs that the sailors acquired 'neither usefull nor curious'? How, in one of the first tribal art markets in the world, could anyone judge an object, and say whether its acquisition would be frivolous or legitimate?

For their part, the Maori attached inordinate value to some things that the Europeans produced. Furneaux mentions in passing that 'We had a catalogue of their words' – which would have been based on lists made during the *Endeavour*'s visit – 'calling several things by name which suprized them much. They wanted it much and offered a great quantity of Fish for it.' His account of this interest in the list is too cursory to be fully understood, but it sounds as though its use was demonstrated, as words were read off it, so as to make the working of writing evident to these Ngai Tahu. These Maori must have grasped that the marks on the paper were, in some sense, signs that captured a sort of knowledge. They may have associated writing with the meaningful inscription of tattooing, or with other sorts of marking and carving that went into art forms that were generally prestigious, that generally signified something, in terms of genealogy and political authority. All this is speculation, yet their surprise before this technology, and their desire to get hold of it, are wholly consistent with a Maori style in dealings with foreigners. What was notable already, and what would become a hallmark of the next century's history in New Zealand, was a will on the part of these indigenous people to make themselves masters of introduced resources and inventions. Novelties would be appropriated with alacrity, yet adapted to customary values and purposes.

Cook was struck by the fact that, out of the succession of people encountered, he did not recall a face sighted during his previous visit of three years before, nor did he meet anyone who claimed to have seen him or any of his companions. True, they all asked after Tupaia, but he seemed famous among the Maori, and his name 'as familiar to those who never saw him as those who did'. Cook was led to contrast the modes of life of the people of the north island, encountered during his first voyage, and those of the south. The latter

living thus dispers'd in small parties knowing no head but the chief of the family or tribe whose authority may be very little, subjects them to many inconveniences a well regulated society united under one head or any other form of government are not subject to, these form Laws and regulations for their general security, are not alarm'd at the appearence of every stranger and if attack'd or invaded by a publick enimy have strong holds to retire to where they can with advantage defend themselves, their property & their Country, this seems to be the state of most of the Inhabitents of *Eahei-nomauwe* [Te Ika a Maui, the north island], whereas those of *Tavai-poenammoo* [Te Wai Pounamu, the south], by living a wandering life in small parties are distitute of most these advantages which subjects them to perpetual alarms . . . the greatest part of the Inhabitants that were here in the beginning of the year 1770 are drove out of it or have on their own accord removed some were else . . . certain it is that not one third of the people are here now that were there then.

Cook was becoming increasingly aware of the heterogeneous character of Maori societies, and of their potential for rapid change. He was disturbed, as I noted at the beginning of this book, by a shift in sexual mores that responded to the desires of his own crew. During the *Endeavour*'s sojourn here, there had been a little but not much sexual traffic. Now, as both he and George Forster remarked in the passages that I discussed earlier, prostitution was engaged in more systematically, and at least a few men appear to have forced women to participate.

It was a commerce that resonated closely, but horribly ironically, with Cook's instructions. The great aim of the programme of voyaging that the

Admiralty had prosecuted with the blessing of the King had been the discovery of new lands and peoples with whom trade could in due course be opened up, to both honour and enrich Britain. A trade was getting under way here very quickly that neither honoured nor enriched anyone. The Maori did not have to be coaxed into commerce. They leapt into it. This commerce promised not the longer-term refinement of civility that many theorists thought it engendered. It instead produced immediate and patent damage that was not only moral.

It is notable that Cook remarks while the *Resolution* is still at Meretoto that 'we interduce among them wants *and perhaps diseases* which they never knew before'. This suggests that he was already aware that it was possible or even probable that sexually transmitted diseases had been communicated to the Maori population by his crew. What, some weeks later, surprised and appalled Johann Forster – the discovery that a seaman had been infected by a Maori woman, meaning that the Maori were infected by Europeans – may have troubled Cook but cannot have shocked him. George Forster's published *Voyage* did not follow his father's journal in making a villain of the sailor responsible, but instead contrived an argument against the introduction of the ailment by any European crew, proposing instead that venereal diseases must have been endemic among the Maori before the arrival of the mariners. Cook would have been reassured had he found this at all convincing. It looks as though he did not.

In Britain, by the last quarter of the century, political writers exercised by the evils of commerce had worn out their favourite metaphor: the corruption of the body politic by a lust for luxuries. On the beaches of New Zealand in 1773, people were debilitated by new sorts of pain and pus: the commercial distemper of their body politic was not at all metaphoric. Cook suffered not from the clap but from a troubled conscience. Less than a year into his second voyage, it seemed that his expeditions' impacts upon native peoples, at any rate upon the Maori, were not mixed or ambiguous but plainly evil.

At the same time as he realized this, Cook acquired a deeper sense of the difficulties of describing other people. He made this manifest in a passage noting that some Maori volunteered to go away with the ships, but then changed their minds. 'It was even said that some of them offered their Children to sale but this certainly had no foundation in truth, the report took rise on board the Adventure where they were utter strangers to their Language and Customs.' Not an 'utter stranger' to the Maori language or Maori customs, Cook himself misinterpreted the practices that had given rise to this report. 'Yesterday morning a Man brought his son a boy about 10 years of age and presented him to me and as the report was then currant I thought he wanted to sell him, but at last I found out that he wanted me to give him [the boy] a shirt which I accordingly did.' He added later that 'This story, though extreamly trifling in its self, will show how liable we are to misstake these peoples meaning and to ascribe to them customs they never knew even in thought.' At first, the seasoned explorer asserts the ignorance of his fellow-voyagers, but acknowledges, on reflection, that he is no less liable to mistake meaning and invent an entirely unreal 'custom' out of misread gestures, acts or statements.

The King's birthday was celebrated with a double allowance of alcohol. Parting gifts were made and Cook was ready to put the next phase of his plan into execution. He would cruise eastward between around 41° and 46° south, and then to Tahiti. He conceded that it might seem 'an extraordinary step' to attempt southern discoveries 'in the very depth of Winter' but he thought it essential that something was done, 'in order to lessen the work I am upon least I should not be able to finish the discovery of the Southern part of the South Pacifick Ocean the insuing Summer'. His sense of how to go about his mission was adaptable. His sense that it had to be comprehensive and complete was not.

The ocean to the east was empty, and, as Forster put it, 'the total want of interesting incidents united to make this run extremely tedious to us all'. By the beginning of August, the ships had crossed Carteret's track, thus establishing that there was no land in this sector of the Pacific at this latitude. Cook had already 'formed some judgement concerning the great object of my researches (viz) the Southern Continent. Circumstances seem to point out to us that there is none but this is too important a point to be left to conjector, facts must determine it and these can only be had by viseting the remaining unexplored parts of this Sea.' It was just as well that there was no point in going further east. Rigour in exploratory method mattered little to anyone else on board. The cold cruise was widely resented. The *Adventure*'s cook had died of scurvy and others were in a bad way. The ships travelled north into warmer weather, and the 'much exhilarated' 'sailors diverted themselves with a variety of plays every evening'. A cautious course was found through atolls, some new to Europeans, others charted already by Bougainville. On 15 August Tahiti was sighted and Vaitepiha Bay on the south-east approached. Cook thought it worth trying for provisions here before moving to the more usual anchorage of Matavai.

Just about everyone aboard the ships appears to have approached the island with a sense of mounting euphoria that was matched by the excitement of Tahitians. One canoe ventured out, the occupants shouting *tayo!* The big green leaves of a plantain were passed up to the ship with the instruction that they should be prominently displayed. This was understood as a symbol of peace and great crowds began to gather on the beach. Something like 100 canoes came off to the *Resolution* and *Adventure*, even while the ships were finding their way towards an anchorage. Coconuts, plantains and breadfruit were enthusiastically exchanged for beads and nails. Tahitian fish-hooks, axes and tools were eagerly acquired. Equally avidly, the Forsters trafficked through their cabin windows for fish and birds, among which they were delighted to discover a few new species. The scene was amicably hectic. As Forster put it, it was 'a picture of a new kind of fair'. Whereas he had only grudgingly acknowledged that the young Maori woman of Tamatea had agreeable features, he here found the women 'pretty enough'; the people generally possessed 'mild features, and a pleasing countenance'. They were affectionate and curious. They wanted to hold the mariners' hands, they leaned against them, they embraced them and they pulled their clothes aside, to inspect the whiteness of the skin and the forms of their bodies. The Tahitians were immediately pleased when the visitors tried to pronounce the words they already knew. They corrected them, they talked at them and they taught them more. Accomplished comparative linguists, the Forsters immediately realized that Wallis and those on the *Endeavour* had mistranscribed names such as Otaheite and Oberea. The O, they understood correctly, was in fact an article. The island was properly just Tahiti, and the prominent woman just Purea. For enlightened philosophers, this was just right. From the very first moments of the encounter, the prior knowledge that peoples enjoyed of each other was improved and enlarged.

The excitement was such that Cook's instructions about the approach to the shore had been neglected. Though the course was altered, the failure of an offshore wind and strong inshore tides brought the *Resolution* into a perilous situation. One officer was fully occupied trying to persuade the high-ranking woman Marorai that the sheets she wanted were worth 'a special favour', one that she was reluctant to bestow, but at length ready to concede. Just, however, as she was being led towards his bed, there was an awful shudder as the ship struck the reef. The man was obliged to rush back up to the deck, to attend to his duty. Had the surf been strong, or the waters just off the coral as deep as they commonly were, the situation could easily have been catastrophic. As it was, repeated knocks were alarming, but it was possible to put out a boat, to anchor and, in something like an hour, to haul the ship off. The perception that these Islanders were real friends was reinforced as they pitched in, 'manning the capstan, hauling in ropes, and performing all sorts of labour'. Marorai, however, seized the opportunity to filch the sheets, relieved of the need to make a sex-worker of herself.

Over the subsequent days, hundreds visited the ship and immense quantities of vegetable foods, as well as barkcloth, baskets, mats and tools were exchanged for beads, nails and knives. There was some pilfering. Some people identified as culprits were whipped, or chased off the ship with a whip, which, according to Forster, 'they bore very patiently'. Whether they really did so, this violence does not appear to have offended the Tahitians generally. Despite his prior experience here, Cook must have made himself susceptible to manipulation by repeatedly asking after chiefs or kings, whom he hoped would regulate trade and organize a supply of pork. Tahitians of higher rank were, however, in no rush to renew their relations with the British, but some men of the commoner class obviously amused themselves by playing the part. Cook went as far as to entertain 'one of these sort of Arrees' for most of the day in his own cabin, liberally distributing gifts through the man to his supposed followers, and was incensed when he realized that his guest possessed no real status, and was stealing everything he could.

I was so exasperated at his behaver that after he had got a good distance from the ship I fired two Musquet balls over his head which made him quet his Canoe and take to the Water. I then sent a boat to take up the Canoe, as soon as she came near the shore the people from thence began to pelt her with stones, the Boat still persuing the Canoe and being unarm'd I began to be in pain for her safety and went my self in another boat to protect her and order'd a 4 pounder to be fire'd a long the Coast, this made them all retire back from the shore and suffered me to bring away two Canoes without the least shew of opposition and in a few hours after the People were as well reconciled as if nothing had happen'd. The Canoes I return'd to the first person who ask'd for them.

Cook makes no claim that this show of aggression was motivated by a considered judgement that theft might be discouraged if a man was chased and frightened and people reminded of the power of cannon. He frankly acknowledges that it was rather the expression of his own anger, perhaps his anger at his own gullibility. If it is true that the shots were aimed above rather than at the man, he was at least exercising some restraint; as were the Tahitians on the beach if Forster is right when he says that they 'took up stones, which they levelled at our boat's crew' but, by implication, did not actually throw. Yet it was perhaps just lucky that no one was injured or killed, that nothing went badly wrong and escalated here.

Cook was probably struggling to recall his Tahitian. Yet he learned quickly that the island's military and political balance had changed as dramatically since his first visit as it had between Wallis's and his first. Five months earlier, Tutaha, the Matavai chief with whom he had developed considerable rapport, had been killed in a disastrous battle against what Cook thought were the forces of a second and opposed Tahitian kingdom, but were in fact the people of the Taiarapu district. 'Otoo' or Tu was in fact not 'now the Reigning Prince', but was an ambitious and innovative chief who had visions of political power on a new scale. On this occasion, Cook's dealings were at first not with Tu but Vehiatua. He dominated the south-eastern part of the island, was said by the common people to be the owner of all the pigs, which they were therefore not at liberty to give away and which they, for the most part, kept out of the mariners' sight. An *ari'i nui* or great chief would customarily have been entitled to solicit pigs from the populace in general, especially when a major ritual or ceremony was due to take place, but he did not 'own' them. It is possible that people were misrepresenting Polynesian property relations, to give themselves a convenient excuse for refraining from barter. It is also possible that Vehiatua did discourage his people from giving away what were, in fact, their most vital and reproductive animal assets.

Eventually, eight days after the ships' arrival, Cook was able to see the high chief, whose attendants had to beat apart a great crowd of watching commoners to make space for their meeting. Vehiatua remembered Cook well from his first visit, and moved to the edge of his stool, requiring Cook to sit on it with him. He was apparently delighted by his gifts, entertained with news of Banks and Solander and keen to converse for some time about the visit of some Spanish ships that had taken place two years earlier. He was intrigued by Cook's watch and wanted to understand its workings. He said he hoped that Cook would stay for some months, and when Cook retorted that because he could not obtain pork he was departing immediately, Vehiatua asked that they remain at least for five days. He did not, however, provide them with any feast, and the Europeans went back to their ships to dine. When Cook and Furneaux returned afterwards, they were finally each given a pig. The chief presumably encouraged other people to produce some of theirs for sale. Enough were gathered to provide a meal for every man on each of the ships. But it was clear that little more would be obtained here, and they moved on to Matavai, where Cook spent some

23. Hodges's portrait of Tu, 1773.

time with Tu. His records from here, like those from Vaitepiha, are primarily concerned with his diplomacy and his efforts to obtain provisions. His prose is not as sparse as it once was, but it was primarily practical. Yet there are glimpses of another sort of person, for whom *tayo* friendships were not merely contracts of strategy or convenience, but emotionally burdened relations. Bringing Tu, and some of his suite, in the pinnace,

I had no sooner landed than I was met by a venerable old Lady mother of the late Toutaha, she seized me by both hands and brust into a flood of tears saying Toutaha Tiyo no Toute matte (Toutaha the friend of Cook is dead). I was so much affected at her behaviour that it would not have been possible for me to refrain mingling my tears with hers had not Otoo come and snatched me as it were from her, I afterwards disired to see her again in order to make her a present but he told me she was Mataou [fearful] and would not come, I was not satisfied with this answer and desired she might be sent for, soon after she appeared I went up to her, she again wept and lamented the death of her son. I made her a present of an Ax and other things and then parted from her and soon after took leave of Otoo and return'd aboard.

The *tayo* relationship, in Tahitian society as well as across the Polynesian–European divide, was always formed for mutual alliance, but was also potentially profound. It often entailed an exchange of names, which meant exchanging aspects of identity, even if only jokingly. It suited Cook if friendships developed; the stronger and more predictable relationships were here, the better. But even the most interested of friendships acquired the tincture of feeling.

The temporary treatment of navigators as visiting chiefs was marked by public performance. On 29 August Cook, Furneaux and some officers visited Tu again. After giving him a broad sword and some other presents, they 'were conducted to the Theatre where we were entertain'd with a Dramatic Heava or Play in which were both Dancing and Comedy'. Cook could not follow it, but gathered that some scenes were 'adapted to the present time as my name was mentioned several times, other parts were certainly wholy unconnected with us'. He could see, in other words, that his visit was being represented; it was entering a local theatrical repertoire. What he could not tell was how the story was supposed to end.

On Cook's first voyage, Sydney Parkinson produced intriguing images of Tahitians, tattoos and Maori carvings. But he was a drawer of flies and flowers rather than an accomplished artist. Tahitians now played host, for the first time, to a professional European painter. William Hodges's record of the place is remarkable for being both precisely empirical and suffused with sensuality. It is carefully descriptive in some respects – Hodges went to a great deal of trouble to capture the singular expansiveness of Oceanic seas and skies – and romantically imaginative in others. Though he brought a European vision to these islands, he did a remarkable job, as he had in both the Antarctic and the far south of New Zealand, of grasping and reproducing

24. *Hodges's* The Resolution and Adventure in Matavia Bay, Tahiti,
*painted back in England in 1776, would, with its pendant view of
Vaitepiha Bay, become an iconic image of Polynesia.*

environmental conditions that were quite unlike any that he had ever encountered in Britain. On a cool morning, the slopes just inland of Point Venus remain in damp shade; the lagoon's water is glassy; the breeze has not yet risen, and coconut palms are like limp ornaments. Later in the day, the thin cloud has vanished in the glare, a canoe is poised between the great hemispheres of sea and sky, and a wedge of land threatens to evaporate in the haze, or with a high tide. By late afternoon, the scene is more benign and humane. A tattered pandanus sail, the sides of a long low house, and a man's shoulder are absorbed in lazy sunlight and lengthening shadow.

In Hodges's *Vaitepiha Bay* the fertile affluence of the land is in perfect harmony with an alluring and exotic femininity. His figures were posed according to convention, but the tattooed bottom which is surely the painting's eye-catching feature says immediately that these are not European women. Their self-ornamentation is patently remote from the Western aesthetic traditions that classical postures connoted. In fact, the very use of these postures, and the equally conventional clutch of drapery, compounds the shock of the unfamiliar: classical beauty was supposed to be unblemished, yet these beautiful and semi-civilized people had marked their buttocks with arches, which seemed designed to do nothing other than invite and arouse.

*

25. *William Hodges,* Oaitepeha [Vaitepiha] Bay, *also called* Tahiti Revisited, *1776.*

This painting provided a certain synopsis of the idyllic qualities of this island, from the perspective of a young, aesthetically imaginative, intellectually sophisticated and of course *male* visitor. Because features of this vision – the sexual voyeurism, the erotic treatment of the environment and the interest in Tahitian pagan art – recur in Gauguin's Polynesian art and in increasingly bland and stupid twentieth-century evocations of an 'island of love', it is easy to forget that participants in Cook's voyages saw much more than the erotic here. Like Hodges, George Forster was infatuated with Tahiti, and he too may have enjoyed himself sexually here. But when he came to write, he was concerned to do something quite other than evoke a permissive paradise. What he has to say is all the more interesting because it owes nothing to his father's journal, which George's book is generally based upon. Indeed it is somewhat at odds with his father's reflections. The seed of a grandly theoretical discussion appears to have been gleaned during an inland excursion. It began in the refreshingly cool early morning of 19 August. For the first time, Forster and his father encountered a group of women beating barkcloth, who paused to explain the details of their technique, the sort of glue used and so forth. They proceeded further into a narrow valley and were welcomed by a man, who had them seat themselves on banana leaves in the shade before his house, while he brought them breadfruit, baked in a fashion which Forster considered 'infinitely superior to our usual way of boiling them'. They drank from fresh coconuts. There was something in this friendliness, something in the 'cool limpid liquor' freely offered just when refreshment was needed, that made this an instance of pure generosity, in Forster's mind. 'We continued our walk into the country from this seat of patriarchal hospitality.' 'Patriarchal' here meant benign and fatherly, not oppressive.

George did not, however, go on to suggest that the perfect sociability manifest in this man's behaviour was typical of Tahiti. Two days later, he described a further, equally delightful walk, this time in the company of William Hodges, who sketched, for perhaps the first time, the covered platforms upon which corpses were exposed, featured in finished paintings such as *Vaitepiha Bay*. As before, people were friendly, gave or bartered food, and explained, in so far as the poor Tahitian of the visitors permitted, the ritual precautions observed around the dead. Yet this tour culminated in a spectacle Forster found offensive. After walking along the shore past a further *marae*, the party encountered an obese man presumed to be a chief, who was being fed by a servant.

His countenance was the picture of phlegmatic insensibility, and seemed to witness that all his thoughts centred in the care of his paunch. He scarce deigned to look at us, and a few monosyllables which he uttered, were only directed to remind his feeders of their duty, when we attracted their attention. The great degree of satisfaction which we had enjoyed on our different walks in this island, and particularly the pleasure of this day's excursion, was diminished by the appearance and behaviour of the chief, and the reflections which naturally arose from thence. We had flattered ourselves with the pleasing fancy of having found at least one little spot of the world, where a whole nation, without being lawless barbarians, aimed at a certain frugal equality in their way of living, and whose hours of enjoyment were justly proportioned to those of labour and rest. Our disappointment was therefore very great, when we saw a luxurious individual spending his life in the most sluggish inactivity, and without one benefit to society, like the privileged parasites of more civilized climates, fattening on the superfluous produce of the soil, of which he robbed the labouring multitudes.

Although the Polynesian religious concept of *tapu* was noticed in the course of Cook's voyages, and the idea of 'taboo' consequently entered Western theory and common usage, the elusive and subtle effects of *tapu* in Tahitian life were not well understood. This man was being fed not because he was too lazy to help himself, but because the sacredness of his body would have been imperilled by contact with cooked food. Had his *tapu* been dispersed or lost, he would have become ill, and his illness might well have caused wider misfortune. Hence, from a Tahitian perspective, there was ritual necessity, not indolent luxury, in this feeding operation – which was probably as oppressive for the recipient as for the servant. George could not have known either this, or that Tahitian men and women of chiefly rank were ideally fat because their bodies were thought to exemplify the abundance and well-being of the land. The man's size and the seemingly servile quality of the relationship told him instead that he had met an instance of a political type, an 'Oriental despot'.

Forster returned to the theme when commenting upon Cook's meeting with Vehiatua, whose disingenuous promises of a supply of pork were unfavourably contrasted with 'the real benevolence of the middle class, which manifested itself towards us in hospitality and a number of good and noble actions'. But, by the time he came to distil his responses to Tahitian society, his censorious attitude to the privilege of individuals and the false hospitality of the elite had undergone some qualification. He observed that 'The evident distinction of ranks which subsists at Taheitee, does not so materially affect the felicity of the nation, as we might have supposed.' 'The simplicity of their whole life' redressed inequalities, in part because people's wants, in this climate, were modest and few. Clothes were not needed to the extent they were in colder climates and food was easily obtained, hence no one here was truly impoverished or miserable; 'there is not, in general, that disparity between the highest and the meanest man, which subsists in England between a reputable tradesman and a labourer'. He had noticed, also, that chiefs were held in genuine esteem by their people, that they in their turn were actively interested in their subjects' lives.

Yet if, George Forster conceded, rank in Tahiti really was mitigated by 'an happy equality', he believed that this society nevertheless contained the seeds of its own destruction. The chiefs were already indolent; their class could only grow in number; the landless people who worked the gardens could, over time, only become more exploited, and this exploitation would, he luridly anticipated, manifest itself in the degeneration of their bodies. 'They will grow ill-shaped, and their bones become marrowless: their greater exposure to the actions of a vertical sun, will blacken their skins, and they will dwindle away to dwarfs, by the more frequent prostitution of their infant daughters, to the voluptuous pleasures of the great.' Quite why the impoverished and enslaved peoples of Europe were not already shorter and darker, Forster did not explain, but he does predict confidently that the tendency can only go so far. In due course, the common Tahitians will 'perceive these grievances' and 'a proper sense of the general rights of mankind awaking in them, will bring on a revolution'.

These reflections are remarkable for their easy steps from the apparent dispositions of a few individuals to a theory of social trends and upheavals. But they are notable also because they reverse the operation so magnificently accomplished in Hodges's painting. *Vaitepiha Bay* had played up what was exotic in Tahiti. One of the key words of the voyage – curiosity – responded to what was new, different, singular and inexplicable in the peoples and circumstances encountered. Banks had never tired of exclaiming that something was indescribable or incommunicable. But in these reflections upon Tahitian society and its fatal future evolution, Forster concedes no strangeness at all. He takes it for granted that the tensions that divide and drive this tropical society are universal relations of status and inequality, that you know, that I know, that for his readers were as banal as the disparity between 'a reputable tradesman and a labourer' in England.

On the course east and then north to Tahiti, Cook's men had been bored, cold and discontented. Cook had promised them diversion and pleasure, which they got. He too enjoyed Tahiti, but was preoccupied from the start by the tricky management of trade and the issue of how theft could be discouraged and prevented; and whether and how far, once it had occurred, it had to be tolerated or punished. Not least, he had to manage his own exasperation. He had to deal with the crisis, happily resolved soon enough, on the reef; he had to pursue chiefs and persuade them to do business; he had the stresses of keeping his own people, and trying to tease out Tahitian politics, simultaneously. As the voyage progressed, his ways of dealing with these sorts of problems shifted, not because he learned from experience and rationally arrived at different strategies, but because he changed. The ground of his loyalties and feelings towards people eroded and formed again.

This happened in subtle ways over time, which are barely noticeable from moment to moment. But there were also turning-points in his personal history and one of these occurred soon after his departure from Matavai. Perhaps the encounter with Tutaha's mother and an interrupted moment of shared grief were catalysts of a sort. On 3 September the ships arrived at Fare, the anchorage on the island of Huahine, in the leeward group of the Society Islands. Cook had been here in 1769. There's a sheltered bay, the water is blue and deep beside the shore, and the view across to an irregular cliff and low mountain might have been designed for a landscape painter. This is as congenial a place as any in the Pacific. Here, also, in 1773 there was no shortage of food. Cook was not only received 'by the natives with

26. Hodges's *view of Fare, 1773.*

the utmost cordiality' but a distribution of presents produced a 'plentifull supply of fresh pork and Fowls'. The demands frustrated at Tahiti were at last met here.

Cook heard, too, that his 'old friend Oree was still living and chief of the Island and that he was hastning to this part to see me'. The next day the protocols of meeting were observed. Cook's boat touched the shore near the chief's house, five young green plantain trees, 'their Emblems of Peace' were placed separately 'and with some ceremony' in the boat, pigs and a dog accompanying each but the last – on each occasion with a particular name and significance that Cook was unable to understand. Finally Ori sent the inscribed piece of pewter that Cook had left with him in 1769. Some man who was guiding Cook through this ritual advised him to decorate the plantains with nails, mirrors and medals. These were then carried ashore and towards the chief. The mariners were told to sit down and the gift-bearing plantains then presented to the chief, 'one was for Eatoua or God, the second for the Arree or King, and the third for Tyo or friendship'. Cook writes, in one of the versions of his journal, 'I wanted to go to the King, but was told that he would come to me, which he accordingly did.' In the other, he has 'This being done Oree rose up and came and fell upon my neck and embraced me, this was by no means ceremonious, the tears which trinckled plentifully down his Cheeks sufficiently spoke the feelings of his heart.' Cook proceeded to make the present 'I had prepared consisting of the most Valuable articles I had for this purpose for I regarded this old man as a father', or, as he put it in his log, for 'this brave old chief who receiv'd me more like a son he had not seen these four years than a friend'.

On succeeding days there was much trade. Ori sent Cook gifts of food every day. Yet not all the people of Huahine were as friendly as the chief. On 6 September, a trading party was harrassed by a warrior who brandished a club in each hand. Cook challenged this man himself, seized his clubs, broke them and with some difficulty sent him away. At about this time, Sparrman, botanizing on his own, was attacked and stripped of his clothes by a couple of men. Cut about with his own sword, which they had also taken, he was lucky to encounter a kinder man who gave him a piece of barkcloth, with which he covered himself, and showed him the way back to the other Europeans. Cook then went to Ori, taking this man to confirm Sparrman's complaint. Ori then proposed to go with Cook in his boat in pursuit of the culprits, which greatly alarmed his people. 'When the people saw their beloved chief wholly in my power they set up a great outcry and with Tears flowing down their cheeks intreated him once more to come out of the Boat. I even joined my intreaties to theirs, for I could not bear to see them in such distress, all that could be said or done availed nothing'. Ori insisted on directing or accompanying a party in search of those he thought had committed the offence. Although this expedition was initially fruitless, and though his people again protested, when Ori proposed to join Cook aboard the *Resolution* for a meal, Sparrman's sword and part of his clothing were returned in the course of the afternoon. Cook mentioned in passing that other officers out shooting had also had things stolen from them – some of which were returned – but emphasized that friendly relations were restored and that the 'Brave old Chief' had placed great confidence in him. This all showed how far 'Friendship is Sacred with these people'. The next day, before departure, they had a further meeting. Gifts were again exchanged, and Cook thought it better to say nothing about the remainder of Sparrman's clothes. 'I judged they were not brought in and for that reason did not mention them lest I should give the chief pain about a thing I did not give him time to recover.' Johann Forster was incensed by Cook's unwillingness to either take further steps to retrieve the goods or to punish the thieves. He expostulated that letting the matter drop would in future 'encourage the Natives to all manner of acts of Violence . . . to much lenity is absolutely dangerous'.

*

Here Cook suffered more than welcomed a further supernumerary 'whose name was Omiah'. But 'Omai' or Mai would join the *Adventure* rather than the *Resolution*; Furneaux was 'desireous' of having him and Mai was supposedly keen to see England. Soon afterwards, however, Cook himself recruited a young man named Hitihiti or Mahine, who he thought might 'be of use to us' if they visited further islands to the west. This prospective usefulness was, he stressed, his only motive for taking the youth on board. It's as though Cook was concerned that there were too many trivial reasons for receiving Polynesian passengers that he needed to dissociate himself from. Quite why these passengers – or many others, who were ready to volunteer – were so eager for their part to join the voyage and visit Britain, no one seems to have inquired, understood or at any rate recorded. The implication is that they were merely curious, which suggests that the mariners saw them as men motivated much like themselves. But this cannot have been the whole story. The political antagonisms that consumed the leeward islands at this time seem to have played some part. One, if not both, these young men joined the ship to look for new allies as well as new sights.

The ships proceeded to the nearby island of Raiatea, where Cook hoped to procure 'an addition of Fruit'. Here, at Haamanino harbour, on 9 September, he encountered another chief, Orio, whom he knew from the previous voyage. This man too 'express'd much satisfaction at seeing me again, desired that he might be call'd Cook (or Toote) and I Oreo which was accordingly done'. As before, presents were exchanged, much barter took place, and provisions were obtained in abundance. The following day, Cook was invited ashore to be entertained with a *heiva*, a play which turned out to be along the same lines as the one they'd seen acted in Tahiti. On this occasion, the most entertaining passage dramatized a theft – it is unfortunately unclear whether this was supposed to be a theft from the mariners or just one among the Tahitians – which was discovered, contested and scuffled over, but Cook was surprised to see that it concluded with the triumph of the thieves. 'I was very attentive to the whole of this part,' he wrote, 'in expectation that it would have quite a different end, for I had before been told that . . . the Theift was to be punished with death or with a good Tiparrahying (beating) but I found myself misstaken in both.'

The drama prefigured events. Cook's account diverges strangely from those of some of the officers and naturalists. Charles Clerke and William Bayly refer to persistent pilfering and even to the flogging of one offender. Cook says nothing of this, reporting instead that his people everywhere met with 'Sevel' (civil) 'treatment from the natives'. On 13 September Johann

Forster's journal angrily records a violent encounter with a Raiatean man during a botanizing excursion, who, after an abusive disagreement about lending a canoe in exchange for some present, struggled with his son George and grabbed his gun from him. The father, still smarting over Cook's failure to revenge the attack upon Sparrman, chased the man, claiming hyperbolically that he was ready to 'stand to the last drop of my blood in defence of my property' and to punish any perpetrator 'in a manner proportionate to the act of violence' (though George admitted that the fight started after he had insulted the man). Johann got in one shot, it seems, and – according to Lieutenant Cooper, who saw the man later – inflicted some superficial wounds. Cook's journal entry for the day consisted of just five words: 'Nothing happen'd worthy of note.'

That evening, however, the tension between Cook and Forster senior erupted. Forster claims that the captain at first laughed about the altercation with the Raiatean – as though no great harm had been done – but later took him to task for shooting at the man. The cranky scientist, who scarcely ever passed up an opportunity for self-justification in his diary, was on this occasion uncharacteristically ready to acknowledge that the fault lay partly on his own side. 'The Dispute went however too far, & though I had once desired to drop the affair as insignificant, Cap^r *Cook* however went on, having been exasperated by some false Insinuations from his first Servant . . . & so some hot & unguarded Expressions came out on both sides & he sent me by Force out of his Cabin.' Three days later, tempers cooled. Furneaux and George Forster mediated, and the two somehow apologized and shook hands.

This squabble is too easily reduced to the tale – one often rehearsed by commentators on Cook's second voyage – of just how impossible Johann Forster was. He was indeed over-sensitive and difficult. In Cook he encountered someone as stubborn as himself. What is striking over these few days, however, is not this collision of personalities, but a certain waywardness in Cook. At both Huahine and Raiatea, the navigator appears emotionally transported by encounters with prominent men whom he has met before, men who are on their part affected, at any rate pleased, to see him again. He writes as lyrically as he ever does about their civility and generosity. He scarcely wants to know of the proliferation of petty thefts that are perpetrated against his men, which he for the most part neglects to record and refrains from punishing. The same man who, only weeks before, has shot at and chased a Tahitian thief in a state of fury is now furious with one of his scientists for having acted in precisely the same way. The thread that connects the two incidents is that of the hospitality of Polynesian chiefs. In the first case, Cook was angry because he had been conned by a man who pretended to be a chief. In the second, he enjoys the friendship of genuine *ari'i*. Whatever this friendship meant for the chiefs, it had come to mean something to Cook, something more important than the trifling misdeeds of their subjects or the annoying grievances of his gentlemen. He was no longer just Cook or 'Toote' but a compound self: the *tayo* of a Raiatean Cook, he was a British Orio.

13

We are the innocent cause of this war

Departing from the Society Islands, Cook began a discourse, 'We will now leave the Sloops for a while and take a short View of the isles we have lately touched at.' It sounds as though he was fancying himself as a writer. No doubt, during the tedious Antarctic passages and the uneventful cruise to the east from New Zealand, he had been reading a good deal: the books in his great cabin naturally included maritime narratives such as William Dampier's *Collection of Voyages*, Antoine Frézier's *Voyage to the South Seas*, and Bougainville's lyrical *Voyage Round the World*, in the translation by Johann and George Forster, published shortly before the ships had departed London. In the Society Islands he had been going over Bougainville closely. He thought his book 'the most usefull as well as entertaining Voyage through these Seas yet published', but went to considerable trouble to interview people about human sacrifice among other matters that he believed Bougainville had got wrong.

In his account of these inquiries, we come close to one of Cook's conversations, one that took place beside a *marae* at Matavai. He was with Furneaux and the marine Samuel Gibson, who was supposed to be the best speaker of Tahitian. They talked with a number of local men, one of whom struck Cook as especially intelligent and knowledgeable.

I began with asking questons relating to the several objects before us: if the Plantans &c^a were for the Eatua; if they sacrified to the Eatua Hogs, Dogs Fowles &c^a to all of which he answered in the afformative. I then asked if they sacrified men to the Eatua, he answered Taata eno they did, that is bad men, first Tepararrahy or beating them till they were dead; I then asked if him if good men were put to death in this manner, he answerd no Taata eno . . . I asked him several more questons, and all his answers seemed to tend to this one point that men for certain crimes were condemn'd to be sacrificed to the gods provide[d] they have not wherewithall to redeem themselves which I think implies that on certain occasions human sacrifices are necessary, when they take such men as have committed crimes worthy of death and such will generally be found amongst the lower class of people. The man . . . took some pains to explain the whole of this Custom to us but we were not masters enough of the language to understand them.

Though the conversation confirmed most of what Bougainville had reported on this topic, Cook rejected other statements of the French navigator's, such as that fruit trees were held in common; 'I much doubt if their is a fruit tree on the whole island that is not the property of some individual,' he wrote. He went on to remark that such mistakes were inevitable: a visit of ten days was far too short to permit any adequate study of a people's customs. The issue of whether Bougainville was right or wrong prompted Cook to inquire more closely and systematically than he had done before. It prompted him to try to be as careful in such questioning as he had always been in surveying. Perhaps it gave him a new sense of how large accounts of customs might loom, in the most 'useful and entertaining' voyage narratives. Maybe it also gave him the idea that if Bougainville had written a good book, a discoverer who had been to the Pacific twice and spent many more than ten days with Tahitians could write a better one. This is why Cook's manuscripts from the second voyage are far more complex than those from his first. On the *Endeavour*, he kept a journal, of which there are a few copies. On the *Resolution*, a journal was composed, revised, copied and rewritten. Many of the changes were inconsequential, but others manifest reflection, reconsideration and a huge amount of work on the part of a writer.

As a kid, I had an image of Cook on his quarterdeck, his eyes scanning the horizon for signs of land. He certainly did a good deal of this, but there were 100 other men and boys on the *Resolution* doing it too. When he was not giving directions to his officers, haranguing chiefs for hogs or inquiring into sacrifice, he spent more of his time, I now realize, facing sheets of paper, trying to get the better of recalcitrant words, alone with the problem of transcribing the combination of the banal, the routine, the curious and the unprecedented that constituted his voyage round the world.

It is the evening of Friday, 17 September; the *Resolution* and *Adventure* are sailing west; Raiatea has dropped out of sight. Cook has written up his reflections on Tahitian sacrifice, but remains anxious to correct misconceptions of Polynesian life. He proceeds to note that 'great Injustice has been done the Women of Otaheite and the Society Isles, by those who have represented them without exception as ready to grant the last favour to any man who will come up to their price'. Like Wales and George Forster, who join him in vindicating the characters of Tahitian women, he protests that married women, unmarried women of higher rank and even many unmarried commoner women 'admit of no such familiarities'. He acknowledges that there are perhaps proportionally more prostitutes here than in other countries and that such women are not subject to censure to the degree they are in England. He reflects upon the travesty of truth that travellers' generalizations are apt to produce. 'On the whole a stranger who visits England might with equal justice draw the Characters of the women there, from those which he might meet with on board the Ships in one of the Naval Ports, or in the Purlieus of Covent Garden & Dury Lane.'

Cook might have known that it was too late to press this qualification upon London's lurid imagination. Ironically, in the course of Orio's hospitality at Raiatea, he had witnessed confirmation of his argument. This would be distorted in the visual record of his voyage, into an innuendo of the sort he sought to dispel. On 11 September, at Hanaminino, the chief had visited the ship and 'presented' several women to Cook, including his daughter Poetua. This presentation was clearly akin to what Cook had earlier noticed among Maori. The point was to solicit gifts for these women, who charmed the officers and took their offerings, but who had no intention of permitting physical intimacies. 'The ladies very obligingly received their addresses, to one they gave a kind look to a nother a smile, thus they distributed their favours to all, received presents from all and at last jilted them all.' The instance of Polynesian politesse receives a different accent in the first cheap edition of Cook's voyages, in which many of the plates based on Hodges's sketches and paintings were freely adapted and altered. Hodges produced no image, as far as we know, of the meeting on 11 September, and there was no representation of it in the official 1777 edition of Cook's *Voyage*. But Anderson's 1784–6 popular serialization made the encounter the subject of a plate in which Orio is not simply introducing Poetua to Cook, but plainly offering him her hand. Perhaps, in another context, this gesture might be ambiguous, but at this time readers were predisposed to see promiscuity as the order of the day in the South Sea. Hence the word 'presenting' now implied that Orio made a gift to Cook of his daughter. The visual imputation was at once alien to the actualities of the moment, and delightful to a British public, for whom Cook was all the more romantic for his imagined entanglements with Pacific princesses.

The *Resolution* and *Adventure* took a slightly southerly course, aiming to avoid routes previously explored and to establish whether there was any land in the latitude of Tasman's 1643 discovery of the islands he had called

Middleburgh and Amsterdam. *En route*, a few atolls were sighted. Cook at first named them after the Earl of Sandwich, but when he later found a more impressive island to name after the first lord, instead honoured another profligate and promiscuous Admiralty grandee, Augustus John Hervey. On 2 October Tasman's islands, known to their inhabitants as Eua and Tongatapu, were sighted. The ships first anchored off the former, where people appeared in great numbers, traded enthusiastically and welcomed Cook and a party ashore. They examined fields and houses, were treated to a kava ceremony and a dance, and proceeded the next day to Tongatapu, where people were equally friendly. Cook was annoyed, as he had been in New Zealand, by the eagerness of the crew to trade for 'Cloth and curiosities, things which I did not come here for and for which the Seamen only bartered away their clothes'. He absolutely prohibited traffic in artifacts and the like and was gratified when, the next day, the Tongans instead brought fruit, pigs and fowl to barter.

The course of contact here seemed to take a familiar course. Cook met 'a chief, or man of some note', 'Hatago by which name he desired I might be called and he by mine (Otootee)'. Officers and scientists were taken for a walk around the country, and all were impressed by the density of carefully fenced and gated plantations, which were generally separated by pleasantly shaded public roads. Cook was intrigued by a 'house of worship', in fact a chiefly burial place, known as a *faitoka*. He asked whether carved figures he saw were gods and whether people were buried at the place. His intuitions were right but he could not understand the responses to his questions. He was puzzled to gather that the man he refers to several times as 'my friend Otago' (the same 'Hatago', in fact Ataonga) was subordinate to another man, reputedly a higher chief, before whom other Tongans had prostrated themselves and otherwise exhibited 'extraordinary respect'. This man, however, displayed none of the vitality that Cook was accustomed to, in Islander leaders. To the contrary, he was 'seated with so much sullen and stupid gravity that I realy took him for an ideot which these people were ready to worship from some superstitious notions'; Cook saluted him and spoke to him. The man said nothing and ignored him. Cook was about to walk away, perhaps offended, though he does not say so. Another Tongan, 'an intelligent youth', 'under took to un deceive me' and somehow explained that this was, in fact, 'the principal man on the island'. The captain then accordingly gave him presents he had intended for another apparent 'chief'. The great man made no acknowledgement of these, 'nor did he so much as turn his head or eyes either to the right or the left but sit like a Post stuck in the ground'. Cook again tried to pay homage to the same man the next day, but left the

27. Ngatu, *decorated barkcloth, Tonga.*

island without gaining further insight into his status, or indeed into the nature of chiefly rule in the Tongan islands.

Material acquisitions were more considerable. Once Cook judged sufficient food had been obtained, he relaxed the rule against trading for curiosities, at which point, it appears, officers, naturalists and common seamen alike were carried away in a sort of orgy of collecting. Cook, who makes no mention of seeking or obtaining anything himself, observed that 'it was astonishing to see with what eagerness every one catched at every thing they saw'. The indiscriminate enthusiasm appeared ridiculous to the Tongans, who parodied the mariners, 'offering pieces of sticks stones and what not to exchange, one waggish Boy took a piece of human excrement on the end of a stick and hild it out to every one of our people he met with'.

Cook here sides with the Tongans in finding his crew's passion for curiosities so avid as to be ludicrous, but does not mention that the shells, natural specimens, ornaments and weapons brought back from his first voyage had quickly acquired a market among antiquarians and dilettantes. Such objects were also regarded as appropriate gifts to superiors and patrons in the naval hierarchy. Cook himself gave Sandwich a set of pieces from Tahiti, New Zealand and elsewhere; and other officers no doubt also presented their unusual souvenirs strategically. The enthusiasm thus had a rational basis – a basket, mat, club or spear had exchange as well as curiosity value – but it nevertheless seems here to have outrun any profit motive, to have had a crazy and obsessive quality. Collecting was, perhaps, a common seaman's way of making the voyage his own, not through maps or discourses, but through assembling a set of odd and interesting things that he could personally discover, delight in and control. To collect was to prise the business of exploration out of its official order. It was to privatize it. It is perhaps no wonder that Cook resented this.

The ships spent less than a week at these two islands. Yet Cook's tendency to write more reflectively about the peoples he encountered was again manifest in a description of Tongan products, persons and practices of some 3,500 words, which he appended to his journal entries from here. He noticed similarities with Tahitian customs that he discussed with Mahine, for whom he had increasing regard. Although Cook failed to recognize that the workings of rank and chieftainship in Tonga were quite different to the Tahitian system, his report of less abstract matters was precise, so far as it went. Knowing the pain that tattooing on any part of the body produced, he must have been astonished to learn that the men were marked not only on their thighs and hips but on 'their gentiles'. He was more positively impressed by the size and workmanship of Tongan canoes, which Hodges evoked in a beautiful watercolour. Cook had long been aware that the peoples of the South Sea were related, and had at some time migrated from island to island, but seeing these great double canoes, 'not only . . . Vessels of burdthen but fit for distant Navigation', brought it home to him that these movements were not necessarily those of some remote and mysterious antiquity. Islanders remained navigators, perhaps as capable of traversing this ocean as he.

Summer approached, and the ships sailed south to renew the search for the continent. On 21 October, the coast of the North Island of New Zealand was sighted. Cook aimed for a northerly landfall because he regarded the people around Poverty and Tolaga bays as 'more civilized' than those of Queen Charlotte Sound, and he wanted to improve them further. He was

28. *Hodges's* Tongan canoe, *1774.*

pleased to meet with a few canoes, one containing men who seemed to possess some status, to whom he gave boars, sows, cock, hens and the makings of a veritable market garden: 'Wheat, French and Kidney Beans, Pease, Cabages, Turnips, Onions, Carrots, Parsnips, Yams &cᵃ &cᵃ' all of which Cook counselled the Maori to look after, hoping 'to stock the whole Island in due time'. This accomplished, they proceeded south without landing. On 25 October mountainous seas and heavy gales ripped the sails and rigging, and pushed the ships away from their course. The *Adventure* lagged and on 30 October was lost to the sight of those on the *Resolution*, which continued to struggle through adverse winds and did not enter Queen Charlotte Sound (again the agreed rendezvous in case of separation) until 3 November. Here, in the wake of the storm, repairs to rope and iron work 'were absolutely necessary occupations'. Cook was frustrated to hear that the boar and sow he had left earlier had been taken in opposite directions, and the goats killed and eaten, though he gave fowl and a further pair of breeding pigs to some people 'who seemed as if they would take proper care of them'. The mariners' efforts to fish with the seine net were unrewarded, though considerable catches were purchased from the Maori, who bartered engagingly and pilfered liberally.

Over the following days, 'our friends' again visited, selling fish, sometimes stealing and stimulating a trade that Cook again thought reflected a want of discrimination among his crew. The favourite articles were now pieces of greenstone, which appear to have been bartered in an unprocessed form rather than as finished ornaments. Cook thought the stuff to be 'of no sort of Value, nevertheless it is so much sought after by our people that there is hardly any thing that they would not give for a piece'. His mood, however, is tolerant. He is no more bothered by this behaviour than he is by petty theft. Here, in the early summer, despite the rough edges to these relationships, despite his anxiety about the whereabouts of the *Adventure* and the promiscuity he does not mention in his journal, Cook is comfortable. He thinks he knows the Maori, he hopes his gifts of stock and model gardens will help eventually to civilize them, but he can live with them as they are.

Early in the morning of 21 November, 'a number of women and children' who visited the ship communicated their anxiety about a party of men. The next day, Cook reported that a group of Maori, some familiar, some strangers, came to the ship and 'offered us various curiosities in exchange for Otaheite cloth and Red Baze, &cᵃ'. Forster adds that they would not part 'with any thing, unless they got a piece red cloth for it & as no body but the Capᵗ had any; he got all the Curiosities that day'. After lunch, on 23 November – a fine and calm day – Richard Pickersgill went ashore with a number of other officers to purchase curiosities. They found warriors 'just risen from feasting on the Carcase of one of their own species', they believed. They encountered, at any rate, the head of an enemy youth, some organs lying on the ground and his heart on a cleft stick, tied to the prow of the principal canoe. 'One of the Natives with great gayety struck his spear into one lobe of the Lungs, and holding it close to the mouth of one of the Officers' – Pickersgill – 'made signs for him to eat it; but he begd to be excused, at the same time taking up yᵉ Head and making signs that he would Accept of that which was given to him, and he presented them with two nails in return,' reported Wales.

Pickersgill brought the head aboard, set it up on what was called the tafferal – a raised part of the stern rail which was usually ornamented with carvings – where a group of the officers and scientists chatted and looked at this trophy. At this moment a few Maori men came aboard and, seeing the head, expressed an 'ardent' desire to buy it, making gestures that made it clear that they wanted to eat it, we are told. Pickersgill would not sell, but was prepared to cut a piece off. According to George Forster, the Maori seemed satisfied with the prospect of eating this, but made further gestures, communicating that it had to be cooked, rather than eaten raw. The journal of Charles Clerke, the lieutenant who actually grilled the portion of flesh, has a different emphasis and suggests that the Maori were actively encouraged to eat, there and then. In any event, Clerke prepared the meat and recorded that the man 'not only eat it but devour'd it most ravenously, and suck'd his fingers ½ a dozen times over in raptures'.

Cook had been on shore, and returned just this happened. He says that

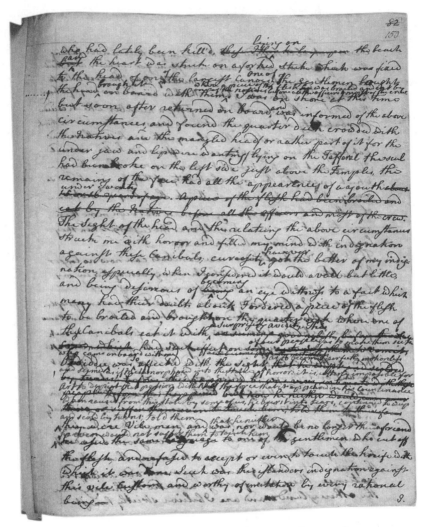

29. *Cook's revision of his journal entry on the 'proof'*
of cannibalism in Queen Charlotte Sound.

he was shocked and indignant, but reflected that nothing he could say or do
would be of much 'avail' – meaning that it was neither his task nor was it
in his power to censure or punish the customary conduct of peoples he
visited, however repulsive their practices seemed. He was mindful, too, of
the incredulity of acquaintances in Britain. Though he had been sure after
the *Endeavour*'s visit here in 1769 that the Maori did practise cannibalism,
'the account I gave of it in my former Voyage was partly founded on

circumstances and was, as I afterwards found, discredited by many people'. He had often been asked, he noted, 'after relateing all the circumstance, if I had actualy seen them eat human flesh my self, such a question was sufficient to convence me that they either disbelieved all I had said or formed a very different opinion from it'. If Cook felt aggrieved that his creditworthiness had been questioned, even by his scientific collaborators, it is perhaps less surprising that as this chain of events unfolded during the November visit, Cook took the extraordinary step of calling for a cannibal encore. He demanded that the warriors make him personally an eyewitness 'to a fact which many people had their doubts about', by eating a further part of the head. This too was accordingly grilled. By this time the whole crew had gathered, to see 'one of the Canibals eat it with a seeming good relish'.

This astonishing performance 'operated very strangely and differently on the beholders', George Forster wrote. Some of the sailors, though regarded as brutal themselves, were so appalled they vomited. Some were so outraged that they proposed to shoot the Maori, who only laughed back, manifestly acting up in the face of this avid disgust. Others made jokes and proposed to join in the feast themselves. The Society Islander, Mahine, was possessed with terror from the moment he saw the head. When the piece was eaten 'he became perfectly motionless, and seemed as if Metamorphosed into the Statue of Horror: it is,' wrote the astronomer, William Wales, 'utterly impossible for Art to depict that passion with half the force that it appeared in his Countenance.' He would later have nothing to do with either the Maori or Lieutenant Clerke, who had cooked the flesh. It was obvious to him, if not to his fellow-voyagers, that this shocking scene was a Maori–European co-production.

The Maori did indeed consume the bodies of their enemies, at least occasionally, but what was witnessed was a highly staged 'fact' – a performance contrived by its European participants to display barbarity, and by the Maori to inspire real horror. Maori social life has always been, and still is, replete with rituals of defiance, such as the well-known *haka* dance which was employed to frighten enemies in the nineteenth century, and to awe guests, foreigners and rugby teams in many situations since. When Pickersgill was urged to eat a bit of lung dangled in front of his mouth, he was being challenged in a similar way. What Cook and his crew witnessed were peculiarly powerful improvisations to the same effect. The British had urged the Maori to show them a bit of savagery. They saw it, and felt savaged by it.

Though Cook recorded his own horror and indignation before the sight, his reflections sustain the mood of the preceding days. He is philosophical and does not censure 'Maori cannibals'. He treats cannibalism as one topic, and Maori character and civility as a separate one.

The New Zealanders are certainly in a state of civilization, their behaviour to us has been Manly and Mild, shewing allways a readiness to oblige us; they have some arts a mong them which they execute with great judgement and unweared patience; they are far less addicted to thieving than the other Islanders and are I believe strictly honist among them-selves. This custom of eating their enimies slain in battle (for I firmly believe they eat the flesh of no others) has undoubtedly been handed down to them from the earliest times and we know that it is not an easy matter to break a nation of its ancient customs let them be ever so inhuman and savage . . .

He thought however that 'as they become more united they will of concequence have fewer Enemies and become more civilized and then and not till then this Custom may be forgot'. This anticipates a theme later elaborated upon by Johann Forster, who discussed cannibalism at some length in his *Observations*, arguing there that such barbarities were ameliorated as societies joined together under more settled governments. It sounds as though the British navigator and the German scientist had, at least for the moment, put animosities behind them and shared a passion to make sense of this practice – whatever practice it had been – in terms that set aside, that even forgot, the moment of instinctive revulsion. They did not judge but instead wondered why the Maori had adopted the practice, what made them sustain it and whether and when they might abandon it. They rejected the theory that the custom originated in hunger. Cook saw it as a symptom of an anti-sociality, that inverted the idea of charity: 'at present they seem to have but little idea of treating other men as they themselves would wish to be treated, but treat them as they think they should be treated under the same circumstances'. Johann Forster saw it as an extreme expression of a warrior ethos, stimulated by the frenzied rage of battle and a desire to inflict absolute and posthumous humiliation upon an enemy, that became habitual. For William Wales, the fact that Maori men could consume flesh well after fighting meant that the practice could not be merely impulsive; it was the product of a 'Choice, and the liking which they have for this kind of Food'.

These 'explanations' had varying emphasis but one thing in common: they took cannibalism as a cultural or historical accident – a thing that required an explanation. Though Wales comes closest to the idea that some people choose cannibalism – and are perhaps themselves as 'horrid' as their custom – none of the three can simply start with the idea that certain peoples are simply cannibals. These writers, in other words, cannot classify the Maori as cannibals and leave it at that. The practice is contrary to expectations, even of 'natives' or 'Indians'. It is at odds with other qualities, civil qualities, of these particular people and requires investigation and explanation. None of the understandings in fact came close to the Maori logic that licensed and necessitated the practice. Reciprocity, in Maori society, was not only about exchanging gifts and acknowledging the life-giving work of gods and priests. It had a negative as well as a positive register. Transgressions had to be recompensed, and insults, thefts and aggressions had to be revenged. The imperative to seek *utu* or vengeance was vital to the identities of warriors here, and the prestige of their clans. To consume a man was to consummate that vengeance – as Forster understood, without grasping that vengeance was not only a psychic need but part of a flow of gift and debt, of giving and taking, of life and death.

On 23 November, Cook engaged in an investigation that he did not fully report. He questioned the Maori about their expedition against their enemies. He did not believe them when they told him that fifty were killed, but did when they said that the youth was 'killed there and not brought away a prisoner'. It seems that he was committed to the view that while those slain in battle were eaten, no one was executed in order to be consumed. He wrote that 'I could not find the reason for their undertaking this expedition.' This is odd because Johann Forster did.

I am afraid we are the innocent cause of this war. For having bought up all the Curiosities & green Stones, the Natives in the Sound were possessed of, & hearing us constantly ask for more & offering various things, which tempted their desires; They went I believe in quest of them among their neighbours, who they knew had a great many left, & killed several of them in order to possess themselves of these things which are so much coveted by the Europeans.

Forster's report is consistent with what is otherwise known. Cook remarked upon avid interest in greenstone in particular. And, in the wake of the traffic in Tonga, the craze for collecting appears to have been at its height. By the third week in November, the *Resolution* had been at Meretoto for more than a fortnight. Many out of the 100-strong complement had been engaged in daily barter with some 150 Maori. It is entirely conceivable that these people had exhausted their supplies of personal ornaments and precious greenstone, and plausible that they should renew conflict with customary enemies, in order to gain further supplies. The likelihood that trade with Europeans was the stimulus for this aggression is enhanced by the very keen interest that some Maori here evidently had in their acquisitions from Europeans. Both the Tahitian barkcloth and the red baize that Cook alone could give seemed special forms of their own highly valued clothes and capes. Some, who had things they had acquired stolen back from them by the seamen, were sufficiently aggrieved to take their complaints to Cook, who flogged one of the sailors responsible, but was unable to retrieve the things that now belonged to the Maori.

The scene of cannibalism on the deck of the *Resolution* was therefore an expression of intertwined Maori and European desires in more ways than one. I've suggested that the Maori were repeatedly exposed to the European fascination with the subject and could not resist acting up in response. This was no 'Maori custom', any more than Purea's live show represented a Tahitian 'custom'. It was a form of behaviour that indeed existed, but was here staged and exaggerated. Yet, beyond this, the violence that provided the unfortunate youth's corpse would apparently not have occurred in the absence of the mariners. To be sure, the Maori did engage in warfare periodically. No one now knows how often these particular people did, when they had last done so, and when they might have done so next, had Europeans not been here.

In many places at many times, new external contacts have exacerbated conflicts between tribes. What is notable about Queen Charlotte Sound is that this occurred so quickly. Long before any regular trade was established, long before the Maori were buying muskets, a new but ephemeral commerce provided a new reason for war. What is notable, too, is that in his journal entry for 23 November, Cook omits to mention this, even though the circumstance underscores the melancholy observation he made almost six months earlier, that European visits only disturb and damage native lives. He does not say anything of this cause because he knew nothing of it. When Forster says that 'The natives told us they had been in Admiralty-Bay on Sunday & fought there a battle and killed many', and Cook writes, 'they had gone from hence into Admiralty Bay and there fought with their enemies many of whom they killed', there can be no doubt that they are reporting the same conversation. Moreover, in one version of the journal entry for the previous day, Cook notes that the strangers who had bartered for baize 'have been out on some war expedition, and those things they sold us were the spoils of their Enemies'. The fact that the Maori sold things looted from their enemies does not of course mean that they undertook the expedition in order to obtain those things. Bear in mind that while his knowledge, and Forster's knowledge, of the Maori had improved considerably since the first visit to this region, and been aided by a month's exposure to closely related Tahitian dialects, neither was in any sense fluent. Cook heard, and was disturbed by what he heard. Forster heard, perhaps a little more acutely, and perhaps knows a little more of Maori grammar. He told Cook, but Cook was not happy. This was the sort of crucial matter that he had to have heard for himself. That may be wrong, but that is how I imagine what happened. It might be why Cook chose these words: 'I could not find out the reason for their undertaking this expedition, *all I could understand for certain* was that they had gone from hence into Admiralty Bay,' and so forth. He was not bearing false witness, but he refrained from reporting a possibility or probability, that manifested the intimate, deepening connection between what he saw as the worst of native society, and the shameful consequences of his own expedition.

The following day the *Resolution* was unmoored. 'Some of our old friends the Natives came to take leave of us,' Cook wrote. He left a letter in a bottle for Furneaux, but thought it most likely he had tired of beating against the gale and sailed away towards Cape Horn or Cape Town. No further rendezvous had been set out and Cook thus presumed his ship would be on its own for the remainder of the voyage. He maintained that 'not a man was dejected' by the dangers of proceeding alone to the south 'or whever I thought proper to lead them'. Proceed alone to the south was what the ship indeed did. Cook read the swells. Birds were closely observed, but only those such as albatrosses and petrels, known to fly great distances from land, were sighted. On 7 December, at half past eight in the evening 'we reckoned our Selves Antipodes to our friends in London consequently as far removed from them as possible'. On 12 December the first ice island was sighted. A few days later it was necessary to alter course to avoid a field of loose ice. It became 'dark and gloomy and very cold'. The passage proved still more gruelling than the first Antarctic cruise. Writing on Christmas Eve, 1773, Cook made no effort to understate the ordeal:

Our ropes were like wires, Sails like board or plates of Metal and the Shivers froze fast in the blocks so that it required our utmost effort to get a Top-sail down and up; the cold so intense as hardly to be endured, the whole sea in a manner covered with ice, a hard gale, and thick fog . . . The bad weather continuing without the least variation for the better which made it necessary for us to proceed with great caution . . . we were continually falling in with large ice islands which we had enough to do to keep clear of.

The mariners must have felt not only at an absolute remove from friends, families and homes, and displaced into the harshest of possible conditions, but transposed also into an upside-down calendar, in which frigid summers succeeded hot winters. Yet they probably felt blessed the following day: it became a couple of degrees warmer, the wind dropped, the sky cleared and Christmas was celebrated as usual. George Forster remarked that many sailors had been saving up their brandy allowances, 'being sollicitous to get very drunk, though they are commonly sollicitous about nothing else'.

The next day the party went on. For Johann Forster, the icebergs 'look like the wrecks of a destroyed world, everyone of them threatens us with impending ruin, if you add our solitary Situation & being surrounded by a parcel of drunken Sailors hollowing and hurraing about us, & peeling our Ears continually with Oaths & Execrations, curses & Dam's it has no distant relation to the Image of hell, drawn by the poets'. The year's end was marked by a good deal of illness. Johann Forster and a dozen others were badly afflicted with rheumatic pains, a few were beginning to develop scurvy, Cook himself was 'likewise pale and lean', and without appetite. At least one man simply snapped. The unpopular Charles Loggie, whose misbehaviour had already led to his demotion from the quarterdeck, was drinking with two midshipmen, whom he quarrelled with and tried to stab, or at any rate cut with his knife. He was flogged on 2 January. The ship sailed north to intersect with Cook's first voyage track towards Tahiti. The possibility that there was land in that region was discounted, and a course towards the south-east resumed. Fresh provisions were exhausted, no fish could be caught, the crew were discontented about rotten bread and the fact that, to spin supplies out, rations had been reduced to two-thirds of normal allowances. After the first mate expressed widespread grievances, Cook agreed to restore them to the usual levels. There was a moment of excitement on 26 January, when many people believed they saw land to the east. That, however, soon afterwards disappeared into haze.

The *Resolution* continued south. The temperatures were a little less severe than they had been in mid December, and the weather on 30 January was clear and pleasant. At four the following morning the clouds ahead appeared unusually bright, and by eight it became evident that a vast body of ice blocked the ship's route south. It seemed to extend way out of view to both east and west; it was closely packed, and ice hills and mountains – some ninety-seven were counted – could be seen beyond its edge. There was no going further here. In the longest of his journal entries for the Antarctic cruise, Cook described the approach to this extraordinary frozen rampart, evoked the pure extremity of the environment and insisted on its incomparability with any Arctic seascape – 'Such Ice Mountains as these are never seen in Greenland' – which made the navigation of these waters a project utterly unlike anything that anyone had attempted in the north Atlantic. Judicious qualification only underscored his claim that he had reached an absolute limit, a place that admitted no human passage: 'I will not say it was impossible anywhere to get in among this Ice, but I will assert that the bare attempting of it would be a very dangerous enterprise and what I believe no man in my situation would have thought of.' He proceeded to make the famous statement that I quoted at the beginning of this book:

I whose ambition leads me not only farther than any other man has been before me, but as far as I think it possible for man to go, was not sorry at meeting with this interruption, as it in some measure relieved us of the dangers and hardships, inseparable with the Navigation of the Southern Polar regions. Sence therefore we could not proceed one Inch farther South, no other reason need be assigned for our Tacking and stretching back to the North . . .

This blunt reference to a resolution to accomplish as much as it was possible to accomplish is one of the few significant passages in Cook's journals that was scarcely amended in his published text and that tended to be quoted verbatim in digests and abridgements of his voyages. It has always been treated as a straightforward expression of this explorer's dauntless perseverance, as a characteristically matter-of-fact and unselfconscious revelation of the unflinching commitment to discovery that motivated the man.

Cook's navigation was, indeed, characterized by methodical rigour. He saw that there were blank spaces on a chart and he worked out a track that criss-crossed them. Once he had laid down that course, he followed it single-mindedly, with no more variation or compromise than he could avoid. But when he wrote of his ambition and accomplishment, he was not baring his soul. He was doing something he had been doing increasingly over the course of this voyage, which was *writing*. And, as writers do, he was making an allusion. He was claiming a position. He was even inflicting a sort of put-down on a fellow-writer, a would-have-been discoverer.

Cook's journals are replete with evidence that he read and re-read a great deal at sea. At times there was not much else to do. Among the maritime works that he studied most closely over the course of this passage was Alexander Dalrymple's *Historical Collection of the Several Voyages and Discoveries in the South Pacific Ocean*, published in London in two volumes in 1770 and 1771; this was his most valuable sourcebook for the Spanish and Dutch voyages. In his preface, Dalrymple freely confessed that 'The *discovery* of a SOUTHERN CONTINENT' was the 'great passion' of his career. He bitterly related his maritime experience in the East Indies, the range and the many years of his preparatory research, and his exclusion from the voyage of the *Endeavour*, which occurred because 'he was not bred up in the *Royal Navy*, and for this reason only', he claimed, though the Admiralty lords had never opposed his participation in the voyage, only his demand to be given command. After negotiation on this point had broken down, the commission had, of course, been given to Cook. Many eighteenth-century books began with pompous and self-serving declarations, packaged as philosophical discrimination. Dalrymple's preliminary waffle was no exception:

True heroism is not the mere contempt of life, or pleasure; there is required to constitute this character, a *sublimity* of *conception*, supported by *dauntless* and perseverant *resolution*; whence the soul, possessed with the *possibility* of effecting, what *it alone* had *energy* to *conceive*, disregards the obstacles which little minds would think *insurmountable*, and though not insensible to difficulties and dangers, acquires a confidence superior to them.

This question will determine the relative dignity of any character, 'What has *he* done which no one else ever *did* before, or *can do* after him?'

Cook does not derive the wording of his Antarctic declaration – 'not only farther than any other man has been before me, but as far as I think it possible for man to go' – from this passage. But there is a direct echo of Dalrymple's sense. Cook uses related wording in a later passage in his journal. He liked the phrase and its resonance; he turned it over in his mind and fine-tuned it. Cook, like most people, thought about what he wanted to do, what he had done, and how he hoped to be regarded. He cannot have been oblivious of the extent to which his second voyage had indeed set a new standard in systematic exploration. Whatever one thinks of other aspects of his behaviour – of the uglier incidents of his voyages, of histories of invasion that followed in Australia and elsewhere – one cannot deny that he made his predecessors look like naïve amateurs, so far as the business of maritime investigation was concerned. He had not only what twentieth-century management-speak called 'vision' – Dalrymple called it, more appealingly, 'sublimity of conception' – but also the ability to make a plan work, which was the ability to push his crew hard without pushing them over the brink. I am sure that Cook thought about all this. He knew that his voyage had established more in two years than a score of predecessors had over the past two centuries. His maps were the measure of his accomplishment. He could not help sizing himself up against Dalrymple's definition of a hero, and could not resist the irony of appropriating Dalrymple's terms to celebrate, not the discovery of the southern continent, but his mounting proof that the great land was no more than myth.

14

The varieties of the human species

In early February 1774, Cook took stock and 'now came to a resolution to proceed to the North and to spend the insuing Winter within the Tropick'. Already sure that there was no continent in the south Pacific, he could very reasonably have shaped a course towards the Atlantic and home. He was ill, it was snowing, yet he was inordinately determined to tie up a series of loose ends. There was a rumoured land of Juan Fernandez. There was Easter Island, perhaps the same as Davis's Land. There was the Tierra Austral del Espiritu Santo, which had been bloodily but briefly colonized by Quiros in 1606 and revisited by Bougainville in 1768, who had neither confirmed nor refuted Quiros's claim that that island was very large. 'I think it a point well worth clearing up,' Cook wrote, as though the task entailed referring to a map rather than traversing a quarter of the globe in order to produce one. He was not altogether candid about the responses of his fellow-mariners to this project, which would mean extending the duration of the voyage by at least a full year. In one draft of his journal, he says that Furneaux, with whom he discussed plans prior to the ships' separation, 'seem'd not to approve of it, but was inclinable to get to the Cape of Good Hope, afterwards he seem'd to come into my opinion'. In the revision of this manuscript, the reference to Furneaux's dissent was excised. Towards the end of his long entry for 6 February, Cook indicated that

Great as this design appeared to be, I however thought it was possible to be done and when I came to communicate it to the officers I had the satisfaction to find that they all heartily concur'd in it. I should not do my officers (*who till now thought we were bound directly to the Cape of Good Hope*) Justice if I did not take some oppertunity to declare that they allways shewed the utmost readiness to carry into execution in the most effectual manner every measure I thought proper to take. Under such circumstances it is hardly necessary to say that the Seamen were always obedient and alert and on this occasion they were so far from wishing the Voyage at an end that they rejoiced at the Prospect of its being prolonged a nother year and soon enjoying the benefits of a milder climate.

The words in italics are scored through. In his later recollections of the voyage, Lieutenant John Elliott wrote, not of this occasion but of a change of course the previous month, that 'At this time we all experienced a very severe mortification . . . we had all taken it into our heads that we were going streight for Cape Horn, on our road home . . . Many hints were thrown out to Capt. Cook to this effect, but he only smiled and said nothing, for he was close and secret in his intentions at all times . . . In this instance, all our hopes were blotted in a Minuit, for from steering East, at noon, Capt. Cook ordered the Ship to steer due South, to our utter astonishment, and had the effect for a moment of causing a buz in the Ship, but which soon subsided.' A buzz, in this context, can only have meant mutinous consternation. If Elliott is talking about what occurred on 11 January, it is highly doubtful that on 6 February, officers and seamen who were more diseased, more exhausted and more fed up with deteriorating provisions really 'rejoiced at the Prospect' of a further year of the same – though they may well have been pleased to gather that they would soon be spending more time at Tahiti. Cook's dissimulation was double-edged, however. If he refused to record the true feelings of his subordinates, he put their loyalty and spirit beyond reproach. Many naval commanders probably adopted this approach to journal-keeping, which presented people's conduct as it should have been rather than as it was. If, in general, this economy with the truth made captains sound like better leaders and made seamen less fractious than either in fact were, it obscures, in this case, Cook's capacity to win his officers over to a course that had 'very severely mortified' them only a month earlier.

The route that Cook proposed through the tropics resembled the one followed the previous winter. It began in the Antarctic, in this case from a position further east, it proceeded north and east into the warm latitudes just south of the equator, then west through the groups of islands known to be scattered across the Pacific tropics, and then again to the south towards New Zealand, which would once again provide a last base for refreshment before a final traverse of the southern oceans. But on this occasion the arc through the tropics would be considerably wider. Cook aimed to venture substantially further east, where Juan Fernandez and Easter Island were supposed to be located, and then much further west. Neither Cook himself, nor the Forsters, who were already provoked and stimulated by diverse

Oceanic cultures, had any notion of just how rich the succession of encounters on this cruise would be. They had no idea yet that in just seven months they would meet the inhabitants of more than twenty islands; some were people they already knew, some were previously unknown to Europeans, and others had been identified and described so vaguely that they might as well have been unknown. The human discoveries of this voyage would have the magnitude, but nothing like the simplicity, of Cook's determination that there was no continent in the south.

In late February, Cook, who had been suffering from constipation, caused by some intestinal complaint, became dangerously ill. He hiccupped uncontrollably, was unable to eat, stand or shit. Neither warm baths, nor induced vomiting, nor camomile tea, nor tobacco glysters were of any use. The surgeon Patten was dead on his feet, tending his first patient night and day. His survival was feared for, but on 27 February a crisis passed: 'the Cap' is easier, having had several stools', reported Johann Forster; though Cook was to suffer relapses and remain weak for a further month.

Cooper, the first officer, was effectively in command. Juan Fernandez was not found. Course was shaped towards Easter Island. Many bonito and flying-fish were seen around the ship, but they had little luck catching them, which was enormously frustrating for people now revolted by their salt provisions, and desperate for any sort of fresh food. On 11 March, after 103 days out of sight of land, everyone was delighted by the appearance of an island. On Sunday the thirteenth, the sight of 'Moniments or Idols' reported by Roggeveen in 1722 left no doubt that this was the same place that he had visited, which is now called Rapanui by its inhabitants. The following day Cook went ashore with a party. A crowd of some hundreds of people neither welcomed nor resisted their landing, but in due course brought sweet potato, plantains and sugar cane in exchange for nails and other gifts. A few women came off in the boats and reached the usual agreements with sailors. A brackish well was found and a few casks filled, but there was no really fresh water, no supply of wood, and no pigs. The land appeared barren, the people were relatively few, their gardens small, their houses rudimentary and the place generally destitute of provisions. Cook decided that there was no point in remaining at the island, but did send a surveying party ashore on 15 March, which gave the Forsters and others a chance to inspect the great statues that would in due course become famous.

An ink sketch that Forster loosely inserted into his journal was probably the first European image of these huge figures. 'In what manner they con-

30. *The first European representation of the famous
Easter Island statues, an ink sketch by Johann Reinhold
Forster, 1774.*

trived these structures is incomprehensible to me,' he wrote, 'for we saw
no tools.' This puzzlement prefigured much idiotic speculation about the
'mystery' of Easter Island, which in fact was solved before it was invented,
without recourse either to the aliens or the migrating native Americans

proposed by various twentieth-century authors. Forster recorded that the 'pillars' they inspected, later painted by Hodges, were named Kotomoai, Kotomoiri, Koho'u, Morahina, Umariva, Uinapu and Uinapa. Wales, like Forster, understood correctly that these were chiefs' names, and that the sculptures were 'errected to the Memory of some of their Ancient Chiefs'. Though their monumental scale indeed made them unique among Oceanic stone sculptures, there was nothing basically unfamiliar about the commemoration of *ariki* in Polynesian ritual and art. What was perplexing was that human images on this scale had been produced by people who were evidently few in number, and generally impoverished. Forster believed that 'These pillars intimate that the Natives were formerly a more powerfull people, more numerous & better civilized.' If by 'better civilized' he meant more socially stratified, the inference would be confirmed some two centuries later. Investigations into the archaeology of Rapanui would establish that from about 800 to 1600 AD the island supported a larger and generally peaceful population ruled more like the Tahitians by semi-divine chiefs who were indeed commemorated by the statues, which people had stopped carving, perhaps a century or more before the *Resolution*'s visit. George Forster guessed that some catastrophe lay behind current poverty, but was wrong to suppose that volcanic eruptions or earthquakes had brought an end to relative opulence and stability. Rather it seems certain that over-cultivation and erosion led to an ecological crisis. Gardens were no longer sufficient to feed everyone, and thin soils did not even support trees out of which canoes of any reasonable size could be built. Hence, here and nowhere else in the Pacific, native people were desperately short of wood, and were less awestruck by the size of the *Resolution* than by the sheer quantity of timber that the ship incorporated. Mahine's judgement was *taata meitai, fenua ino:* a good people, a bad land.

Cook too was astonished by the statues, but reasoned that people 'wholy unacquainted with every mechanical power' could nevertheless have set them up, 'by raising the upper end by little and little, supporting it by stones as it is raised and building about it till they get it erect, thus a sort of mount or scaffolding will be made up which they may roll the Cylinder and place it on the head of the statue after which the stones may be removed from about it' – which is precisely how it was done, so far as we now know.

Cook was still more impressed by something else that became apparent even before he landed. The Islanders who ventured out to the vessel looked like those encountered elsewhere. They were tattooed, they had pieces of tapa, their weapons were like those of the Maori, and most conclusively, the words they used were immediately recognized as variants of Tahitian,

Tongan and Maori words. The staggering thing was that Rapanui lay thousands of miles from Tahiti. 'It is extraordinary,' Cook wrote, 'that the same Nation should have spread themselves over all the isles in this Vast Ocean from New Zealand to this Island which is almost a fourth part of the circumference of the Globe.' Over time, he remarked, each group of settlers had 'become as it were different Nations each having adopted some peculiar custom or habit', but any perceptive observer would 'soon see the Affinity each has to the other'.

This understanding marks the distance between Cook's sense of Oceanic people, and Bougainville's. Bougainville had visited Tahiti briefly, and only once. He therefore had no sense of how this society changed over time, as a result of its own seasonal and cyclical shifts, or in response to the visits of Europeans. Cook had encountered Tahiti in different states. Here at Rapanui he found evidence that pointed towards longer-term change, from a 'more' to a 'less' civilized order. Bougainville's limited, idealizing perception was conducive to the notion of the 'noble savage'. Towards the end of his first Pacific passage, Cook had responded to Aboriginal Australians in similar terms, but by now he and his companions knew too much about Oceanic people to dwell upon obvious qualities of their lifestyles, such as a 'simplicity' relative to Europe. The changes that Islanders had brought about or suffered made their societies real and subject to historical accident, rather than ideal and available to rhetoric.

These perceptions would be reinforced at the Marquesas Islands, which the *Resolution* reached three weeks later, after sometimes encountering calms during a passage generally north and west. The scurvy of those briefly refreshed by the Rapanui visit began to return, as did Cook's weakness. The harbour of Vaitahu on the island of Tahuata, which Cook knew from Quiros's report of the only previous European visit in 1595, was open to squalls and frustratingly difficult to enter, and once the ship had anchored, those Islanders who came off had frustratingly little to trade. A small pig was bought for a broken knife. Nor did the people approach exchange in a way that the mariners considered honest or straightforward. They 'frequently keep our goods and make no return' Cook complained, and was prompted to fire a musket ball 'Close past one man' who seemingly understood that this was a protest against him reneging on his side of a deal. He was frightened enough to 'run to the other end of his boat for the fruit' he had been offering, which he then passed up to the ship. Barter continued and some men came aboard, but Cook was concerned by their apparent disposition. He told officers to watch them closely. 'These words were no sooner out of my mouth' than some iron was taken. 'I told the officers to fire over the Canoe till I could get round in the Boat but not to kill any one, but the Natives made too much noise for me to be heard, unluckily for the theif they took better aim than I ever intend and killed him the third Shott.' Another man in the canoe seemed to be laughing hysterically as he baled blood and water out of it. A third, a youth of about fourteen or fifteen, 'looked at the dead man with a serias and dejected countenance and we had after wards reason to believe that he was son to the disceas'd.'

Somewhat later 'a man who seem'd of some consequence' came out and sold a pig. The next day a cautious and fearful trade took place on the beach. Cook met a man he thought was a chief, exchanged presents and thought that 'a good under Standing Seemed to be settled between us'; further trade took place. A village was visited, and Cook taken to the house of the man who had been shot. He was sorry that the man's son had fled upon their approach. 'I wanted much to have seen him to have made him a present and by other kind treatment convinced him and the others that it was not from any bad design we had against the Nation we had kill'd his father.' How the youth might have responded is anyone's guess.

Certainly, the values that European gifts possessed were uncertain. Cook took a boat to another bay to the south and obtained eighteen pigs. When he came back he found that trade had somehow become 'spoil'd' in his absence; he learned that officers had been ashore exchanging things, which were new to Marquesans and which interested them keenly. These new things seem not to have been European objects, but things obtained from other Polynesian islands that they recognized as singular forms of their own artifacts, or things that they valued that were much rarer here than elsewhere. 'What ruined our Market the most was one of them giving for a Pig a very large quantity of Red feathers he had got at Amsterdam [i.e. Tongatapu], which these people much value and which the other did not know, nor did I know at this time that Red feathers was what they wanted, and if I had I could not have supported this trade in the manner it was begun one day.' In fact, Cook had learned elsewhere that Polynesians generally valued red things – red was a *tapu* colour associated with intense sanctity, and high rank – and he had seen people wearing feather ornaments, and seen highly valued things adorned with feathers. But neither he nor anyone else on this voyage understood that feathers were intimately associated with gods and demi-gods, who were supposed to be born as bloody miscarriages, covered in feathers. In the Marquesas, chicken feathers were commonly used in head-dresses but were not special. The bright yellow and red feathers of small parrots, which were sought and caught in deep forests and high valleys, were considered potent, as the stuff of divinity. 'A very large quantity of Red feathers' was an unprecedented thing.

Once this had happened, there was no chance of obtaining pork in any quantity, nor was the open bay the easiest place to get wood or water out through surf. Cook resolved to leave it and 'seack for some other place that would supply our wants better'. His purpose, apart from obtaining food, had been to determine more accurately the situation of this island; he had accomplished that. As the ship zigzagged past the coast of the neighbouring island of Hiva Oa, he distilled his observations, as he usually did. He wrote about cloth, ornaments and houses. He believed that the people he saw did not prepare food as 'cleanly' as the Tahitians did, and they had laughed at him when he showed that he disliked eating dirty food. Reporting this, he hastened to add, 'I know not if all are so, the actions of a few individuals are not sufficient to fix a custom to a whole Nation.'

Physically, he thought the Marquesans 'as fine a race of people as any in this Sea or perhaps any whatever'. 'Tattouing like a coat of Mail', he wrote on a separate slip of paper, catching fortuitously at the indigenous rationale for the intricate and dynamic full-body tattoos of men. The images that covered their bodies were not only marks of membership in feasting societies organized around prominent men, they were also sets of eyes and faces that symbolically multiplied their vision and knowledge, that armed the body against attack.

Others were impressed, similarly, by Marquesan bodies and tattoos. Clerke wrote, 'the Men are punctuated (or as they call it tattow'd) from head to foot in the prettyest manner that can be conceived'. This, and Gilbert's more general observation on Polynesian tattooing, that it was 'curious and exceeding handsome Nay so becoming in those people that to a European they wou'd appear naked without it', are surprisingly appreciative. This mode of marking the body was radically strange to Europeans. I would have expected these midshipmen to have responded more as George Forster did, when he remarked that Tahitians of both sexes were 'adorned, or rather disfigured' by the singular black stains. The stains Clerke saw at Tahuata were far less restrained than Tahitian tattoos. He was responding to bodies wrapped comprehensively in images, in heavy and asymmetrical patches and diagonals across the face, in further faces, arcs, and solid fields around shoulders, knees and arms. The statements of Clerke and Gilbert suggest that they have become accustomed, even aesthetically attuned, to this form of adornment and are now capable of recognizing and responding to what was indeed its most frenetically elaborate Oceanic expression.

Despite the interest in tattooing manifest in the written statements of

Clerke, Gilbert, Cook and others, we now know the early Marquesan manifestation of the art, not through any drawing of Hodges, but from images produced during the first Russian circumnavigation that took place nearly thirty years after this visit. During the few days in the Marquesas, Hodges painted a fine view of Vaitahu, and some sketches of canoes, but oddly refrained from any image featuring Marquesan tattooing – apart from one portrait of 'a chief' of Tahuata, whose forehead features some stray lines, curly characters and a kind of grid. If this man was tattooed in anything like the fashion recorded in later drawings and photographs, the drawing conveys the effect inadequately. The squiggles, intriguingly, imply that Hodges might have thought (as many later theorists did) that tattooing was a proto-script, a system of esoteric writing rather than a powerfully organized design.

It is odd that this artist made no greater effort to represent this visually extraordinary and truly exotic art of personal presentation, and there is something consistent in his failure to do so. In New Zealand, his portraits either omitted the *moko* of men and women, or presented them weakly. He did not attempt to depict tattooing in Tonga at all, and in Tahiti only did so through the alluring buttocks of the Vaitepiha bay painting (perhaps an exception that proves a rule, given that they did not compromise the presentation of the face). It is as though this professional painter confronted a limit that nothing in his training or his dealing with the human body enabled him to transcend, as though he had been taught always to respond to form, and had no pictorial language for 'punctures'. Parkinson, during the first voyage, had had no trouble at all, but he was more of a draughtsman than a painter and was less encumbered by the business of art.

After the departure from Tahuata, Cook sailed south and west. His plan, though he did not say so at the time, was to pass through the Society Islands again, where he must have been more confident that he could obtain supplies of fresh food. On 17 April an atoll was sighted. Never having visited any one of 'these half drown'd' isles, Cook thought it worth attempting to anchor and land. No navigable gap into the central lagoon was found, but people were sighted, boats were sent ashore, and a landing was made without opposition. When Cooper and Pickersgill tried to distribute presents, however, they were 'received with great indifference which plainly shew'd that we were unwelcome Visitors'. This is not surprising because it was here, at Takaroa, that Byron had killed two or three people ten years earlier. Cook saw that armed men nearby were being reinforced, and sent another boat to the shore to reinforce his party in turn. Fortunately, by the

31. A Chief of Santa Christina, *engraving after Hodges,*
from Cook, Voyage Toward the South Pole, *1777.*

time they reached the beach 'the day was far spent'; those who arrived did not land, and those already ashore chose to re-embark and return to the ship. This withdrawal probably forestalled fatal violence, since Cook's orders 'not to fire upon the Natives if it was possible to avoid it' had failed to prevent killing just ten days earlier. Cook had a point to make before he sailed away. 'As soon as the boats were hoisted in I ordered two or three Guns to be fired over the little isle the Natives were upon in order to shew them that it was not their own Superior strength and Numbers which obliged us to leave their isle,' he wrote, adding with satisfaction that they ran away 'as fast as their legs could carry them'.

His brief notes on the people and their disposition manifested the Forsters' axioms that environment and mode of subsistence shaped bodies and temperaments. The atoll-dwellers, though of the 'same Nation' as all the other

Islanders, occupied islets 'where Nature has not bestowed her favours in that profusion she has done to some of the others'. The soils would certainly have been poorer and drier than those of wetter, hilly, high islands. The people indeed depended to a greater degree on marine resources than, say, the Tahitians or Marquesans. They were probably more exposed to sun and sea and may well have been darker-skinned as a result. When Cook says that they seemed 'to have a more ferine disposition' he is responding not to their 'disposition' but only to how they responded to him. Here, his reflective turn failed him. Because of the hostility, he has forgotten his care in consideration. He readily attributes a 'disposition' to them collectively, though he admittedly says it is a thing that they *seem to* have, not one that they just have.

From here a course was taken towards Tahiti, and on 22 April Cook visited Matavai Bay for the third time. He reported simply that old friends 'express'd not a little joy at seeing us'. Wales conceded that 'if there be any truth in Physiognomy they were extreamly glad to see us, from what Motive I will not pretend to say'. If the astronomer sounds ungenerous, he recognized that there was something nebulous, something never fully explained, about this sequence of encounters that his commander was less willing to acknowledge. Although Cook was often suspicious of appearances, he wanted Polynesian affection to be what it seemed. Wales was almost certainly right to suspect that something deeper was going on, that Cook chose to overlook.

Cook understood, of course, that Polynesians befriended Europeans in part because they wanted the things they could get from them, just as he befriended them in order to facilitate gifts of food. But *taio* friendship and name-exchange entailed much more than a flow of trifles or food, and to recognize that these relationships had a utilitarian side was to stop short of grasping their appeal or their effect. There was something going on in these islands, a sea-change in politics, that capitalized upon new cults such as that of 'Oro, and the appearance of new voyagers, new artifacts, new kinds of cloth, and new trade relations. This sea-change began before the arrival of Europeans. Although not a product of European contact, it was dramatically accelerated and distorted by it. It was not Cook's nails, knives and axes that high chiefs such as Tu really needed. What they were trying to collect, control and assimilate was rather his name, his image and an idea of his prestige. This name or idea was not something Cook had made, or deliberately introduced. It was not a British invention but a Tahitian one, something that they valued in their own terms, that could be circulated and held up, with feather sashes that signified claims to *marae*, to titles, and to tribute.

Whatever Cook represented to Tahitians before he arrived, he quickly amounted to something more. The red feathers that had been obtained in Tonga, which he had never brought to Tahiti before, which had so much excited the Marquesans, now provoked intense and unprecedented interest. These 'they admired and coveted amazingly', Johann Forster wrote. Cook reported that once word got out that the ship brought a supply, 'all the Principal people of both sex endeavour'd by every means in their power to Ingratiate themselves into our favour in order to obtain these Valuable Jewels'. As George Forster noted, the line between what might be and what might not be trafficked suddenly changed.

I have observed . . . that the women of the families of chiefs never admitted the visits of Europeans; and also that whatever liberties some unmarried girls might with impunity allow themselves, the married state had always been held sacred and unspotted at Taheitee. But such was the force of the temptation, that a chief [Potatou] actually offered his wife to captain Cook, and the lady, by her husband's order, attempted to captivate him, by an artful display of all her charms, seemingly in such a careless manner, as many a woman would be at a loss to imitate. I was sorry, for the sake of human nature, that this proposal came from a man, whose general character was otherwise very fair.

The Forsters father and son were fully aware that feathers – red feathers in particular – had ritual uses, but they seem to have been determined to forget this, in their eagerness to draw a moral from the unseemly conduct of Potatou and his wife. While George Forster mentioned that the feathers were used in warriors' costumes and 'on some other solemn occasions', he compared the 'extatic joy' of a Tahitian receiving a single one with that of a European 'who should unexpectedly find the diamond of the Great Mogul'. Neither Potatou nor anyone else at Matavai was desperately eager to acquire feathers because they were the latest things in town, because there was any sort of fashion or craze for them. Feathers, rather, were things that had existing value. They were worn, and they were attached to garments, artifacts and costumes on certain occasions, but they were not 'ornaments' if an ornament is just a pretty thing. They were sought by people whose lives revolved around the manipulation of power, and who grasped the making, the acquisition and the display of certain feathered art forms as techniques of sacred power, just as western politicians today instinctively understand, use, and try to control televised images.

On this occasion, the Forsters knew more than was convenient. They had to overlook their own observations, in order to jam a particular pattern of behaviour into a European mould. In general, there was something positive in their approach to anthropological reporting. They emphasized the common humanity, rather than any supposed racial distinctness, of the people they visited, but this emphasis upon essential uniformity also had a negative side. Just as George Forster had insisted on seeing Tahitian inequalities as variants upon European class conflicts, both Forsters now presumed that consumerism afflicted Polynesia as it afflicted Europe. The presumption enabled them to write lyrically and at length about the refinements as well as the flaws of Tahitian society, but in the end blocked their understanding of what made that society, and what mattered to Tahitians.

Cook was less concerned by the moral implications of the eagerness for feathers than pleased that they were in such demand. The island appeared to have recovered from the state of post-war scarcity it had been in during the previous visit. There were plenty of pigs, but the *Resolution*'s stocks of trade goods were much reduced. Had feathers not been collected in Tonga, had they not fortuitously possessed such value here, Cook would have found it difficult to obtain the quantities of food he needed. He decided to remain longer than he had first intended. Casks and sails were brought ashore, the forge was set up to repair ironwork, the ship was caulked and the rigging overhauled.

On 26 April the mariners were astonished to see a massed fleet of

32. Hodges's *view of the great Tahitian canoe fleet, 1774.*

elaborately decorated war canoes. Forster gathered, probably correctly, that the introduction of iron tools had enabled them to be built more quickly and elaborately than would have been so before; Cook understood that one of the chiefs on the island of Moorea had 'rebelled' against 'his Lawfull Sovereign', Tu, which perpetuated the misunderstanding that the island was organized like a feudal kingdom. It is perfectly possible, though, that Tu had obtained tribute from Moorea, or part of Moorea, that had been withheld for some reason, and that the forces now being drawn together for these displays were intended for an expedition to reassert that relationship. Cook was at first frustrated that confusions prevented him from interviewing Tu about the nature of naval operations, but a few days later he was able to witness what he understood were exercises. He was impressed by how swiftly canoes could be landed and carried ashore.

Tu's older brother, Teari'ifa'atau, was aware that Hodges drew anything remarkable and 'desired of his own accord that he might be sent for'. In response to what was almost a native commission – though we have no record that Hodges left any of his pictures with locals – the painter produced several lively sketches, and later finished paintings, that suggest that the fleet impressed itself upon him, as a dazzling spectacle. Cook was increasingly impressed, not only by the skilfulness and sophistication of the canoe-borne fighting force, but also by Tu personally, who he now regarded as 'a brave, Sencible, and intelligent Chief'. He went so far as to offer his support in the expedition against Moorea, which help several of the prominent men of Matavai had initially solicited, before changing their minds. By 14 May, when Cook was ready to leave, 'they certainly wanted us to be gone before they undertook any thing' for reasons that were not clear to him then, and that remain a little puzzling now.

While Charles Clerke and others continued to record their feelings for Tahiti in the most effusive terms, the visit was not trouble-free. Cook went to considerable lengths to secure a stolen musket, and proposed to flog a Tahitian caught trying to take a cask. Tu and others were alarmed and 'beg'd hard for the Man', but Cook was inflexible. He delivered a tirade against local thieves, and insisted that since sailors who committed crimes against Tahitians were punished, this thief would be dealt with in the same fashion. 'I said more to the same purpose most of which I believe he pretty well understood as he was satisfied and only desired the Man might not be kill'd,' Cook claimed. A huge crowd witnessed the violence – two dozen lashes with the cat of nine tails – which the offender 'bore with great firmness'. They then listened attentively as the prominent warrior Taua 'harangued' them. If we are to believe Cook, the speech recapitulated what he had said himself, stressing the 'several Advantages they had received from us' and condemning the incidence of theft. Tu 'on this occasion spoke not one word', perhaps less reconciled to the show of discipline than Cook would have us believe. It is possible that it was this intervention that gave him the sense that the British could not be counted upon or controlled, that made him think he did not want them in any way involved in his mission against Moorea.

On 15 May, as the *Resolution* sailed from Matavai, John Marra, the gunner's mate, leapt overboard and tried to swim towards a canoe that seemed to be waiting, to pick him up. The ship was brought to, a boat put out, Marra captured and brought aboard. Cook discovered that there had been a preconceived plan, which Tu had been party to. He kept Marra in irons until they were clear of the islands, but decided not to punish him further. 'I did not think him so culpable as it may first appear,' Cook wrote. He regarded the Irishman as a good seaman, he had neither 'friends or connections to confine him to any particular part of the world, all Nations were alike to him, where than can Such a Man spend his days better than at one of these isles . . . I know not if he might not have obtained my consent if he had applied for it in proper time.' Maybe Marra was unusual for his detachment from Europe, for being as ready to make a home here in the South Seas as in any other part of the world. But perhaps many of his fellow-seamen were hardly less dislocated. The nations that eighteenth-century intellectuals took to define people – that made a Briton as different to a Frenchman as a dog was from a cat – really 'were alike to them', they belonged anywhere or nowhere. Perhaps Cook felt also that had his own life been different, had he not had friends and connections and a naval mission, he could likewise have wanted to live here.

They proceeded to Huahine. As before, those who ventured away from the ship were harassed by locals. On this occasion Cook did not overlook the 'outrages' but took them to Ori, his old friend from previous visits. The chief proposed that they undertake a punitive expedition against some men supposed to be responsible, who had formed themselves into a group of 'Banditi'. Cook was willing, perhaps because he again attributed greater structure to local political institutions than they possessed. He probably overestimated Ori's legitimate authority, and categorized as 'bandits' people who had always been independent of the chief, and who may well have resented him monopolizing contact and exchange with Cook. But Cook was again ready to get involved in local conflict. On this occasion, a party at first consisting of some forty-eight of his people, Ori and a few supporters, grew very rapidly as they marched into the interior; Mahine tried to tell Cook that many of those with them were in fact the supposed enemies, and were leading them into a trap. Cook was reluctant to believe this, but when they arrived at a deep and rocky gully, he saw that they could easily be encircled and stoned. He refused to go further. Though the excursion sounds like something of a shambles, he believed that it had caused some alarm, which he tried to reinforce by putting on a demonstration of musket fire on the beach. This was all consistent with his theory that it was vital that indigenous people always understood the superiority of European weapons. The problem here at Huahine, as he understood it, was that too many Islanders had seen officers trying incompetently to shoot birds. Most were 'but indifferent sportsmen and Miss'd generally two Shott out of three, this together with their pieces missing fire, being Slow in charging' and so forth had diminished indigenous fear before European firearms. The issue, then, was a technical one. Cook was not able or willing to entertain the idea that there might be a wider problem, in the domain of local politics, that might need to be studied and negotiated.

As before, the *Resolution* proceeded next to Raiatea. The visit coincided with a gathering of *'arioi*, marked by much festivity, many theatrical performances, more thieving, and a gratifyingly brisk trade in pork and provisions. As they were leaving this place, on 4 June, Orio

asked the name of my *Marai* (burial place) a strange quiston to ask a Seaman, however I hesitated not one moment to tell him Stepney the Parish in which I lived when in London. I was made to repeated it several times over till they could well pronounce it, then Stepney Marai no Toote was echoed through a hundred mouths at once. I afterwards found that the same question was put to Mr F[orster] by a Person a Shore but he gave a different and indeed more proper Answer by saying no man who used the Sea could tell were he would be buried.

The question was not as narrow as Cook took it to be. Orio wanted to know where Cook would be buried because he wanted to know where his land was; who his ancestors had been; he wanted to know the place that made him a person. Had this Polynesian man known Cook's circumstances, he might have expected him to answer 'Marton'; though he would have been surprised to discover that a man of Cook's consequence had no rights to gardens, animals or trees in the place of his birth; and that there were no stones that commemorated his forebears there. Polynesians did, of course, voyage, but to voyage was generally to settle and to make new *marae*

Cook did not understand himself in relation to his genealogy, either as a descendant or a founder, but he was gratified by this interest. 'What greater proof,' he wrote, 'could we have of these people Esteeming and loving us as friends whom they wishd to remember [than them wanting] to know the name of the place were our bodies were to return to dust.'

Because Cook could not promise that he would return, Mahine decided to remain at Raiatea rather than leave his land for ever. 'Just as he was going out of the Ship he ask'd me to Tattaow some Parou for him in order to Shew to any other Europeans who might touch here.' The request – that Cook 'tattoo some talk' – tells us not only that Mahine anticipated a career as a cross-cultural go-between and wanted a letter of reference, but that, even as mariners made the word 'tattoo' their own, it meant something new to Tahitians, who began to use it to refer to the art of writing. Cook was a little sad, it seems, to see the last of the young man. He had not much knowledge of religion or tradition, and was no Tupaia, but was 'Docile, Gentle and humane': a better specimen of a Society Islander, Cook thought, than Mai, who was by now God only knew where, on the *Adventure*.

Exchanges of words such as *tatau* involved appropriations of ideas rather than a flow of commodities. They did not exactly enrich either side, but they changed them, for better or worse. Both sailors and Islanders were changed because they were, in peculiar ways, open to one another. Cook had become accustomed to that openness. He celebrated it, and wrote frankly in his journal that the 'good People' of Raiatea had 'indeared' themselves to him. The *Resolution* took a course towards the west, where 'new' people would be encountered, but nothing like the same more-or-less happy mutual engagement.

The island of Niue is like a jagged coral platter. Niueans knew invasions and their myths and their society were shaped against them. When they saw a great canoe, they saw a further set of people, here to try to take their land. They were angry but not alarmed. The island was a sort of citadel. In some places you could get ashore across the coral, but it was nowhere easy to get from the shore up the coral cliffs. To reach the plateau meant struggling up a fissure here, or at best a steep valley there. The advantage lay with the defenders. They thought that the people in the great canoe had little chance of gaining the level ground, of walking among their coconuts, of finding the village of Tuapa, where houses were neatly organized around an open green, where people would feast on birds and coconut crabs. They were right. A few of the intruders landed and began to interfere with canoes. A handful of men threw stones. The intruders made noises, but got back into their boats and left.

Cook unfortunately called the place Savage Island. He sailed from here to the Tongan archipelago, this time falling in not with Eua and Tongatapu, which he had visited before, but Nomuka, further to the north, where the people and products, however, seemed much the same. Here, Tongans were troublesome. Two muskets among other things were stolen, and returned only after Cook seized two canoes. Relations became a little more cordial. A man and an older woman, who seemed to possess some seniority, brought Cook a young girl, whom they wanted him to retire with. Cook declined, as he always did, and the older woman vigorously berated him, 'I understood very little of what she said, but her actions were expressive enough, and shew'd that her words were to this effect, Sneering in my face and saying, what sort of a man are you thus to refuse the embraces of so fine a young Woman.' It was a question that remains hard to answer. Cook had a moral sense, but was not moralistic. Perhaps it is surprising that he should not have joined just about every other man on his ship in occasionally enjoying physical intimacies with women he thought attractive. Cook, however, was a literal man. Perhaps even when he was as remote from home as he was in the Pacific, he took his marriage vow as seriously as he took his superiors' instructions. But the issue was probably rather his understanding of his own authority. He liked it to remain unambiguous. He felt that control, an example and self-denial were things he had to display.

Despite the difficult character of contact at Nomuka, Cook named the island group the 'Friendly Archipelago' as they sailed away, 'from the extraordinary courteous and friendly disposition of their inhabitants'. He was convinced that, had they stayed longer, the people would have given no further trouble. His frame of mind was optimistic.

Just over two weeks later, 'Quiros's land' was sighted – or rather the islands of Maewo and Ambae, the north-east extension of the chain that is now Vanuatu. No anchorage was feasible here, but a few days later a harbour was found on the coast of the great island of Malakula. On 22 July, people came out in canoes, some ventured aboard, but an altercation occurred and shots were fired. The Islanders, frightened away by the four-pound cannon, left the ship. A little later Cook took a party ashore, to land 'in the face of about 4 or 500 Men . . . arm'd with Bows and Arrows, Clubs and spears'. So far from attacking the intruders, however, 'one Man gave his Arms to a nother and Met us in the water with a green branch in his

33. *William Hodges,* Mallicolo, *1774.*

hand, which [he] exchanged for the one I held in my hand'. This was thought
to be a token of peace, and shortly afterwards a small pig was presented to
Cook, which he hoped marked the beginning of a trade. It was probably,
however, a sacrifice, offered because Cook and his men were presumed to
be ghosts. They were repeatedly addressed as *tamar* or *tamach*, which meant
spirits in the local language. Some men splashed water over their heads as
boats approached, to ritually dispel dangerous sacredness. Others were
blackened, which was a sign of mourning, and perhaps thought appropriate
to the reappearance of the dead.

These people did allow the Europeans to cut some wood, but they had
no desire to trade. They did not actually threaten any of the mariners, but
'were very unwilling that we should go into the Country and very desireous
for us to go on board', Cook noted. The following day, he and Forster, but
no one else, were permitted to go a few yards inshore to see houses and
gardens. They landed in another part of the same bay, Cook thought by
invitation, but just five minutes later people wanted them gone.

We can be sure that the Malakulans were perplexed by their visitors. If
these white-skinned people seemed at first to be ancestors returned from the
dead, the mode of their appearance and the demands they made were not
consistent with the usual sorts of ancestral anger and power. The Europeans
were equally confounded, for different reasons. They had become accustomed to people who spoke Polynesian languages, who differed in many
small and some significant ways from one another, but who had many things
in common, such as light skin, tapa and tattoos. These islands – which Cook
would call the New Hebrides – were situated between Tonga and New

Zealand, and it would have been reasonable to expect them to be inhabited by other tribes of that great Oceanic nation. But, as Cook was surprised to remark, 'we understood not a word they said, they are quite different to all we have yet seen and Speak a different language, they are almost black or rather a dark Chocolate Colour, Slenderly made, not tall, have Monkey faces and Woolly hair'. Although George Forster thought the Malakulans quick-witted, and was impressed by the apparent density of population – always supposed to be a sign of civilization – most people agreed with Cook in considering these Islanders ugly. Forster regretted that their colour and features 'often provoked us to make an ill-natured comparison between them and monkies'.

Cook now encountered people he was unprepared for, and made a distinction that tended to bestialize these people. While his discussion was not wholly preoccupied with physique – he described Malakulan weapons and ornaments, and the elaborate wrappers that did not so much cover the penis, as make it conspicuous – he was specific about two indicators of racial distinctness, one being colour, and the other the nature of men's hair. He acknowledged that the beards of Malakulan men consisted 'rather more of hair than wool', but described their heads as 'Woolly' which was to associate them with the African peoples who were classified as 'negroes', and frequently denigrated in order to justify their enslavement. In a revision of the same passage, he made a qualified comparison explicit: 'They are rather a Diminutive Race and almost as dark as Negros, which they in some degree resemble in thier countenances, but they have not such fine features. Thier hair is short and curled, but not so soft and wooly as a Negros.' Hodges's depictions of these people are at odds with the written record. He neither gives them features which could be said to be monkey-like, nor does he seem to make them ugly. The man he has standing in a canoe, his club casually held over his shoulder, is, to the contrary, a commanding and dignified figure. It might be argued that the painter presents people in this way not because he lacks the prejudices of his shipmates, but because he has always dignified the human form. But these portraits are also naturalistic ones, that do not assimilate Malakulan bodies to standard European types. If Forster is right in claiming that those 'easily persuaded to sit for their portraits ... seemed to have an idea of the representations', the images cannot have been so idealized as to be unrecognized by the people depicted.

The *Resolution* sailed south, following the trend of the archipelago and plotting the positions of various islands within it. Cook, still in need of wood, tried to land on Erramango. People here presumed that the visitors were dangerous ghosts, whom they tried to get rid of as quickly as they could. Cook came ashore but thought that the people meant harm. His suspicion seemed justified, in so far as they seized a gangplank and oars as he re-embarked, and tried to capture his boat. He says he was 'very loath to fire upon such a multitude' and tried to shoot only the chief who seemed to be directing the operation 'but my Musquet at this critical Moment refused to perform its part'. So he ordered the boat's crew to fire. One sailor was injured by a spear and another very slightly by an arrow; one or two Erramangan men – including the chief Narom – were killed. Hasty and violent as the meeting had been, Cook had observed that 'These Islanders are a different race of people to those on Mallecollo' and that their women 'wore a kind of Petticoat made of Palm leaves'.

He called the place Traitors Head 'from the treacherous behaviour of the inhabitants'. He had forgotten the Earl of Morton's strictures, or at any rate did not feel that his own landing here was any sort of aggression that they might legitimately resist. He proceeded to the neighbouring island of Tanna, dominated by the active volcano, Yasur, that gave parts of the island a preternatural porosity. Sulphurous waters bubbled forth in one place, mud boiled at another. Nights were illuminated by explosions. The rain came laden with ash. Yet the bay that Cook called Port Resolution provided the ship with a safe and convenient anchorage. On their arrival vast numbers of Islanders came off, trafficked and pilfered. Cook responded by ordering muskets and the four-pound cannon fired, aiming to do no injury. While most people withdrew, one old man plied back and forth between ship and shore in a small canoe, bringing yams and coconuts. Cook landed, filled two water-casks, distributed presents, and received some coconuts. He found that none of the men would barter their weapons, which they rather 'held in constant readiness'. He realized that it was possible to bring the ship considerably closer to shore, and considered this desirable, not only in order to make it easier to get wood and water off, but also to 'over-awe the Natives'. The following day there were around 1,000 armed men on the beach. Cook feared an attack and fired over the group, who appeared only momentarily alarmed. 'One fellow shewed us his back side in such a manner that it was not necessary to have an interpreter to explain his meaning'; further shot were fired which in the end dispersed the people. Cook landed again, marked out lines which he indicated that the Tannese should not cross, found the same old man who made them gifts on the first day, and presented him with cloth and other things. Gradually people became a little more friendly, climbing palms and throwing down coconuts, without expecting or requiring a return. Their attitude of caution was like that of the Malakulans, though it came to be qualified over the days the *Resolution* remained at the bay.

They had no desire to acquire any of the Europeans' goods, and went so far as to bring back an axe that one seaman had accidentally left in the forest. Still, 'many of the younger sort' remained 'very daring and insolent'. They frequently challenged the marines who were keeping guard on shore. 'Insolent' was a word that Cook had used before. It was how he described the behaviour of the Maori at Poverty Bay – not a word that suggested that he wanted to understand why Islanders were 'insolent'; it was not a word that promised mutual accommodation.

Yet both the old man, whom they learned was called Paowang, and a younger one perhaps named 'Whaagou' came on to the ship, tried their food, and drank with them. If these men had begun, as the Malakulans had, by supposing that the British were ghosts, they had probably changed their minds by now. It became possible to conduct conversation of a sort. 'They gave us to understand in such a manner which admited of no doubt that they eat human flesh, they began the subject themselves by asking us if we did, otherwise we should never have asked them such a question.' If this information reinforced the negative views that many of the crew had already formed about the people of this archipelago, the people continued to become more familiar. Though they preferred the Europeans not to venture beyond the beach, they began to permit them to do so. Cook considered the part of the island that he at length saw to be 'well cultivated open and airy'. On an excursion on 14 August, he was treated with civility and encouraged to rest at one place, where people brought coconuts, plantains and sugar cane. This kindness led him to conclude not only that they were essentially 'Civil and good Natured when not prompted by jealousy to a contrary conduct' but to reflect that one could not blame them for that 'contrary conduct'. He was almost ashamed of the intransigent and aggressive turn his thinking had taken, in the aftermath of the trouble at Erramango.

. . . when one considers the light in which they must look upon us in, its impossible for them to know our real design, we enter their Ports without their daring to make opposition, we attempt to land in a peaceable manner, if this succeeds its well, if not we land nevertheless and mentain the footing we thus got by the Superiority of our fire arms, in what other light can they than at first look upon us but as invaders of their Country; time and some acquaintance with us can only convince them of their mistake.

If in this reflective mood, Cook meant that time would tell Islanders that he personally was not there to seize their lands and stay, this was reasonable. More time, however, would tell them that other men of his kind in other ships would do just that. Even in the short term, however, his expectation was naïve. If Islanders feared that Europeans meant harm, 'some acquaintance' gave them mixed messages, and would hardly convince them that they had made a simple mistake.

On Tanna, Cook's perception, and that of the Forsters, who walked further inland to collect plants, was becoming more positive, but they were in a minority among the Europeans. The officers, seamen and marines were troubled by the place and the people: the women were kept at a distance, the men were always armed, the rumbles and the smoke alarmed and irritated them. Muskets were discharged at a few boys who had merely thrown stones. Cook was 'much displeased at such a Wanton use being made of our fire arms'; he 'took measures to prevent it for the future'; what measures he does not say, but they entirely failed, for, just before the ship sailed, the marine William Wedgeborough, one of the sentries on the beach, shot a man dead. Cook was incensed. 'I who was present and on the Spot saw not the least cause for the commiting of such an outrage and was astonished beyond Measure at the inhumanity of the act, the rascal who perpetrated this crime pretended that one of the Natives laid his arrow across his bow and held it in the Attitude of Shooting so that he apprehended himself in danger, but this was no more than what was done hourly and I beleive with no other View than to let us see they were Armed as well as us'. Most of the people fled. Cook prevailed on a few to remain, sent for the surgeon, and was taken to the injured man, who soon died. He had Wedgeborough taken back to the ship, placed in irons, and brought to the gangway to be flogged. Here, however, the officers protested vigorously. After a good deal of angry debate, Cook agreed not to proceed with the punishment, but did keep the marine confined, in the end for two months. He resented this shooting, especially, because he believed that the man who had been killed was not the one who had actually made the threat.

The injustice which troubled most of those on board was not the killing of the Tannese, which Lieutenant Cooper and others considered no more than the consequence of the Islanders' 'insolence'. Elliott thought the occasion one of Cook's rare lapses – a moment when 'He lost sight, of both justice, and Humanity' in punishing a man who had merely defended himself. The officers appear to have been united in the view that the bowman's threat was real and Wedgeborough's conduct justifiable, but Cook had been an eyewitness, and merely saw an Islander level and draw his bow after Wedgeborough had pointed his gun. If Cook was correct in his belief that the wrong man had received the bullet, he was very likely also right to think that there was no real danger, since the shooting would not have prevented the arrow being fired. Cook dropped his insistence upon punishment probably not because he was convinced that the circumstance had been different, but because he learned, in the course of this heated debate, that either Clerke or the lieutenant of marines, Edgcumbe, had given orders different to his own, indeed contrary to his own, that directed the sentries to shoot if they thought themselves threatened. He cannot have liked this, but if Wedgeborough's action had this sanction, he could hardly flog the man for it.

Cook had tried to kill a man at Erramango, and failed only because his musket failed him. From his perspective, he had to try to land; if he knew this looked like invasion, for those men on the beach, if they reasonably saw it as provocation, he saw that as unavoidable. He gambled on his ability to dispel their perception. At Erramango, the bet had been bad. In most places it was a case of neither simply winning nor losing, but some mix of success and failure. Cook knew that when he reached somewhere new, as often as not, some shooting would take place. In some cases warning shots, or small shot, would pacify people to the degree he required. In others lives would be lost. Cook would try to contain and restrain violence, but knew he could not prevent it. He managed it, in his own mind, by drawing a line between what he had tried to do, at Erramango, and what Wedgeborough had succeeded in doing, at Tanna. His officers agreed that the issue was necessity, but did not see the line that he did.

The *Resolution* left Tanna, proceeded further south, and then north to extend the survey of the archipelago. A landing was made at Espiritu Santo, in the north, where the people resembled those of Malakula, and course was then shaped towards the south-west. On 4 September, an extensive land, not known before, was sighted. The following day its coast was followed, an entry found through a reef, and in due course a sandy anchorage located. Here, the people were familiar and less cautious than they had been throughout the 'New Hebrides'. They appeared without weapons, they massed about Cook's party when they landed on 6 September, but seemed curious rather than threatening. Cook noticed that women seemed not much regarded among them; one man, whom he took to be a chief, gently prevented him from giving some of them beads and medals. Speeches were made, which the Europeans could not understand. They were later shown where to get water, were permitted to walk as far as they wished. They were impressed by the intensity of agriculture and the complexity of irrigation systems. They obtained little food, but much in the way of weapons. Cook again acknowledged and disparaged this traffic:

... indeed these things generally found the best Market with us, such was the prevailing Passion for curiosities, or what appeared new. As I have had occasion to make this remark more than once before, the reader will think the Ship must be full of such articles by this time, he will be misstaken, for nothing is more Common than to give away what has been collected at one Island for any thing new at a Nother, even if it is less curious, this together with what is distroyed on board after the owners are tired with looking at them, prevents any considerable increase.

If he remained reluctant to regard native manufactures as valuable or interesting, he revealed the uncertainty of their worth. On the one hand, curiosities were simply things that appeared new; yet some new things are said to be *less curious* than the old things used to buy them. But how did one know whether a piece of tapa or a club was interesting or remarkable, or more interesting and remarkable than another? As this voyage proceeded, it must have seemed that its discoveries became less, rather than more, definite.

The lack of any linguistic competence meant that little was understood of the people at Balade. However, Cook thought they behaved with 'all the civility imaginable', though his servant was presented with a toadfish that, it transpired, was poisonous. Because George Forster was in the process of drawing the fish, he, his father and Cook ate only some of the liver and roe. Yet they woke feeling the effects around three in the morning. 'We were seized with an extraordinary weakness in all our limbs attended with a numness or Sensation like to that caused by exposeing ones hands or feet to a fire after having been pinched much by frost,' Cook wrote, 'I had almost lost the sence of feeling nor could I distinguish between light and heavy bodies that is such as I had strength the move, a quart pot full of Water and a feather was the same in my hand'; after vomiting and sweating they each recovered, and Islanders aboard the ship the following day saw the rest of the fish hanging up and 'immidiately gave us to understand it was by no means to be eat'. Cook presented men he took to be chiefs with breeding pairs of both dogs and pigs, animals until then unfamiliar to them, and 'went a shore and by Vertue of our being the first discoverers of this Country took posession of it in his Majestys name'.

Given the brevity of the visit, Cook wrote at length concerning products and appearances, describing the appearance of the country – which, where it was not cultivated, was generally barren – houses, ornaments, weapons and canoes. He noted that the women here, as at Tanna, were 'far more Chaste than those of the Eastern islands', and that, so far as he knew, none of the seamen had succeeded in obtaining 'the least favour' from them. He was unable to learn any name for the land as a whole, which was therefore called New Caledonia. Its coastline was followed to the south, and Cook would probably have proceeded back to the north to chart it fully had not a maze of coral reefs made its southern extremities very dangerous.

The *Resolution* proceeded from here to New Zealand; the ship arrived at Queen Charlotte Sound just eleven months after having left it. The people the mariners encountered were delighted to see them, but 'talked a great deal about killing which was so variously understood by us that we could gather nothing from it', Cook reported on 24 October. Repairs were made and fish were bought, as before. Some of the crew picked up stories from Maori concerning a shipwreck, a dispute between survivors and a battle between them and Maori. Cook was alarmed, thinking that this might have been the *Adventure*. He interviewed people as systematically as he could, and found they denied the report. He got one chief, whom he knew from earlier visits and called Pedro, 'into a communicative mood' and established to his satisfaction that the *Adventure* had been at Ship Cove not long after his previous departure, had remained ten or twenty days, and had not been wrecked or stranded on the coast, yet he 'did not wholly set aside our doubt of some disaster having happened to some other strangers'. On 8 November, Cook left a further sow and boar on shore. 'Its hardly possible for all the methods I have taken to stock this Country with these animals to fail,' he thought. On 9 November, he gave 'Pedro' a parting gift of an empty oil jar 'which made him happy as a prince'. He jotted down some notes on government around Totaranui. His view was that 'the head of each Tribe or family seems to be respected and that respect may on some occasions command obedience, but I doubt if they either have a right or power to enforce it'. Cook thought that he would never again see the sometimes squally, sometimes tranquil, waters of this sound, the tree ferns on the slopes around Ship Cove, nor visit his 'friends the Natives' once more. There was a gentle breeze from the west-north-west. At eight in the morning the temperature on deck was just under 60° Fahrenheit. His final thought was this: 'Notwithstanding they are *Cannibals*, they are naturaly of a good disposission and have not a little share of humanity.'

15

The Southern Hemisphere sufficiently explored

The wind veered; a penguin was sighted. The *Resolution* was a month and a week crossing a marine desert, grey dune behind grey dune. This ocean was so featureless that the discovery of a patch of seaweed counted as a remarkable occurrence. From time to time albatrosses and petrels flew about the ship, and four seals were seen in as many weeks. Yet favourable winds made the passage swift, and at times the ship made 140, 160 and even 183 miles a day. It mattered to Johann Forster, maybe to everyone, that they reached an anchorage, which meant Tierra del Fuego, for Christmas. On 17 December 1774, Desolation Island, near the Pacific entrance to the Strait of Magellan, was approached. Cook remarked that this passage from New Zealand had been the most uninteresting he had ever undertaken. Nothing apart from the variation of the compass had been worth noticing.

He did not propose to sail through the strait, but around the south of Tierra del Fuego, 'as the world has but a very imperfect knowlidge of this Coast'. Its mountainous and lifeless aspect he found peculiarly depressing. 'This is the most desolate coast I ever saw, it seems to be intirely composed of Rocky Mountains without the least appearence of Vegetation, these Mountains terminate in horroable precipices . . . hardly any thing in nature can appear with a more barren and savage aspect than the whole of this coast.' They proceeded into an overshadowed harbour that Cook considered gloomy, and called Devil's Basin. Remains of huts and fires indicated that the place was inhabited, by people who may not have considered the place so bleak and lifeless. Nor was it in fact so for the mariners, who soon found vast flocks of breeding shags and geese. On 24 December, two shooting parties were sent out, one led by Pickersgill and the other by Cook himself. It proved difficult to land through heavy surf, and still more difficult to clamber beyond the bouldery water's edge. As the men, now 'sportsmen', struggled over and around great rocks, many more geese escaped than were shot, but enough were killed in the end to 'make a distribution to the whole Crew', just in time for Christmas dinner. Though an eighteenth-century cleric wrote that the goose was 'a silly bird, too much for one and not enough for two', these seamen were delighted to share one among three. They could eat and drink 'in Plenty & could now, as their Expression is, celebrate the Feast & live *like Christians*, or as people of Sense would call it, *like Beasts*: for the little sense they have was soon lost in Liquor', wrote Johann Forster. The common sailors' approach to entertainment always attracted his censure, but on this occasion forty-eight hours' rowdiness and fighting was enough even for Cook, who put most of the men ashore, 'to recover' as George Forster put it, in the bracing open air.

In the midst of this disorder and revelry, some twenty Fuegians came off to the ship in four canoes. Cook thought they were 'of the same nation' as those he had encountered six years earlier in Success Bay, though they were in fact a different group, the Yaghan. Cook's repugnance in the face of the landscape carried over to these people, whom he regarded as 'a little ugly half starved beardless Race'. He noted that the women 'cover their privities with a flap of Seal skin' but were otherwise dressed just like the men in sealskin capes. He observed that small children at the breast were naked, 'thus they are inured from their infancy to Cold and hardships'. He saw bone harpoons that he assumed were used to kill seals and possibly whales. He said that the people stank. This was not an occasion for the sort of reflection that George Forster often, and Cook occasionally, engaged in, on the variety of human customs and ideas of taste. It was not an occasion to consider how effectively the oil that caused the odour ameliorated the cold. These oiled bodies were repulsive and that was that.

Johann Forster differed from Cook on points of detail. If he was right, the Yaghan men did have beards, 'thin & cut short'. He recorded more about their ornaments and weapons, and collected one of the sealskin capes, a spear, and a shell necklace. But he responded to the people in the same way. He blamed them for his failure to obtain words in their language; 'though I pointed to many things, in order to get the Names of them, they seemed to be too stupid for the signs'. His judgement echoed Cook's 1768 verdict upon the Haush: 'They . . . seemed to be the most wretched & dirty of all human beings I ever saw in my Life.'

Throughout the Pacific, the *Resolution*'s second and subsequent visits to people – to the Maori, the Society Islanders, and the Tongans – fostered more nuanced senses of their dispositions, beliefs and institutions. Cook was now visiting Fuegians for the second time. On a different occasion, I imagine, he might have noted that these families belonged not to the same, but to an evidently related 'nation'. He might have exhibited interest in the contrast between their canoe-based fishing and the shore-based foraging of the Haush. But there was no accumulation of knowledge, no deeper insight. It is, at first sight, not easy to reconcile this attitude with the same man's observations on indigenous Australians. Both peoples were fisher-gatherers, both had limited material possessions, yet one attracted Cook's admiration and the other his antipathy. The discrepancy may be easier to understand if we recall that he approved of the consonance between clothing and climate around the Endeavour River. In such a warm place, the people possessed as much as, and no more than, they needed. At the southern extremity of America, on the rim of the Devil's Basin, so-called, the people seemed to need a great deal more than, they possessed. Their want of better garments and shelter made them desperately miserable, Cook and Forster thought; they were somehow too ignorant or indolent to better protect themselves.

No doubt, indigenous life along this coast was tougher – objectively – than it was in tropical Australia. But these explorers were oddly unwilling to put two and two together. They had just caught more good eating birds in a day than they'd got anywhere else in the course of the voyage, but did not reflect that this environment was in fact rich. Perhaps these 'miserable' people ate geese a lot more often than the average sailor or the average Briton did. Maybe they were not miserable at all. But neither Cook, nor either of the Forsters, could countenance this. However far they had been able to go, in grasping the non-European values and preoccupation of some Pacific Islanders, an understanding of the lives and self-perceptions of Fuegians meant going rather further. It meant seeing bodies and faces differently. It meant not being bothered by oil. It was out of their reach.

On approaching Tierra del Fuego, Cook wrote that he had 'done with the SOUTHERN PACIFIC OCEAN, and flatter my self that no one will think that I have left it unexplor'd'. Still, he was mindful that, though discussion of the southern continent had focused upon the south Pacific, there were tracts of the south Atlantic that had not been exhaustively investigated. As recently as 1769, Dalrymple had republished a sixteenth-century chart marking a 'Gulf of St Sebastian', a great indentation into a southern land, in the mid Atlantic east of Tierra del Fuego. Cook's crew were exhausted, but the existence of this and other rumoured lands remained to be established.

On 9 January, as the ship cruised into this hypothetical gulf, Johann Forster reported that most 'dread to fall in with Land, for fear that this might retard our early arrival at the Cape'. He was not concerned himself: on the one hand a new land would mean new plants, birds and fish. On the other, the brandy was running out, and he was confident that whatever Cook would do, he would not cruise for longer than the liquor lasted. By

13 January, the imagined coast of the Gulf had been sailed through; but a day later something was seen ahead. Some bet ten to one that it was ice, others five to one that it was land. In due course it became apparent that the latter were right. Seas were high, it was miserably cold, 'the Snow makes the Air thick, we cannot see ten yards before us', wrote Forster, who would have been delighted to have left the exploration of these places to another time and ship altogether. The pathetic thought crossed his mind that 'If a Capt, some Officers & a Crew were convicted of some heinous crimes, they ought to be sent by way of punishment to these inhospitable cursed Regions, for to explore & survey them.' He is unlikely to have been the only one aboard who, by now, was regarding the business of discovery as a degrading ordeal rather than an honour.

The country before them was unprepossessing, high, wild, rocky and frozen. Remember that it was midsummer: but 'the head of the Bay, as well as two places on each side, was terminated by a huge Mass of Snow and ice of vast extent . . . Not a tree or shrub was to be seen, no not even big enough to make a tooth-pick,' Cook wrote, though he landed, displayed the flag, and took possession. On 20 January, they sailed along the north, then around the eastern end of this land, which they saw then turned back to the west; it was hence no more than an island. Cook wrote that though he 'still had hopes of discovering a Continent' 'I must Confess the disappointment I now met with did not affect me much, for to judge of the bulk by the sample, it would not be worth the discovery.' He named the place South Georgia, and continued to sail to the east, encountering some small rocky islets and then a further land, which the voyagers considered still more awful. Cook thought its aspect that of 'the most horrible Coast in the World'. Clerke wrote that it was 'as wretched a Country as Nature can possibly form – the shores are formed of rocky and Icy Cliffs and precipices – we've not yet seen a Hole we cou'd shove a Boat in, much less the Ship . . . we see Mountains of immense bulk and height . . . totally cover'd with Snow as is the whole face of the Country throughout'.

Several people were ill with colds and rheumatism, Johann Forster noted on 30 January; but Cook continued to sail to the east for a further three weeks, in search of the 'Cape Circumcision' (named after the Catholic holy day) that de Lozier Bouvet thought he had discovered in 1739. Bouvet had mischarted the island that he had in fact found, which Cook was hence unable to relocate. Finally, on 21 February, the commander resolved 'to steer for the Cape of Good Hope'. His statement came at the end of a lengthy journal entry that took stock of his findings, and reflected on a host of questions of geography and exploratory method, ranging from the use of seabirds as signs of land, to the nature of ice. The theory of how ice was formed was vital, because the prevalent but incorrect view was that seawater could not freeze. (Melting sea-ice produced fresh water; people therefore understandably assumed that it was frozen fresh water, though it was just being established experimentally that the salt was precipitated out of salt water as it froze.) From this misapprehension, it was conjectured that ice had to break away from some coast and masses of ice meant that land lay somewhere behind them. The reasoning was spurious, but Cook was led to the correct conclusion, that there was in fact a southern land, albeit one near the pole that was inaccessible, virtually lifeless and uninhabitable. It was hardly the temperate, rich and potentially populated continent that de Brosses and Dalrymple had in mind. Observing that he had proven, quite conclusively, that no accessible continent existed, and had also 'settled the situation of some old discoveries [and made] many new ones' in the tropical Pacific, Cook summarized his accomplishment:

I flater my self that the intention of the Voyage has in every respect been fully Answered, the Southern Hemisphere sufficiently explored and a final end put to the searching after a Southern Continent, which has at times ingrossed the attention of some of the Maritime Powers for near two Centuries past and the Geographers of all ages . . .

This man is under no modest illusion concerning the monumentality of his findings. On the most important issue they are negative. They may be disappointing, but they are *complete*. They bring a history to an end. It is no surprise to find their author restating the claim that he had made just over a year before. 'I can be bold to say, that no man will ever venture farther than I have done and that the lands which may lie to the South will never be explored.' Repeating that the far southern lands were inexpressibly horrid, the climatic conditions appalling, and the navigation acutely danger-ous, he concluded drily, 'after such an explanation as this the reader of this Journal will hardly expect to find me much farther to South'.

In his 21 February entry Cook conceded that 'We had been a long time without refreshments, our Provisions were in a state of decay and little more nourishment remained in them than just to keep life and soul together.' As was his custom, he reiterated that his crew 'would cheerfully have gone wherever I thought proper to lead them', which was less true than ever. Yet the rosy distortion enabled him to say that abandoning exploration at this point was an act of indulgence that their good behaviour merited. It also happened to be an act necessitated by the fact that the ship was falling apart. 'Some thing was giving way every hour and we had nothing left either to repair or replace them.'

The winds were not favourable. The *Resolution* was obliged to sail north-east and tack back. On 2 March they changed direction. People hoped to see the Cape in a few days, but conditions kept changing. On 11 March Johann Forster wrote that spirits and expectations had fallen, 'All the Effects of the foul Wind! How difficult it is to bear disappointment with any degree of philosophical temper.' The following day it was quite calm. The frustration must have been acute. Forster expected letters at the Cape and became increasingly anxious and apprehensive that family, friends or patrons might have died during his three years away. 'Those therefore who send people out upon such a long Expedition do not think, that we lose so many valuable connexions in Life. I am no more young, if I should be unfortunate enough to have lost in my Absence my best Friends & Patrons I must begin life as if it were again . . .' At this moment, the scientist was utterly depressed by the protracted, cold and tedious southern cruise, which had given Cook a place in history and himself scarcely a specimen or an observation of interest. He was exercised by what he could have done in London. He could have secured supporters, published more, and perhaps obtained an appointment at the British Museum. The voyage, he thought miserably, had meant great loss for little gain.

On 16 March 1775, a Dutch ship, 'a homewardbound Indiaman' was sighted and lost sight of. Other than the *Adventure*, this was the first European vessel that those on the *Resolution* had had any contact with since late November 1772. Two days later, this vessel was within view again. Though still some six miles away, 'we were too impatient after News to regard the distance'. Boats were sent from the *Resolution*, which returned in due course with the report that, as Forster put it, 'every where there was universal peace' – he meant no war in Europe. Gratifying as this information no doubt was, Cook was more concerned by the report, from English sailors aboard the Dutch ship, 'that the Adventure arrived at the Cape of Good Hope Twelve Months ago and that one of her boats crew had been Murdered and eat by the People of New Zealand'.

This, Cook now understood, was what lay behind the 'talk of killing', behind the stories that had been told, denied and repeated by the Maori around Totaranui. He would not obtain any fuller account until he was back in London. What had happened, from the perspective of those aboard the *Adventure*, was this. After the ships had been separated, the top-heavy consort tried and failed for several days to get to the south of Cape Palliser to enter Cook Strait and then Queen Charlotte Sound. In the end Furneaux had decided to bear away for Tolaga Bay on the North Island, that he knew, from the reports of Cook's first voyage, to be a convenient anchorage. There they rested until the gales subsided. They obtained water and wood, made repairs, and then sailed laboriously southward, reaching Ship Cove just six days after the *Resolution* had departed. They repaired casks, sought further wood and water, and saw a good deal of local Maori, who were occasionally aggressive. On 16 December 1773 they were all but ready to depart. William Bayly, the astronomer, had got his tent and instruments on board. The next morning, a boat was sent to Grass Cove, named after the greens which helped prevent scurvy that had been gathered there before. This boat was commanded by one John Rowe, Jack to his friends, a cousin of Furneaux's by marriage, from a Cornwall family connected also to Samuel Wallis, who had taken the *Dolphin* round the world. If we wanted to know who Rowe was, in Maori terms, and demanded to know his *whakapapa*, we'd understand his genealogy, not only as a naval, but as a distinctly exploratory one. Either despite or because of this, he was impetuous. He'd spent time in north America, and was confident that he knew how to deal with native peoples, which for him meant forcefully. At Tolaga Bay, confronted by a numerous and hostile crowd, he'd wanted to take a couple of Maori captive to secure the return of a stolen cask of liquor. The view of others present was that this would have been stupidly dangerous, the risk more than the grog was worth.

Rowe's boat was expected back by three in the afternoon, on 17 December. It did not appear and still had not done so the following morning. Lieutenant James Burney took the launch out to search. It was thought that some accident might have happened around the rocks, so he took a sheet of tin to make a temporary repair. He followed the shore of the sound inland, looking into every bay as they proceeded. They had lunch and paused at a Maori settlement, where they searched some canoes and houses, finding nothing suspicious. He proceeded further and met more Maori, who were friendly and traded some fish. Further inlets were investigated, but no boat, and no canoes or inhabitants, were sighted. By mid afternoon the party reached a small beach by Grass Cove. Here, a large double canoe was hauled up. On sighting the Europeans, two men near it ran into the brush. Burney and his marines came ashore, thinking something had gone on here, but with no inkling of what they would find. At first all they saw were some shoes, which had recently been issued to Woodhouse, one of the midshipmen, and 'one of the Rullock ports of the Cutter'. But then

One of the people at the same time brought me a piece of meat, which he took to be some Salt Meat belonging to the Cutter's Crew – on examining this & smelling to it I found it was fresh meat – Mʳ Fannin, (the Master) who was with me, supos'd it was Dog's flesh & I was of the same opinion, for I still doubted their being Cannibals: but we were Soon convinced by most horrid & undeniable proofs – a great many baskets (about 20) laying on the beach tied up, we cut them open, some were full of roasted flesh & some of fern root which serves them for bread – on further search we found more shoes & a hand which we immediately knew to have belonged to Thoˢ Hill one of our Forecastlemen, it being marked T.H. which he had got done at Otaheite with a tattow instrument.

Burney found a place where it seemed that something had been buried. He began to dig awkwardly with a sword, but then realized that some people had lit a considerable fire in the next bay. He abandoned the excavation of what may well have been an earth oven, got everyone back into the boat, and made way into Grass Cove itself. There were many people on the beach, and the hill above 'thronged like a Fair'. As they approached the shore they began firing. The Maori on the hill dared them to advance, but then ran off, some injured by shot. Burney then landed, found bundles of 'Cellery' that Rowe's party had gathered, and a broken oar but no boat. What he did find was so literally unspeakable that he was unable to describe it at all, even in his report to Furneaux.

We found no boat – but instead of her – Such a shocking scene of Carnage & Barbarity as can never be mentiond or thought of, but with horror. – whilst we remained almost stupified on this spot, Mr Fannin call'd to us that he heard the Savages gathering together in the Valley . . .

As it became dark, Burney's party withdrew. They destroyed several canoes on the beach, and fired a volley in the direction of the Maori, but he and Fannin judged that there would be 'poor Satisfaction' in killing 'some of the Savages'. Or, as Burney rephrased it, he considered it not 'worth while to proceed where nothing could be hoped for but revenge'. As they rowed away, 'we imagined we heard somebody calling'. They rested their oars, listened, but heard no more. They shouted 'but to little purpose the poor Souls were far enough out of hearing – & indeed I think it some comfort to reflect that in all probability every man of them must have been killd on the Spot', Burney wrote. They did not get back to the *Adventure* until almost midnight. If those on board suspected no more than some minor mishap, their anxiety had no doubt mounted while the launch was away. Furneaux can only have been doubly devastated, by the killing of the men and of his kinsman in particular, but was not much of a writer and communicated nothing of his feeling, beyond noting that Burney returned 'with the melancholy news' of the loss of the boat and her crew. He must have accepted Burney's judgement that the massacre was unlikely to have arisen 'from any premeditated plan'. The most compelling evidence for this was that people from Grass Cove had met Rowe on his way into the sound, and then spent the morning near the *Adventure*, in Ship Cove. Had they any inkling of events that might have provoked reprisals, they would hardly have exposed themselves so directly to the ship's cannons. In any case, Furneaux undertook no punitive raid. He seems not to have seriously considered doing so, and to have been satisfied that there was 'not the least probability' of any member of Rowe's party remaining alive. For Burney, the twilit discovery of the indescribable residue of the fight was permanently traumatic. The private voyage memoir he kept for his family and friends alluded only cursorily to the tragedy. At home, he spoke of it only in a whisper.

Off the Cape on 18 March 1775, Cook learned the barest essentials of what had occurred, and wrote, 'I shall make no reflections on this Melancholy affair untill I hear more about it. I must however observe in favour of the New Zealanders that I have allways found them of a Brave, Noble, Open and benevolent disposition, but they are a people that will never put up with an insult if they have an oppertunity to resent it.' He was using 'resent' in an eighteenth-century sense, meaning 'to revenge it'. Precisely what the Maori would not do would be to harbour resentment, without acting upon it.

The news may not have come as a complete shock. When Cook left Queen Charlotte Sound, he said he was satisfied that the rumours of shipwreck and killing did not concern the *Adventure*, but must have continued to suppose that they had some substance, that they must have arisen from some violence between some mariners and the Maori. If he was prepared for the report by a nagging doubt, he must nevertheless have been stunned by it. Europeans including the first circumnavigator, Magellan, had been killed by Pacific Islanders before, but nothing like this had happened in the course of recent discoveries, so far as Cook was aware. He did not yet know that just before his second voyage had departed England, the French navigator Marion du Fresne and nearly thirty of his crew had also been killed by Maori. He would meet Marion's second in command a few days later, and discuss the sorry details with him. But at the time he heard of the Grass Cove killings, they seemed unprecedented.

In response to the news, Cook expresses no anger or antipathy towards the perpetrators. He is not prompted to go back to the incidents of hostility that marked his earliest meetings with them and cite these as instances of a characteristic belligerence. He does not complain about the aggressive qualities of their warrior ethos. He does not begin calling them 'savages', as even the liberal and literate Burney does; still less does he fulminate about the wickedness of cannibalism. His first reaction is instead to remind his reader that the qualities of these people are essentially good. Despite his statement that he will wait on fuller information before reflecting upon the tragedy, he is immediately concerned to excuse and explain away the event – and he does so with some perspicacity, since evidence obtained later indicated that it was precisely an 'insult' on the part of the impetuous Rowe that provoked the violence.

Cook's comment was consistent with his personality and thought, as it had been shaped by the first voyage, and as it had evolved over the course of the second. His understanding that Maori cannibalism was 'customary' was peculiarly important to him. This proposition dissociated people he liked from a particular practice that repelled him. If the practice was a 'custom', that meant that it was a national habit, necessarily something that people would be attached to, and would not relinquish easily, but that provided no guide to their 'disposition'. Cook claimed he knew their disposition, and he was sure that it had nothing savage about it. Hence, whenever he mentioned Maori cannibalism, he added the sort of qualification we notice here. He insisted that it was a fact, but was equally insistent that the people were good. 'Nevertheless I think them a good sort of people', was how he put it when he wrote to John Walker, soon after his return to London.

Cook's response to the Grass Cove report was consistent with the way he acted and wrote in another sense. During his second voyage, he had been entirely capable of being angered by native behaviour, and of resorting to violence, when he was affronted, or when he saw his expedition prejudiced. Yet, when Pacific Islanders made trouble, not for himself personally or for himself as commander, but for others of the ship's company, he exhibited an increasing propensity to disregard supposed mischief, or to take the side of the Islanders. Cook did this at Huahine and Raiatea, not overly bothered that he mortally offended Johann Forster. He did it most divisively at Tanna; he did it in smaller ways at many other places. He had a realistic sense of the deep harm that 'civilized Christians' did to native peoples, but nevertheless got on with his job. His shift in loyalty was a more singular mutation. It was a partial withdrawal from the responsibility that he sustained over 'his people', his officers and crew. It implied an alienation from the people he shared an unusually confined space, but perhaps little intimacy, with. It suggested a romance of adoptive kinship with indigenous aristocrats, a real regard for independent warriors and a subtle, perhaps a contrived, sense of cross-cultural justice. His allegiance was, in the end, neither to mariners nor Maori, but to the line that he alone charted, between just and unjust violence, between punishment and outrage.

On 21 March Cook went ashore at Cape Town. He waited upon the Dutch governor, found a letter from Furneaux (which does not appear to have survived) and arranged supplies of fresh bread, meat, greens and wine. Extensive repairs were made, and the ship's rigging almost completely replaced. Officers and sailors enjoyed themselves. 'It was no uncommon thing,' Elliott wrote, 'in our Rides in the Coutry, to see three of the Sailors on a Horse, in full sail, and well filld with grog.' Five weeks later, when they departed in the company of a Danish frigate and an English East India company ship, they were saluted and music was played in Cook's honour. He was not yet home, but the range and reach of his voyage were becoming known to a public. He was on the cusp of fame.

And, he feared, of notoriety. On 16 May he arrived at St Helena, where he, the Forsters and other gentlemen were liberally entertained by the governor and others of the English establishment. At the Cape, Cook had seen and read Hawkesworth's *Account* for the first time, and found it 'mortifying'. 'I never had the perusal of the Manuscript nor did I ever hear the whole of it read in the mode it was written, notwithstanding what Dr Hawkesworth has said to the Contrary in the Interduction,' he complained. This was bad enough, but he had not reckoned on the book having reached St Helena, nor on it having 'given offence to all the principle Inhabitents' there. They were angered by a passage on their treatment of slaves, and the suggestion that they were too stupid to make use of carts or wheelbarrows – observations that Hawkesworth extracted from Banks's journal. The residents of St Helena did not content themselves with spirited verbal objections, they also, according to George Forster, 'studiously placed' carts and wheelbarrows 'before captain Cook's lodgings every day', embarrassing him to such an extent that he not only attested to the use of wheeled vehicles on the island, but wrote about *how well* the slaves were in fact treated before embarking on remarks that celebrated, as effusively as he ever did, the gentility, civility, neatness and good order of the place.

Here, Cook had to think of his place in society rather than in history. Coincidentally, the governor, John Skottowe, was the son of the Yorkshire gentleman for whom Cook's father had worked; his family had owned the

Great Ayton farm on which Cook's parents, and Cook himself, had lived. The profoundly stratified social order into which Cook had been born, and which had shaped him as a child, suddenly reappeared in the time of his mature accomplishment. He encountered a man who might at times have been physically proximate, but socially remote. A young Cook might have got off a path hastily, out of Skottowe's way, as he rode past. Cook would have remembered Skottowe; Skottowe would have had little reason ever to know Cook, let alone to remember him. Cook had no problem about who he was and where he came from, but he wanted his status measured by what he'd become, not where he'd started. Yet he was deferential before social superiors and his considerable ambition was discreetly channelled. When he wrote that he was mortified, he meant it. He was instinctively apologetic, not because factual mistakes had been made. Maybe they had not been with respect to the treatment of slaves, maybe he did not even think that they had been. He regretted the report as published, because of who it offended. Proprieties made his world work; he was careful to acknowledge them; they had been violated.

During the voyage, and well before these events, Cook's ambition had turned from geographic to literary accomplishments. He never says so in so many words, but his greater attention to his writing, his redrafting, his expansion, his reflection, and his address to his reader, say so again and again. He revisited the ugly incident at Tanna. The killer, Wedgeborough, had since fallen overboard and drowned, but Cook did not regard this as reason for letting the matter drop. To the contrary, he was concerned to describe it more fully, and make his case for the injustice of the action incontestable. Whereas he had initially written merely that 'unfortunately one of [the natives] was Shott by one of our Centinals, I who was present and on the Spot saw not the least cause for the committing of such an outrage', he now explained the context and the succession of events as minutely as he could. He returned to the landing-place, he attested,

just as our people were geting some large logs into the boat; At the same time four or five of the Natives steped forward to see what we were about, and as we did not allow them to come within certain limmits unless it was to pass along the beach, the sentery ordered them back, which they readily complied with. At this time I had my eyes fixed on them and observed the sentery present his piece (as I thought at the men) and was just going to reprove him for it, because I had observed that when ever this was done, some or another of the Natives would hold up their arms, to let us see that they were as ready as us, but I was astonished beyond measure when the sentry fired for I saw not the least cause ... The rascal who perpetrated this crime, pretended that a Man had laid an arrow a Cross his bow and was going to shoot it at him, so that he apprehended himself in danger, but this was no more than what they had always done, and I believe with no other view than to shew they were armed as well as us, at least I have reason to think so, as they never went further.

Concerned about the management of conflict throughout the voyage, Cook was now concerned about it in a new way. He had read Hawkesworth's introduction, with its reflections on violence; whatever he made of it, he saw that incidents of this kind would be closely scrutinized; people who had not been on his voyage would discuss thefts and landings and shootings and death in coffee houses and over dinners. He wanted it understood that some people had been shot because he considered it unavoidable, some had been shot because his orders had, in the heat of the moment, been misunderstood, and one had been killed by a 'rascal' who had acted contrary both to his order and to natural justice. Cook would not obscure the crime but would make it public and censure it. He knew that he was representing not only his voyage, but his own conduct and character. He would be what he wrote: a dedicated discoverer, a thorough and consistent one, a man who would leave no room for doubt, and no tract of ocean unexplored – he would be all that, but he would also be humane. This is not to say that Cook invented a humanity or a conscience that he did not in fact possess. He did have humane impulses, which he sometimes acted upon, and at other times forgot or suppressed. But these impulses, and his actions, were raw happenings; how they were selected, shaped and valued in a narrative of the voyage was another matter altogether. Cook knew his choice: he would announce his humanity, he would make out of it a fact that would be as distinct as his track around the southern ocean.

On 29 July 1775, the *Resolution* sighted the coast near Plymouth, 'Having been absent from England Three Years and Eighteen Days,' Cook noted. Clerke lost no time writing to Banks, 'in a very few Hours we shall anchor at Spithead from our Continent hunting expedition'. He did not give him particulars but hoped to visit him soon, to tell all, to present him with the curiosities he'd obtained. The lieutenant plainly cared not only about Banks's patronage, but also about Banks. 'God bless you send me one Line just to tell me you're alive and well, if that is the case ... you know I never despair, but always look for the best, therefore hope and flatter myself this will find you alive and happy, which that it may, is the sincerest Hope and Wish Dear Sir Yours Gratefully Oblig'd & most H:ble Serv' Cha' Clerke. – Excuse the Paper, its gilt I assure you, but the Cockroaches have piss'd upon it.'

16

Now I am going to be confined

In 1771, the avid journalistic interest in the *Endeavour*'s return from the Pacific had owed much to Banks's participation and to his ambitions. No one on the second voyage had anything like his status or his singular self-publicizing abilities. Hence the press coverage of the return of the *Adventure* in July of 1774, and of the *Resolution* just over a year later, was sparse. London was, in any case, preoccupied with, confused and divided by the grim news of the outbreak of war in America – the beginnings of what would become the War of Independence. But a few reports of Cook's return did appear. One published in *Lloyds Evening Post* was short and scrambled but significant:

We hear by Capt. Cooke, who is arrived in town from his long voyage round the world, that they discovered in 71.30 [i.e. 71°30 S] an amazing face of perpendicular rock, with a large chain of country; but the ice was so thick, the weather so inclement, and the sea so very high, that they could not land. They also called again at New Zealand, where the Savages treated them with civility, attention, and hospitality; and they clearly informed them of murdering their people before, and having eaten them. The reason they assigned was, because they had killed, unprovoked, some of their people.

We would not usually attach any weight to a journalist's claim to have a story direct from the commander of an enterprise, but the item does start by singling out what was certainly the great moment of the voyage, from Cook's point of view: the moment that prompted him to announce his own heroism in having gone as far as it was possible for man to go. Oddly, while the latitude the *Resolution* reached is reported correctly, the newspaper muddled matters, suggesting that the ship found a landmass, rather than simply a wall of ice. But it is the rest that can only have derived from conversation with Cook himself. He was his own spin doctor, and he put it the way he habitually put it: he celebrated the civility of the Maori first, and acknowledged their warrior violence second. He again excused the Grass Cove killings, sure that provocation must have come from the European side. Furneaux and others on the *Adventure* concluded that the massacre had not been planned, but Cook alone was certain that it had been sparked off by some British aggression or over-reaction. Though subsequent inquiries proved him right, this view was, in 1775, no more than an informed guess. The newspaper was anticipating a Maori explanation that had not yet been provided. It was also presenting an understanding of the event that must have looked idiosyncratic, blaming an outrage upon its British victims. The following month, the line was restated in the *London Magazine*, where a commentator added, 'and indeed no people, if not properly restrained by their officers, are more wanton in their wickedness than the English sailors'.

For those who'd sailed on the *Adventure*, this view of the incident may have been provocative. Some may have seen it as an insult to their friends' memories. An account, perhaps deliberately intended as a rejoinder, appeared in another paper. It claimed to be an extract from the journal of one of the men who accompanied Burney. The level of detail suggests that it was in fact drawn from a log or journal written soon after the events, though it corresponds with none of the known *Adventure* manuscripts. This telling is distinguished by its animosity toward the 'cruel barbarians' who perpetrated the massacre, who were very justly fired upon. The British aimed 'to kill as many of them as our guns could reach', and the writer was satisfied that 'many' were wounded 'and some killed'. The report fully revealed the horror of the scene that Burney had been unable to describe. Those who advanced inland 'beheld the most horrible sight that ever was seen by any European; the heads, hearts, liver and lights, of three or four of our people broiling on the fire'; a few yards away they encountered bowels and mangled limbs. Furneaux's journal suggests that it was the discovery of the men's 'intrails' lying on or near the beach that Burney found so numbingly shocking. The claim that these were actually in the process of being cooked must have been concocted for or by the newspaper. Whereas Burney left the scene despondent, and resigned to the uselessness of revenge, this printed account airs resolute anger. It does not raise the question of why the killings might have occurred, excluding the possibility that the evil extravagance of cannibalism could be somehow explained, let alone excused.

Those in London in 1775 who cared to think about the people of the South Pacific were presented with startlingly inconsistent notions. The 'savages' of New Zealand were on one assessment civil and hospitable; on another they were capable of indescribable cruelty.

In the meantime many ladies and gentlemen around town had encountered another sort of Islander in the person of 'Omai' or 'Omiah'. In so far as this man figures in the letters and publications of the period, he is less the Raiatean Mai than a sort of walking projection of English fantasies. One early report celebrated his will to travel in search of knowledge about other lands, as if he were a native counterpart to Cook or Banks, but the tenor of comment changed quickly. Ironically, this was precisely because Mai was taken charge of by Banks, but associated with the morally dubious rather than the praiseworthy aspects of the natural historian's persona. Banks lost no time in presenting Mai to the King. The widely reported encounter ensured that the exotic visitor was quickly absorbed in a whirl of fashionable engagements. Though Cook and the Forsters had thought him foolish and a poor specimen of a Society Islander, others considered Mai intelligent, or at least remarkably well-mannered. His pleasant company was cited by Fanny Burney (James's sister, later renowned for her novels), among others. But most people were patronizing: at best, Mai represented a diverting amusement. Or they were censorious because they were censorious of Banks – who had been and was still the target of much satire. Given that he was indeed promiscuous, and that botany was commonly regarded as a sexy hobby more than a field of serious inquiry, he was a front-runner among candidates for prurient parody; and it is not surprising that this extended to criticism of the idle entertainment provided to Mai, who joined his rakish circle, was taught to play cards, kiss a lady's handkerchief, and take a fancy, supposedly, to trivial and useless curiosities. He was represented as the priest of a cult, which he was not. He was painted, several times. One of the paintings was printed, on large paper appropriate to a drawing-room wall. He was paraded. When Mai prepared later to return to the Pacific, George Forster among others lamented that he had not been taught useful, mechanical arts that would have helped improve the lives of Polynesians: the implication was that he would have been more appropriately adopted by a middle-class tradesman than by a macaroni like Banks.

Yet Mai in fact had a clear idea of what he could usefully take home. The moment he was introduced to George III, he promptly hailed him as King of England, Tahiti, Raiatea and Borabora. He explained that he had come 'here for Gunpowder to destroy the Inhabitants of Bola Bola, who are our Enemies'. He was inaugurating a tradition: Islanders from all over the Pacific would, during the course of the nineteenth century, seek powerful allies and arms in Sydney, Honolulu, San Francisco and just about anywhere else they could reach. They were occasionally lethally successful, in obtaining them, and changing the balance of power back home. This is less striking than the

34. *Francesco Bartolozzi after Nathaniel Dance*, Omai,
a Native of Ulaietea, *1774, engraving.*

fact that Mai understood that the British assumed sovereignty over the
islands that he and his ancestors had occupied for generations. He must
have known that this was a nonsense so far as Polynesian social and political
realities were concerned. There could have been no question in his mind

that the *ari'i* retained their glorious feather sashes and the pre-eminence that possession of those objects proved. And he knew that Cook had mostly behaved and been treated as an honoured guest, albeit one who committed occasional outrages when he was trying to recover property. Yet Cook had never pretended to own the islands, and never acted as though he represented a foreign chief who claimed to do so. So, what Mai grasped was not only the claim, but the point that it meant nothing in Polynesia, for either the inhabitants or the British, but perhaps something in London. In any case, he capitalized on it whenever anyone would listen, repeating his hope to engage in a war of liberation. Though we know him now above all as the dusky prince of Reynolds's and Dance's portraits, he was (needless to say) never exotic in his own eyes. He was as ordinary as anyone who harboured a national grievance.

If Cook's return was not much noticed by the press, it aroused a good deal of excitement in other circles. Lord Sandwich cut short a yacht cruise, visited the *Resolution*, announced promotions and gave the officers dinner. Cook was promoted to post-captain and to a sinecure at Greenwich Hospital. One journalist cited this honour as an instance of Sandwich's corruption: 'some men in power leap over all rules and institutions; and dispose of places according to the pulse of interest, and the complexion of the times'. Later in the year Cook was put up for election to the Royal Society. The nomination form, signed usually by only a few Fellows, was endorsed by twenty-five, including Banks, Solander, Maskelyne and Forster, among a spectrum of astronomers, architects, physicians and natural historians. They included the anatomist John Hunter, who purchased from Pickersgill – perhaps through Cook or more likely Banks – the head from Queen Charlotte Sound that had starred in the cannibal experiment staged some two years earlier. Cook saw a good deal of these scientists. He prepared a paper on the health of seamen for the Society. He was invited to dine by its president, Sir John Pringle. He sat for the Nathaniel Dance portrait that Banks had commissioned. His status had changed after his first voyage, but it was now enhanced further. His naval rank was elevated, he was on good and easy terms with his most powerful superiors, and he was a respected member of a scientific and social elite. But unlike his fellow-explorer Constantine Phipps, he was not of that elite. Unlike the next generation's naval hero, Nelson, he had no wish to cut a flamboyant figure within it. Cook preferred the modest respectability but absolute unfashionability of Mile End, where he resumed domestic life; where I guess he enjoyed his wife's company, where he let the prospect of retirement, like a navigational problem, nag at him. He wrote to John Walker in Whitby, 'my fate drives me from one extream to a nother a few Months ago the whole Southern hemisphere was hardly big enough for me and now I am going to be confined within the limits of Greenwich Hospital, which are far too small for an active mind like mine'.

At the time he wrote – August, 1775 – a further voyage was already anticipated. It was presumed that Mai had to be taken home, but the expedition would have far broader ambition. Its conception, in several senses, reflected that of the second voyage, in that it aimed to resolve an equally long-standing geographic question, to potentially spectacular commercial advantage. Trade with Chinese ports was of considerable and growing importance to the eighteenth-century European economy; yet east Asia could be reached only via a slow, often fatally unhealthy passage around southern Africa and across the Indian ocean. It had long been imagined that a northern route from the Atlantic and Pacific was there to be found, which would enable quicker voyages and a more profitable trade. By the 1770s, some fifty voyages had at one time or another set off to search north American coasts for this North-West Passage, but the moment was one of renewed optimism, in both England and France.

Forster's patron, Daines Barrington, was one of those who was preoccupied. His confidence hinged on the tenet that seawater did not freeze. If ice was therefore found mainly around river entrances, on the northern coasts of America and Asia, it ought to be possible to sail across the pole and into the north Pacific, tending either west over America or east over Asia. Barrington set aside other pressing concerns – which ranged from the observation of trout in Wales to early English legal history – to publish his *Probability of Reaching the North Pole Discussed*, in 1775. He talked up the subject in coffee shops, and even in Parliament – which voted a handsome prize to the discoverer of any passage. He was not unduly bothered that the theory had already been tested by Phipps in 1773, who had reached Spitsbergen and some 80° north, but whose ships had been very nearly trapped in advancing ice. If that did not augur well for any new attempt from the north Atlantic, a map hot off the press admittedly suggested that a search for a passage from the Pacific side could very well succeed. Russian colonists and traders had been increasingly active in Siberia, around the peninsula of Kamchatka, and in the north Pacific. An essay and chart published in Germany in 1774 that purported to describe their recent discoveries was much discussed, translated and republished in London. It indicated that Alaska was an island, separated by a broad expanse of open water from the American mainland. This was unproven but exciting.

It was expected, at first, that Cook would not command the new voyage. He had done enough to earn retirement, or at least respite. But he was to be closely involved in the expedition's planning. Though the *Resolution* would sail again, the *Adventure* had been dispatched elsewhere, and Cook therefore helped select a new ship, again a Whitby collier, in early January 1776. Soon afterwards he was asked by Sandwich to dinner with the Admiralty Secretary Philip Stephens, and Sir Hugh Palliser, to discuss the choice of commander. These men, it is said, felt that they could not ask Cook to undertake the service, but hoped that he would, and succeeded in enthusing him. According to Andrew Kippis, Cook's first biographer, Cook became 'so fired' by the notion of a mission 'that he started up, and declared that he himself would undertake the direction of the enterprise'. Not because he was like Barrington and carried away by the 'probability' of the passage, but because the voyage would give 'completion . . . to the whole system of discoveries'. Beaglehole believes that Cook's friends failed to fully grasp what he had been through, neglected his need for real rest, and made a disastrous mistake in luring him into a further voyage at this point. Though Cook was obviously older than he had been, we do not, in fact, know that he was desperately tired or strained. No one who met him at this time suggests that he was. In any event, it is not hard to imagine that he found the prospect of completing a 'whole system of discoveries' irresistible. He would, I suspect, have been irritated by the thought that a former subordinate such as Clerke or Gore might succeed and might in due course be a hero on an equal footing, having done for the north Pacific what Cook did for the south.

Over the winter of 1775–6, Cook was concerned as much with packaging the past as shaping the future. He would have gathered quickly that he was far from the only person 'mortified' by Hawkesworth's publication, but the question of how and by whom the second voyage was to be published was by no means straightforward. Johann Forster believed that the task was to be his. Probably, before the voyage, Barrington had assured him that it would be. The honour and the reward he was desperate to secure. The philosophically informed travel narrative was at once a noble genre – in this case not least because it would be framed patriotically, as a narrative of British naval and scientific accomplishment – but also a tremendously popular and notably lucrative one. Forster wanted his name on the sort of book that the second voyage indeed became. If you handle these volumes in the hushed rare-book room of a library, or procure them from the locked case of some antiquarian dealer, you can see why. The paper is thick, the quarto pages are generous, the print is large and opulently spaced, the many folding maps and illustrations have been beautifully drawn and carefully engraved. The whole production is a world away from the crude efforts that were the usual stuff of the book trade.

Forster had a case, not least because he had earlier translated a whole series of scientific travel narratives. However, Cook, over the course of the second voyage, had deepened his knowledge, not only of the places and peoples in the Pacific, but of the business of writing. From September 1775 onward there was a great deal of discussion, involving Sandwich, Forster, Cook and others, that presupposed that the writing, the credit and the cash would be in some way shared. At first, Forster would write on the basis of Cook's journal. He was asked to prepare a sample, which he duly did, covering the stay in Dusky Sound. His written English was thought to be inadequate. Some people put it to Sandwich that he was not the right person for the job. There was much to-ing and fro-ing, and as early as October, Sandwich was 'almost convinced' that the natural historian was 'what he has been represented to me to be, an utterly impracticable man'. At about this time, it was determined that the literary cleric Dr John Douglas, Canon of Windsor, would tidy Cook's narrative, while Forster, kept in the dark about this arrangement, might proceed to publish a parallel account – still with official blessing – that would present the voyage's scientific findings.

During the first few months of 1776, Forster and Cook both proceeded with the revision of their journals, apparently in a climate of mutual misunderstanding. Sandwich tried to dispel the confusion at a meeting in mid April, where a formal agreement was drawn up and signed. The document stipulated that a two-volume work would appear, consisting of Cook's narrative and Forster's philosophical observations. They were supposed to co-operate, and to share the costs and profits. But difficulties arose very soon afterwards, when Forster submitted his first chapters, which were in a narrative form: Sandwich and perhaps others had assumed that 'observations' would be arranged more discursively. As negotiations broke down, Forster desperately attempted to retrieve some financial advantage from the situation, but offended Barrington by insisting that seawater could freeze. True to form, he would never let his need for patronage prevent him from putting his view, which on this occasion as well as others happened to be right. He thus lost both Barrington's support, and any purchase in negotiations. Sandwich's attitude hardened, and Cook was advised that he should publish on his own.

It is sad that a thinker as brilliant as Forster should have seen his aspirations collapse around him. The 'utterly impracticable' man was treated more badly than he deserved, at great cost to his family, already well used to debt and insecurity. But the outcome was not all bad. The official narrative would be emphatically Cook's own book, and, though Forster had been reluctantly divorced from the Admiralty, he was perforce also freed from editorial control. Those who still had some regard for his science looked forward to his findings. Cook, when he gathered that Forster would publish independently, may well have been perturbed. The captain had a precise sense of the morality that the voyage should exhibit; he knew that there were accomplishments that he wanted to own, and accidents he wanted to disown. He wanted no repetition of the murk, contention and indecency that Hawkesworth's book had stimulated. The one specific directive he made to Douglas was that 'With respect to the Amours of my People at Otaheite & other places; I think it will not be necessary to mention them atall'; though his enhanced sense of the importance of anthropological observation led him to add, 'unless it be by way of throwing a light on the Characters, or Customs of the People we are then among'. He had no idea what Forster might write, but he did know that Forster would be nothing if not a loose cannon, in the subtle struggle to refine the voyage's reputation. The matter bothered him. The ups and downs of his relationship with the quirky and fractious man, over the course of the voyage, crystallized into resentment.

On 10 February 1776 the process of mustering the companies of the *Resolution* and the new vessel named the *Discovery* began. A good many of those first recruited had sailed with Cook before. They included the American William Ewins, the Scottish gunner, Robert Anderson, and the Irish quartermaster, Patrick Whelan. The master's mate, William Harvey, had sailed in both the *Endeavour* and the *Resolution*, as had William Lanyon from Cornwall, William Peckover from London, and John Ramsay of Perthshire. Lieutenant John Gore, renowned for being an intrepid character and outstanding sailor, but no intellectual, had sailed on the *Endeavour* but not the *Resolution* – he had instead accompanied Banks on a private trip to Iceland. At the time of the first voyage, Gore had been more experienced than Cook, and there is thought to have been tension between them. By 1776 this ought no longer to have been an issue. If there were residual misgivings on either side, Gore for his part always wanted a piece of the action, while Cook knew that he needed lieutenants he could depend upon. It was they after all who routinely managed the ship. His second lieutenant would be James King, a clergyman's son, who evidently had sufficient financial security to undertake periods of private scientific study, in Paris in 1774, and subsequently in Oxford, where his brother was a student. King knew

Edmund Burke, was widely read, and was a competent astronomer. His earlier naval experience had included service around Newfoundland, under Palliser. He was barely more than half Cook's age, but they had points of connection, and things to talk about – though King was shocked by one of their early conversations. Something like 'Curse all science!' was what Cook angrily replied, when King asked whether there would be natural historians on the new voyage. He could have had no idea that the contention pierced Cook's most sensitive nerve, it threatened his effort to define his accomplishment.

Charles Clerke would command the consort. As a veteran of Byron's voyage as well as Cook's first and second, he had, like Pickersgill and Gore, sailed around the world three times. He knew the range and variety of Pacific seas, islands, peoples and experiences as well as any European then alive. He was devoted to Banks, for whom he collected things. However, Banks's own abilities to be fascinated by the novel, to notice all kinds of things, to pursue inquiry doggedly and to write it all up never rubbed off on Clerke, whose second voyage journal was admittedly richer than his record of the first, but never as full as Cook's – let alone as wide-ranging and revealing as that of Banks or Forster. From Cook's point of view, he was no doubt the best of possible people for the job: Clerke had not only experience, but experience of voyaging with Cook. He knew Cook's style and expectations, which Furneaux had not known when he embarked in the *Adventure*. This epitomized the ways the third voyage differed from those that came before – just as a third or second marriage differs from a first. The project would still be an experiment, but by now Cook and his companions knew what sort of experiment it was. They had spent more time with each other than with wives, girlfriends or children, and if they did not each know their own strengths and failings, they never would.

Among the others who knew each other, to some extent, were James Burney and George Vancouver. Vancouver, now nineteen, had been a midshipman on the second voyage and would later become the famous commander of a further Pacific expedition. Yet neither he nor William Bligh, appointed master, subsequently notorious as the supposed despot overthrown by the *Bounty* mutiny, would be particularly visible in the course of the third voyage. William Anderson, the surgeon, about twenty-eight, had caught the infection of natural history, the crazy passion for things new, that led him not only to look and inquire relentlessly but to write with almost excessive particularity. Anderson too had been on the second voyage. He had compiled some sort of zoological tract, and it is tantalizing to find him mentioning 'a Manuscript I have by me intitled The General History of

a voyage made in the Resolution in the years 1772, 1773, 1774, and 1775',
which seems never to have reached any collection or archive. In any event
it has never been sighted by any Cook voyage scholar. If this document
survives, if it is ever rediscovered in the recesses of a cupboard or an
attic, our already rich but patchy knowledge of the second voyage will be
dramatically enhanced; I would like to know, for example, what Anderson
made of the tragic shooting at Tanna, and Cook's supposedly unjust treatment of the perpetrator.

Anderson, as surgeon, was assisted by two 'surgeon's mates'. The first
was David Samwell, who would also write a detailed and highly engaging
voyage journal. Though this is often cited for Samwell's frank exposé of his
sexual activities – he made the most of opportunities at just about every
Pacific landfall – Samwell was as much an intellectual as either Anderson or
King, but of a basically different sort. He belonged to radical and literary
circles. As poet, antiquarian and romantic Welsh nationalist, he had an
interest in folklore different from any other Cook voyage participant, and was
prompted to transcribe Maori songs. But if he would be the first European to
make this sort of effort – the first to do more than list words and phrases – his
observations on some other counts were less empathetic than Cook's. Those
who travelled on the third voyage would carry an extraordinary resource – a
collective, but unevenly shared, unevenly valued memory of months of discussion with fellow-voyagers Tupaia, Mahine and Mai, complemented by
recollection and reflection upon many meetings on many islands. It remained
to be seen whether, in the end, these remarkable encounters between Europeans and Pacific Islanders would exhibit the limits, more than the scope,
for understanding between such different peoples.

Just before the Resolution's return, Banks, Mai and others had set out to visit
Constantine Phipps's estate in Yorkshire. As it happens, Castle Mulgrave is
just north of the port of Whitby; it does not exactly overlook the town, and
today is discreetly located, out of view in well-planted grounds. Yet in the
eighteenth century there would have been no ambiguity about what the
house represented: suffice to say that its incumbent would typically have
been a Member of Parliament, a person whose life scarcely intersected with
that of the local population. En route there, their coach, overloaded with
Phipps's nautical and Banks's botanical baggage, had stopped frequently to
inspect and collect any remotely unusual plant that Banks sighted; they
travelled by way of Scarborough, where Mai exposed his tattoos while
plunging into the sea. As Phipps's guest, he amused himself by going out
shooting and on at least one occasion dug an earth oven to roast the ducks,

geese and partridges that the vigilance of gamekeepers preserved from the natives of the region.

This excursion to Cook's home country exhibited certain ironies of eighteenth-century mobility, which brought people from the harshly class-stratified societies of the north Atlantic into contact with the less deeply divided, but nevertheless unambiguously hierarchical communities of Polynesia. In Cleveland, Cook had been a nonentity, a landless lad of the commonest sort, who migrated to the sea, who could easily have vanished among the marine proletariat, as common men soon afterwards would vanish into the factories of Manchester and Leeds. The last place that this younger Cook would ever have contemplated visiting was Castle Mulgrave; yet on the other side of the world, the man he happened to become had been embraced as a son by a high chief on Huahine, and would be treated as an aristocrat often enough in the South Seas – but nowhere else. Mai, for his part, came from a landholding family, but one of low status, and one that was in any event dispossessed by the invasion that he desperately wanted to avenge. Even when he travelled with Furneaux and Cook, he tended to be ignored by the prominent Polynesian men and women they encountered; he would receive a modicum of attention in Tonga, far enough from Tahiti for his true status to be obscured, but only in England was he genuinely honoured by an elite, who re-invented his genealogy with the fancy and facility they employed in re-inventing their own. The so-called 'Priest of the Sun' was hence further upgraded to a 'Chief of Otaheite' in the title of one painting.

Through the first half of 1776, Cook revised his journal, sending samples, revisions and bottles of wine – some of which had been around the world – to Canon Douglas. Over the same months, a small army of engravers, including the most distinguished practitioners of the period, got to work on Hodges's drawings, Cook's maps, Forster's plants, and sundry other curiosities. The book would be lavishly illustrated with some sixty prints – the bulk of them after Hodges's sketches. The reader of the *Voyage Toward the South Pole* would be also the viewer of a whole gallery of 'new' men and women, some of whom – Tu, Potatau and Mahine among them – were identified individually, and others as the 'Man' or 'Woman' of Easter Island, Malakula, Tanna, New Caledonia and Christmas Sound, among other places. These were portraits of individuals – some of whom looked grave and dignified, some benign and friendly, others perhaps uncouth and strange to eighteenth-century English men and women. But the plethora of characters would not necessarily be easily recognized as a set of distinct nationalities. As we've seen, there was much disagreement about what sort of people 'New Zealanders' among others were. There was moreover a good deal of dissonance between written portraits of beauty here and ugliness there, and these visual images, which made a few people – notably the Tierra del Fuegians – look wild and I suppose savage, but not actually ugly or physically 'primitive'. Hodges was professionally incapable of depicting ugliness, as he had been unable to draw a disfiguring tattoo. The *Voyage* might be a scientific book, but from his point of view it also had to be a handsome one.

Many of the illustrations were based not on Hodges's field sketches, but on paintings and drawings that he produced after his return to London. At some point a decision was made that the engraved views would include representations of Cook's initial landings on several islands – Eua, Malakula, Erramanga and Tanna. The first of these islands, in Tonga, had been sighted but not visited more than a century earlier by Tasman, and the *Resolution* was the first European ship to call at the other three, in Vanuatu. Though not every 'first contact' was treated in this way, these places, rather than Point Venus or Ship Cove, were certainly selected because they had been sites of new encounters. Whoever had the idea, Hodges adapted it brilliantly. Two quite different peoples face each other for the first time. The Islanders are supposed to be in a state of awe and astonishment before the unprecedented spectacle of great ships and white men; their attitudes exhibit trepidation, consternation, excitement, and – in the case of the people Cook had called Friendly Islanders – an essential civility and generosity, manifest in offerings of food. The Tannese, in contrast are more hostile, the Erramangans actively belligerent, while the men of Malakula respond with guarded civility, as they in fact had.

These images included authentic touches – one of the women at Eua has a finger missing, amputated to mark the death of a relative or chief, as Cook's reader will learn – but they are essentially imaginative, in that seamen and Islanders alike are presented classically, with the dignity of actors in an antique drama. Despite the deliberate idealization of the scenes, the Eua picture is notable for making it evident that the meeting is actually not the very first encounter between Europeans and these Tongans. The active figure in the boat that is about to reach the shore is not Cook, but the chief named Ataongo, who has come off to the *Resolution* some time earlier, and who then guides Cook's pinnace to a convenient landing-place. None of the journals explicitly indicate that he held aloft the plantain or banana leaf that would have been recognized as an emblem of peace, though it is quite characteristic of Polynesian diplomatic improvisation that a local might step over to the side of the visitors – to do whatever needed to be

35. The Landing at Middleburgh *(i.e. Eua), engraving after Hodges,
from Cook,* A Voyage Toward the South Pole, *1777.*

done, that ignorance or linguistic incompetence prevented them from doing. Invented or not, Ataonga's presence in Cook's boat, so dramatically central to this image, was striking for its implication that an Islander might be instantly enlisted, to help inaugurate a peaceful commerce. There could surely be no stronger sign of the civility of these people, a sentimental reader would have concluded. Those more sceptical might have doubted the idealization; I do not know if, in the eighteenth century, an English reader would have guessed that Ataonga had a project of his own. This was no innocent civility, but a way to parade prestige. Perhaps Cook was a recruit rather than a recruiter.

Whatever was going on, the scene was a grand one. Even the violence

36. *William Hodges,* The Landing at Malakula, *1775–6.*

of the Erramangan and Tannese landings has an impressive and significant, rather than a confused or merely unfortunate, character. As Cook acknowledged in his journal during the visit to Tanna, the people of these islands could very reasonably suppose that Europeans were aggressors and invaders; though he hoped that time and good treatment would convince them that they were mistaken, it was inevitable that in some places he would come into conflict with their hostile patriotism. These scenes, as much as the peaceful arrival at Eua, further underscore the momentous character of the voyage's history. It had one face, in the remarkable venture into the regions beyond human life, beyond almost all life, in the far south, and another altogether in the encounter with unprecedented human novelty in the tropics.

Because they had him making history, Cook liked these engravings. The book that contained them would not appear until well after his departure on the third voyage, but he saw proofs, and would take a number of prints with him. Some Pacific Islanders had manifestly enjoyed the business of sitting for Hodges, and Cook no doubt anticipated pleasing them with their portraits, though he gave away a few even before he left England. About to depart one world for another, he remained sensitive to the gestures that one made, in the subtle system of patronage, respect, rank and favour that was the Royal Navy. If we believe an eighteenth-century inscription, six of the prints were 'presented to Paul Henry Ourry Commissioner of Plymouth Dockyard by the celebrated Navigator Captain Cook himself'. These, perhaps much admired and consequently in a tatty state, recently appeared on the market, at an astonishing price.

Perhaps because Hodges was fully occupied with work towards the *Voyage*, his reappointment to the *Resolution* seems never to have been considered. Cook would instead be accompanied by John Webber, a twenty-four-year-old painter of Swiss descent, who had been represented in the Royal Academy's 1776 exhibition. His work there impressed Solander, who called on the artist a few days later, in late April or early May, and promptly recommended him to the Admiralty. An artist who might bring back work that was both accurate and attractive to polite society would help ensure the success of the voyage. By now it had become clear that success or failure depended not only upon avoiding shipwreck in the South Seas, but also – once back home – on the navigation of taste.

So far as the third voyage was concerned, dealing with all that would have seemed a long way off to Cook in early July 1776, when Webber joined the *Resolution*. The great forthcoming book that reported his second voyage was no doubt still on his mind, but by now he was most exercised by final preparations for the new voyage, and by reflection upon its plan, set out in the official instructions that he had no doubt helped frame, but had just received in their final formal state. These specified that Cook should sail via the Cape of Good Hope, search for some islands south of Mauritius, supposed to have been discovered by the French, and to proceed from there to Tahiti, to repatriate Mai, and to refresh the ships. He was then to approach the north American coast, far enough north to avoid touching at any point claimed by Spain, and follow that coast north, exploring any possible passage, to reach around 65° – more or less the latitude of the Bering Strait, which separates north-east Asia from north-west America – by June, 1777. In this area, it was thought, the search for the passage should begin in earnest:

... you are very carefully to search for, and to explore, such Rivers or Inlets as may appear to be of a considerable extent and pointing towards Hudsons or Baffins Bays; and, if from your own Observations, or from any information you may receive from the Natives (who, there is reason to believe, are the same Race of People, and speak the same Language, of which you are furnished with a Vocabulary, as the Esquimaux) there shall appear to be a certainty, or even a probability, of a Water Passage into the aforementioned Bays, or either of them, you are, in such a case to use your utmost endeavours to pass through with one or both of the Sloops, unless you shall be of the opinion that the passage may be effected with more certainty, or with greater probability, by smaller Vessels, in which case you are to set up the Frames of one or both the small Vessels with which you are provided, and when they are put together, and are properly fitted out, stored, & victualled, you are to dispatch one or both of them under the care of the proper officers ... But nevertheless if you shall find it more eligible to pursue any other measures, than those above pointed out, in order to make a discovery of the beforementioned Passage (if any such there be) you are at liberty, and we leave it to your discretion, to pursue such measures accordingly.

Beyond this point, everything was left to Cook's discretion, and the plan begins to sound like a global inversion of the search for the southern continent. 'At the proper Season of the Year' Cook was to turn back to the south, to Kamchatka or wherever else he thought appropriate, for winter refitting and refreshment, to renew the search in far northern waters the following spring. If there seemed to be no passage to the north of America, he might try above Asia. He should sail as far north as seemed prudent. He should in due course return to England via whatever route he thought best 'for the Improvement of Geography and Navigation'.

The instructions reflect Oceanic experience, first in imagining that affinities between the natives of Alaska and those of Greenland implied the possibility of travel between these regions, and second in supposing that the great geographic puzzle might be solved with information obtained from these 'Esquimaux'. These hopes recall Cook's astonishment when confronted by the affinities between peoples dispersed across Oceania, his admiration of the 'distant navigations' that he knew Polynesians had undertaken, and his attentiveness to conversation with Tupaia, Mahine and many others. Perhaps across the far north, as well as in the South Sea, people who belonged to a single 'great nation' were dispersed. Perhaps they not only had travelled, but still travelled; and perhaps among them there were knowledgeable and curious men who were ready to name islands, draw maps and talk passages.

The third voyage would be a passage-hunting, rather than a continent-hunting, one. But it had subordinate aims that stemmed from Joseph Banks's longstanding interests in the rearrangement of nature. In December 1775, a publisher understood that the voyage would not only return Mai, but export a useful gift of plants and animals 'to our *tropical allies*', and 'bring in return the bread-tree for our *West Indies*, and *St. Helena*'. As if the plantations of the Caribbean were not already profitable enough, the possibility that breadfruit might be transplanted to provide cheap food for slaves had been raised soon after the return of the *Endeavour*, but was probably ruled out at this time by war in America. The project would eventually be attempted by Cook's sometime midshipman Bligh, first in the *Bounty*, and then after the mutiny and subsequent proceedings successfully in the *Providence*. For the time being, though, the idea remained on Banks's extensive wish list. But the improvement of the noble Tahitians would not be forgotten. On 10 June, Cook took on board 'a Bull, 2 Cows with their Calves & some sheep . . . at His Majestys Command and expence with a view of stocking Otaheite and the Neighbouring Islands with these usefull animals'. Though goats and sheep, as well, of course, as chickens, dogs and cats, had travelled before, this enlarged maritime farmyard had consequences for what we might call the quality of life aboard the *Resolution*. This Cook rather airily passes over, in his evocation of regal benevolence. Think of the sheer volume of shit, the mess of damp and rotting feed, the inadequacy of ventilation below leaky decks, the already cramped accommodation, the tendency of these barge-like boats to roll.

Back in London in a house near St Pancras crowded with specimens, children and impecunious visitors, Johann and George Forster were getting to work on books that they would publish with or without the approval of the Admiralty. Johann could not legally publish a narrative of the voyage, but George had been a minor at the time they joined the *Resolution*, had signed no agreement and was in no way constrained. If he were able to bring out a book before Cook's *Voyage* appeared, it was just possible that he would capture the lion's share of the market and ease the family's financial plight, especially if his father were able to negotiate translation rights in France and Germany. The task was formidable, given that Cook's book was already in almost its final form; but George sat down, and can have done almost nothing but write for nine months. Over 300,000 words, over 1,200 pages, his *Voyage Round the World* ruined his health, but betrays none of the anxious rush of its composition. The best-written of the many published accounts of Cook's voyages, it would later be recognized as one of the liveliest travel books of its time. Today, the idea of a 'wonder of nature' is a cliché. Then, the attitude of romantic astonishment before spectacular, daunting or unusual natural phenomena was in its infancy. The notion that scientific interest and aesthetic surprise might often come together in one's feeling before a beautiful or wild scene was equally new. In many lyrical passages, Forster revelled in the positively sensual evocation of places and sights, such as the cascade of Cascade Cove.

The first object which strikes the beholder [who has clambered up the slope, from the shores of Dusky Sound, to the base of the waterfall], is a clear column of water, apparently eight or ten yards in circumference, which is projected with great impetuosity from the perpendicular rock, at the height of one hundred yards. Nearly at the fourth part of the whole height, this column meeting a part of the same rock, which now acquires a little inclination, spreads on its broad back into a limpid sheet of about twenty-five yards in width. Here the surface is curled, and dashes upon every little eminence in its rapid descent, till it is all collected in a fine bason about sixty yards in circuit, included on three sides by the natural walls of the rocky chasm, and in front by huge masses of stone, irregularly piled above each other. Between them the stream finds its way, and runs foaming with the greatest rapidity along the slope of the hill to the sea. The whole neighbourhood of the cascade, to a distance of an hundred yards around, is filled with the steam or watery vapour formed by the violence of the fall. This mist however, was so thick, that it penetrated our clothes in a few minutes, as effectually as a shower of rain would have done. We mounted on the highest stone before the bason, and looking down into it, were struck with the sight of a most beautiful rainbow of a perfectly circular form, which was produced by the meridian rays of the sun refracted in the vapour of the cascade.

37. *William Hodges*, Cascade Cove, Dusky Bay, *1775*.

Forster continued to describe the tinting of the steam with the 'prismatic colours', the steep brown rocks above the stream on one side, the rough landslide on the other; the mosses, ferns and grasses of the shaded gorge; and the deafening noise of the cascade that all but drowned out 'the shrill notes of thrushes, the graver pipe of wattle-birds, and the enchanting melody of various creepers' that 'completed the beauty of this wild and romantic spot'. This sort of writing goes to some trouble to take the reader to the place described. Nature's own animation – manifest in the vigorous flow of the water, as well as in plant and animal life – is almost palpable in this animated prose that deftly follows not only the eye, but all of the sensitive observer's senses – from the striking spectacle of the fall itself, through the vapour, around the vicinity, up towards the brush and light at the top of the bluff. This was prose that would be appreciated, that some readers thought remarkable and exemplary. Alexander von Humboldt, the pre-eminent natural historian of the romantic period, would later single out Forster's *Voyage* as the book that inspired his interest in the subject.

Perhaps, therefore, it was unfortunate that Forster wrote equally vividly about the behaviour of British sailors. The harshness of their lives reduced them from thinking beings to insensible creatures, 'incapable of feeling for others', driven by 'gross animal appetites', fond of killing, occasionally susceptible to 'a horrid eagerness' to fire upon natives. Though they came from a civilized society, they were really 'a body of uncivilized men, rough, passionate, revengeful, but likewise brave, sincere, and true to each other', was Forster's considered assessment.

The idea that these European men had degenerated into a sort of savagery was not just an idle thought, but a recurrent theme of his narrative. In an offensive passage, he claimed that the women of New Zealand were dirty, smelly and commonly infested with lice; 'it is astonishing,' he thought, 'that persons should be found, who could gratify an animal appetite with such loathsome objects.' Elsewhere, Forster tended to acknowledge that peoples had different ideas of what was and what was not attractive. Islanders who anointed themselves with oils obviously liked an odour that repelled Europeans. But on this occasion, he refrains from this sort of qualification, and degrades Maori women with the same horridness that he imputes to seamen. He does so because he is carried away by his own rhetoric: the women's supposed 'loathsomeness' reveals the true degradation of the British sailors.

At many points, Forster was frankly critical of officers as well as ordinary seamen. His account of the voyage's most contentious incident was deftly crafted, to heighten a sense of their inhumane propensities. On Tanna, he takes a long walk into the hills and is profoundly impressed by the beauty of the countryside, the industry manifest in native agriculture, the felicity of local domestic life, and so on ('The cheerful voice of the labouring husband-man resounded very opportunely to complete this idea', etc.). He rests and reflects upon human goodness, the growth of friendship with the Tannese, and the merits of civilized society but this sentimental stuff is contrived to accentuate the shock which hits Forster and his reader on their return to the beach and the awful news that a sentry has peremptorily shot a man dead. An afternoon is thus shown to encompass the finest possibilities in meetings between peoples – and the ugliest of actual outcomes.

Thus one dark and detestable action effaced all the hopes with which I had flattered myself. The natives, instead of looking upon us in a more favourable light than upon other strangers, had reason to detest us much more, as we came to destroy under the specious mask of friendship, and some amongst us lamented that instead of making amends at this place for the many rash acts which we had perpetrated at almost every island in our course, we had wantonly made it the scene of the greatest cruelty. Captain Cook resolved to punish the marine with the utmost rigour for having transgressed his positive orders, according to which the choleric emotions of the savage were to be repressed with gentleness, and prudently suffered to cool. But the officer who commanded on shore, declared that he had not delivered these orders to the sentry, but given him others which imported, that the least threat was to be punished with death. The soldier was therefore immediately cleared, and the officer's right to dispose of the lives of the natives remained uncontroverted.

This made for a powerful and engaging narrative, but one that was also, needless to say, offensive to people who saw the voyage, and the particular incidents, very differently. It incensed William Wales, who prepared an eighty-page polemic, intending to demolish the book and the reputation of Forster senior, who Wales took to be the true author of the *Voyage*. A decidedly unflattering and unfortunately plausible account of Johann's character prefaces Wales's *Remarks on Mr Forster's Account of Captain Cook's Last Voyage Round the World*, highlighting the excessive weight that the naturalist placed on his appointment by the King. Forster was, we gather, constantly engaged in a quarrel with some person on board the *Resolution* or another and far too ready to

threaten him with complaining to the k—g at his return; and he assured us that he had interest enough to prevail on his majesty to discard him for ever from his service. A threat, which he was so weak as to employ against almost every person on board the ship at one time or other, and so often, that it became a bye word among the seamen, whom I frequently heard threaten one another with the same dreadful denunciation on the most common and trifling occasions. Can it be supposed, that such a man did not render himself cheap, and that he would not sometimes find the ill consequence of being so?

If Forster had indeed made himself unpopular, his pretensions were most bitterly resented by Wales, who was now assiduous and venomous in drawing attention to every possible slight error, who contested every account of any contentious matter in the *Voyage*. Fairly enough, he drew attention to inaccuracies in maps and erroneous transcriptions of latitude and longitude. His personal stake in the case became manifest in extended disputation of whether a watch stopped, or *was stopped*: his own responsibilities, as astronomer, to maintain and monitor the timepieces were at issue. But his fullest acrimony was reserved for Forster's accounts of incidents of violence between mariners and seamen, which in each case Wales took to be inflated and distorted.

Of the violence at Erramango, Wales considered that Forster's description inexcusably branded 'Captain Cook and his party with indelible infamy' and 'wanton barbarity', because Forster had written that, after muskets had been fired, and the men on the beach had retreated behind a dune, they continued to appear and 'annoy our people', who in turn 'amused themselves to fire at them as often as their heads appeared'. We have no way of judging whether marines and seamen 'amused' themselves in firing, though we might recall that Parkinson had made precisely this complaint, five years earlier: if this had been true at Matavai, in 1769, it was perhaps also true of Erramango in 1774. Wales did not quote what Cook proceeded to write. Although the captain considered that the display of two oars on a nearby headland represented 'a Sign of Submission' – who knows why he interpreted it that way – he was subsequently 'nevertheless prevailed upon to fire a four pound Shott at them', which fell short, but terrified the people on the shore. If, for Wales, the charge of 'wanton barbarity' stood or failed on whether firing continued after the people had been driven back, the facts of the matter are worse rather than better than Forster suggested: a heavier gun was used, albeit ineffectively, even after Cook thought that the people had sued for peace.

Wales proceeded to rehearse the already much-disputed Tannese shooting, 'one of the most malignant pieces of misrepresentation and abuse in his whole book', and 'a strange composition of absurdity, falsity, and malevolence'. He went over the details, insisting that the sentinel legitimately shot the man, who was apparently about to fire an arrow at him. He adds that his witness, the master's mate, Whitehouse, was absolutely certain that Captain Cook was 'mistaken in saying, that there was room to suppose that it was not the man who drew the arrow that was shot'. This marked the extent to which Cook's view differed from Wales's, and was in some cases closer to Forster's, though Cook's interest was not Forster's. Cook would slant stories, and occasionally suppress the most culpable details, which Forster disclosed and amplified, in an account of the voyage that was not malevolent, as Wales had it, but was certainly passionate. The business of arguing about the violence of these expeditions, inaugurated by John Hawkesworth, was booming, but had nevertheless only just begun.

PART 4:
TO THE NORTH PACIFIC

17

I allow because I cannot prevent it

Four years to the day after leaving Plymouth to search for the southern continent, the *Resolution* departed the same port on 12 July 1776. 'The Singularity of yᵉ circumstance made Us look upon it as an Omen of a like prosperous Voyage,' observed James King – who had not known the 'prosperity' of the bitterly extended Antarctic cruises. Yet the mood was optimistic, though it was already apparent that the ship had been badly refitted, that the caulking of decks and sides reflected 'barbarous Neglect', meaning much leakage into cabins and spoilage of stores.

The *Resolution* sailed alone. Clerke was bonded to his brother's creditors, who could not be persuaded that their cash was less important than maritime exploration. He had to stay in London to sort the situation out, and would follow when he could. Cook made for Tenerife, in the Canary Islands, thinking that it might be a better place than Madeira for obtaining supplies, and was courteously received by local officials. He stocked up on pigs, sheep, goats, poultry, fruit and vegetables, and was generally satisfied. The wine, though much inferior to what he'd bought before at Madeira, was at least also much cheaper. He met Jean-Charles Borda and Don Joseph Varela y Ulloa of the French frigate *Boussole*, who were making astronomical observations, aiming to fix the position of the Peak of Tenerife with exactitude, an exercise after Cook's heart which they pursued with his sort of rigour; he noted their 'kindness' in sharing their findings, and regretted that the exigencies of his plan left no time for cosmopolitan, mathematical, exploratory conversation.

Sailing past Bonavista, the ship's course was poorly reckoned. Very nearly too late, Cook and Anderson, looking to the starboard, together realized that they were 'close upon' the surf, close upon some sunken rocks off the south-eastern point of that island. Only desperately quick action, and some luck, prevented wreckage; 'Our situation for a few Minutes was very alarming,' Cook acknowledged; the situation deserved the 'severest reprehension', wrote Anderson, but qualified an apparent criticism of Cook, on the grounds that 'the true reason' for the near miss 'does not appear'.

Over subsequent weeks the crew were given fruit punch, to stave off scurvy. When the weather was dry the caulkers were constantly at work, trying to do what should have been done in the Deptford yard. Mai diverted himself fishing for dolphins. The passage to the Cape was uneventful. There, Cook paid his respects as usual to the Dutch governor, and established a camp and observatory on shore. The livestock was landed, and some sheep promptly stolen. Cook was annoyed that though the police were renowned for their efficiency – no slave, however cunning, would succeed in escaping the colony, it was said – they could not or would not help him recover his flock. Always versatile, he resorted to 'employing some of the meanest and lowest scoundrels of this place, who, to use the phrase of the person who recommended to me this method, would for a Ductatoon cut their Masters throat, burn the house over his head and bury him and the whole family in the ashes'. With what standover tactics I do not know, but these persons did secure the return of most of the flock. Cook mentions that one Mr Hemmy, an English settler, offered to make up his loss with a Spanish ram, and that Hemmy's 'pains to interduce European sheep at the Cape' had been frustrated by Boer obstinacy; the farmers liked the animals they already possessed, which appear to have been unusual in possessing fatty thick tails. In any case, he went on to remark, European sheep would not produce the wool that they did in Europe, and even if they did, the labour shortage made it impossible for the colonists to manufacture even their own clothing. 'Was it not for the slaves that are continually importing here, the Dutch settlement at the Cape would be thiner of Inhabitants than any habitable part of the world whatever.' All this was symptomatic of the moment: a set of sheep stolen and recovered with the help of thugs, race unspecified, prompted reflection on the varieties of sheep and the success and failure of colonies. In the southern hemisphere, wool and inhabitants alike became thinner: Cook was exercised by the future fecundity of his own seaborne farm, and the state of his own maritime population.

He adjusted that population by sending one man home on an East India company ship. He described William Hunt, the armourer, as an 'invalided' man, which seems to have been a way of covering up the serious offence of counterfeiting, theoretically a hanging crime, but one that might have troubled the Dutch authorities more than it prejudiced Cook's mission. Cook's approach to naval discipline remained selective. He must have felt that there was no need or point in making an example. Perhaps he excused Hunt because he even had some liking for him. But on that point I can only speculate: the emotional contours of these voyages are for the most part as distant and hard to imagine now as the outlines of the north Pacific were then.

Clerke arrived on 10 November. The *Discovery*, he reported, was 'in want of caulking'. The men who had just done as much as they could on the *Resolution* got to work on her consort. The bakers who had promised bread were chided. Rather than risk further thefts of stock, Cook re-embarked the sheep and cattle, and moreover enlarged the menagerie: 'To which I added two young Bulls, two Heifers, two young stone Horses, two Mares, two Rams, several Ewes and Goats and some Rabbits and Poultry' – which apparently included turkeys, geese, ducks, guinea fowl, '& one Peacock and Hen' – 'all of them intended for New Zealand, Otaheite, and the neighbouring islands' or wherever 'there was a prospect that the leaving of some of them might prove usefull to posterity'. Given that the care of these animals on board entailed much additional work, inconvenience, fouler air and general unpleasantness – which by now had been experienced rather than just anticipated – it is remarkable that Cook should have gone so far beyond his obligation to carry the stock supplied by the King, so far as to supplement it with four horses as well as further cattle and diverse other creatures. It is notable that he does not see the beasts simply as usefully prestigious gifts to Polynesian chiefs: he might have thought that they would be surprised, impressed and pleased to receive them, but he would have said so, had some equine or bovine diplomacy been uppermost in his mind. We cannot avoid concluding that the prospective contribution 'to posterity' was of peculiar personal importance to him: he was understanding his voyage as a charitable one, he wanted his actions to be understood as charitable ones, and his imagining of charity had been inflected, his old interests and inclinations I suspect been reinforced, by further conversation before departure with Banks, who had remained as restlessly interested as always in the introduction of 'useful' animals and plants to appropriate climates and populations. Over the London winter and spring, Cook's ambitions had become wider. The 'completion' of the whole system of discovery certainly loomed large among them, but the improvements he sought would not be exclusively in the domain of geography, but also that of 'oeconomy' (a capacious notion that encompassed sociality and morality as well as economics): Pacific Islanders would enjoy more and better foods, and have more and better to trade; more trade, maybe more civility. There was no mercenary scheme here, but a grander notion, and Cook had his eye on it.

By the end of November, both ships were caulked and provisioned as fully as was possible 'for two years and upwards', Cook wrote. They were equipped with everything 'we could think of for such a Voyage, neither knowing when nor where we should come to a place where we could supply our selves so well'. The course and duration of the mission were indeed uncertain, though Cook was already at this early stage writing for posterity, reminding his reader of the poignancy of this departure from the civilized world.

The larger plan was to sail for America's north-west coast, via New Zealand and the Society Islands, but reports had reached London of new French discoveries in the southern ocean. Cook knew that these could refer to lands of no great extent or consequence but, almost by way of postscript to his second voyage, wanted their situations defined. The information he had was vague. He knew of Kerguelen's first voyage, but not his second. The former had brought back excited reports of a southern land; the latter, which led to the navigator's disgrace, acknowledged that these had been overstated, if not quite concocted. Once again, it had been a case of islands rather than lands, and cold and desolate ones at that.

The cruise south-east from the Cape was at once 'tedious and dangerous': the weather generally 'nasty, raw, wet, disagreeable', Clerke thought. Cook wrote – as he had at Tierra del Fuego on his first voyage, and in the Antarctic seas on his second – that this southern summer recalled 'the very depth of Winter' in England. He, but only a fraction of his crew, were accustomed to this antipodean perversity: the seasons were reversed, but the weather the same, at the bottom of the world. Not only was the ocean vast and stormy, but it was strangely invisible. Fogs persisted for days, making the approach to Kerguelen's islands hazardous. The ships frequently lost sight of each other; no one knew whether the islands sought for might be struck, or missed altogether. Those like King who had not seen, and had not been told, what the voyage's instructions were, were frustrated by the possibility that search for this subsidiary object would set back the larger plan. His fear that 'yᵉ smallest delay would hazard yᵉ loss of a season' was prescient.

Finally, on 24 December, an island was sighted, then a second and then others. Fog remained thick, the sea was high, and the surf on their shores 'frightfull'. The *Resolution* barely got by one rocky dome that was called Bligh's Cap, probably the same, Cook considered, as Kerguelen's isle of Rendezvous, 'but I know nothing that can Rendezvous at it but fowls of the air for it is certainly inaccessible to every other animal'. The following day a bay was reached, where grass was cut for the cattle, water replenished, and nets tried without luck, though many birds shot. All were at work on both 25 and 26 December. The crew were given the freedom to celebrate on the twenty-seventh, when most went for walks ashore. He had 'never before experienced Christmas day so little noticed', one seaman complained.

The country was found to be 'barren and desolate in the highest degree'. What had appeared from the sea to be verdure extending over the hills turned out to be a sort of moss, widely dispersed over what was basically bare rock. Though a kind of edible cabbage was gathered and boiled, there were no trees, and nothing that could even be called a shrub. These islands were not horribly frozen as those of South Georgia and the South Sandwich Islands had been, but the place seemed similarly lifeless. It seemed to spurn human interest and attention. Reporting an excursion to a hill-top in search of a view, Cook repeated himself in his journal, as he often did: though his view was impeded by fog, such country as he could see was 'naked and disolate in the highest degree'. Just as the stereotypic savage lacked clothing, the land itself here lacked the civil dress of forest, it was naturally unsociable and unwelcoming.

John Webber met his first test as expedition artist. Here, of all places, he began illustrating un-European scenes. His view of the anchorage is at first sight a pretty unremarkable drawing of a bay, a beach and a mountain. A closer look suggests a good eye, a graphic intelligence, even a trace of dry humour. The drawing is attentive to the meagre vegetation, the strata of the rough slope above the opposite shore, the waterfall, the basalt outcrop and, in the distance, the oddity of the natural arch, that made the bay unmistakable from the sea. There is a sensitivity to geology that a Banks or Forster would have approved of, but there is also a sense of composition in the moody shadow of the foreground, in the disposition of ships, boats and men venturing ashore, and in the formal echo, between the flattened arc of penguins, and the flattened triangle of the mountain-top. And there is something faintly ironic in the penguins, posed as though engaged in polite conversation at an afternoon garden party. Their self-absorbed congregation, indifferent to the arrival of humanity, marks the sort and the extent of such wretched sociality as is imaginable here. The bleakness of the place, Edgar thought, was compounded by 'the Melancholy Croaking of Innumerable Penguins'.

On Friday, 27 December, one of the seamen out for a walk came across a bottle. Inside was a Latin inscription on parchment recording the French discovery that had alerted the Admiralty to these islands. Cook had one of his Latin-literate officers write on the other side, 'Naves Resolution &

38. *John Webber,* A View of Christmas Harbour, *1776.*

Discovery de Rege Magnae Brittaniae Decembris 1776', then 'display'd the British flag and named the harbour Christmast harbour as we entered it on that Festival'. Anderson remarked, 'a flag was hoisted as I believe to signify our taking po'session of this place for his Majesty, a circumstance not only contrary to the law of nations but if seriously meant to the law of nature, as being in itself not only unjust but truely ridiculous, and perhaps fitter to excite laughter than indignation'.

If Anderson's 'as I believe' is not merely a turn of phrase, it is extraordinary that there might be uncertainty about what was being done on this occasion. We would surely expect the participants in a voyage to *know* whether a place visited was being taken possession of, or not. Cook's own journal leaves the matter obscure. He certainly gave places names without taking possession of them. When he did take possession, he generally did so in a more ceremonious way. The men, or at any rate the officers present, would have a drink and a toast to his Majesty's health, and perhaps shout three cheers. No drinking and no cheering on this occasion, apparently. What effect could a declaration of possession have that was ambiguous before its witnesses, that was not even explicitly recorded in the possessor's journal?

We do not know Anderson's understanding of either the 'law of nations' or that of 'nature', and it is therefore unclear what specifically he meant by asserting that the action contradicted both. The feeling of injustice here was not that of a late twentieth- or twenty-first century liberal, whose first concern would be with the non-recognition of indigenous tenure. It was rather with the pre-emption of actual and deserving possession by persons who might inhabit or use this land. Yet Cook carried out his instructions with a certain impartiality: ugly or inconsequential islets, barren as well as luxuriant places, would be named, charted, and often possessed. If it is not clear exactly why Cook took possession when he did, this is nevertheless the Cook we know, who has steadily refined a certain insensibility, whose taste is neither for pleasure nor profit, but for method and completeness.

For those who had experienced the extended discovery of nothing, during the antarctic cruises of the second voyage, this week must have reinforced an ambivalent sense of exploration, as a miserable struggle to reach places that were harsh and inhospitable that seemed to offer nothing in the way of diversions, riches, natural resources or future trade. The visit was perhaps more depressing for those who had not voyaged this far before, and had been encouraged by newspaper reports and sailors' gossip to form the most fantastic notions, of islands of ripe fruit and ripe women. Though this place was, in reality, not desolate at all – certainly not so for seabirds – its supposed sterility must have seemed contrived to cruelly dampen these expectations.

It would not be long before expectations met further actualities. But first, during January, the ships made sail across the southern Indian ocean, towards Australia. The passage was monotonous but dangerous. Continually foggy, visibility was commonly reduced to a half or even a quarter of a mile. Cook had nothing to report but the character of air, wind and his reflection upon the wholly unavoidable peril of such conditions. It was safer to sail on a clear night, if a proper watch was kept, than through such fogs. At any moment, the vessels might either be remote from any sort of threat, or on the point of sailing into a small island or isolated rock. In the latter case, 'no fortitude or dexterity could save a ship running perhaps six or seven knots from instant destruction'. But his instinct was that these waters were empty. 'We us'd then to be more cautious', he wrote, referring to his earlier voyages, when 'the notion of land being in unknown seas seem'd more universal, at least with us'. The expectation that blank spaces on maps might be replete with the hazards as well as the promises of coastlines had receded.

The land that did in due course appear was anticipated and known as Van Diemen's Land – so-called by Tasman, now Tasmania. It had been visited by Furneaux in 1773 after his first separation from the *Resolution*.

His landmarks were recognized, and anchorage was made, in Adventure Bay, named after his ship. The bay is a broad and spectacular opening in the east coast of what is now Bruny Island, just south of Hobart. The weather was warm, and the long beach of fine white sand beautiful. Parties were sent ashore. Wood and water were easily obtained, and a huge catch of fish netted. As was usual, whenever port was reached, problems of discipline arose. One group of marines stole some liquor before landing 'and made themselves exceedingly drunk, for which they receivd a dozen lashes each', Clerke recorded. Cook was hardly interested in this reciprocity of minor offence and minor punishment, but was anxious to obtain grass for the cattle: what was found was coarse, but for the want of better was cut anyway. Smoke inland had been sighted. On the afternoon of 28 January, the second day ashore:

> we were agreeably surprised at the place we were cuting Wood, with a Visit from some of the Natives, Eight men and a boy: they came out of the Woods to us without shewing the least mark of fear and with the greatest confidence immaginable, for none of them had any weapons, except one who had in his hand a stick about 2 feet long and pointed at one end.

These were the first indigenous Australians Cook had seen for over six years. He might immediately have sensed an affinity, since they seemed as uninterested as the Eora of Botany Bay and the Guugu Yimidhirr of the Endeavour River in gifts or barter: 'They received every thing we gave them [meaning beads, trifles and some ironware] without the least appearance of satisfaction.' They gave back or threw away some bread and appeared disgusted by fish, but did keep some birds they were offered '& gave us to understand they would eat them'. But Cook did not remark that this indifference or resistance to presents recalled his experience with the people he had met in 1770. He was struck, rather, by dissimilarities in language among other domains; his eye for human variety had become finely adjusted.

The meeting with these people was brief. Cook wanted to know how accurately the man with the stick – presumably a throwing club – could deliver it. This interest was communicated with signs, and the man performed, but failed to impress, missing a target that lay only twenty yards away. Mai fired his musket at the mark, in order to demonstrate the superiority of European guns, Cook tells us, as if to insist that this competition was part of his rational plan, to ensure that these native people were fully aware of their visitors' strength, and of the imprudence of any belligerence on their part, perhaps an unnecessary revelation, since no inclination towards aggression had been expressed, nor any propensity to theft. In any case, the distinction between an educative exhibition and an actual aggression was lost on these people, who were terrified by the blast and who all ran away 'not withstanding all we could do or say to prevent them: one was so frightened that he let drop an ax and two knives that were given him'. This same afternoon, these people or others visited a group cutting wood, who gave them a few things. They were perceived to be sociable and friendly, and some went as far as to help, lending their strength to the cross-cut saw. But they were especially curious about the boat that lay offshore, and picked up the rope and tried to haul it in. Some waterers in the boat were alarmed and fired a shot in the air. The Aboriginal people then fled. After they had gone, Cook took a boar and sow into the woods, leaving them by a stream. The Aboriginal people had seen them, and seemed to want to kill and consume them immediately; Cook thought that if he thus secreted them, they might survive long enough to reproduce.

The next day, a larger group appeared and spent several hours in the vicinity of some of those cutting wood. They had apparently not been more than momentarily intimidated by the guns of the day before. They did not express 'the least fear or distrust', Cook wrote. He was struck by one man, 'much deformed, being humpbacked, he was not less distinguishable by his wit and humour, which he shewed on all occasions and we regreted much that we could not understand'. Cook noted again that people set no value on iron, and was perplexed that they seemed not to understand the use of fish hooks that they were offered. 'We cannot suppose but that people who inhabit a Sea Coast must have ways and means to catch fish.' Though he knew that they had rejected all the fish they had been offered, he concluded that they must simply have had an abundance, and no need for it. In fact, all indigenous Tasmanians observed a taboo on eating fish, for reasons that remain puzzling and controversial among archaeologists and anthropologists.

After Cook left this group, some women and children arrived. The latter were said to be finely formed and pretty, but the former judged unattractive, though evidently not to everyone.

Some of the Gentlemen belonging to the Discovery I was told, paid their addresses and made them large offers which were rejected with great disdain whether from a sence of Verture or for fear of displeasing the Men I shall not pretend to determine. This thing was certainly not very agreeable to the latter, for an elderly man as soon as he observed it, ordered all the Women & Children away, which they obeyed, but not without some of them shewing a little reluctancy. This conduct to Indian Women is highly blameable, as it creates a jealousy in the men that may be attended with fatal consequences, without answering any one purpose whatever, not even that of the lover obtaining the object of his wishes. I believe it has generally been found among uncivilized people that where the Women are easy of access, the Men are the first who offer them to strangers, and where this is not the case they are not easily come at, neither large presents nor privacy will induce them to violate the laws of chastity or custom. This observation I am sure will hold good throughout all parts of the South Sea where I have been, why then should men risk their own safety where nothing is to be obtained?

Cook, we can only suppose, was so habituated to his own restraint as to naïvely imagine that other men might calculate when and when not to pursue sexual opportunity, on the basis of what was in fact a complex and dubious generalization about the people of the 'South Sea'. His 'uncivilized' people were not those of Tahiti or those related to them in the neighbouring Society Islands or Marquesas. In these places, sexual commerce had been volunteered, acquiesced in, or refused by women, who were neither 'offered' nor restrained by their men. True, the obverse of the proposition had been sustained by experience at Malakula and Tanna, where men seemed to actively sequester women and where, all the evidence suggests, no sexual contact whatsoever was permitted. Women had been offered most conspicuously to the mariners by their menfolk in Queen Charlotte Sound, but there the latter had not been 'the first' to do so, as Cook's tenet stipulated. Rather, as he was disturbed to record, the men had begun to do so only after they had acquired an appetite for European things, and after they had gathered that women were obtaining ironware and other things in exchange for sexual favours. The issue was further complicated: which South Sea peoples were civilized and which uncivilized? Who exactly was this proposition meant to apply to? Cook never made any categorization, or any ranking explicit. His tendentious argument was more indicative of frustration with the risky passion of his men – here, moreover, officers rather than understandably unreflective Jack Tars – than a stab at an Oceanic sexology.

The remarks are, however, resonant of the arguments of Johann Forster, who placed particular emphasis upon whatever he took to be the status of women in the places visited. His larger principle was that 'the more the women are esteemed in a nation', the closer they were led towards 'the blessings of civilization'. Conversely 'the more debased the situation of a nation . . . the more harshly we found the women treated'. The paradox was that 'esteemed' Tahitian women were free to commercialize their bodies, while 'debased' Malakulans were compelled to be virtuous. But this was only the same paradox that afflicted commercial civilization itself, that simultaneously refined and corrupted everyone from Maori – infected by their first taste of trade – to the venal and syphilitic politicians of London and Paris. Not for the world would Cook have travelled anywhere with Forster again, but he was not opposed to sailing with his ideas, which remained inconsistent, censorious and suggestively powerful. Cook had no particular interest in their philosophical elaboration, but they shaped his sense of incident in this case of sexual commerce, or rather its refusal.

The friendliness of the Tasmanians impressed itself upon Charles Clerke. 'There was a harmless Chearfullness about them,' he wrote. But he, among other observers, yoked this pleasant simplicity to a lack of wants and to a state of nature. That remark was preceded by the statement that 'The inhabitants seem to have made the least progress towards any kind of Improvement since Dame Nature put them out of hand, of any people I have ever met with.' The midshipman Martin wrote that 'They have few, or no wants, & seemed perfectly Happy.' These conventional observations were easily rephrased in negative terms, however. Anderson agreed with others that they 'were mild and chearfull without reserve or jealousy of strangers', remarkable since that 'jealousy' was otherwise 'almost constantly observed' among indigenous peoples, on initial contact with Europeans. But, Anderson thought, this was perhaps so, not because these people were simply good-tempered or benevolent, but because they possessed so little 'to loss or care for'. He proceeded to note 'with respect to personal activity or genius we can say but little of either [though] they do not seem to possess the first in any remarkable degree, and as for the last they have to appearance less than even the half animated inhabitants of Terra del Fuego'. The surgeon Ellis, who later published a voyage narrative, agreed disparagingly that 'they seem to be nearly on a par with the wretched natives of Terra del Fuego'; John Rickman, a lieutenant on the *Discovery*, who also rushed out a book for the printer's money, did not repeat this comparison, but asserted that the Tasmanians 'were wholly insensible' to the 'blessings' of their luxuriant country. They 'seemed to live like the beasts of the forest in roving parties, without arts of any kind'. He conjectured that they were 'a sort of fugitives who have been driven out from some more powerful community, and subsist here in a state of banishment, as it is hardly possible otherwise to conceive so fine a country possessed by a people wholly destitute of all the arts of civil life'.

Cook himself ventured neither any negative nor positive characterization of these people, as occupants of a state of nature, though Clerke's and Martin's remarks recall the gist of what he himself had said some years earlier of the Guugu Yimidhirr happiness observed at the Endeavour River. But that celebration of Aboriginal life in Australia's far north had turned upon the climate. The tropical heat made clothing and elaborate shelter unnecessary, but here, in the temperate south, the conditions were less benign. Cook had, moreover, seen many peoples since. He occasionally still came out with idealizing generalizations, but had gravitated rather towards particular description, and more nuanced judgements of customs and temperaments. These assessments inevitably remained limited, in this case most obviously by the lack of linguistic understanding. Neither Cook nor anyone else could possibly have gained any insight, under the circumstances, into issues of property among Tasmanians. Much of what they had to 'loss or care for' was not fenced land, but was intangibly related to rights in stories and sacred sites. Yet, even if he had seen natural simplicity become complicated, Cook was disinclined to denigrate these people, though near the end of his second voyage, he had again all but bestialized the Fuegians. Here, however, he did not see the parallel that Ellis, Anderson, and others did. He went out of his way to note that 'where ever there was a heap of shells there remained the marks of fire, an indubitable sign that they do not eat their food raw' – a point emphasized, perhaps, because others on board proposed that the Tasmanians did. He acknowledged that their hair was 'as woolly as any Native of Guinea' – which in the heyday of slavery was to liken them with the Africans most subject to a dehumanizing racism – but insisted that they were otherwise different, 'they were not distinguished by remarkable thick lips nor flat noses, on the contrary their features were far from disagreeable'. If the comparison subscribed to the worst stereotypes of the time, it did so in order to exempt these people from them.

On the first voyage, the artists had been part of Banks's team. On the second, Hodges had been his own painter. But back in London, in the course of preparing his book, Cook, collaborating with Hodges and Douglas, and advised by Sandwich, Banks and others, had hit on a new, and heightened, sense of the work that printed pictures could do. They would provide visual information, of course, and would attract a readership beyond maritime and philosophical circles, through carefully engraved images of exotic places, peoples, scenes, and plants. In 1777 the published *Voyage* would set an entirely new standard, for the range and quality of illustration in a travel book, and the wider readership was indeed attracted and excited. Some of the prints were much more than attractive illustrations, they dignified the voyage, celebrated its transactions, and defined it as historic. On the third voyage, Cook was more mindful than ever of history-making, and John Webber would be his artist. Webber was as familiar as Hodges with the tradition of history-painting. The meeting with the Tasmanians gave him his first subject appropriate to this treatment. From his perspective, this was not simply an incident but a dramatic encounter analogous to the 'Landings' that Hodges had depicted. Webber's pencil and ink study would not have been drawn on the spot, but was probably composed soon afterwards on the basis of his field sketches; it featured the 'humpbacked' man who impressed Cook with his wit and humour. But it was also a contrived scene, which juxtaposed the parties theatrically – the Tasmanian men on one side and members of Cook's company on the other.

Webber might have depicted the people running away, frightened by Mai's musket, or the local women, rebuffing the officers' proposals, but it is hardly surprising that he did not. Those moments were just as much a part of this meeting, but they were not the right ones to memorialize. The event was picked out, but it was also distorted. In the sketch, which was never finished, Webber paid most attention to the stances and expressions of the indigenous people, who appear hesitant, and in awe before the strangers. But Cook is explicit that the group approached without 'the least mark of fear and with the greatest confidence immaginable', indicating not only that their mood was different, but that they took the initiative, in emerging from the bush to greet or confront the visitors. We know from David Samwell that so far from the indigenous people being scared, it was one of the marines who was 'struck with Terror & Astonishment' on first sighting the natives. The German seaman, Heinrich Zimmermann, admitted that, on hearing 'the laughter and the cries of joy' of the Tasmanians, 'we ran in alarm to the boats, in which we had left our guns'. None of this quite suits Webber, who has no doubt about who is the lead actor in this scene: Cook moves purposefully towards the principal Tasmanian, who is trepidatious but ready to receive this benevolent stranger's gift.

On the morning of 30 January a light westerly breeze sprang up, and the ships put to sea, and sailed towards New Zealand. The winds were light, and the sailing straightforward. It's slightly mysterious that George Moody, a marine belonging to the *Discovery*, fell overboard 'and was never seen afterwards' on the calm night of 6 February. A few days later the coast of Te Wai Pounamu came into view, and for the fifth time in seven years, Cook entered Ship Cove.

Soon after the ships anchored, canoes appeared, 'but very few of them

39. *John Webber*, An Interview between Captain Cook and the
Natives, *1777.*

would venture on board; which appeared the more extraordinary, as I was
well known to them all', Cook wrote; but it was clear that

they were apprehensive we were come to revenge the death of Captain Furneaux's
people: seeing Omai on board whose first conversation generally turned on that
subject; they must be well assured that I was no longer a stranger to that unhappy
affair, and I did all in my power to assure them of the continuence of my friendship,
and that I should not disturb them on that account.

The people it seems accepted this, or at any rate were reassured when the
Europeans embarked on no aggression. They began trading, much as before.
Cook set up an observatory on shore, began brewing beer from what he
called spruce, probably the New Zealand *rimu*, the carpenters cut wood
and parties were sent to obtain grass. These parties were, for the first
time, guarded by marines. Cook observed that he had never taken such
precautions before, 'nor were they, I firmly believe, more necessary now',
he wrote, implicitly reiterating his view that the Grass Cove massacre was
provoked by its victims. Boats that ventured any distance from the ship,
Cook placed 'under the direction of such officers as I could depend upon
and who were well acquainted with the Natives'. It sounds as though his

concern was not to protect their crews from attack, but to prevent them from emulating Rowe, in committing some stupid aggression that provoked attack. Cook was pleased that 'a great many' Maori families soon settled in Ship Cove. He was impressed by the rapidity with which they constructed a temporary village; they provided the ships with fish in abundance, they traded curiosities to seamen as acquisitive as they always had been, they offered women, but desire had been dampened. We know from Samwell that some sexual commerce continued, but Cook implies that it was all but abandoned:

the Seamen had taken a kind of dislike to these people and were either unwilling or affraid to associate with them; it had a good effect . . . A connection with Women I allow because I cannot prevent it.

Cook's position on this issue was not only moral. He mentions no moral angle on this occasion, but notes that though some men believed that such 'connections' provided security among 'Indians', he considered that to be the case only if one settled among them.

. . . but with travelers and strangers, it is generally otherwise and more men are betrayed than saved by having connection with their women, and how can it be otherwise sence all their View are selfish without the least mixture of regard or attachment whatever; at least my observations which have been pretty general, have not pointed out to me one instance to the contrary.

The issue had, apparently, been on Cook's mind. He did not merely report this refusal of an offer. He generalized about frontier and voyage sex. He argued that it heightened risks. Maybe he remained conscious of just how large the issue had loomed in the scandal around Hawkesworth's book and in popular treatments of his first voyage. He had asked Douglas to censor this aspect of his second voyage narrative. He was thinking now, not about managing the record, but trying to limit the damage. He was at odds with his crew, who detested and feared the 'cannibals' that Cook liked and respected; but this was oddly convenient if it meant that they, or most of them, kept away from the women.

Cook's ambiguous construction, 'their View are selfish', probably refers to the travelling men rather than the women who were party to these connections. But if it was true that sailors mostly sought quick satisfaction, the categorical claim was not in fact supported by the voyage experience. At the end of the first Tahitian visit, relations with Tutaha and others had been upset because Cook felt compelled to take chiefs hostage, in order to recover two men who had deserted. When they were retrieved and questioned, it transpired that they'd done so because of 'two Girls, to whome they had strongly attache'd themselves was the sole reason of their attempting to stay behind'. Apparently the same motivation lay behind other attempts to desert. If sexual commerce was certainly disruptive and contentious, it also produced odd intimacies, that Cook knew of, that undermined his generalization.

Webber was busy. He sketched people and the swiftly constructed huts that had impressed Cook and he put a good deal of work into a representation of Cook greeting a chiefly man on the shore before this settlement. Though the artist handled this meeting slightly less theatrically than the event at Adventure Bay – the latter had been treated as a moment of first contact, which this was not – the scene was nevertheless again contrived to convey historic significance. Burney mentions that the crews were desperate for curiosities and it sounds as though many men, aware of the collecting opportunities that would arise, had joined the ships 'much better provided than in any former voyage'. The terms of traffic changed, much in favour of the Maori, who now required an adze for things they would previously have sold for a nail. James King was among the collectors. He obtained a fine comb made from whalebone, on which he later inscribed his name.

In his journal entry for 14 February, 1777, Cook mentions that among the many Maori visitors is a chief named Kahura. This warrior, he gathered, 'headed the party that cut off Captain Furneux's boat and who himself killed the officer that commanded it', that is, Jack Rowe. Other Maori told Cook that Kahura was 'a very bad man'; they encouraged him to kill him and were surprised that he did not. Revenge or *utu* was a central element of Maori life. It was the obverse of the fundamental social obligation to repay a gift. The flow of generosity, indebtedness, honour and violence that these principles between them generated were in effect the substance of Maori history, and the axes out of which sacred power or *mana*, and political prestige, were produced. A failure to take revenge would generally have been interpreted as a sign of weakness or cowardice. Had Cook not manifestly been a powerful man, local Maori would not have tried to capitalize upon the situation, by informing him that various enemies of theirs had perpetrated the massacre, 'the people of each Hamlet or village by turns applyed to me to distroy the other'. They probably found it all but incomprehensible that he did not punish Kahura, and perhaps began to think that he

40. *John Webber,* Captain Cook in Ship Cove, Queen Charlotte
Sound, *1777.*

was not powerful after all. There is no hint of this in Cook's own journal, but others report that those vigorously engaged in trade were more assertive and demanding than they ever had been. 'It seemed evident that many of them held us in great contempt and I believe chiefly on account of our not revenging the affair of Grass Cove', wrote Burney. He may well have been right, but he was also the man who had been on the spot during the second voyage. He had discovered the bodies, he had been one of those most affected by the horror. He was thus not quite an impartial commentator.

Two days later, on 16 February, Cook took five boats up to Grass Cove, simply to collect grass, but the occasion was dominated by the memory of the affray. The inquiry that newspapers, more than a year earlier, had claimed had already taken place took place now. Curiously, its findings were more or less along the lines that had already been reported. Through Mai as interpreter, Cook understood that Rowe's party had rested for a meal. When some Maori among or near them stole or snatched some bread, they were assaulted in return, which led to a fight and two were shot dead. Before the muskets could be reloaded, all were clubbed, or seized and then clubbed. The last man killed, several agreed, had been James Tobias Swilley, a black servant of Furneaux's, who had been left to guard the boat. Anderson felt for him, since he 'must certainly have felt the most horrid sensations on seeing his companions murder'd before his face without the least hopes of giving them assistance or prolonging his own fate'.

Parenthetically, it should be mentioned that our manuscript of Cook's 'journal' does not in fact consist of a series of daily entries. It was certainly based on such a series but was rewritten – probably soon after the departure from Ship Cove, but perhaps also subsequently. Cook's account of this interview is informed by hindsight. He clearly conducted further inquiries over subsequent days, but does not detail the whole intermittent inquest. He is content, rather, to report that though there were variant versions, what he heard first 'was confirm'd by the testimony of many people who I think, could have no intrest in deceiving us'. He summed up:

all agree . . . that the thing was not premeditated, and that if the thefts had not, unfortunately, been too hastily resented no ill consequence had attended, for Kahoura's greatest enemies, those who solicited his distruction the most, owned that he had no intention to quarrel, much less to kill, till the quarrel was actually commenced.

The rights and wrongs of the matter were clearly much debated. Despite the near-unanimity of the testimony, many on board both ships did not accept Cook's view that the assault had not been planned. They believed rather that the affair had been 'a concerted Scheme', agreeing with those Maori who wanted Kahura killed. Mai, too, was vociferous in this opinion, perhaps because he had been on the *Adventure* at the time of the tragedy and regarded those killed as kin of a sort. Shortly before the ships were to leave Meretoto, Kahura visited twice, the second time with his extended family. The second time, Cook was in his cabin. Mai alerted him to the warrior's arrival and Cook told him to invite Kahura in.

. . . he interduced him into the Cabbin, saying 'there is Kahourah kill him' but as if he would have no hand in it himself, retired immidiately, but returned again in a short time and seeing the chief unhurt, said 'why do you not kill him, you till me if a man kills an other in England he is hanged for it, this Man has killed ten and yet you will not kill him, tho a great many of his countrymen desire it and it would be very good.' Omais arguments, tho reasonable enough, having no weight with me, I desired him to ask the cheif why he killed Captain Furneaux's people.

Kahura then feared he would be killed, but cheered up when assured that he would not. At length he ventured an explanation consistent with what Cook had already heard, except that he claimed that the trouble began when one of the mariners refused to pay him for a stone hatchet he had offered. This, Cook considered, was merely an invention that made 'the English appear the first aggressors'. The conversation was relaxed. Kahura was in no hurry to leave. He saw 'a Portrait of one of his countrymen hanging up in the Cabbin, he desired to be drawn, and sat till Mr Webber had finished, without the least restraint. I must confess,' Cook wrote, 'I admired his courage and was not a little pleased at the confidence he put in me.'

When I started writing this book, I pinned some dozen pictures on to a cork board. They included a Hawaiian feather god, one of Cook's Tahitian maps, and a few snapshots from Tahiti, Cooktown and Whitby. The board has been by my desk; the pictures have been like landmarks, enabling me to find my way. Out of them, though, one has been peculiarly enigmatic and compelling. It depicts a slightly pensive, but seemingly alert and agile man, whose hair is captured in a tight and neat topknot, who wears four fine white feathers and indeterminate ornaments – I guess of greenstone or bone, and perhaps again feathers – that hang from his pierced ears. He wears a full flax cape – Webber's brush suggests a certain sumptuousness – and is a man marked by *ta moko*, by the painfully chiselled, curvilinear face tattoo that signalled something of his genealogy, that enhanced his *mana*. The disconcerting and awe-inspiring effect of the design can only have been accentuated in this case by its asymmetry, presumably its incompleteness. Yet there is no incompleteness in the man, who lacks neither poise nor intelligence, who is his own sort of aristocrat.

Perhaps Webber, like Cook, admired Kahura. Certainly this sketch, the one that Webber drew on the morning of 25 February 1777, seems to do more than merely acknowledge the warrior's sense of his own dignity. This does not look like the 'very bad man' that many Maori wanted dead. Nor does it look like the leader of the 'infernal Savages' (Samwell called them) who not only killed, but devoured the crew of an English boat. There is a glaring inconsistency between all the talk that twirled around a hated cannibal and an essentially empathetic portrait, but also something larger than this. What is larger is paradoxical, but it epitomizes the whole of Cook's experience, maybe the whole of eighteenth-century European experience, in Oceania. And there is not one paradox, but several. The man's actions were inconceivably horrible, but also justifiable. That was as obvious to Cook as it was incomprehensible to others. Men from one side of the world, intruding on men from the other, fell out and fell to blows. They did so not because they misunderstood one another, not because they were representative of different cultures that are prone to 'clash', as the cliché has it, but arguably because these particular men, Jack Rowe and Kahura, had a good deal in common. They were similarly proud, similarly violent, similarly courageous, similarly impetuous. The two cultures might have had two opposed views

41. *Webber's portrait of Kahura, 1777, drawn in*
Cook's cabin on 25 February 1777.

about how the survivor of the bloody contest deserved to be treated.
Yet many Maori agreed with many Europeans that Kahura ought to die.
Those who dissented were Kahura himself, we presume his kin, and Cook,
who among the Europeans was not quite in a minority of one, but in a

minority that authoritatively outweighed the majority of common seamen and gentlemen.

The picture and its circumstances do not add up, but that is in a way consistent: the circumstances themselves did not add up. Moments of friendship and moments of violence could never quite be reconciled; nor could the senses of human affinity, difference and antagonism that they at various times engendered. In Cook's imagination, friendship and understanding loomed larger than hostility and estrangement. Minor trouble he refrained from reporting, and major confrontation he explained away. His thinking this way his company could not follow. His action on this basis, his people often resented. Cook was adhering to rules of his own that he'd invented during his second voyage, that suspended the loyalties that his loyal crew thought they were due. At Raiatea and many other places, he had refused to avenge thefts and insults perpetrated upon sundry officers and men who walked off and were silly enough to end up in trouble. Cook's overriding loyalty was to his own judgement, to almost esoteric principles he worked out that identified one theft as inconsequential and another as an insolence that had to be punished. Between Ship Cove and Grass Cove, this sort of squabble was writ large. The assault had not stopped at stripping clothes or seizing a sword. It had entailed stripping flesh. It had reduced British subjects to the savages' victims. The argument that it had been an outrage was 'reasonable enough', Cook conceded, yet it had 'no weight with me'.

I had always declared to those who solicited his death that I had always been a friend to them all and would continue so unless they gave me cause to act otherwise; as to what was past, I should think no more of it as it was some time sence and done when I was not there, but if ever they made a Second attempt of that kind, they might rest assured of feeling the weight on my resentment.

This was noble, though probably entirely unintelligible from a Maori point of view. Here, it is worth recalling that the very word 'Maori' emerged only during the nineteenth century, to distinguish indigenous New Zealanders generally from foreigners. In the 1770s, the various peoples Cook encountered – though certainly aware of their shared affinity and difference from the Europeans – did not see themselves as 'Maori'. Their identities, relationships and antagonisms were tribal or still more local and particular. Hence even Cook's seemingly straightforward proposition that he was a friend 'to them all' was nonsensical, since to be a true friend to one *hapu* or sub-tribe should have meant joining and supporting that people against another. Cook's explanation and warning, which excused a first attack on his own tribe, but promised that a second would be vigorously avenged, was, I suspect, still less clear in translation as it was unclear to Cook's men. They must have thought that their captain cared more for Kahura than he did for Rowe's memory. They were probably right.

18

An act that I cannot account for

William Anderson must have been active on every one of the crowded twelve days of the visit of the *Resolution* and *Discovery* to Ship Cove. Conscious that there was no Banks or Forster on board, he was anxious to make the most of opportunities to botanize, and to observe. On the last voyage he had fallen out with the Forsters, but he'd learned a lot from them first, not least that a natural historian's vision extended to just about everything, as his now did, around Totaranui.

He situated the sound: 14° south, 'Longitude 184.45 W from London, though the accuracy of this is disputed by the Astronomers', a 'cavil' of no consequence to the navigator. He proceeded to talk sailing directions, landforms, mountains, beaches, rocks. I find his remarks, even on the most ordinary of geographic points, peculiarly remarkable. When he says that the rock along the shore is 'a brittle yellowish sand stone which acquires a blueish cast where the sea washes over it', I feel a weathered bit of this stone breaking up between my fingers, I see the grey water of Totaranui lapping against a blueish boulder on a wet and cloudy afternoon, I imagine the thick scrub up the slope behind it.

What Anderson also learned from the Forsters, especially from George Forster, was a naturalist's aesthetic. The yellowish soil, formed out of the rock he's just described, supports 'luxuriant growth'. The hills are covered by 'one continued forest of lofty trees which flourish with a vigour almost superior to any thing imagination can conceive, and afford an august prospect to those who are delighted with the grand and beautiful works of nature'. This sublime magnificence, he thought, derived from the mildness of the climate. He proceeded to describe the winds and weather, and in more detail the trees and plants. He singled out useful ones, such as the wild celery, a certain scurvy grass, and what he called Philadelphus; the last 'we drank the leaves . . . as tea and found they had a pleasant taste and smell, which might make an excellent substitute for the oriental sort, as it is well known fashion has a greater share in making such things generally useful than the palate'. He was talking about the well-known manuka or New Zealand tea tree, used medicinally by the Maori, and subsequently by bush settlers in lieu of 'the oriental sort'.

Anderson itemized and described birds, fish, shellfish and insects, whose Linnean species names he gives in footnotes to his manuscript. He distilled what was known of the Maori, beginning with their physique and appearance; he was careful to point to variety in skin colour, which ranged 'from a pretty deep black to a yellowish or olive tinge'. He noticed that among young people the countenance was 'generally free and open', but that many men looked 'serious', or displayed 'a sullenness or reserve'. He went on to write about dress, ornaments, ochre, tattoos and houses, which he thought were squalid. He was more impressed by the canoes and, like Banks, Parkinson and others before him, particularly taken with the prows. The *waka* often had 'a large head ingeniously carv'd and painted with a figure at the point, which seems intended to represent a man with his features distorted by rage'. When he got on to their temperament, he stressed, like Cook, a Maori sensitivity to insult, and commitment to revenge: 'No people can be more susceptible of an injury done them and none more ready to resent it.' He lacked Cook's qualifying, almost romantic regard for their openness and bravery. What he saw as a Maori tendency to mistrust was, however, 'in some measure to be expected where there appears to be but little subordination and consequently few if any laws to punish transgressions'; which was to say that the political environment – here the lack of political union or regular government – was what accounted for the dispositions of the men.

Anderson fully acknowledged the terrifying power of Maori war dance, marked by the 'frantic fury' of participants and 'the most horrid distortion' of their eyes, mouths and tongues. The excess of the whole performance 'almost foretold' the 'horrid, cruel and disgracefull' practice of cannibalism, which, as a fact of human society, perplexed Anderson. He could not understand what its origin could have been, he could not understand its limit, he could not see that it would not, in the end, lead to the extirpation of whole peoples. He was also baffled by what he saw as the inconsistency of Maori character: the awful practice suggested that they were 'destitute of every humane feeling', 'yet we find them lamenting the loss of their friends with an excess which would argue the most tender remembrance of them'. He could cite a variety of other signs of strong affection. On one point, Anderson lapsed into silly self-contradiction: he argued quite soundly that cannibalism had nothing to do with hunger, or any environmental scarcity, but went on just a few pages later to propose that the way to reform the people, to break them from the awful practice, was by 'substituting plenty of animal food', perhaps cattle (which Cook carried with him, but did not leave here, so unconfident was he that they would survive). But this little absurdity expressed a real anxiety, a proto-missionary zeal to see the Maori elevated somehow. Anyone who had been face to face with their aggressive independence could only clutch at straws, in planning the amelioration of this awesome, energetic, martial society.

Cook imagined no amelioration or improvement of the Maori. Occupied as he often was by practical matters during this visit, he made further inquiries about their manners and again thought through what he knew. His sense that they were a people profoundly divided, and mutually hostile, was reinforced. He gathered that injuries done to a father would never be forgotten, that the grievance would be nursed by the son, for however long, until the opportunity for revenge arose. Though people were mutually hostile, he saw that they had a system of calling on each other to trade. They traded various things, but most notably the *pounamu* or jade. This was highly valued, and came, he thought, from only one source. He was sorry not to have the chance to visit it, 'as we were told a hundred fabulous stories about this Stone'. He had previously admitted that he had no idea what, if any, religion the Maori had. He now made some tentative observations, making implicit comparison with Tahitians. Unlike them, they had no *marae* 'or other places of publick worship', but there were priests, who would address the gods, soliciting success in war, fishing and other enterprises. He understood that prohibitions upon eating were on some occasions very rigorously observed. He saw pieces of hair attached to the branches of trees, near their houses, and guessed this was done for some religious reason, 'but what these notions are I never could learn'. To these sorts of miscellaneous observations he added that women who were unmarried lived unprotected, in 'but a forelone state', 'so that Polygamy is perhaps more justifiable here than in any other part of the World'. But his conclusion was that the New Zealanders were perfectly satisfied with what they possessed. They had no yearning for knowledge or improvement. They were not surprised by new objects, they would listen to Mai, 'but like people who neither understood nor wished to understand what they heard'.

In other words, they would be what they were. Yet Cook's sense of these people was differentiated. He responded to distinct personalities, and he had real regard for some, such as a young man named Te Weherua. From the start of the visit, he had attached himself to Mai, and wished to join the vessel. Cook thought at first that he would change his mind. When it seemed he did not, he had it explained to the youth, to a servant who would accompany him, and to the community, that there would be no coming back; yet this seemed not to trouble them. Inquiries established that Te Weherua's father had been killed a few years earlier, though his mother was alive and lamented the prospect of his departure. These circumstances, and what Cook took to be a puzzling indifference on the part of others to whether the young men remained or disappeared, satisfied him in the end that 'the boys would not be losers by the exchange of place'. Once again, Cook's company would incorporate non-Europeans. Once again they would share histories and tell tales. Like Tupaia, Te Weherua took up the pencil, to illustrate his account of a monstrous, man-eating being – probably the well-known *taniwha* of Maori myth – he 'with his own hand drew a very good representation of a Lizard on a piece of paper, as also a Snake in order to shew what kind of animal he meant'. Maybe, when they sat about, the Maori used a stick in the sand to draw descriptively, but it sounds nevertheless as though Te Weherua was a ready practitioner of an unfamiliar art. His drawing does not seem consistent with Cook's claim, that the Maori had no interest in trying anything new. The Maori would, in fact, try all sorts of new things, but on their own terms. What Cook responded to was not their resistance to innovation, but an intractable independence.

The ships took a north-easterly course towards Tahiti. The winds were light and unfavourable and by mid March Cook began to worry that the food for the horses and cattle would not last. Moreover, the likelihood of reaching north America in time to use the summer months for exploration was diminishing. At the end of the month, an island previously unknown to him was sighted. It proved to be densely inhabited by people who chanted like the Maori, and who appeared to be hostile. A canoe approached. An offering was made. Mai demanded to know whether the people were cannibals. They were disgusted to be asked, but wanted to know in return whose ship this was, and whence it came. These were the usual Polynesian questions, which Cook had been asked nearly eight years earlier on his intrusion into Poverty Bay, and often subsequently. Cook put out a boat to look for an anchorage. The canoe promptly pulled alongside, and one of the men stepped into the boat. His name was Mourua. Thought to be 'the Kings brother', the nineteenth-century research of the missionary William Wyatt Gill tells us that he was in fact his *toko* or 'support', his warrior deputy. He appeared friendly and directed Cook's boat towards landing-places, perhaps in order to give those on shore the chance to attack. According to their own traditions, the people of this island, Mangaia, regarded arriving strangers as invaders, and generally killed them. The Europeans may thus have been lucky that the surf was too heavy. A good many people swam out to the boats. Several climbed into them, and were 'impudently Troublesome', taking whatever things they wanted. To forestall more of this, Cook took the boats back out towards the ships. Only Mourua remained with them, and came on board, somewhat uneasily. He had conversed with Cook and Mai, and was given a knife, which he thrust through a slit in his ear. He was drawn by Webber. 'We were obliged to leave this fine island which seemed capable of supplying all our wants,' wrote Cook, without knowing how fortunate he probably was that there was no anchorage or safe landing here. He mentioned that 'their' forearms were tattooed. Perhaps he meant only that Mourua's was. He judged the people closer to Maori than to Tahitians, not I think because he detected any greater physical affinity, but probably because their warrior propensities put him in mind of Maori.

A few days later they reached another island, like Mangaia a part of the group later called the Cook Islands – today the independent nation of that name. Atiu was slightly smaller than Mangaia, but likewise densely inhabited by Polynesian peoples related to those already known to Europeans. John Gore took boats to investigate the shore. At the same time canoes came off, people came aboard, and there was some gift exchange, though Cook was later to understand that the man he tried to 'compliment' with presents had been disappointed. He wanted 'an Animal they had not on the island, though they knew very well what they were'. On the *Discovery*, another man tried similarly to obtain a dog in barter, and 'met with the like disappointment'. Given the lengths that Cook was going to to try to introduce various animals to various islands, it would have been enormously ironic if those Islanders who actually sought specific animals were not able to obtain them from him. The people returned the next day with a pig, some plantains and some coconuts, for which they 'demanded a Dog and refused every other thing that was offered'. Cook mentions with some irritation that one of the officers had a dog and bitch, that were 'a great nuesence', that 'might have been desposed of here to some essential purpose', but the owner would not part with his pets. Mai, however, was less selfish, and gave away his own; they left 'highly satisfied,' with this one creature, but without the breeding pair that would have been useful to posterity.

Though there was no likelihood of a boat landing, John Gore thought it might be possible to ply about outside the surf and persuade people to bring provisions off in their canoes. What was wanting, especially, was grass for the cattle, which, as Anderson noted, 'seem'd to droop from being continually fed on dry food'. Cook approved the idea. Gore took three boats, and found the people did come off in canoes. They may have assented to trade,

42. *John Webber*, A Man of Mangaia, *1777*.

but wanted the Europeans ashore, and used small canoes to take first Gore and Mai, then Burney and Anderson, towards the coral reef, upon which the waves pounded. The Islanders watched the 'motions of the Surf' carefully and seized the moment to deposit their passengers, who were then taken hold of and led across the coral to a great throng of curious people. Anderson and Burney, separated from the other two, were led to visit one chief, who wore ear ornaments consisting of great bunches of red feathers. Then they were taken to other places to be presented to a second and a third. They were fatigued and hot in the midst of a great crowd, but were propelled onward, to a group of dancing women, like the chiefs decorated with bunches of red feathers. The dancers seemed to pay no attention to the visitors as they sang a slow and serious song; they moved their feet slightly, but their fingers 'very nimbly', and clapped periodically; their choreography was 'in exact concert', Anderson reported; the spectacle took his mind away from his tiredness, though he was wondering where Gore and Mai had got to.

At length they appeared. Mai, extraordinarily enough, had encountered some of his 'country men' (whether from Raiatea specifically or the Society Islands generally, we do not know), who had been blown off course in their canoe and reached Atiu eventually, some dying during a passage of around 600 miles. This had occurred, Anderson judged, more than twelve years earlier, since the men had no knowledge of European visits to Tahiti. (It may well have been through these men that Atiuans had heard about dogs.) While intrigued by this discovery, the party was troubled by the conduct of the Islanders, who deliberately separated them from each other, took things from them, and prevented them from either rejoining each other, or moving back towards the shore. Yet they were not unkind: Anderson, who sounds as though he was on the point of fainting, was fanned by the chief himself, while a woman brought coconuts, breadfruit and pudding. He worried that the people had 'some intention of keeping us amongst them'. Mai became increasingly alarmed as he witnessed those by him digging an earth oven. His New Zealand experience convinced him that he faced the worst of possible fates. 'He even went so far as to ask them the Question, at which we were rather angry as none of us had thought of such a thing.' For most of the day, people crowded about them, gazed at them, wanted them to uncover parts of their skin, 'which commonly produc'd a universal murmur of admiration', no doubt because, through much of tropical Polynesia, lighter skin was associated with chiefly rank, and sometimes sought or enhanced by bleaching. Mai was relieved to see a pig brought to the earth oven. Time went by. They tried again to reach the shore, but were held back, and plants and pieces of coral that Anderson had picked up were pretty roughly taken from him.

Mai counselled them that they 'were wrong in taking up any thing, for it was not the custom here to admit freedoms of that kind till they had in some measure naturaliz'd strangers to the country by entertaining them with festivity for two or three days'. They felt affronted, decided to do what people wanted anyway, but persisted in asking to be allowed to leave. They were eventually given some food, there was some kind of kava ceremony, and the chief kept suggesting that they stay the night. Finally, as it became dark, he agreed to provide a canoe to take them off to their boats.

Anderson was at once enormously relieved to be away, and frustrated and thrilled by the chance he had 'long wish'd for, to see a people following the dictates of nature without being bias'd by education or corrupted by an intercourse with more polish'd nations'. He had imagined an opportunity to observe such people 'at leisure, but was here disappointed'. He might have added that the problem was that the Islanders were no less curious about him than he was about them. Unfortunately for Anderson's science and his comfort, not one or two but hundreds of them were curious, and their crowding and looking and poking converted him from an inquirer into an object of inquiry. Yet Anderson had perforce seen many of them. He had noticed the differences between chiefs and commoners that existed elsewhere in the islands. He had admired a physique he thought nearly perfect, and glimpsed their temperament: 'Many of the young men were perfect models in shape, of a complexion as delicate as that of the women and to appearance of a disposition as amiable,' he wrote, despite the pushy treatment he'd suffered. He'd also seen canoes, that 'were most curiously staind or painted all over with black in innumerable small figures'. Here care was devoted to this art, he thought, rather than to tattooing. What he did not see was anything of the country. At no point had any member of the party been allowed much more than a hundred yards from the place they'd landed.

Among other things, the long day here had revealed the inherent impossibility of observing peoples 'uncorrupted' by contact with Europeans, especially the impossibility of observing them in a leisurely, that is to say a sustained and unconstrained way. Precisely because they were 'uncorrupted' they controlled their lands and their lives. They would also control European visitors, who might be welcomed or allowed to stay, who might be warned off or killed, who might at best see this or that by accident, but who would not be suffered to go wherever they pleased, to inspect things and take things, without being 'in some measure naturaliz'd'. The poignant thing was that as soon as visitors began to be 'naturaliz'd', hosts began to be 'corrupted' – as they had been in Tahiti, Tonga, New Zealand and elsewhere. By 1777, those peoples could – after moments of violence, pacification and much trade – be observed at leisure, but observations of them were no longer salient to the same thing, they did not display the 'dictates of nature'. With his second voyage experience, Anderson must have known this. He had been party to moments of first contact, or what might as well have been first contact, on other shores. He knew that meetings with 'new' peoples were always awkward, suspicious, hedged about in some way; they never opened up the space for extended study that he sought.

At this time, Cook was frustrated less by the limits of knowledge than by the failure to obtain any grass. He had things to say about the visit here, and thought the accidental voyage of Mai's 'countrymen' explained how some remote islands had become settled. But he was preoccupied with the need for provisions. Fortunately, the next day a smaller island that appeared unoccupied was sighted. Gore remained intrepid, managed to land a boat through rough surf, and was able to collect greens and some 100 coconuts. Huts made it evident that the place was visited from time to time, and in one of them Gore 'left a hatchet and some nails to the full Value of what we took from the island'. Cook knew the niceties of Polynesian property and wanted to place himself above reproach.

Now it was almost the middle of April. Cook faced the fact that he had no chance of reaching northern waters in time to do anything over the summer of 1777. He knew that he also had to act if he was to save his stock. Light and adverse winds meant he would not get them to Tahiti alive. He 'therefore determined to bear away for the Friendly Isl^{ds} where I was sure of being supplied with every thing I wanted', he wrote. They sailed westward, called at the uninhabited atolls of Palmerston (discovered but not visited during the previous voyage), where more grass was obtained, and where Anderson was transported, by the varied luxuriance of the coral, and the 'yellow, blue, red, black &c' tropical fish, 'playing their gambols amongst the little caverns', easily seen in the bright and still lagoon water. The place prompted speculation about the formation of islands. Less than a fortnight later, the *Resolution* and *Discovery* reached the Tongan island of Nomuka.

Cook had, it seemed, been right. Even before harbour was found, vegetables were traded from canoes, and King went off with a couple of boats and brought back seven hogs. Two chiefs, Kepa and Tupoulangi, appeared with further gifts of pigs; wood pigeons, fowl, shaddocks (a sort of island grapefruit), breadfruit and yams, as well as small baskets, flutes, clubs and spears were offered. Samwell reports a typical specimen of ship humour; they thought Kepa was 'of such weight and consequence', they called him Lord North, after the English prime minister. He made himself busy, organizing 'the commercial Interests of his Countrymen'. 'It was remarkable', Cook was surprised and no doubt gratified to report, that 'the

Indians would hardly part with any one thing to any body but me'. His first anxiety had been to control traffic, and he immediately gave orders that certain people were to have the exclusive management of barter, that no one else was to trade either off the ship or on the shore, and expressly that 'no curiosities should be purchased till the Ships were suppled with Provisions and leave give for that purpose'. He had been favourably impressed by his 'Friendly Islands' in 1773 and 1774. The sense that there was an unusual standard of civility here was quickly reinforced in many ways, though the order behind that civility was obscure. Lord North's apparent authority notwithstanding, a higher chief named Finau appeared. He was introduced to Cook as king of all Tonga. They exchanged further gifts, and Finau dined on board, several times. The horses were landed to graze. Precautions were taken, but people felt secure.

Yet this pleasure was neither unblemished nor uncomplicated. 'They behav'd in the most civil manner to us (if we except their attempting to thieve every thing),' Anderson wrote. His parentheses are symptomatic of an effort that mariners made to define this encounter as perfect, although incidentally flawed, by the energetic and ingenious efforts of Tongans to appropriate every possible novelty or foreign valuable. On some occasions, Cook asked Finau to have consequential stolen objects returned, which he sometimes did. But chiefs themselves were thieves, until Cook had even some associate of Kepa's flogged, and then required his kin or friends to provide a pig before he would be set free. This occasioned some disquiet. Cook had rarely flogged Islanders before. Still worse, the result was only that people of rank generally commissioned their servants or slaves to take things for them. Many of them were flogged, 'which made no more impression than it would have done upon the Mainmast', Cook wrote, though he nevertheless continued to flog frequently and with increasing severity without reporting particular punishments in his journal. Instead he writes about the superb fish soup, made with coconut milk, that Finau brings him, 'probably done in a wooden vessel with hot stones' he conjectured. It was so delicious he had it imitated 'and found it very good though my Cook did not come up to theres'.

By 11 May it appeared that they had obtained just about everything that Nomuka could provide, and Cook therefore sailed on Finau's advice north towards the Ha'apai group. They reached Lifuka on 17 May. Here Finau and Kepa introduced the British. They 'harangued' people or at any rate made extended speeches, which Cook thought explained his visit, told people not to steal, and encouraged them to bring goods to trade. The next day they were provided with grand entertainment. Some 3,000 people (Cook's estimate), appeared to watch boxing matches – which disappointed the mariners when fights took place between women. Great piles of food had been assembled for presentation. Cook was told that one pile was for Mai – who was clearly playing a central role, as go-between – and the other for himself. Then the next day, Finau asked Cook, in effect, to stage a British festival in return: he wanted 'to see the Marines go through their exercize'; after they had performed, some 100 Tongan men demonstrated a dance with paddles, with 'flourishes', variety, regularity and quick time, which Cook and other witnesses found utterly astonishing. 'It was the opinion of every one of us that such a performance would have met with universal applause on a European Theatre.' He candidly acknowledged that it 'so far exceeded any thing we had done to amuse them that they seemed to pique themselves in the superiority they had over us'. In Tongan eyes, their own dance was not only outstanding, they also considered Cook's musical instruments to be derisory, relative to their own; Cook admitted that people had been indifferent to his French horns, at other islands as well as this one. That evening, 'in order to give them a better opinion of English amusements, I ordered a set of Fire works to be got ready'. Though some of these were spoiled, Cook was confident that the 'sky and Water Rockets' had been captivating, they 'intirely turned the scale in our favour'.

It appears that another scale was tilting back and forth. Cook was oblivious, almost fatally so. Nearly forty years later, William Mariner survived an assault upon the ship *Port au Prince* in this same harbour, and lived among the Tongans for four years. He was adopted, tattooed, and generally looked after. He eventually returned to Britain, and his memoirs were written up as *An Account of the Natives of the Tonga Islands* by John Martin, an ethnologically minded doctor, who had interviewed him extensively, confirmed the text with him carefully, and who incidentally went on to dedicate the book to Banks. The *Account* is unlike nearly every other beachcomber's story. In so far as it can be checked against other sources it is remarkably precise. Hence what might otherwise be dismissed as a sensational story has been, I think justly, accepted by most commentators. Mariner was told by Finau's son and by other men that the chiefs had conspired to kill Cook and his company. The plan was that they would be invited ashore to witness a night dance, and then Cook, those with him, and the marines massacred on a signal. The ships could then be seized, and those remaining on board killed. The best timing was however disputed. Most preferred the night, but Finau thought that it would be difficult to assault the ships then. Minds were changed once or twice, Finau was offended that

43. Cook *witnesses the perfection of Tongan choreography:* Webber,
A Night Dance by Men in Hapaee, *1777.*

his view was not accepted, and caused the whole scheme to be abandoned, we are told.

If we cannot be absolutely certain that there was a plot of this kind, its possibility, even its likelihood, are jarring to the reader of Cook's journal. Cook's propensity here, as in many places before, is to play up the sociality and friendliness that he feels subsists between himself and prominent Polynesian men. He likes to think that they have great regard for him, he dwells upon their signs of affection. No doubt some did regard him highly. His great boats and his things were impressive. And there are signs that on some occasions the attitude was actually affectionate. But Cook consistently underestimated, or at any rate understated, the profoundly political and pragmatic dimension of the behaviour he met with. Many of these men, and certainly Finau, had led hazardous lives. They were as adept at manipulating meanings, resources, family connections and debts as any English politician. Their experience was moreover already international, in the sense that they regularly travelled, dealt and fought with Samoans and Fijians, as well as with Tongans from all parts of the archipelago. Their friendliness was not necessarily always duplicitous, but it was never naïve. Cook understood this, up to a point, though he never worked out what made Tongan politics tick, he never understood quite how the various chiefs he met were ranked or related. He was on the outside looking in, and hence the rationale and the possibility of a real assault eluded him.

*

In 1777 the British had no notion that there had been this degree of danger. Rather, the place was a paradise. At Nomuka, Samwell had enjoyed duck-shooting ashore and sex on the ship. So far as he was concerned, the 'enchanting Prospects' of the isle could 'be said to realize the poetical Descriptions of the Elysian Fields in ancient Writers'. Anderson had been delighted by the 'spirit and exactness' of the dances they had witnessed, which he described minutely, in his own way lyrically. For his part Cook was increasingly impressed by the etiquette and ceremony that he saw, especially when a further supreme chief appeared. Paulaho was more or less what Finau had falsely been represented to be. He held the title of Tui Tonga, and was the highest-ranking, sacred chief of the whole archipelago. The Europeans would continue to be confused by meeting further high chiefs, by a complex division of rank and power that split aspects of status and authority in ways that simple models of feudalism or monarchy could neither specify nor explain. Paulaho visited the ship, and surprised Cook by asking 'several pertinent questions one of which was "what brought us to these islands"'. His response emphasized, according to the surgeon William Ellis, that he came from a 'great and mighty prince' who wanted friendship and had things to trade. Paulaho allegedly was well satisfied, though he might have been more impressed had the great prince appeared in person. They ate on board. Cook accompanied the chief ashore, where they entered a house and Paulaho received a number of people, including some who offered up things they had obtained through trade with the ships. He heard their reports, he seemed to approve, he gave their things back, apart from one glass bowl. Cook saw that those who brought the Tui Tonga gifts were careful to squat as they did so, that no one addressed him while they were standing, that those who took their leave first approached, knelt, and brought their heads into contact with the sole of his foot; he wrote that 'I was quite charmed with the decorum that was observed, I had no where seen the like'.

At Lifuka, again briefly at Nomuka, and then during June at the southern island of Tongatapu, there was much sociable interaction. Seamen had themselves shaved by the Tongans, who used sharp shells, and Tongan men had themselves shaved by the barbers on board. These experiments with razors suggest a good deal of mutual trust. Yet at the same time thefts were continually perpetrated. Islanders were flogged when they were caught. Seamen too were flogged for the neglect of duty that losing things represented.

As they arrived at Tongatapu, Cook witnessed a further manifestation of Paulaho's superiority to the people in general. The king was cruising about in his great canoe, while many people in smaller vessels crowded about the ships; 'two who could not get out of his way he run quite over with as little concern as if they had been bits of wood'. Samwell seems to have been unimpressed by the 'decorum' that charmed Cook, and still less by this sort of thing. He saw something outrageous in the 'barbarous treatment of the common People' that was permitted by 'an exorbitant Power' that the chiefs had somehow acquired. He understood that Paulaho, Finua and others could have a man put to death, for no particular reason, if they so chose, but conceded that Paulaho at least had never acted upon this entitlement. He was unclear what laws they had, but they seemed to place commoners 'intirely at [the chiefs'] Disposal in respect both to their Lives & Property: of the latter it may be doubted whether they have any!'

Samwell was right to estimate that the powers of Tongan chiefs were considerable. To a greater degree even than at Tahiti, high chiefs were quasi-gods, they were closely identified with the fecundity and prosperity of the land and the sea. They were profoundly revered, and also widely feared. Samwell, something of a radical, sees the behaviour that reflects a huge gulf of status, and is offended. He does not, of course, grasp the cultural underpinnings of these inequalities. He has no sense of what chiefs were to the Tongans, who understood humanity as inherently differentiated by genealogy, as ranked in relation to deities, kings and conquerors. Their notion, that people were of fundamentally different sorts, was deeply seated cosmologically, in a way that even the most reactionary of European ideas of the natural entitlements of aristocrats were not. The Tongans saw life itself as conditional upon the life and the ritual work of the chief; the remoteness of chief and commoner, the greatness of a king, and the awfulness of a king's anger, were only consistent with this, they were only natural. Cook does not understand much more of this than Samwell does, but he has no objection to what he sees. He has a stake himself in hierarchies. A hierarchy that places captain above crew is nearly natural to him.

Cook continued to marvel at both the environment and the social order that he encountered. In search of a further high chief, he had a fruitless visit to the village of Mu'a, but thought the place 'most delightfully situated on the bank of the inlet'. It was primarily an aristocratic settlement, where many of 'the great men of the island' had a house 'in the midst of a small plantation, with lesser houses and offices for servants &cᵃ'. These estates were all neatly fenced and gated. There were always public paths between plantations, 'so that no one trespasseth upon another'; there were fine open greens, said to belong to the king, and used for 'publick assemblies'. It is plainly the punctilious regulation of private property that made the place attractive to Cook – though he was no doubt also delighted by the beauty of the gardens, beauty that I might add is real not imaginary, and that can still be found in many parts of the Pacific today. Yet what was especially pleasing was the spectacle of an aristocracy attached to the land, that subsisted around working gardens, that had a tranquil and rural seat. Perhaps only momentarily, Tongan rulers seemed to possess the calmness, authority and authenticity that the propertied classes of Europe so patently lacked. Cook was no political theorist, but he had absorbed common notions of the gulf between ideal and real aristocrats. He cannot have helped admiring people who appeared to exemplify an antique ideal better than any modern British representatives. And he liked it that they treated him well, and took him into their homes.

On 15 June, Cook gave a number of the high chiefs gifts, and tried to give them dinner, but when the meal was served, not one of them would sit down and eat. 'Every one was *Tabu*, a word of a very comprehensive meaning but in general signifies forbidden', he wrote, citing for the first time a Polynesian term that would in due course enter common use, in European languages, and later assume a special burden in fields such as anthropology and psycho-analysis. It is at first surprising that the concept had not been recorded earlier, since prohibitions of various sorts had often been observed, but this was because the religious ideas, and the ranges of their meaning, were somewhat different from island to island. In Tahiti and New Zealand, in the places the Europeans had got to know best, they were probably not routinely told that this or that – their tramping over consecrated ground, for example – was *tapu*. They would have been told not to do this or that, but the word would not have been used, as it was in Tonga, regularly in negotiation about what they could do, in explanation of what their hosts could or could not do. It was the double meaning of tabu in Tonga – its 'very comprehensive' signification of sacredness, and its related, but confusingly distinct sense of 'forbidden' – that suddenly brought this aspect of Polynesian religion into view.

At Tongatapu there were further displays of dancing, which again were aesthetically impressive. Cook was impressed, also, by the public order that was maintained in a crowd he probably overestimated, when he claimed it was of 10–12,000. The great number went some way to excusing the thefts that were continually suffered: 'Amongst such a multitude there must be a number of ill disposed people and we hourly experienced it.' Virtually every day people such as the sailmakers, who worked ashore, were 'plundered' from in 'daring and insolent' ways, but also sometimes with great contrivance and ingenuity. The officers were certainly exasperated, but could not help admiring the 'genius' and the 'finesse' of some thieves, who worked together to create diversions. Many of the things stolen were of no great value in themselves, and Cook could not apply to Finau or Paulaho to have every piece of fabric, needle, pair of scissors or chisel restored; rather, he resorted to increasingly severe punishment. Both on the ship and shore, Tongans were subjected to two, three and even six dozen lashes; by naval standards these numbers were illegal and extreme. But he went further; the ears of some thieves were cut off, and one man's arms were cut with crosses through to the bone, to mark him out permanently, and to horrify and deter others. This general pattern of increasing violence is well documented in many logs. Cook admirers among the crew were shocked. The cutting to the bone, Gilbert wrote, 'was an act that I cannot account for any otherways than to have proceeded from a momentary fit of anger as it certainly was not premeditated.' In so far as this was a justification, it makes sense – the commander was prone to fits of rage – and it is ironically reminiscent of Cook's apologetic explanation of the Maori killings at Grass Cove. Intriguingly, Gilbert also describes Cook's general approach to punishment as 'rather unbecoming of a European', as though it became too unpleasantly like the callous brutality that marked some chiefs' treatment of some common men.

Perhaps Cook was driven to act the way he did because he could make no more moderate dissuasion work. Yet the pitiless escalation of punishment here is unprecedented. And it is difficult to know quite how Cook reached this point, and made sense of it to himself, since his own journal nowhere acknowledges the sustained severity of punishment. He restated his prescription, 'I would not allow the sentries to fire lest the innocent should suffer with the guilty', meaning that he prohibited the use of musket balls which would have killed. This must have been effective, since none of the log-keepers record any fatal shooting, despite much tension and stone-throwing, no doubt fuelled by commoners' anger over the floggings. In other words, he drew a new line in his own mind: the principle that it remained necessary to observe was that Islanders would not be killed for theft. But he would go as far as seemed necessary, to suppress 'ill disposed' actions by other means, and in Tonga, where common men were perhaps compelled to steal for their masters, that meant going places his officers and men did not recognize. The astronomer Bayly, who was no sentimentalist, thought that 'in some instances' Cook could 'be said to have been guilty of great cruelty'. Perhaps Cook felt the same. Had he not, he would have acknowledged and examined

44. Kato mosi kaka: *basket, Tonga.*

the issue in his otherwise copious journal; but now the waters of his own practice were a confusion of shoals that he had no way of mapping and making a course through.

To forestall the stock being stolen, Cook made a public distribution of the animals he intended to leave: the event was announced in advance, and most people of the district were present. To Paulaho he gave 'a young English Bull and Cow', to Finau he gave a horse and mare, and to another chief a cape ram and two ewes. Mai was

desired to tell them that there were no such animals within many Months sail of them, that they had been brought them at vast trouble and expence, and therefore they were not to kill any till they became very numerous, and lastly, they and their Children were to remember that they had them from the men of Britane; he also explained to them their several uses and what else was necessary for them to know, or rather as far as he knew for Omai was not very well versed in these things himself.

Exactly how this was translated, we have no notion, but it reflects Cook's interest in a particular posterity. On this occasion, or another, the commercial value of future beasts was communicated to Paulaho, if not also to the others. 'It always was a favourite conversation of the King's, the riches he should gain by these Animals, inquiring of us how much Iron & other things future ships would give for a Bullock,' James King recorded. For Cook, the breeds would provide the Tongans with both food and trade, but they would become also living monuments to the generosity of Britain. He was mindful of the 'vast trouble' that they had given him, but here, as in the Antarctic, it took trouble to make history.

Unfortunately some Tongans were not satisfied and the next day stole a goat and two turkey-cocks. Cook was 'determined to have them again'. He immediately impounded several canoes, went ashore, and finding Paulaho, Finau and other chiefs together in a house, 'put a guard over them', and told them he would not let them leave, until these creatures and other things that had been stolen were brought back. The chiefs maintained their composure, 'sat down and drank their Cava without any measure of restraint', and assured him that everything would be returned. Yet armed men began to assemble behind the house. Some marines forced them away, but Cook must have felt that it was too dangerous to remain there, so he asked his aristocractic hostages aboard for dinner, which some agreed to. Others, however, did not want the king to go, though he did not resist. They did all go, remaining on board until mid afternoon, when Cook took them back to shore, 'and soon after the Kid and one of the Turkey-cocks was brought back, the other they said would come the next Morning, I beleived them and released both them and the Canoes'. Cook presents this as a success story, but it does not take much acuity to read between the lines, to discern that the action engendered much anxiety, among Tongans in the vicinity, who quickly gathered what was going on, and thought of mounting some sort of counter-assault. The day ended without bloodshed, as had those days at Matavai years earlier, when Tutaha and others had been held hostage, but like those days it was close to ending differently.

It certainly left a residue of tension. Soon afterwards, on 22 June, some officers on an inland excursion, without Cook's authorization, had various things stolen from them. Cook was plainly annoyed to report that on their return

they got Omai to complain to the King, he not knowing what step I should take and fearing the worst, went off early the next morning and also Feenough so that we had not a Cheif of any authority left with us. I was very much displeased at this and gave Omai a reprimand for meddling in it and put him upon his mital to bring his friend Feenough back, which he did towards the evening, but not before he was well assured I should take no step to oblige them to return what had been taken from the gentlemen. This declaration of mine brought back the King the day after. Both these Chiefs very justly observeyed to me, that when any of my people wanted to go into the Country they ought to be made acquainted with it, when they would send people along with them and then they would be answerable for their safety. And I am convinced from experience, that by observing this method a man and his property is as safe amongst these islanders as most other parts of the world.

Williamson, one of the officers concerned, fulminated; he could not 'pass over the strange conduct of Capt Cook on this occasion'; Cook had been displeased by efforts on the part of James King to retrieve stolen muskets, which Williamson thought entirely reasonable; Cook had unaccountably told Finau he could keep a gun, 'it being a very handsome one'; 'at the same time telling him that provided the natives did not steal from him, they should not be ill treated'; Williamson in other words thought Cook gave them a licence to steal from anybody but him.

If a small nail was stolen from Captn Cook, the thief if taken was most severely punished, if of a little more consequence than a nail, then the Chiefs were immediately seized . . . I was much more affected by such arbitrary proceedings, than with the loss of my gun, although it was great, I could have no redress.

Cook was doing precisely the same thing here that he had done at other places during the second voyage. He was preventing and policing thefts carried out against the ships, against any sort of official property. But he would not be bothered if things were stolen from individual men, or officers who went off on private pursuits. Cook was drawing the line he had drawn before. It angered his officers, making them think that he placed the interest of a native chief ahead of theirs.

On Sunday, 6 July, Cook was ready to sail, but was waiting on a flood tide during daylight that would take the ships safely through a narrow passage. The necessity of remaining a few further days at Tongatapu gave him the chance to take up an invitation of Paulaho's 'to be present at a public ceremony'. Cook had witnessed indigenous ritual of one sort or another before, but he had seen nothing on the scale that he was now to encounter, and he became its attentive, almost obsessive, observer.

On 8 July, he took two boats to Mu'a, the village he had already visited, following Paulaho and his party, who had travelled by land the evening before. The men were found drinking kava, as they commonly did, but at about ten in the morning people began to congregate around a great open space, into which men brought yams, each tied to a pole, while other men, armed, began to sing. Those who brought yams assembled in small parties, then marched to present them before the *fa'itoka*, the royal tomb and temple, that faced the open green. Here the yams were made up in bundles 'but for what purpose [we] could not learn, and as our presence seemed to give them uneasiness we left them and returned to the Cheif', who told them to walk about for a time, since the ceremony would not yet start. Cook betrays an anxiety to miss nothing: 'the fear of loseing part of this Ceremony made us not be long absent'. When he and his companions came back, Paulaho told him that the boat crew were not 'to stir from the boat' because everything 'would very soon be *Tabu*, who ever as found walking about would be *Mated*, that is killed or beat'. Cook was more concerned to be told that neither he nor other visitors could be present at the ceremony, though they would be taken somewhere they might see it. The obstacle, they were told, was their dress; 'to be present it was necessary we should be naked as low as the breast with our hats off and hair untied'. Mai offered to conform, but 'other objections' were then raised. While discussion and preparations proceeded, Cook himself 'stole out', and tried to join men moving towards what he calls, using the Tahitian term, 'the Morai'. Some of these men, he noticed, carried four-foot sticks, with shorter twigs tied across them; the significance of these, among other aspects of the proceedings, he did not understand.

His presence and movement made people increasingly anxious. They all cried 'tabu' until, on coming into view of the ritual edifice, he was urged so strongly to go back that he thought he had better comply. 'I had observed that those people with the sticks passed this Morai or what I may as well call church, and thinking something was going forward beyond it, which by taken a turn round I might get a sight of, but I was so closely watched by three men that I could not put this in execution.' He tried to shake them off, and tried to approach the *fa'itoka* again, where a mass of men were now seated; he realized that he would have a reasonable view from what he called 'the Kings Plantation' and withdrew to there, 'very much to the satisfaction' of the men who were gently trying to keep him away from the *tapu* place. From here he was able to witness a procession of men in pairs, each pair carrying one of the sticks he had seen before between them; 'The small pieces of sticks that were tyed to the others we were told were yams, so that probably they were used to represent this root emblamatically.' All seemed to bend as they walked, Cook noted, as though unable to support the notional weight of the yams that were signified; he counted 108 couples, 'all or most of them men of rank', who passed close by – 'we had a full view of them', he stresses.

This phase of the event having concluded, Cook and his party proceeded to a place they had been allocated, among many other people, and behind a fence which was intended to block their view; they 'took the liberty to cut small holes to peep through'. They saw people bringing more pieces of wood, and coconut fronds; a man 'made a set oraison', an oration, and a small shelter was then constructed, on the ground before the *fa'itoka*; those who had built it then withdrew. Paulaho's son appeared with some attendants; a group of women brought sheets of barkcloth, and wrapped him in them; Paulaho himself arrived, and was seated some distance from 'the Prince'; and the procession that Cook had seen earlier appeared, came right up to the young chief, and deposited their offerings, 'being the sticks before mentioned'. All this time, three men 'continued to make an Oraision'; once all the symbolic yams had been presented, another man made some sort of speech, and at intervals got up and broke a stick that had been presented. His speech concluded and with it the rite; 'we were at liberty to go where we pleased', Cook wrote. He went and confirmed that what were tied to the poles were not yams, as they had been repeatedly informed, but only small sticks, that were hence 'only the representation of these roots'.

Most of the European party now returned to the ship; Cook 'and two of three more' remained to see the conclusion of the ceremony, which they understood took place the following day. That evening, they ate and drank brandy with Paulaho, 'who went to bed grogish'; they shared his house and slept. The following morning Cook first visited Paulaho's son, who stayed elsewhere, and visited other chiefs, who were all drinking kava, as they commonly did in the morning. Around the middle of the day, Cook and Paulaho ate together again; they were told that the ceremony would soon resume, and that they had to seclude themselves as before. But Cook 'however had resolved to peep no longer from behind the Curtin but to make one of the number in the Ceremony if possible'. He therefore left the plantation, where he had been encouraged to remain, and made his way to the company of seated men, who seemed to be taking turns to make informal speeches, while others laughed and applauded. Cook was asked several times to go away; when they saw he would not do so, they wanted him to bare his shoulders, 'with this I complied after which they seemed no longer uneasy at my presence'. Williamson, though, was uneasy.

We who were on ye outside were not a little surprised at seeing Capt Cook in ye procession of the Chiefs, wth his hair hanging loose & his body naked down to ye waist; no person being admitted covered above ye waist, or with his hair tyed; I do not pretend to dispute the propriety of Captn Cook's conduct, but I cannot help thinking he rather let himself down.

Nothing further happened for an hour, until 'the Prince, the Women and the King' all arrived, as they had the day before. Some parties of men ran back and forth; a speech was made, and Cook's group together ran, and seated themselves before Paulaho's son and his attendants. Cook was now 'partly under the management of a man' who seated him advantageously, where he might have seen everything, 'but it was necessary to sit with down cast eyes and as demure as Maids'. There was again a procession, like that of the day before, though this was followed by a second, where the men carried baskets, and a third, where they brought 'in different kinds of small fish'. Cook described the presentation of these offerings minutely, observing a curious tug-of-war over some of the fish offered, moments of aclammation, some 'speaking or praying by different persons', and an occasion when the company of men among whom Cook sat had to leap or run a few paces, and sit facing away from Paulaho's son. Though watching what went on was obviously forbidden, 'Niether this commandment nor the remembrance of Lots wife discouraged me from facing about,' Cook wrote, though the crowd of those who did remain in attendance precluded him from seeing, in any case; he was afterwards told, however, that 'the King and Prince were each presented with a piece of roasted yam'. This was evidently the climax of the occasion, which may have formally concluded at this point, though Cook's impression was evidently that a wrestling competition that followed immediately, was part of the ceremony, rather than a supplementary entertainment. When this finished, in any event, things were no longer *tapu*; the baskets 'became simply what they realy were, viz. empty baskets, so that whatever they were supposed to Contain was emblematically represented, and so indeed was every other thing they brought in except the fish'. Cook tried hard to have the meaning of the whole ceremony and its various elements explained to him. It is odd that Mai was unable to help; and he was told little more than what he already knew, that the proceedings had been *tapu*. He presumed that some 'Oath of Alligiancy' to the prince and future king was central to it, but was evidently less interested in the purpose of the event than in the 'Ceremonious solemnity' and 'great deal of Religion' with which it was conducted, manifest particularly in concerns about the 'dress and deportment' of the Europeans, which nowhere else had 'been called in question on any account whatever'. But now, as he recapitulated,

it was expected that we should be uncovered as low as the waist, that our hair should be loose and flowing over our shoulders; that we should like them sit cross leged and at times in the most humble posture with down cast eyes and hands locked together, all of which they themselves observed; lastly every one was excluded but the Principle people and those who acted a part. These to me were a sufficient testimony that they looked upon themselves to be acting under the immediate eye of a Supreme Being.

Cook's account of his own behaviour over these extraordinary two days has a resonance, for anyone who has ever done anthropological fieldwork, and witnessed for the first time a ritual, ceremony or happening, that is patently important and patently meaningful, but also complex and confusing, if not almost opaque, to the outsider. The anthropologist would today be supposed to be far more ready to defer to local feeling about where he or she should be, and what he or she should see. But there is an anxiety that is otherwise the same, to be near the scene of the action, to avoid missing some crucial act, gesture, moment or pronouncement, that prompts precisely the intrusiveness that characterizes Cook's behaviour here.

Cook did not simply record facts or gather new information: he had an agenda. He gives this away in the offhand reference to the 'Morai or what I may as well call church', and in his emphasis upon the 'emblamatical' character of the offerings. He makes explicit in his conclusion that the Friendly Islanders understand themselves as 'acting under the immediate eye of a Supreme Being'. It is as though he sees parallels between sticks and baskets and bread and wine. He convinces himself that there is not only religion here, but a religion not so remote from Christianity, based on an idea of divine omniscience.

Cook made this effort, we can only suppose, because it helped him affirm the status of people that he admired, in religious terms rarely explicit in his journal, but that must have remained implicitly important to him. Because his general claim was motivated in this way, it is not surprising that it was off from the mark, as an account of Tongan religion – which postulated crowded otherworlds, occupied by many spirits, divine ancestors and principal gods, rather than a single supreme being. These gods were moreover propitiated and invoked, they empowered the projects of the present. They were not heavenly headmasters who watched out for bad behaviour. The proper interpretation of the *'inasi* itself remains an unresolved problem. What puzzled Cook has continued to perplex analysts of Tongan culture, including the Tongans themselves, because Tongan rites evidently changed, even before the Christian missionaries worked for their suppression. Hence the *'inasi* was not sustained beyond the early years of the nineteenth century, hence no other observer, and no linguistically competent observer, was ever able to study it more fully. Certain of its features, notably the sharing of food between the Tui Tonga and his son, stand as dramatic violations of the usual protocols; some analysts in effect take up Cook's notion that the ceremony featured an 'Oath of Alligiancy', seeing the son's inclusion as a political improvisation, intended to strengthen a succession that might otherwise have been problematic. It has also been suggested that this dramatization of the father–son bond was wholly consistent with the themes of agricultural fertility, regeneration and succession, which were central to this ritual, as they were to many similar Polynesian harvest rites. Cook had by now seen so much that we might expect him to have put pieces together, to have grasped the fecund spirituality of Oceania, to have seen the links between prosperity and political power. Out of his contemporaries, Forster came closest to grasping Polynesian culture as a sort of whole, as a harsh and energetic symphony of warrior ceremony in New Zealand, and a more polished political pageant in Tahiti. For his part, Cook witnessed an actuality before him, but made sense of it through faulty Christian translation; he looked here and there at once. And once again he was both close to and far away from his Polynesian hosts.

19

They may fear, but never love us

Cook talked to Anderson about Tongan ritual. They shared the view that the great ceremony had been not only political but religious, that it had much solemnity about it. The Friendly Islanders were, in their own way, god-fearing people. Cook and Anderson also saw eye to eye on a great blight that gave the voyage as a whole a rotten taste. Cook grimly reported that he had 'the Mortification to find that all the care I took when I first Visited these islands to prevent this dreadfull [venereal] disease from being communicated to them, prove enefectual'. In the course of Anderson's ethnographic excursus on the Tongan people, he remarked on prevailing ailments but found that 'the most destructive is a European one introduc'd amongst them most probably by the ships that visited them in 1773' – the *Resolution* and *Adventure* – 'which has already begun to make fatal ravages amongst them, many having lost their voice and a great part of their noses . . .' Though some of the horrible facial lesions and corrosions that shocked and disgusted this surgeon were probably caused by yaws, which was already endemic, rather than syphilis, there is no doubt that Tongans were by now suffering from venereal diseases for the first time. The pain and misery of the effects, Anderson knew professionally if not personally. The criminality of their introduction, he found unimaginably atrocious.

The injury these people have receiv'd from us by communicating this certain destroyer of mankind is not to be repair'd by any method whatever: for it is not barely depriving them of life at last that forms the greatest part of the misfortune, but it is by rendering them completely miserable while alive from their not knowing how to stop its progress, and depriving them at the same time of that intercourse between the sexes which most probably is a principal ingredient of happiness in a country where custom has laid but little restraint upon it . . . The man who has rob'd, murder'd and been guilty of all the Catalogue of human crimes is innocent when compared to the one who did such a thing knowingly. An adequate punishment may be found perhaps for a fault, however heinous, that may be committed upon an individual, but is it in the power of man to invent tortures equal to those felt by a whole nation that the aggressor in this case might be properly repay'd? Humanity itself must startle at the thought of making a single object miserable in this respect, even for a short time, but what must be said when we reflect that in present circumstance the misery is not only entaild upon thousands who now live but must of necessity be convey'd to endless generations?

It's as though Anderson begins to imagine a kind of tribunal that would measure the horror of this sexual holocaust, and invent a punishment of equivalent awfulness, that would somehow match the sufferings of a whole people – but he then stops short. The ramifications of the crime reverberate into the future, without end, and commensurate justice is accordingly indescribable.

Cook's regrets were accentuated by the great admiration he had for the knowledge and art, as well as the civility and religiosity, of the Tongans. A few years earlier Cook had admired the great double canoes they built, but he now learned that they were used to travel not only within the extensive Tongan archipelago, but to the neighbouring but nevertheless distant Fijian and Samoan islands. He obtained a rough idea of Fiji's location. He gathered that the Fijians were warlike, that they practised cannibalism, and he met a few who were on Tongatapu at the time of his visit. He had wanted to learn more of the great *va'a* – the word was the same as the Tahitian, a variant of Maori *waka* – and went aboard one under sail. But Cook's biographer, J. C. Beaglehole, is surprised that he made no effort to learn more of Fiji, and sees this as symptomatic. Would not the Cook of the second voyage, he asks, have gone after these islands, and 'fastened them down securely on his general chart, even at the cost of minor disorganization of his time plan?' He answers the question posed by apparent indifference to an exploratory opportunity by raising a further conundrum, of whether the 'long but unsuspected strain on [Cook's] mind' was 'beginning to affect his attitude to the human situation, to make him the victim of his own exasperation' in dealing with Tongan thieves, and diminishing his energy and enterprise more generally. Was Cook, Beaglehole asks, 'beginning to experience a certain inner tiredness?'

The issue is important, because – notwithstanding its tentative phrasing – Beaglehole's view has become an orthodoxy. It is widely repeated, perhaps most surprisingly by postcolonial scholars, who reject Beaglehole's idealizing view of his subject, but rephrase this argument that conjures up a tired, angry, violent, and irrational Cook, a Cook increasingly fallible. But in fact there is nothing unprecedented or unexpected in Cook's decision not to search out the Fijian islands. ('Decision' is not the right word: in fact, the question never arose, for good reason.) During the first voyage, Cook became aware that Borabora was an important island not far from Huahine, but he took no trouble to visit it, either then, or when he had two further opportunities, in 1773 and 1774. Nor did he trouble to investigate the 'Navigators Islands', the Samoan group, which Bougainville had incompletely identified; nor did he make efforts to find various other islands that he knew of, through Tupaia among other Polynesian fellow-travellers. During the second voyage Cook had, of course, made particular efforts to identify and chart all southern lands, because that task was integral to his mission; but despite his own rhetoric, about the 'completeness' of his south Pacific discoveries, he had never otherwise pursued possible islands exhaustively.

There is, moreover, a very straightforward reason why Cook would not have wanted to sail west towards Fiji. He saw the settlement of his cattle, horses and other stock in the Society Islands as a central objective and a dignifying one of his mission. True, he might have been able to obtain more greens in Fiji. But he had been told repeatedly by Tongans and by Fijians themselves that Fijians were warlike people, and even cannibals. He could presume no easy access to supplies; given his recent experience at Mangaia and Atiu, he might expect rather the reverse. But even if further provisions were to be obtained, he would certainly have embarked on an uncertain and extended cruise. Cook had known that his stock would survive no further delay. The question of why he did not sail towards Fiji is a non-problem; neither a temper, nor a tiredness so mysterious that Cook was unaware of it himself, had any bearing on his interest in the accomplishment he anticipated.

En route to Tahiti, the ships passed the island of Tupuai, south-west of Tahiti; the sense of an ocean replete with Polynesian people, related but varied, was reinforced: here again people understood Tahitian, they wore barkcloth, and they had artfully decorated canoes that seemed to resemble those of New Zealand. A few days later Tahiti came into view. David Samwell was at first disappointed by Vaitepiha Bay: the clouded hills did not match up to his expectations of a paradisical place. He soon changed his mind, but Cook would be annoyed and disappointed by new realities, rather than old fantasies, in this place.

It transpired that Spanish ships had not only visited since his last visit, but left four settlers – two priests, a servant and one 'Matimo' – the marine

Maximo Rodriguez. They had arrived, after a comparatively short voyage from Lima, some four months after Cook's last visit, in late 1774. The notion had been that they would spread the Catholic faith, which the frightened fathers apparently made no effort whatsoever to do. The whole party had been taken back to Peru twelve months later. During their stay, however, Matimo had learnt the language quickly, toured the island, mixed with the people, and told stories about the British, which they found it highly offensive to hear repeated. Anderson seems to have been genuinely dismayed to hear that England had been represented as a small, defeated and inconsequential island. The Tahitians may not have believed all that they were told, but they had been impressed by the Spanish frigates, which were rather grander vessels than the Whitby cats; and 'their Officers being better dressed which we took but little care about at those places', Gilbert recorded. These foreigners also behaved differently to the British: they had maintained their distance, refraining from sexual contacts. They had not allowed people on their ships, and there had been no killing. Yet Samwell was entirely confident that whatever comparisons the Tahitians made were entirely in favour of the British. 'They all unanimously condemen'd the flesh-subduing Dons, for that self denial which may be deemed meritorious in Cells & Cloisters, but will be always looked upon with Contempt by the lovely & beautiful Nymphs of Otaheite,' he wrote, having wasted no time in making local acquaintances – who probably indeed found the Spaniards' sexual renunciation hard to fathom.

Cook, of course, saw this differently. He would have been pained to learn that national enemies had somehow sustained a discipline he had been unable to sustain and had exempted themselves from violence that Tahitians now associated particularly with the English. But most of all, he must have been appalled to gather that the Spanish had already brought cattle. He does no more than report the point, in his own journal. From James King we learn that they were told their rivals had brought 'over with them cattle much finer than ours; the disappointment & vexation on this last information was visible on all our Countenances. We saw that our Act of benevolence from its being too long deferred, had lost its hour, & its reward; We saw the loss of a season & an immence deal of trouble all thrown away to no purpose.' There was no excitement; these animals had been seen before; there would be no scope for the sort of oration Cook had delivered in Tonga, which called upon natives to witness and remember an act of British benevolence. As in the business of discovery itself, there was no prize for second place.

Cook was irritated, too, at Mai's indiscretion, in handing out too many gifts too quickly, to the wrong people. But Mai and many others had the upper hand in exchange; now well knowing the value of red feathers here, stocks had been obtained in Tonga, and the news of what the ship carried spread like wildfire; 'not more feathers than might be got from a Tom tit would purchase a hog of 40 or 50 pound weight, but as every one in the Ships had some, they fell in their value above five hundred per cent before night but even than the ballance of trade was much in our favour,' Cook tells us. News as well as pigs and sexual services were bought. Purea was dead. Clerke 'felt severely for the loss of this good old Lady'. Mai's sister appeared, and they had an 'extreamly moving' reunion, 'better concieved than discribed'. The ships had been leaking badly, again, and the caulkers got to work, again.

Cook gathered together the company on the quarterdeck of the *Resolution*, and formally announced to them the purpose of their expedition. Samwell says 'he told them that he supposed they all knew the Destination of the Voyage' 'which was to try to find a northwest passage'. Cook made the announcement at this time because he wanted them all to understand the necessity of reserving provisions. One summer's exploration in the north might not suffice, and the voyage might well extend to four years. Hence the supplies of spirits would not last, hence he proposed not only a half allowance, but that the men give up their liquor altogether, while in the Society Islands, except once a week. Cook can only have been gratified: 'the readyness wth which they consented to this was a little surprizing', Lieutenant Williamson wrote, 'as a Seaman in general would as soon part his life, as his Grog'. By now, though, Cook knew the ups and downs of collective mood, better than this, or perhaps any other of his officers. If he had to impose restraint at some point, there could not have been a better time to do so than when all were carried away by the euphoria of a return to Tahiti. The exception was made on Saturday nights, 'when they had full allowance to drink to their feemale friends in England, lest amongst the pretty girls of Otaheite they should be wholy forgotten', Cook wrote, patronizingly, as he pretty consistently did, of his 'people'. The half pint of liquor they mixed to their great satisfaction with coconut milk.

Around 18 August, Cook met the chief called Vehiatua – young successor to, rather than, the titleholder he had met before. There were speeches about his previous visits and about the Spanish, who had told them that Cook should not be allowed into Vaitepiha Bay again, but they now paid no regard to this and made Cook 'a formal surrender of the Province and every thing in it the meaning of which I perfectly well understood'. They exchanged names. What Cook understood 'perfectly well', I think, was that 'the Province' had been offered to him in a nominal and rhetorical sense, as part and parcel of that business of exchanging names; just as his ship remained his, the land and the produce remained, in every consequential sense, the property of the chiefs and people who lived upon it. Not even a piece of firewood could be removed, without permission and payment.

A few days later they moved on, as they had before, to Matavai. Here they were met by Tu and his kin, in the midst of 'a prodigious number of people'. Mai, dressed in his best outfit, knelt before the chief, but was taken little notice of. A huge gift of food was received, and presents made in return; in due course, as people gathered what Mai had, they began to regard him, they solicited things from him. Cook – writing his journal entry for 24 August, but evidently with hindsight – tried to contrive a closer relationship between Tu and Mai, since he hoped to leave the stock with Tu, and thought Mai might help manage them. But Mai's imprudence becomes a motif of his journal, over subsequent weeks. He returns to his early disparaging judgement of the man's character, which he had to some degree put aside while Mai had interpreted so usefully in Tonga. He laments the young man's silliness, his lack of diplomacy in his own land. Yet there may have been more to Mai's activity than met Cook's eye; there may have been strategy that he did not see.

Cook visited Pare, called on Tu, and saw the Spanish bull; he conceded that 'a finer beast than he was I hardly ever saw'; he may have consoled himself, that however fine, the bull was little use without the cow that had been given with him, but lost; he made his own presentations, of peacock and hen, turkeys, drake and ducks.

The next day I sent the three Cows I had on board to the Bull, the Bull, the Horse and Mare and Sheep I put a shore at Matavai. And now found my self lightened of a very heavy burden, the trouble and vexation that attended the bringing of these Animals thus far is hardly to be conceived. But the satisfaction I felt in having been so fortunate as to fulfill His Majestys design in sending such usefull Animals to two worthy Nations sufficiently recompenced me for the many anxious hours I had on their account.

This philanthropy accomplished, a camp was established, the *Discovery*'s damaged mainmast got ashore, sails and water casks were repaired, the usual tasks proceeded with: since nothing could be undertaken in the north until the warmer months of the following year, this would be an extended visit, the longest of any of Cook's visits to the Society Islands. At Tahiti the experience was, in general, more comfortable and less fraught than before, because the abundance of the most desired trade goods, and apparent abundance on the island, meant that chiefs and people were no longer unwilling to trade pigs and bring other sorts of provisions; because Cook no longer had to cajole, associated tensions diminished. At the end of August there was a report that Spanish vessels had returned to Vaitepiha, which caused brief alarm. Cook even had cannons mounted, in preparation for hostilities; but it transpired that these and similar subsequent stories were concoctions, that all issued from people from that part of the island, who were once again put out, that the Pare chiefs more or less monopolized the mariners. Hence, if only briefly, Tahitian and European rivalries were fused and aggravated. But such jostling as took place had little impact on most common people, and on the pleasant routine of the mariners, which Samwell summed up. One day was much like the one before; men were occupied

watering the Ship, drying our bread and repairing the Sails, while at the same time we were trading with the Natives for Provisions which they brought to us in great Plenty and we never wanted fine Girls on board. Those who have leasure amuse themselves ashore among the Houses or in paying Visits to their particular friends or Tayo.

Even the incidence of theft was tolerable. The robbery of a man by his supposed *taio* caused some alarm. Cook happened to come ashore soon afterwards, frightening Tu, who must have anticipated that he would take hostages as he had before, but Cook reassured the chief. From his point of view the matter was a private one, he was uninterested.

During his last visit, Cook understood that the people of Eimeo, Tahiti's much smaller neighbour, generally now called Moorea, were engaged in what he then understood was a 'revolt' against Tu. This conflict had broken out again; it is interesting that he now calls it a 'war' rather than a 'revolt', suggesting that he had finally grasped that Tu was a powerful chief, not a king who had legitimate sovereignty of any sort outside his own districts. Cook attended a gathering where the campaign was discussed and his assistance solicited; in the absence of Mai, he had no interpreter, and had to explain as best he could that because he was 'not thoroughly acquainted with the dispute', because the Eimeo people had never 'offended' him, he could not participate. 'With this declaration they either were or seemed satisfied,' he wrote, but soon afterwards encountered Tahua, the man who he had before thought was Tu's 'admiral'. In fact Tahua was an independent warrior and chief in his own right, and he roundly berated Cook for failing to lend support to his friends.

The prospect of fighting gave the Europeans an opportunity to observe a rite that they had heard about, but never before witnessed, in the Society Islands. Tahua had killed a man 'to be sacrificed to the Eatua, to implore the assistance of the God against Eimeo'; Cook 'thought this a good opportunity to see something of this extraordinary and Barbarous custom' and asked Tu if he could attend, who readily agreed. Cook knew who he wanted with him on this occasion: he went with Anderson, Webber and Mai. They proceeded by boat to one of the temple complexes in the Atehuru district; on their arrival Tu asked that the seamen remain in the boat, and wanted Cook and his companions to remove their hats. They did so and approached the *marae*, where many boys and men were gathered at a decent distance from four priests, and the 'Corps or Sacrifice', which lay in a small canoe, half dragged out of the water. Tu then received offerings of plantain leaves and feathers. One the priests recited some sort of prayer. 'During this prayer a man who stood by the Priest held in his hands two small bundles seemingly of Cloth, in one as we afterwards found, was the Royal Maro and the other, if I may be allowed the expression, was the ark of the Eatua.' The 'royal Maro' was the sacred feather sash that was intimately associated with the high chiefly title; the 'ark' of the *atua* was a *to'o*, a woven representation of a god, probably of the war god, 'Oro. Potent and treasured figures of this sort were normally left in *fare atua*, 'god houses', on the *marae* and brought out only when rites like this took place. The *to'o* was wrapped in barkcloth.

They witnessed a succession of prayers; at different times plantain leaves were removed from the body and laid before the priests; the body was removed from the canoe, and oriented parallel to the sea; some hair was removed from the head of the victim, and an eye extracted; it was wrapped in a green leaf, passed to Tu, who then passed it, with red feathers, to the priests. 'During some part of this last ceremony a Kings fisher made a noise in the trees, Otoo turned to me and said "that's the Eatua" and seem'd to look upon it to be a good omen.' In due course the sacrifice was brought to the *marae*, further prayers were recited that specifically entreated the destruction of the enemy, and the victim was buried within the *marae*. A dog was then killed, seared and gutted. Its stomach and intestines were discarded but the heart, liver and kidneys and the whole carcass were taken to the priests, who recited further prayers, accompanied by intermittent drumming. It was left on the *marae*, with pigs and other dogs sacrificed before.

The ceremony was over for the day. Cook and his companions were fed and accommodated by Potatou. They understood it would resume, and 'Being unwilling to lose any part of it, some of us repaired thither pretty early, but found nothing going forward, however soon after a pig was sacrificed and laid on the same alter with the others.' Later, when the principal rites resumed, Tu 'placed himself between two drums and desired me to stand by him'. A succession of prayers were recited, and a succession of red feathers placed on 'the Ark of the Eatua'. A further pig was sacrificed; and a bundle untied, to reveal 'the Maro with which they invest their Kings with Royalty'. The sash was carefully unrolled and spread out before the priests, and proved to be 'about five yards long and fifteen inches broad, and was composed of red and yellow feathers', organized in a kind of checked pattern, with projecting sections like pennants, at one end, a black feathered border, and, astonishingly the English pennant that Wallis had displayed and left, when he took possession, he imagined, of the island. The Tahitians had always understood special forms of decorated cloth to be sacred. Their own great canoes and *marae* carried tapa streamers and pennants of a sort; they did not know quite the claims that European flags made, whether on European ships or on Tahitian land, but they were nevertheless entirely used to using cloth to make political claims. Whatever Wallis's pennant had claimed was neutralized and forgotten, as this exotic and extraordinary cotton thing was literally incorporated into what we may literally call the fabric of Tahitian sovereignty.

This operation was finished, and the other bundle 'which I call the ark', opened; but Cook was kept at a distance from it, while understanding that 'the Eatua was concealed in it, or rather what is supposed to represent him'. He does not use the word 'emblamatical' that he had rather savoured in his description of the Tongan rites, but he remains interested here, in discerning religion in 'representation'. Although he could not see the god, he gathered that it resembled others that he had seen. Smaller figures, presumably of less important gods, had been obtained in barter, and his description of these is easily reconciled with the *to'o* in museum collections: 'This is a thing made of the twisted fibres of the husk of the cocoa-nut, shaped something like a large fid [a conical pin], that is roundish with one end much thicker than the other.' The god unwrapped, the entrails of the pig sacrificed earlier were examined, 'and from their appearences some favourable Omens were conceived'. The god was wrapped up again, and the ceremony ended.

Sketches that Webber probably made over these two days are lost, but he worked these up into an elaborate finished composition which itemizes the features of the site, the priests, the drums, and the dead pigs and dogs. At

45. *Cook as the civilized witness to a barbarous practice:* A Human
Sacrifice at Otaheite, *by Webber, 1777.*

the centre of the picture is the body of the man sacrificed. The moment when
he is about to buried is depicted. Cook is included, standing beside Tu, an
attentive but grave witness. It is not only this strange and disturbing occasion
that Webber thinks he needs to depict. Somehow Cook's presence here is as
important. Somehow, human observation has become historic, too.

While the Tongan *'inasi* left Cook with an impression of a benign ritual of
political legitimacy, the Tahitian ceremony was a 'barbarous' custom, and
one of a number, associated with Tahitian war. Cook and others believed
that Tahitians had at one time been cannibals (though if this was true, it
was only so of the remote past); he had seen many skulls at *marae*, attesting
to frequent sacrifices; and he understood that when Tuteha and other great
chiefs had been killed in the last war, their bowels had been cut out and the
bodies distributed, parts to be buried in different *marae*.

On their way back to Matavai, Cook had occasion to express his displeasure. He was asked by Tahua what he had thought of the ceremony, 'what
our opinion was of it and if we observed such Customs in our own Country'.

During the Ceremony we were silent but as soon as it was over we made no scruple
in giving our sentiments very freely upon it and of Course condemned it. I told the

Chief that this Sacrifice was so far from pleasing the Eatua as they intended that he would be angry with them for it and that they would not succeed against [their enemy on Eimeo] Maheine. This was venturing a good deal upon conjecture, but I thought there was little danger in being misstaken; for I found there was three parties in the island, one extreamely Violent, one perfectly indifferent about the Matter, and the third openly declaring themselves friends to Maheine and his party. Under these circumstances it was not likely such a plan of operation would be settled as would insure even a probability of success. Omai was our spokesman and entered into arguments with so much Spirit that he put the Cheif out of all manner of patience, especially when he was told that if he a Cheif in England had put a man to death as he had done this he would be hanged for it; on this he balled out 'Maeno maeno' (Vile vile) and would not hear a nother word; so that we left him with as great a contempt for our customs as we could possibly have of theirs.

If Tahua was offended, the row seems not to have bothered Tu, who soon afterwards made a great offering of cloth to Cook, and followed it up with presentations of food. Cook was treated also to a sort of play, he went to see a chief embalmed; he was disappointed to miss a further human sacrifice; 'I would have been present at this too had I known it in time.' Likewise he regretted not knowing of some business, 'Otoo giving or restoring lands &cᵃ to the friends and followers of the late King Tootahah, which had been withheld from them ever since his death.' Throughout September, Cook's chief interest was evidently to see more of Tahitian custom, and his constant companions were Mai, Anderson and Webber – who interpreted, co-interpreted and illustrated, respectively.

There was time for recreation, however: one evening, Cook and Clerke took a horse ride 'round the plain of Matavai to the Very great surprise and astonishment of great train of people'. The activity gave the Tahitians, Cook thought, 'a better idea of the greatness of other Nations than all the other things put together that had been carried among them'. Their use understood, the intensity of local delight in the horses perhaps diminished Cook's disappointment that he had failed to be the first to introduce cattle. He made further presentations to Tu of English and Cape sheep. He tried to negotiate some distribution of the cattle between Tahiti and Raiatea, but failed and decided to leave them all with Tu.

Preparations for the campaign against Eimeo were well advanced; Cook was able to witness a sort of Tahitian naval review, and persuaded Tu to stake mock fights, so that he could see how canoes engaged in each other, and warriors on raised stages would flourish their weapons and fight. Though he had declined repeatedly to participate in the action, Cook, who was curious to visit Moorea or Eimeo, thought he would sail over in company with Tu's fleet, and preparations were made for departure, just at the point when it was announced that Tahua had already fought, and a peace had been concluded, on unfavourable terms. Tu was blamed for failing to join the fray earlier, and Tahua threatened to attack him next; 'this called upon me to support my friend by threatening to retaliate it upon all who came against him when I returned again to the island'. There were a range of recriminations, but differences were, at any rate for the time being, resolved.

Just before departure, Tu's mother and sisters, and some other women, came aboard the ship, and explained to Cook that they proposed to sleep in his cabin

and to cure me of the desorder I complained of, which was a sort of Rheumatick pain in one side from my hip to my foot. This kind offer I excepted of, made them up a bed in the Cabbin floor and submitted my self to their direction, I was desired to lay down in the Midst of them, then as many as could get round me began to squeeze me with both hands from head to foot, but more especially the parts where the pain was, till they made my bones crack and a perfect Mummy of my flesh – in short after being under their hands about a quarter of an hour I was glad to get away from them. However I found immediate relief from the operation, they gave me a nother rubing down before I went to bed and I found my self pretty easy all the night after. They repeated the operation the next Morning before they went a shore, and again in the evening when they came on board, after which I found the pains intirely removed and the next Morning they left me.

Such was Cook's physical intimacy with Tahitian women. Their attention attests to the genuine kindness that was as much a part of these meetings as the interested friendliness of *taio* that Cook represented sentimentally, when the *taio* were his, and complained about, when Mai was asked for too much, by people he did not rate. But he was forced to acknowledge that just before they departed, 'Our friend Omai got one very good thing here for the many good things he gave away, this was a very fine double Sailing Canoe, completely equiped Man'd and fit for the Sea'. It was in fact one of the most valuable of Tahitian manufactured things, and its acquisition suggests that Mai had not frittered his wealth away quite to the degree Cook had believed. At the same time, a presentation was made of another canoe, which Tu wanted Cook to convey to George III. Cook was delighted by this expression of Tu's friendship; 'it was a thought intirely his own'; but was taken aback to gather that the gift consisted of a sixteen-foot double canoe, a model of the grandest sort, that 'seemed to have been built for the purpose, and was decorated with all those pieces of Carved work they usually fix upon their Canoes'. Cook considered it too big to transport, which disappointed the chief, and is in hindsight really unfortunate, since the great Tahitian canoes, which featured prominent and elaborate sculpture, as well as a host of more ephemeral decorations, that appear so magnificent in Hodges's and Webber's paintings, were no longer built after the early years of the nineteenth century, and no examples were ever either preserved locally or acquired by any northern hemisphere museum. If museums got hold of many things that they had no right to collect, there would have been no harm in this singular *va'a* – the first, perhaps, of many model canoes intended for export – ending up somewhere like the British Museum.

On departure, Cook mulled over the Spanish visit. He was content that the lies that had apparently been told had been refuted, since his reappearance. He was reassured by the failure of the settlement and the efforts to convert people to Catholicism. Tu assured him that although the Spanish had promised to come back and establish a new settlement, of men, women and children who would bring houses and animals and live and die there, he would not permit them to come to Matavai, because it 'belonged' to Cook. 'But', Cook wrote,

it was easy to see that the idea pleased him, little thinking that such a step would at once deprive him of his Kingdom and the people of their liberties. This shews with what facility a settlement properly conducted might be made among them, which for the regard I have for them I hope will never happen; indeed it is no ways likely as there is no one inducement that I can see.

The inducements to colonial settlement would prove, unfortunately, to be more various than Cook foresaw. The dispossession and unfreedom that he anticipated came about, not 'at once' with the establishment of a settlement, but gradually and relentlessly through an odd concatenation of the intrusions of English missionaries, a motley set of traders and French naval officers. The missionaries would come just over twenty years after Cook wrote these words. He could not know it, but they would choose Tahiti, because his own descriptions and Webber's graphic images of sacrifice and war ignited a passion – not for further knowledge of such 'barbarous' customs, but for evangelism and their abolition.

The visit to Moorea might easily have been uneventful. The Europeans discovered a good harbour; they exchanged things with people; and the chief Mahine (not to be confused with the young man who had joined the *Resolution* during the previous voyage) and 'his Wife or Mistress' came aboard. But on 6 October, as Cook was on the point of leaving, he realized that a goat had been stolen, one of four he had gone to some trouble to obtain from Tu. Two had been destined for Raiatea and two for 'any other island or islands I might meet with in my passage to the north'. (By now, there were a good few goats on Tahiti but as yet probably none on any neighbouring island.) 'The loss of this Goat would have been nothing,' he wrote, 'if it had not interfered with my views of Stocking other islands with these Animals.' Cook gathered that Mahine had the goat. Two older men offered to help recover it. He sent a boat with them, to convey a 'threatening message'. He also tried inducements: Mahine had asked him for goats but been refused, because Cook needed those he had for the other islands. Now he proposed to send another messenger back to Tu with red feathers, to ask him to send another pair to Mahine. As these possibilities were broached, Cook was staggered to hear that a second goat had been stolen. The first was soon afterwards returned, with a man who acknowledged that he had stolen it, he said, on the grounds that breadfruit and coconuts had been taken without his permission. Cook therefore let him go without punishment, but discovered the next morning that the inhabitants of the area, and the chief Mahine, had all retreated to remote parts of the island, clearly anticipating some retributive violence. He used the same old men who had helped retrieve the first goat to make inquiries about the second, and sent men in a boat to where he understood it might be recovered; but the people there appeared to be devious, or at any rate promised to bring the animal but failed to do so before it became dark, and before Cook's men felt they had to withdraw.

Cook was now a hostage to his notion that he had to maintain an appearance of superiority. Maybe he was also a hostage to his own pride, if that was a different thing. 'I was now very sorry I had proceeded so far,' he wrote, 'as I could not retreat with any tolerable credet, and without giving incouragement to the people of the other islands we had yet to visit to rob us with impunity.' This was not quite logical, because it was by no means clear that news of the theft would be conveyed to Huahine and Raiatea, where people had in any case often been 'troublesome'. But Cook was committed to action of some sort, and he asked Mai, and the two unnamed local old men, for advice, which was readily volunteered: it was to head into the country 'and shoot every Soul I met with', which Cook would not do, though if his punitive effort refrained from assaulting individuals, it became absolutely wanton in its destruction of property. On the morning of 9 October, Cook took a group of some forty inland across the island, while sending Williamson with boats to meet him on the other side. Some further attempt was made to get the goat, from people that Cook thought had it, but this proving fruitless he began burning houses and war canoes; he supposedly destroyed only things 'belonging to people concernd in the theft', but he relied on local, inevitably partisan, guides for this information and in all likelihood broke up or burnt canoes that belonged to their enemies, who may or may not have had any part in the theft. This caused much distress: at one point Mai called 'and told us, a great many men were getting together to attack us, we made ready to receive them, but instead of offensive weapons, they were headed by ten or twelve men with plantain trees in their hands, which they laid down at my feet and beg'd I would spare a Canoe that lay close by, which I did'. The party eventually reached the district of Varari, on the opposite side of the island, where Cook damaged nothing because he understood the people were allies of Tu. He then returned to the ships, to the disagreeable news that despite this onslaught, nothing had been heard of the goat.

The following morning, he sent a message to Mahine 'to till him that if he did not send the goat I would not leave him a Canoe on the island and that I would continue destroying till it came'. And he began to do so, breaking up three or four canoes on the shore, and travelling to the next bay, where more were smashed or burnt. That evening, finally, the goat was returned. Cook wrote that the affair 'could not be more regreted on the part of the Natives than it was on mine', which was utterly inadequate, as a summation of the savage strategy he had employed here. The canoes he had destroyed were not ordinary fishing vessels – though even they were finely made, and required hundreds of hours' carpentry, and specialized sewing, carving and caulking. The vessels included large war canoes, some large enough to contain 100 or more paddlers, like the model he had been offered they featured fine sculpture, they were religiously significant, and they were expressions of chiefly prestige, as he well knew. Their loss denuded people; as Edgar among others complained, it would affect them for many months if not years to come; he could not understand why chiefs had not been taken hostage, as had been done before, since this had 'always in these cases been found to succeed'.

Mahine had, perhaps, simply been beyond reach, but it is indeed surprising that Cook neither tested nor even mentioned the possibility of seizing him. The clue to this strange and horrible violence lies, I think, in Cook's passing allusion to the fact that he 'asked Omai and the two old men what methods I should next take'. He had spent the better part of the preceding months closely observing Polynesian practice, and had most recently heard and seen a good deal of Polynesian war. When he'd upbraided Tahua for his human sacrifice, he had cast his criticism, not in an alien moral language, but in approximately Tahitian terms, which focused on efficacy: the sacrifice, Cook had suggested, would not *work*; the attack would fail. If his inclination was increasingly to study and manipulate local strategies, he may now have thought that an exaggerated emulation of local warfare would most effectively secure the quick return of the goat, and reaffirm British superiority. In one sense, he was savagely correct: these aims were realized. But the action appears to have involved much more than this. It was effectively hijacked by his local advisers, who drew him into the sort of game he had avoided elsewhere. On this occasion Mai was particularly vigorous, appropriating canoes as well as destroying them, and plundering a considerable quantity of food.

From Matavai to Poverty Bay and back, Cook had repeatedly been driven to extremes by an unwillingness to qualify or abandon objectives that he had embraced. He had repeatedly pushed his luck, driven by a mix of pride, anger and a theory of encounter that demanded the display of superiority. Anger played a considerable part, and we have his own word for it that he was sometimes incensed by 'insolence'.

On this occasion, he knew himself that he had gone too far. Samwell, who considered that the people of Moorea had brought the misfortune upon themselves, was all but alone in defending it. Even he added a poignant detail, that an officer from the *Discovery*, who had somehow been unaware of what was going on, had wandered inland on his own, and been found by 'three Indians' who had considered taking his life, by way of revenge for the ongoing carnage, but then decided to let him go away 'without hurting him, which reflects Credit upon the Forbearance and Humanity of these people'. It is telling that even Williamson, who mostly thought that Cook was too gentle with Islanders, thought 'the man totally destitute of humanity, that would not have felt considerably for these poor & before our arrival among them probably a happy people, & I must confess this once I obey'd my Orders [to destroy houses and canoes] with reluctance'. James King's protest was among the most reasoned:

I doubt whether our Ideas of propriety in punishing so many innocent people for the crimes of a few, will ever be reconcileable to any principle one can form of justice. At all events plunder should not have been permitted. On a consideration of the very serious & weighty damages they have sustained, I much fear that this event will be a very strong motive not only to these Islanders, but to the rest, to give a decided preference to the Spaniards, & that in future they may fear, but never love us.

Common to much comment was a lack of understanding as to why Cook had acted in the way he had. George Gilbert declared that he could not account for Cook's conduct 'all about such a trifle as a small goat', which tells us that Cook was voyaging almost on his own. King and some others had certainly grasped the importance of the transfer of cattle to Tahiti; and everyone understood and hoped that the voyage would accomplish something great, in the shape of the discovery of the north-west passage, that would bring not only fame but the £20,000 reward. But few shared or even discerned Cook's sense that his voyage was historic, in a broader and higher sense that did not hinge on a single discovery. Webber did know its grandeur, and did much to make it visible, through his images of momentous encounters and extraordinary scenes, which so often centre upon Cook's inquisitive presence. Oddly, Webber produced no representation of Cook's gifts of cattle, horses, goats, sheep or turkeys, yet this programme of stocking the islands for posterity was at the heart of Cook's notion of this voyage, as an endeavour of patriotic benevolence. Hence a goat, however small, was no 'trifle'.

On 12 October the *Resolution* and *Discovery* anchored in Fare harbour, on Huahine's west coast. Cook had already called three times at this magically beautiful port, most recently in 1774. His chief concern now was to settle Mai. He had hoped to reconcile him to the people of Borabora, who had dispossessed his family, but 'he was too great a Patriot to listen to any such thing'. Greetings and ceremonies took place; some land was purchased, a house built, and a good deal of effort put into establishing Mai's gardens. Relations with people here had always been fraught, and Ori, the chief upon whom Cook had previously depended, had now withdrawn to Raiatea. Those who resented the British intrusion had never been particularly restrained; now they were still less so. One man of Borabora stole a sextant, but was caught. Cook, infuriated, ordered his head shaved and his ears cut off, but King or some other officer intervened, halting the barber as he severed one lobe, and letting him swim ashore. This man avenged himself by destroying some of Mai's plantations, and declared that he would kill him as soon as Cook left. Cook therefore had him seized and – one log tells us – apparently thought of shooting him, but confined him aboard the ship, and proposed to remove him to Borabora, or to another island. This proposal 'seemed to give general satisfaction', Cook declared, among whom exactly he does not say; he was again angered when an inadequate watch enabled the man to get hold of the keys to the irons, and escape. Though the man is described as an aggressive 'rascal', there are mysterious indications that he was deliberately set free, which imply that someone on board may have had a higher regard for him. Cook makes no mention of any such mutinous subversion of his little peacekeeping operation; but several of those thought to be at fault for the man's supposed escape were demoted, placed in irons themselves, or flogged. All this speaks a certain disquiet, in the wake of the events at Eimeo.

The time came to leave Mai. The farewell was affectionate. 'He sustained himself with a manly resolution' until he came to embrace Cook himself, when he burst into tears, 'as did most of us who were his Acquaintance' wrote the astronomer Bayly, who was among those who'd sailed with Mai in the *Adventure* and had spent time with him in many parts of the Pacific, the Atlantic and England, more than four years. Cook's parting judgement was patronizing but warm: though the young Raiatean 'wanted application and perseverance' his faults were 'more than over ballanced by his great good Nature and docile disposition . . . I have very seldom had reason to find fault with his conduct.' He could not resist returning to his favourite theme, nothing that the greatest benefit that Society Islanders received as a result of Mai's travels were 'the Animals that have been left upon them, which probably they never would have got had he not come to England; when these multiplies of which I think there is little doubt, they will equal, if not exceed, any place in the known World for provisions'.

They sailed on, as before, to Raiatea, where Cook's old acquaintance Orio was welcoming. The ships, 'much pesterd' with rats, were drawn up close by the shore, and bridges made, with a view to get the rats to pester Raiateans instead. Some astronomical observations were made. 'Nothing worthy of Note happened' until the night of 12 November, when John Harrison, a marine, deserted. Orio promised to send some people after him, but did not bother, Cook thought. Some thefts took place 'that Mataued' most of the many people about the ship; intimidated, they abandoned the vicinity. Cook considered the moment opportune to recover the man, and took two manned boats in search of him. People readily escorted the party to a house in which the poor fellow was found, 'lying down between two Women with his Hair stuck full of flowers & his Dress the same as that of the Indians', Samwell related, maybe enviously. It transpired that Harrison had not left his post until his relief had appeared, and Cook accordingly 'mitigated' his punishment to a dozen lashes on two consecutive days. The time for tropical refreshment and refitting seemed to be running out, and Cook had the ships heeled over. Sheathing was renewed, and some experimental tin plates tried in place of the usual copper. The prospect of a long passage into northern waters yawned open, like an abyss.

Cook was no doubt annoyed when two further men deserted, especially because one was Alexander Mouat, the son of Captain Patrick Mouat, who had commanded Byron's supply vessel, the *Tamar*, during the voyage to the Pacific of 1764–6. If his view had always been that he could not lose a man, he certainly did not want to lose a man with distinguished if perhaps undeserved naval connections. Clerke went after them, but had no luck; his impression was that the people wanted the two to remain on the island, 'and with that view amused him with false information the whole day', sending him on a no doubt otherwise pleasant boat trip, but one in the direction opposite to that taken by the deserters. The following day they were pursued to the neighbouring island of Taha'a, but on arrival there, Cook was told that they had already moved on to Borabora. Cook did not want to pursue them this considerable further distance, at any rate by small boat, so returned to the ship, and the following day instructed Clerke to detain the kin of Orio, the chief whom he knew well, who had even co-operated with him, in attempting to recover the men the day before. 'The chief was with me when the news reached him, and immediately acquainted me with it, thinking it was done without my knowlidge, till I undeceived him and then he was in a hurry to get out of the Ship, not knowing but he was in the same situation himself.' Cook told him, however, that he could go, but should do whatever it took to get his men back, and that if they were not returned, 'I would carry the others away with me.'

Orio seems to have acted promptly, but the hostage-taking caused still more consternation and distress than similar actions had previously. Crowds of women gathered on the shore beside the ships, crying loudly, and slashing themselves with sharks' teeth repeatedly, lamenting the seizure of Poetua in particular, perhaps because she was pregnant. The 'howl' was so melancholy, Clerke reported, 'as render'd the Ship whilst it lasted, which was 2 or 3 hours, a most wretched Habitation'. He tried to get the women away, to no purpose, since they would 'stand and bleed and cry' until they were exhausted.

A reprisal was planned, and on 26 November Cook was disturbed when the people suddenly evacuated the area around the ships. He tried to find out what was going on, and heard that Clerke and Gore had been seized. 'The tables now seemed to be turned upon me,' he wrote, and swiftly sent out a rescue party, and boats to cut off the canoes, that were desperately trying to escape the bay. It very quickly transpired that the story was false, but it was evedent from Several corrobrating circumstances that they had such a design in view, nay they made no secret of speaking of it the next day, but their first and great design was to have got me. It was my custom to go and bathe in the fresh Water every evening and very often alone and always without arms; expecting me to go as usual this evening and had determined to Seize me and Captain Clerke too if he had accompaned me. But I had, after confining their people, determined not to put my self in their power.

Orio had even asked Cook several times if he intended to bathe, which did not make him suspicious; but when it became plain that he was not going, the chief had ventured off with others to try to capture others whom they might find. It had been a close call on several counts. Cook's much earlier reflections on the propensities of local women to either betray or save their visiting foreign lovers were incidentally here refuted. A young woman from Huahine who had remained with some sailor aboard the *Discovery* happened to overhear local warriors discussing their 'disign'; this information she had disclosed; the same warriors later threatened to kill her for spoiling their scheme; and if Cook's report is accurate, these threats were taken seriously, to the extent that her kin came in the middle of the night to get her away from the ship 'to a place of safety'.

The women who lamented Poetua's seizure, whose blood ran freely, must have been deeply distressed on the morning of 27 November, when the *Resolution* and *Discovery* cast off their moorings, and moved some way out of the harbour. Two days later, Orio had still no news from Borabora. He thought to go after the men himself, and Cook planned to follow with the ships. Adverse winds forced him to remain in the harbour, however, and these same winds later brought Orio back with the two men. Cook, exhausted and exasperated, lost no time releasing his hostages. 'This ended this affair which gave me more trouble and vexation than the Men were worth, and which I would not have taken but for the reason before mentioned', that was because others too 'wanted to end their days at these islands', 'and to save the Son of a brother officer from being lost to the World, for I could soon have supplyed their places with Volunteers that would have answered our purpose full as well if not better', he remarked, referring to the many Tahitians and other Islanders who had wanted to join and voyage with his ships, as Mai had done. If Cook's opinion of English sailors had undergone no elevation, he now saw the point of being lenient. Bayly recorded that 'The Ships Company petitioned the Capt to excuse Shaw the Seaman from any more punishment & all hands promised to behave exceeding well, & not to Atempt to escape or desert any more, on which the Capt excused him.'

At about this time, John Webber painted what is undoubtedly his most serene painting, perhaps the most arrestingly beautiful portrait that any Cook voyage artist produced. His subject is Poetua. Brought to us with the most conventional, classical poise, she bears absolute assurance and exotic dignity. Her attractiveness is maybe enhanced, not disfigured, by her small and regular tattoos, which she seems to point towards, as if reminding the viewer of her Raiatean nationality.

We might see nothing in this picture but male fantasy, nothing but a painterly expression of the sexual colonization of these islands, that writers such as Samwell relish in, that Webber probably also played his part in. The flowers behind the ears surely mark the stereotype: this is a dusky maiden of an aroused imagination, if ever there was one. There is no avoiding the paradox. Here indeed is an ideal image, a figure conjured up out of tradition and type. Yet here also is an actual and a particular woman, whom Webber knew, whose rank and accomplishment is as real and evident as that of any of Gainsborough's sitters. He conveys the power of her person as compellingly as he obscures her disempowerment, at the time he painted this. When she sat for him, she was not disposed before a Raiatean landscape, a raggedly luxuriant plantain breaking out of the murk behind her; she was a hostage on board a ship, distressed by her friends' screaming.

They sailed for Borabora, the politically powerful island Cook had never before visited. Now he wanted to recover an anchor that Bougainville was known to have lost there. The ships were running short of scrap iron, needed for trade if new islands were encountered. Accompanied by Orio, and six or eight other men who 'would gladly have taken a passage with us to England', Cook understood, they had a quick passage to what he thought was 'one of the most capacious harbours I ever met with'. Here he encountered the renowned chief Puni, the dispossessor of Mai's family, who was pleased to let him have what remained of the anchor for half a dozen axes. This man had obtained a Spanish ram but had no ewe, so Cook put one of those ashore that he had bought at Cape Town. He added that at Raiatea he had left 'an English Boar and Sow and two Goats, so that not only Otaheite but all the neighbouring islands will in a few years have their breed of hogs considerably improved'. This, he imagined, marked the end of this effort. The voyage's purpose and character swung now around a hinge;

*46. Webber's portrait of Poetua, painted during her
captivity, 1777.*

Borabora fell away into a cluster of cloud on the horizon, and Cook steered
into a great expanse of virtually unknown ocean to the north. He had asked
people if they knew of islands to be found in that direction. They did not.
Cook may have felt a renewed sense of purpose. A good part of his crew
did not. 'We left these Islands with the greatest regret imaginable,' wrote

George Gilbert, 'supposing all the pleasures of the voyage to be now at an end; having nothing to expect in future but excess of cold and hunger, and every kind of hardship and distress.'

20

Squalls and rain and so dark

During the night of 22 December 1777, the *Resolution* and *Discovery* crossed the equator. Cook, for the first time, sailed into the north Pacific ocean, a geographic domain he did not know, where his task would be different from anything he had undertaken before. Yet his first landings were in places that were of a piece, naturally and culturally, with the islands of the South Sea. George Gilbert's expectation that the remainder of the voyage would bring cold and misery was not wrong, but premature.

On 24 December land was sighted, which proved to be 'one of those low islands so common in this sea', a coral atoll that looked barren, but that Cook thought might supply turtle. Over subsequent days, boats were sent to examine the coasts, places to land were found, and turtle were indeed caught in abundance; the crew did a great deal of fishing and fought off rapacious sharks, which they diverted themselves by torturing, 'sometimes two were firmly lashed together by their tails and turned adrift'. On 30 December, Bayly, King and Cook studied an eclipse of the sun; search parties had to be sent out for a man who had become separated first with one companion, then on his own. He had been unable to find his way back to the boats, even though vegetation was sparse and the ships visible from most parts of the islet. As Bayly remarked, it appeared 'scarcely possible' that the men had found the space to lose themselves, 'but a seamen when on shore is in a manner helpless'; some conversation along these lines took place, which left a residue too in Cook's journal. 'Considering what a strange set of beings, the generality of seamen are when on shore, instead of being surprised at these men lossing themselves we ought rather have been surprised there were no more of them,' he observed, airing an assessment of his people's abilities that he did not normally make explicit. Cook did not count himself as a seaman in this sense. He remained a reasoning being, while the 'generality' of them operated on the basis of nautical instinct, which could leave them stranded, like fish out of water. It was a remark that measured the distance – maybe the growing distance, that separated him and his men.

Cook left a bottle containing an inscription; he named the place Christmas Island. He thought the presence of shells and suchlike in its interior proved conclusively that it was formed 'by Marine productions': he meant the growth of coral, which was then hypothesized but not fully understood. At daybreak on 2 January 1778, the ships weighed anchor and proceeded north. The breeze freshened.

Many birds were seen, as were turtles, considered 'signs of the vecinity of land'; on 18 January, one island, then another, and the next day a third, were sighted. These were not inhospitable atolls, but high and substantial islands, and there was much excitement aboard, and speculation as to whether they might be occupied 'with a new Race of People distinct from the Islanders to the Southward of the Line', Samwell wrote. 'We were sometime in Suspense,' he continued, as to whether the islands were inhabited at all; but in due course canoes appeared, and he at least was astonished to find that their language was 'much the same as that of Otaheite'. The people came alongside but would not come into the ship. When they gathered that the Europeans were not immediately hostile, they threw overboard stones that they carried in their canoes, apparently their only weapons. They exchanged a few fish for nails, and further canoes that approached as Cook sailed along the south coast of the island of Kauai brought off pigs and sweet potatoes, 'so that we again found our selves in the land of plenty, just as the turtle we had taken on at the last island was nearly expended'. The ships passed several villages, some right on the shore and others further inland; they saw plantations, gardens and great crowds of people, who seemed to be gathered around vantage points, looking out at the Europeans. The following day the British approached the land, and were met by more canoes. The people would now come aboard, and were amazed by what they saw, more so, Cook felt, than any 'Indians' he had brought on to a ship before. There were a couple of attempted thefts. Cook sent Williamson closer to shore with three armed boats to look for a landing-place, and for water; but he gave the lieutenant explicit directions that the party as a whole should not land; no more than one man was to get out of the boat, if it was really necessary to do so, to locate a source of fresh water.

It was obvious that these Islanders had little or no previous contact with Europeans, and Cook's first concern was to police sexual traffic, to prevent the communication of venereal disease. He gave orders that 'no Women, on any account whatever, were to be admitted onboard the ships, I also forbid all manner of connection with them'. But he was not over-confident.

It is no more than what I did when I first visited the Friendly Islands yet I afterwards found it did not succeed, and I am much afraid this will always be the case where it is necessary to have a number of people on shore; the oppertunities and inducements to an intercourse between the sex, are there too many to be guarded against. It is also a doubt with me, that the most skilfull of the Faculty can tell whether every man who has had the veneral is so far cured as not to communicate it further, I think I could mention some instances to the contrary. It is likewise well known that amongst a number of men, there will be found some who will endeavour to conceal this desorder, and there are some again who care not to whom they communicate it, of this last we had an instance on shore at Tongatabu in the Gunner of the Discovery, who remained a shore to manage the trade for Captain Clerke. After he knew he had contracted this disease he continued to sleep with different women who supposed not to have contracted it; his companions expostulated with him without effect; till it came to Captain Clerke's knowlidge who ordered him on board.

Williamson returned. The ships were anchored, and Cook went ashore at Waimea. Hundreds of people immediately prostrated themselves before him. He can only have been surprised by this extreme deference, which he had not encountered among other Polynesians. The people remained 'in that humble posture' until he 'made signs' that they should rise; they then brought plantain branches and many small pigs, which were presented rather than sold; he located the supply of water, and then went back aboard until the following morning, when he brought back a watering party that he supervised himself. Marines maintained a watch as others traded on the beach. Leaving matters in Williamson's hands, he walked up the valley through taro plantations with Anderson and Webber. They passed a number of villages, and saw what Cook called *marae*, 'like those of Otaheite', as they indeed were, though the Hawaiian term for the analogous ritual precincts was *heiau*. He was struck by elevated timber constructions, partly wrapped in plain barkcloth, 'which seemed to be consecrated to Religious and ceremonious purposes, as a good deal of it was about the Morai and I had some of it forced upon me at my first landing'. The 'some of it forced' is suggestive. Cook saw a good deal of, but never quite understood, Polynesian sacredness; he did not know why, at certain moments, objects and people had to be wrapped or unwrapped; he would not have appreciated that, as a person equated with a great chief, he was not only sacred but dangerously so; he did not see that the cloth contained, diffused and diminished the threat. Yet he had seen enough presentations and rites to intuit that there was something 'Religious' in this action. He now gathered that his person was something to be contended with, in Hawaiian religious terms.

Cook was impressed by a house upon the *heiau*, he saw figures of gods within it, he saw burial places, and burial places which he understood were occupied by 'Tangata Taboo' or human sacrifices. Not only was the word *tapu* – *kapu* in Hawaiian – found here, but there was abundant evidence 'that these people have nearly the same Notions of Religion', the same as Tahitians, it goes without saying. They examined the whole place. Webber drew it; they returned via a different route to the beach, where trade proceeded, marked by great 'honisty' and the absence of any sort of cheating, Cook noted. The following day the wind turned, it rained, and the sea was choppy; landing was impossible, but people came out and traded from canoes. Cook tried to move further offshore, but winds changed again, and he was obliged to sail further away. He tried for an alternative harbour, and ventured around the island's west point, only to find 'a prodigious surf' on the north shore (a coast much renowned today, in surfing circles). For a few days barter was sustained intermittently by boat, as the ships tacked and stood about, but they were unable to regain the anchorage, and moved to the smaller island of Niihau to the west. Here again, the sort of heavy surf that anyone who has visited Hawaii in the winter will recall pounded the beach and impeded landing. Gore got some people ashore, where they did trade, and obtained processed salt as well as yams, but much was lost getting in and out of the boats. According to James King, Cook was 'very uneasy' about what would transpire if the people remained ashore, but there was no getting them off. Gore and some twenty stayed on the island overnight, 'thus', Cook wrote, 'the very thing happened that I had above all others wished to prevent'.

This 'very thing' had probably already occurred, off Kauai. The women there had seemed desperately eager, for probably the same reason that Tahitian commoner women had initially offered themselves to British sailors: this was a way of forming an advantageous affiliation with persons perceived to be of high rank. The evident interest of the women no doubt fuelled the desire of the men, and Edgar wrote that it had been impossible to keep them off the ship: some men had employed subterfuges, such as having the women dressed as men, '& calling them their Tio's'. Samwell acknowledged the seriousness of Cook's injunction on this occasion, but characteristically celebrated a woman named Walako'i, whose apparent status as a priestess was 'no bar to the Performance of her Devotions at the Temple of Venus, for like the rest of her Countrywomen she scrupled not to grant every favour to our people'. He was probably not of the party himself, but appears to have gained almost as much pleasure merely from writing about what he took to be the spontaneous licentiousness of the 'girls', who seemed not to want payment but 'would almost use violence to force you into their Embrace regardless whether we gave them any thing or not'.

The next day, those ashore were retrieved and Cook left goats, 'a Boar and Sow pig of the English breed', and melon, pumpkin and onion seeds with a man who appeared to possess some status. On 2 February, the ships shaped a north-easterly course, towards the coast of America, and Cook reviewed the new and remarkable discovery of what he thought was a group of five islands: Oahu, which he had only glimpsed, Kauai, which he called Atoui, Niihau, and two rocky islets. He did not yet know that the archipelago extended hundreds of miles to the south-east and included five other substantial islands, Lanai, Molokai, Kahoolawe, Maui, and what locals today call 'the big island' of Hawaii itself. Even so, the group was impressive; and Cook would not have named it after the first Admiralty lord, the Earl of Sandwich, had he not rated it among his most significant discoveries.

The first impression was that of affinity between the inhabitants of Kauai and the Tahitians, and this prompted him again to raise the question of 'How shall we account for this Nation spreading it self so far over this Vast ocean?' He had the elements of an answer, in the geographic knowledge that he knew Society Islanders possessed, the great canoes that he had seen Tongans sail, the navigational methods that had been to some degree explained to him, and the incidence of accidental voyages, such as the one that had brought some Society Islanders to Atiu. Yet, if Polynesians carried mental maps, if they had great vessels capable of 'distant navigation', if they knew how to pursue a course, and if they would occasionally be propelled away from their destinations, to find new places previously unknown, Cook nevertheless found the sheer range of their migrations almost unbelievable, and their motivation and accomplishment incredible.

The Polynesian affinities that at first surprised the mariners also brought particular differences into view. Tattooing was practised here, but not to what Cook considered 'a high degree'. The decoration of barkcloth, on the other hand, was much elaborated. 'They have a great variety of patterns and many of them are extremely beautiful.' He was impressed also by red and yellow feather caps and cloaks, though the latter were so highly valued that he was unable to obtain an example through barter. The visit had been too brief for anything of the social order to be clearly discerned, though King recorded an observation that Cook did not, that houses here formed distinct villages, and were not just scattered about, as they were in the

Society Islands. The people encountered were mostly commoners, but Clerke had been visited by a chief, Kaneoneo, who had come off in a great double canoe and (Cook wrote) 'like the King of the Friendly Islands, paid no regard to those who happened to lay in his way but ran against or over them without endeavouring in the least to avoide them; nor could they get out of his way as the people in [other canoes] were obliged to lay down till he had passed'. I don't know whether Cook was comparing only this particular act, or imagining that Hawaiian society resembled Tongan society in other ways: the obeisance that he had met on landing at Waimea might have recalled the 'decorum', the rites of respect and great distinctions between aristocrats and ordinary people, that he had found both striking and attractive in Tonga. Yet no one on either vessel realized that these islands were true kingdoms, dominated by an aristocratic class, the *ali'i*.

Only after sailing from Hawaii did Cook learn that Williamson had concealed what had taken place on the first attempt to land. According to the cooper, Griffin, Cook was angered by the 'Cowardly, dastardly action'. We do not know quite what Cook wrote in his journal, when he initially heard the news; the way he put it, when he subsequently revised the only text that we now have, was that as the boat approached the beach, people 'pressed so thick upon [them] that he was obliged to fire by which one man was killed. But this unhappy circumstance I did not know till after we left', which rather let Williamson off the hook. Williamson himself wrote an extended, self-justifying account of the matter, which emphasized the categorical character of his order to the boats' crew, that they were not to fire without his order. He gave this order twice, he said, 'from ye great wantonness of the inferior people on board a ship, & ye idea they possess that it is no harm to kill an indian'; but proceeded to explain that as the boat grounded, he was surrounded, people jumped in, and seemed inclined to take things, or capsize them; there was clearly something of a panic, and a tug of war over the boat hook, as the crew were attempting to back the boat off and the Hawaiians trying to pull it in. Cook considered later, without having been present, that the people 'were excited by mere curiosity to get what they had from them, and were at the same time, ready to give in return what they had'. He may well have been right that the Hawaiians meant no bodily harm, yet Williamson in fact did more or less what he himself had tried to do, under similar circumstances at Erramango, four years earlier, which was to shoot a man dead.

Williamson provides, literally, a blow by blow account of the affair. He has 'been thus particular', he explains, because he always disagreed with

47. Kapa, *decorated barkcloth, Hawaii.*

Cook over the proper 'manner of treating indians'. Whereas Cook argued for the use of small shot, which would warn, frighten, or injure rather than kill, Williamson was 'determin'd never to fire but when necessity obliged me & then to do execution'; he thought any more moderate response made one seem weak, encouraged 'insolence', and then led to further violence. He reveals, or maintains, that because he and Cook disagreed so fundamentally on this point, he asked Cook 'never to send me on duty where I could not act from reason & ye dictates of my own Conscience'; and he argued that in this case his action had been vindicated the following day, when the people at Waimea had prostrated themselves before Cook: 'such were ye good effects of at once shewing our superiority'. Whenever exactly he wrote this, Williamson contrived to present himself as a man as concerned as Cook to restrain the violence of common seamen, and one with a better theory of how to limit harm. Cook's approach to the sorts of circumstances that had confronted Williamson at Waimea was not really different from Williamson's. He would use ball, and shoot to kill, if the necessity arose. And this is why Cook regretted the incident, but did not censure it, and did not punish Williamson.

Some premonition is hinted at, too, in James King's yoking of the discovery of a further set of South Sea Islanders to patriotism:

The Knowledge of this wide extensive nation, their Manners, their Arts & of the different Islands they inhabit, add a lustre on our nation, & gives it a decided advantage over all others, in her Naval skill & in the Spirit of their enterprises; & which every good subject must rejoice to see; & hope, that no event will ever happen to abate or confine the influence of such a spirit.

The north Pacific seemed to lack life: hardly a bird or an 'Oceanic animal' was sighted for over a month, until around daybreak on 7 March 'the long looked for Coast of new Albion was seen', Cook wrote, employing an old possessive name that dated back to Sir Francis Drake. He had reached the coast of what is now Oregon. He followed the land north, frustrated by the lack of a harbour, and by heavy and unpleasant weather that made it impossible to chart the coast accurately. Though on the lookout for a rumoured Strait of Juan de Fuca, hypothetically an entrance to a north-west passage, he missed the entry into the waters that separate Vancouver Island from the mainland, and sailed up the island's west coast, presuming understandably enough that its great forests and massive snow-covered mountains belonged to the American continent.

In due course, what Cook called an 'inlet' appeared. The word fails to conjure up the scale of Nootka Sound, a place that I felt, when I visited, had undergone some abnormal topographic enlargement: the width and the reach of the waters here, the yawning greatness of the still wintry sky, the bald eagle's long glide, and the sheer bulk in the ranges that rise away to 5, 6, maybe 7,000 feet, only twenty to thirty miles inland, give this place an almost inhuman capaciousness, to my eyes, though not to Cook's, I take it, and certainly not to those of the people who came off in canoes 'without shewing the least mark of fear or distrust'. He had passed a cove that these people, of the Mowachaht bands of the Nuu-chah-nulth nation, considered the centre of the world, a place where the winds blew from all directions, as different seasons brought herrings and whales from the sea, warmth from the south, the salmon back to the rivers, and the scent and smell of cedar, fir and yew from the north. Here, a great creator had produced the first woman, she in turn had produced a boy, and peoples and chiefs had emerged and spread: these people, like the Maori, knew their ancestors and made great carvings of them. The carvings likewise belonged to the very structures of their houses. The ancestors were not dead but present, and embodied in the architecture that their descendants inhabited.

Yet these people were also just another set of 'Indians', perhaps the twentieth or thirtieth set that Cook had met with. They struck him at first as 'mild and inoffensive'; they wanted iron, which they evidently knew, and traded readily, remaining alongside the *Resolution* throughout the night. The following day, 30 March, Cook found a 'pretty snug cove'. Trade continued, marked by 'the Strictest honisty'. The people offered skins and furs of many sorts, bark clothing, weapons, fish hooks, some carved objects, and human skulls and hands, which were probably trophies from inter-tribal war. The British learned a local word: *makook* was an imperative, meaning buy, or reciprocate. Hence, a man would throw them some fish, and say *makook*, give me something in return.

The ships were moored in what Cook, displaying his habitual lack of imagination in the business of names, once again called 'Ship Cove'. It was a shallow but sheltered bay on a good-sized island in the middle of Nootka Sound; parties were sent ashore to cut wood, and an observatory was as usual established. New groups of local people appeared; in each case they 'went through a singular ceremony', paddling vigorously around both ships,

48. *John Webber,* The Resolution and Discovery in Ship Cove, Nootka Sound, *1778.*

while one man stood upright, 'speaking or rather holloaing all the time', 'sometimes this person would have his face covered with a mask, either that of the human face or some animal'. The people would, after this, join the others already trading, they became increasingly familiar, and they began to steal things, which led to tussles but no serious violence. Modern native historians put it this way:

We were able to bind Cook to us through ceremonial welcome and gift exchange, and to establish and maintain excellent relations with the captain and his crews in the hope that we could attract more visitors. We were very pleased with the trade that ensued, being able to exchange a few trifling furs, combs, spoons and hats for items we greatly valued, in particular iron, axes, and cloth . . . our visitors stayed with us longer [than the Spaniard Juan Perez, who had passed the Sound in 1774], and we were able to gain a better understanding of these men in 'floating houses'.

These people, like others of the Northwest Coast – to employ the regional designation that later became standard among ethnologists and tribal art historians – were unrelated to the Pacific Islanders, and no amount of Tahitian or Maori would facilitate any communication with them. Yet the expectations, even the sporadic sensitivities towards native culture, that the succession of Oceanic encounters had engendered were transposed to this place. Burney, who had often been attentive to song elsewhere, wrote of the oratory or chant that Cook had referred to, 'the halloo is a single note in which they all join, swelling it out in the middle and letting the Sound die away. In a Calm with the hills around us, it had an effect infinitely superior to what might be imagined from any thing so simple'. Cook added, 'each strain ends in a loud and deep sigh uttered in such a manner as to have a very pleasing effect'.

The weather was bad; work caulking and repairing masts was hindered; yet people visited regularly and brought plenty of fish, which the mariners appreciated, since they failed to catch any themselves; by 12 April, Cook was talking of being visited again by 'some of our old friends'. Over the following days he had a great tree cut down to make a new mizzen mast; the locals 'looked on with more silent attention than is usual with Indians', he noticed, and gathered that the people they had encountered first had cunningly monopolized trade. Those who arrived from elsewhere were forced, it appeared, to trade through them, they raised the prices of what they had to offer, they went off in canoes for some days to get more of the furs that Cook's crew particularly sought, and they mixed water with the oil that they sold. Yet, Cook considered, 'it was always better to put up with these tricks than to quarrel with them'. Why? 'As our articles of trafick consisted for the most part of trifles,' he explains, as if he feels he should apologize for being imposed upon, before undermining his own excuses by admitting that the people had little regard for beads and insisted upon metal, to such an extent that by the time they departed, 'hardly a bit of brass was left in the Ship', other than in essential instruments.

Cook found that this shrewd approach to commerce extended to the commonest things ashore. He sent a party to cut grass, and did not anticipate that this would trouble anyone; but the men who began the task were stopped by people, who insisted that they had to *makook*, to pay for it. Cook went to the spot himself, and found some dozen men who all made claims. He paid them, expecting that his people then would be able to cut anywhere, yet encountered further demands, 'there was not a blade of grass that had not a seperated owner, so that I very soon emptied my pockets with purchasing, and when they found I had nothing more to give they let us cut where ever we pleased'. 'The very wood and water we took on board they at first wanted us to pay for,' he added, remarking that nowhere else had he encountered the notion that every natural production was 'their exclusive property'. And the people would have been paid, he added, had he been present himself when these demands were made; but they were ignored by the crew, and the people after a while got tired of asking, yet later 'made a Merit on necessity and frequently afterwards told us they had given us Wood and Water out of friendship'. The negotiations and tensions around property were, as they long had been, triangular, since Cook tended to respect native claims that his crew did not; or rather, they probably had many angles, which are no longer all visible to us.

On 20 April, Cook, Webber and others visited the village of Yuquot, in the place also known as Friendly Cove, an open sandy bay just inside the northern entrance to the sound. They had stumbled upon a place of central importance to the native nations, occupied then, as it was until the mid twentieth century, by peoples led by a line of chiefs named Maquinna. Cook did not see the most sacred site here, a shrine associated with the native whaling tradition, but he was treated 'very curtiously', he was invited into houses, he was given a mat to sit upon, and shown 'every other mark of civility'. Webber depicted the line of houses on the rise above the beach, just where houses and ancestral memorials were photographed later, and where two or three remain today. Cook noticed that women wove cloaks, and cleaned and dried sardines, which were smoked suspended in these dwellings; he says nothing of a new sort of women's work that Samwell discloses, paid at the rate of 'a Pewter place well scoured for one night'. The women were amiable enough, the surgeon thought, but it sounds as though he was far from alone in trading all the metal he had, and was then moved to complain that 'No Bankrupt ever found a fair one kind.' If Cook made no particular effort to constrain sexual contagion here, that may be because he supposed 'the venereal' to be endemic already on the American continent.

There was no reason to protract this visit, once the essential repairs had been made, and every reason to hasten further north, to do as much as was possible during the approaching summer. At the end of April the ships left the sound, not before Cook had been given a valuable beaverskin cloak by a chief he took a liking to, whom he presented with a 'New Broad Sword with a brass hilt' in return. 'He as also many others importuned us much to return to them again', and promised to set aside a supply of skins to trade when they did so. The seed of a future fur trade was germinating, for better or worse.

After departure, Cook set out his observations, as he had often done on leaving ports over the decade since he visited Rio, in 1768. He used a series of marginal headings that included: *Nautical remarks, Country and produce, Animals, Inhabitants their Persons and Habits, Manufacture, Ornaments, Songs, Canoes, Food & Habitations, Large Images* and *Government and Religion*. His remarks were the sort he always made, and were as constrained as they usually had been, when next to nothing of the language was known. He thought the people were dirty, 'docile courtious [and] good natured', but also 'very passionate and quick in resenting what they looke upon as an injury'. He described their clothing and cloaks in great detail, and the masks, whose significance was clearly a good deal debated. People including Samwell, who had a functional turn of mind, were sure that those featuring animals were 'decoys' employed in hunting. Others thought they shielded the face and body in war, and still others presumed they were used in 'public entertainments'. Cook remained interested in manifestations of religion, but thought that the 'monsterous large' images 'or statues' commonly found in houses were not gods, because otherwise people would not have proposed to sell them to him, as he maintained they often did. Yet there was some sensitivity over the European interest in these figures. When Webber went into one house, a man was 'seemingly displeas'd' when the artist took an interest in the two carved and painted figures 'of a Gigantic proportion'. He screened them off with a mat, to stop Webber sketching them:

49. *John Webber,* Representations of Animals Used as Decoys, *1778.*

Being certain of no future oppertunity to finish my Drawing & the object too interresting for leaving unfinish'd, I considered a little bribery might have some effect, and accordingly made him an offer of a button from my coat, which when of metal they are much pleas'd with, this instantly producd the desir'd effect, for the mat was remov'd and I left at liberty to proceed, as before. Scarcely had I seated myself and made a beginning, but he return'd & renewd his former practice, till I had disposd of my buttons, after which time I found no opposition in my further employment.

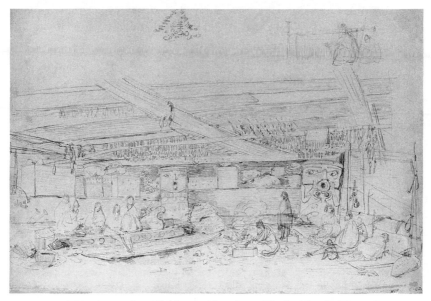

50. *The picture that Webber paid to draw:* The Inside of a House in
Nootka Sound, *1778.*

Which is a stark instance, and the best documented instance, of the
negotiation that Webber had been obliged to engage in throughout the
voyage. Though he could sketch a distant view, perhaps also a village view,
without seeking anyone's acquiescence, he could never produce any more
intimate scene, such as this house interior, without it being apparent to the
people around him, without them at least putting up with the practice, or
maybe encouraging him.

The Yuquot people were to suffer at the hands of those who later took
away a great many of the 'large images' that interested Cook and Webber.
At the end of the nineteenth century, the people of Friendly Cove would be
prodded and cajoled into selling what then remained of the great whalers'
shrine; its components would end up in a New York museum, where they
remain today, though perhaps not for much longer. Other works would be
valued, not in their own hands, but in auction rooms; the masks' styles,
forms and types would be analysed in alien languages; and it would not be
until the very end of the twentieth century that the Nuu-chah-nulth would
again play a significant role in defining the meanings and values of their
own treasures, and having some say in the ways they would be curated and
exhibited. Yet it is in a way encouraging that the very beginning of this
process was an act of exchange rather than appropriation: Webber made a

deal, and took away a drawing. His graphic record remains useful, if limited: it tells us what these figures looked like, and where they were situated; it exhibits a lively regard, if next to no understanding.

Just outside Nootka Sound, the ships encountered an approaching storm. The winds increased, they encountered 'Squals and rain'; it was 'so dark that we could not see the length of the Ship'. By the middle of the following day, it was blowing 'a perfect hurricane', it was too dangerous to run before the wind, the ships were brought to, and the *Resolution* began to leak. This was hardly an encouraging start to the voyage's real business.

The search for the North-West Passage was a counterpart to the search for the southern continent, in the sense that both were long-postulated geographic entities, around which wafted cartographic and commercial fantasies. And Cook's plan, as I noted before, entailed a kind of inversion of his second-voyage strategy: he envisaged far northern explorations in summer months, and winter refreshment in warmer latitudes. Yet in other respects this search was an entirely different one to that of the previous voyage, and moreover a tougher challenge. Though the Antarctic cruises had been miserable and gruelling, their logic was straightforward, and when Cook encountered long rolling seas for days on end, he could be certain that no land lay behind them, even when visibility was poor. For a decade, he had honed his feeling for signs of land and signs of its absence. But now he looked not for land but for passages through land, which he had no concerted experience in seeking out; and he had to do so along the length of a great swathe of the American continent, along a mountainous coast full of fissures. Any broad opening might mark the beginning of a passage; but openings were easily missed in fog or haze, or missed because storms made it impossible to remain close to land; and any opening might need to be traced a considerable distance before it became evident whether it led anywhere. Others trying for passages had placed much reliance upon tides, but neither their flow, nor other currents, were in fact reliable indicators of whether any waterway might possess an outlet: there were few signs of any sort that would help exploration here.

The first weeks of May were unpromising. The coast was found to tend not north but west, and even south of west, at once diminishing the likelihood of a passage, and implying a longer voyage before any route to the north or east might be found. In mid May conditions were threatening, and Cook ventured into what was later called Prince William Sound, to find a harbour and to try to fix the *Resolution*'s leak. Some native people appeared, who at first seemed 'peacable' but then made a bold effort to steal a boat, in full view of many seamen. They then tried subsequently to raid the *Discovery*, climbing on to the deck, producing knives, and seeming inclined to plunder. They withdrew only when alarmed seamen appeared with cutlasses. 'Does not these circumstances shew these people to be strangers to fire arms?' Cook asked, sure that neither attempt would have been made, had the Aboriginal people any notion of the effects of the cannons and guns they exposed themselves to. He was relieved to add that 'We had the good fortune to leave them as ignorant as we found them'; the prudent retreat had forestalled violence.

Though surprised rather than angered by these daring attempts to appropriate things, Cook seems not to have felt the empathy for these people – perhaps of the Tlingit nation – that he had for the Nuu-chah-nulth. He at any rate responds to no individual, he has no impression of civility, ingenuity or refinement. But he was interested in their clothing and canoes. He had noticed immediately that the latter were made of sealskin over a wooden frame, quite different to the bigger, solid wooden boats of Nootka Sound. He 'attentively examined' one kayak 'with Crantz discription of the Womens boat in Greenland before me'. David Crantz's *History of Greenland* had been published in English in 1767. It celebrated the accomplishments of the Moravian mission, but had natural historical as well as evangelical content, and included an extended account of the 'manners and customs' sort. The book had been given to Cook, presumably, as a guide to people he might meet, were he successful in finding a passage through to the Arctic Atlantic; but it now enabled him to ask and tentatively answer the sorts of questions Forster might have asked, had he been here rather than agonizing over his debts in London. Cook found that the canoe before him was built 'in the same manner' as that described by Crantz. He had identified a likeness that linked the north Pacific to the far north Atlantic, that was manifest also in dress, tattooing, and fishing and hunting implements. The latter were 'the very same as are made use of by the Esquemaux and Greenlanders and are all of them very accurately discribed by Crantz; I did not see one with these people that he has not mentioned, nor has he mentioned one that they have not', Cook insisted. So far as physique and appearance were concerned, these 'thick set good looking people' seemed to bear 'some affinity' to Crantz's Greenlanders, but because he had himself never seen 'either a Greenlander or an Esquemaus . . . I cannot be a sufficient judge and as we may very probably see more of them I shall reserve the discussion of this point to some other time'. Cook would comment later on affinities of language rather than physique, but was wondering already whether these people were like Polynesians, who had migrated over icy wastes rather than a great ocean; who perhaps once had greater boats, and had come this far, via a navigable passage.

The leak was stopped, the weather improved, and a north-westerly course taken into the sound. The ships anchored in one arm, where the flood tide came in through the channel the ships had used; 'altho this did not make wholy against a passage, it was however nothing in its favour'. As conditions cleared, the height of visible land diminished hope further, and Cook sent boats out to investigate inlets. Gore was confident that the arm he looked into 'bid fair for opening a communication to some other Sea', but a mate who had accompanied him thought rather that they had got within sight of its end. Cook's guess was that Gore was wrong, and he saw warm months passing, well before he had got far north, while little was accomplished. The ships made way back into the open sea, and followed the coast to the south and west, but soon found a further large opening to the north-east; there were great mountains to the north and west, but these were presumed to belong to an island, and there was renewed optimism on board. Yet Cook himself studied the horizons and thought that the mountains 'were every where connected by lower land', he became sure that all the land that they saw was part of the great continent, yet persevered with investigation 'more to satisfy other people than to confirm my own opinion'. He was mindful that his course and his conduct would be debated on the return of the voyage, and he did not want the conclusiveness of his findings undermined by Gore or anyone else. He would try to leave no one scope to say that a likely inlet had been ignored. At first there were hopeful signs: on 29 May, a clear day, 'in a North North East direction no land or any thing to obstruct us was to be seen'. Without much wind, rapid tides were used to carry the ships further, but by 31 May, it was noted that at low tide the water was partly fresh, hence Cook became convinced that they were in a river, 'and Not a Strait that would communicate with the Northern Seas'. Yet it seemed important to be certain, and two branches were broached, Bligh was sent further and reached a point where the waters narrowed considerably, and it was clear that they did not extend much further inland; the foray was abandoned, not far from the present site of Anchorage.

If the discovery of this River should prove of use, either to the present or future ages, the time spent in exploring it ought to be the less regreted, but to us who had a much greater object in View it was an essential loss; the season was advancing apace, we knew how far we might have to proceed to the South and we were now convinced that the Continent extended farther to the west than from the Modern Charts we had reason to expect and made a passage into Baffin or Hudson bays far less probable, or at least made it of greater extent. But if I had not examined this place it would have been concluded, nay asserted that it communicated with the Sea to the North, or with one of these bays to the East.

As if to compound Cook's frustration, a careless watch led to the ship being grounded on the way downriver and occasioned further delay, relieved only by trade with Aboriginal people, who had manufactured knives, which suggested contact with Russian traders, and who brought good salmon and halibut. Cook wrote that they were 'of the same nation' as the people encountered in Prince William Sound, 'but differ essentially from those of *Nootka* . . . both in their persons and Language'. If he was failing to find a passage, he was mapping human variety, albeit in a rudimentary way.

Negotiating mist and fog, the ships resumed their course westward along the southern coast of the great Alaskan peninsula. On 19 June some native people delivered a small wooden box to the *Discovery* that, Clerke later realized, contained a letter written in Russian, which unfortunately no one was able to read. Some people thought it might be a plea for help from some castaways, but Cook dismissed the possibility and pressed on. On 26 June, visibility was poor but the wind moderate, so he 'ventured to run', until breakers were heard suddenly and the *Resolution* brought to and anchored; when the fog cleared it became apparent that they had been lucky, or, as Cook put it, that 'Providence had conducted us through between these rocks where I should not have ventured in a clear day'. The ships were just off an island. Some native people were seen towing to shore 'two Whales which we supposed they had killed this morning'. They visited, and Cook learned that the name of the island was Unalaska; the people, who sought tobacco in trade, had clearly had some contact with Europeans.

Here the ships had rounded the Alaskan peninsula: Unalaska was one of the Aleutian islands, which extended much further, in a great arc, out into the centre of the north Pacific. Cook had no interest in tracing this arc, but was concerned rather to follow the continental coast first to the north-east, and from mid July onwards back to the north-west. The weather was often foggy, but there were no false passages. Cook consulted Stahlin's map of the 'New Northern Archipelago' and can only have been confused. On 3 August, William Anderson, whose health had steadily declined, died. Cook wrote of his passing that 'He was a Sensible Young Man, an agreeable companion, well skilld in his profession, and had acquired much knowledge in other Sciences, that had it pleased God to have spar'd his life might have been usefull in the Course of the Voyage'; my guess is that the 'Course of the Voyage' became a gloomier prospect in the absence of this companion. The next island sighted was named after Anderson, 'to perpetuate the Memory of the deseased for whom I had a very great regard'.

In early August they neared the Bering Strait, which separates Asia and America, and crossed to the Siberian shore. Here a Chukchi village was visited, where people were at first trepidatious, retreating as Cook approached and tried to put his hand on a man's shoulder, keeping spears and arrows on the ready, until the commander and two or three others managed to mingle, pass out a few beads, and bring 'on a kind of confidence'; 'by degrees a sort of traffick between us commenced'. These people had metal spears and other things of 'European or Asiatic' origin; they carried their arrows in beautifully embroidered red leather quivers; their faces were long rather than round, and they belonged to quite a different nation to 'All the Americans'. Cook inspected both winter and summer houses, he saw large frames, constructed out of bone, that seemed to be built of dry skins. He judged that the people survived on sea animals and fish, since the country was barren. A couple of men performed a kind of dance, which Webber drew Cook witnessing. The attention to detail in both his sketches and Cook's description make it plain that people as well as passages remained objects of exploration here; and that the always uncertain drama of meeting with them remained a matter of exploratory history.

If Stahlin's map was right, this was the great island of 'Alaschka'. But 'it appeared rather more probable' that it was what it in fact of course was, the 'country of the Tchuktschians explored by Behring in 1728'. Which meant that Stahlin's map was either very wrong 'or else a mere fiction'. Cook felt that he was not yet in a position to pronounce such 'a Sentence' upon this chart. But whether the strait he had just crossed separated the 'island' of Alaska from America, or America from Asia, the coasts on both its sides clearly tended to the north, and there was renewed optimism that a route might be found towards Baffin Bay. The ships sailed back towards the American coast and north-east through the Strait, across the Arctic circle, and followed the northern coasts of Alaska. Now, had Barrington been right, it should have been possible to sail towards the pole, through open water clear of any coastal ice that had formed around the mouths of American rivers.

In the middle of the day, on 17 August, both the sun and moon appeared at intervals. It was possible to make observations, which put the ships 70°33' north and 197°41' east. This, coincidentally, was about as far north as Cook had got to the south, on 31 January 1774; and here he encountered a sight that must have recalled that morning, when he got as far as it was possible for man to go. The sight was that of 'a brightness in the Northern horizon like that reflected from ice, commonly called the blink'. It was disregarded, because people thought it 'improbable' that ice would be encountered so soon; in his voyage towards Spitzbergen, Phipps had got fully ten degrees further north before narrowly avoiding destruction in ice. And yet, Cook wrote

the sharpness of the air and Gloomyness of the Weather for two or three days past seemed to indicate some sudden change. At 1 pm the sight of a large field of ice left us in no longer doubt about the cause of the brightness of the Horizon we had observed. At 1/2 past 2 we tacked close to the edge of it in 22 fathoms Water being then in the latitude of 70°41', not being able to stand any farther, for the ice was quite impenetrable and extended from WBS to EBN as far as the eye could reach.

From this position the ships sailed back to the south, and then east, and soon reached a point where the ice shelf met the land; here too were shoals, and both ships were nearly trapped, their situation 'more and more critical' in the narrowing space between ice and shore. They tacked, fortunately the wind proved favourable, and it was possible to make way into the only open water, towards the south-west. The following day they sailed west and north; Cook does not make it clear, but presumably he felt that he needed to test the limits of the ice, and try for any passage that might lead through it. The ice that was found was broken and looser than what had blocked his course the day before, but was nevertheless 'too close and in too large pieces to force the ships through'. Here, however, they found what Cook called sea-horses, meaning walruses, in great numbers, and as 'we were in want of fresh provisions', both ships sent out boats which succeeded in killing a number of these animals. Webber perhaps saw, in the business of blasting away at these huge, helpless beasts, huddled on the breaking ice, a visual anecdote of the extremity that the voyage had reached. He made a whole series of sketches of the subject, and later worked one up into an evocative oil of the strange sport. There was a good deal of debate on board as to whether walruses were edible at all, but the much-resented withdrawal of the salted ration gave them no choice but to try it. Cook, as usual, set an example, and struggled to get others to regard the flesh as delicious. His assertion that 'there were few on board who did not prefer it to salt meat' seems to have been a long way short of the truth.

Two days later it became apparent to Cook that the edge of what he called 'the main Ice' was not static; it 'covered a part of the sea which but a few days before was clear', and 'extended farther to the South than where we first fell in with it'. They had been in this area less than a week, but the ice was clearly advancing southward, and the scope for exploration diminishing. He sailed west for some days, and took boats out to approach and examine the ice. He was sure himself that it was 'intirely composed of frozen Snow and had all been formed at sea'. It seemed utterly improbable that such vast masses could have been formed within, or floated out of rivers, and in any case there was no land matter, no old wood, gravel or soil, incorporated within it. He asked himself also whether this ice was much reduced, and responded, not by the sun, 'altho he is a considerable time above the horizon he seldom shines out for more than a few hours at a time'. Cook thought that it was rather the wind and waves that corroded ice, hence a good deal might be destroyed in a stormy season, 'but that there is always a remaining store, none who has been upon the spot will deny and none but Closet studdying Philosiphers will dispute'. He was now certain, in other words, that Barrington's premises were false and his deductions spurious. Ice did not depend upon land, and there was accordingly no open Arctic sea. He did not yet say, no north-west passage: he must have had a strong sense, yet cannot have been absolutely confident that Stahlin's map was pure concoction. He could not be sure that he had not missed an opening, somewhere further south, somewhere free of ice. He sailed as far as the Asian coast, where the land was desolate, where ice threatened. He had, evidently, considered looking into the possibility of an Arctic passage over north Asia rather than north America; yet it was plain that the same conditions prevailed, and he 'gave up the design' he had formed.

The season was now so very far advanced and the time when the frost is expected to set in so near at hand, that I did not think it consistant with prudence to make any farther attempts to find a passage this year in any direction, so little was the prospect of succeeding. My attention was now directed towards finding out some place where we could Wood and Water, and in considering how I should spend the Winter, so as to make some improvement to Geography and Navigation and at the same time be in a condition to return to the North in further search of a Passage the ensuing summer.

The cruise had failed, but only in the same sense that the exploration of the southern ocean had failed, namely to find a rumoured object. It had succeeded in establishing, for the first time, the general outline of the north-west American coast; it had confirmed a point of decisive importance concerning the formation and extent of northern ice. The Cook who felt dejected and frustrated by the delays of May and June had now learned a good deal, albeit a good deal that pointed to the non-existence of the passage. This was not a finding that would bring a parliamentary prize, it meant no treasure to be shared among officers and crew, but it was certainly nevertheless the sort of 'improvement to Geography and Navigation' that Cook saw as his task, that he wanted to make history by making.

During September, the ships proceeded south and east; they investigated Norton Sound, which looked the most likely candidate for Stahlin's strait between Alaska and America, but its limits were quickly established. Cook decided that he did not want to winter in a Russian port, such as Kamchatka, because that would mean six or seven months' inactivity; he would sail for Hawaii, for the Sandwich Islands, instead. En route the *Resolution* and *Discovery* stopped again at Unalaska, where contact was made with the Russians, whose presence had previously been suspected. The lack of any interpreter made communication difficult – and in hindsight it is surprising that neither the Admiralty nor Cook himself had thought of including a single Russian speaker in either ship's company – but Cook shared his rum and his maps with the fur traders, and such discussion as was possible reinforced his sense that Stahlin's publication had been a jumbled, erroneous imposition. The geographer had referred in passing to the difficulty of deriving accurate information from 'the illiterate accounts of our sea-faring men' but his map, Cook retorted, was one that 'the most illiterate' of these men 'would have been ashamed to put his name to'.

They remained more than three weeks at Unalaska, and Cook took the opportunity to extend and synthesize his observations on these native American peoples. In the course of addressing his usual set of headings, he described their method of making fire, and added that it was the same as that found in Brazil, Tahiti, Australia and many other places, 'yet some learned and inginious men have made use of this custom to prove that this and that Nation are of the same extraction, but accidental agreement in a few particular manners or customs is no proof that two different Nations are of the same extraction, or that a desagreement proves they are different'. He makes the point because he had been trying to get to grips with the question of how one might prove that nations were 'of the same extraction'. He did take 'particular manners or customs' into account, but his south Pacific experience suggested that the strongest evidence would be linguistic, rather than artifactual. People might 'accidentally' produce similar clothes, conceivably even similar canoes, in similar environments, but would hardly

375

use the same or related words, unless their dialects had a common derivation. Cook assembled a comparative vocabulary of American languages and 'such corresponding words' as he could get from the lists he'd been given of 'the language of the Greenlanders, and Esquemaux; from all of which there is great reason to believe that all these nations are of the same extraction'. As it happens, not only modern anthropologists but the people themselves, now represented by the Inuit Circumpolar Conference, would agree. His further inference that there therefore ought to be 'a northern communication of some sort by sea' was wishful thinking, since the migrating peoples might have crossed north America, in whichever direction, over land. Cook was straining to connect his human observations with his mission; he acknowledged in any case that a 'communication' might be 'effectually shut up against Shipping', meaning, I suppose, that it might have, or might once have, been negotiable by kayak, but not by any larger boat. 'Such as least was my opinion at this time,' he added, and further qualified the whole discussion: 'two much stress must not be laid on the following Vocabulry . . . for I have frequently found that two, or more persons, have written down the same words and when compared have differed not a little'.

Cook's third voyage has often been seen as one marked by the growing, indeed the enveloping fatigue of the great navigator. It is supposed that Cook suffered lapses in his abilities, curiosity and decisiveness; more antagonistic commentators claim that he became detached, irrational, and violent. It is not hard to understand why the tale has been told in these terms: we like it when a great character's life exhibits a rise and fall, and may perhaps be seduced by the notion that a colonizer might collapse, like Conrad's Kurtz, into some black hole of his own evil. But Cook's voyages do not exhibit any such trend. Some of the worst violence occurred in New Zealand as early as 1769, when the man was supposedly saner. And the third voyage is marked by ups and downs, not by any sort of downward spiral. The terrorism of Tonga was succeeded by relatively peaceful months on Tahiti, by brief savagery on Moorea, by trauma on Raiatea, and six months of north American contacts with native peoples that were devoid of serious violence, almost devoid of tension. We understand these encounters, not by holding on to a heroic or anti-heroic notion that Cook always played the defining part, for better or worse. Things were awful, in the Tongan islands in part because a peculiarly stratified Polynesian society pressured common people to steal on behalf of their superiors – risking punishment that no commoner would otherwise risk, and that no Tahitian would expose him or herself to. Things went better than they had before at Tahiti because growing familiarity was accompanied by a new abundance of the trade goods that the Tahitians most earnestly desired. As both sides had more to offer, difficulties dissipated. Things were worse on both Moorea and Hua-hine, because the people Cook dealt with knew that his primary allegiances were with their rivals and enemies. On the north-west coast, the Europeans went about barter and soliciting sex in much the same way they had in the South Pacific. It was the native approach to these encounters that was in some cases subtly, in others dramatically, different from place to place. At Nootka, people gained more by hard bargaining than by theft. In Prince William Sound, they were bold but withdrew rather than risk a fight. Many Inuit practised their diplomacy: they sang and chanted and brought Europeans within their orbit. They defined Cook's men as people they could deal with, and they dealt with them.

A dream that we could not reconcile ourselves to

Cook's intuition had somehow told him that there was more to the Hawaiian archipelago than the islands he had sighted in February 1778, and in particular, more that lay beyond Oahu. The southward course he took from the Aleutians was therefore not back towards Kauai, but into what might well have been open water, some hundreds of miles to the east. Yet he was right, and on 26 November the island of Maui came into view. It was massive and impressive, the summits of its ranges were covered in clouds, the visible slopes were fissured by ravines, there were 'beautiful cascades', James King remarked, 'down the Cliffy coast'.

Cook took his usual steps, issuing orders to regulate trade, and again attempted to restrain sexual contagion. 'And Whereas there are Venereal compaints remaining onboard the Ships, and in order to prevent as much as possible the communicating this fatal disease to a set of innocent people, it is hereby ordered that no Woman on any pretence whatever be admitted.' Those who tried to bring women on board, or allowed them on board, were warned that they would be punished, and 'if any person having, or suspected of having the Venereal disease or any Symptoms thereof, shall lie with any Woman, he shall also be severely punished'. A list of such people would be kept on the quarterdeck, none of whom would be allowed onshore, 'on any pretence whatever'. Cook read these directions out, and made what King called 'a sensible speech', urging people to adhere to them. He was no doubt angry and sad but not surprised to find that the 'evil' he meant to prevent 'had already got amongst them'. Over the ensuing weeks, a good many Hawaiians came out to the ship, not just to trade but to complain and to seek help, assuming that the British might have treatments for the illness they had introduced. King recorded that three men 'apply'd to us, for help in their great distress: they had a Clap, their Penis was much swell'd, & inflamed'. There was argument aboard as to whether the infection could really have spread in ten months from Niihau and Kauai as far as Maui, whether it perhaps pre-existed, in these islands, or might have been brought by other Europeans. Some journal-keepers, such as Burney, insisted that the Hawaiians did not blame the British, and could not tell them when or where their disease originated. It is just possible that Burney had not understood the conversations that he had with Islanders; more likely, he was dishonestly denying what was well known, and was reported plausibly by the midshipman Edward Riou, also on the *Discovery*. The people who indeed were venereally afflicted – the surgeon confirmed – 'spoke of the Isle Atowi [i.e. Kauai], as if we had left it at that place the Last year'. Riou, like Cook and King, was aghast that the disease had been transmitted, not unfortunately by some forgotten Spaniards but that 'we ourselves that has entailed on these poor, Unhappy people an everlasting and Miserable plague'.

A 'dreadfull surf' broke against the rocky coast. Cook saw no harbour, but during the last days of October people came off in canoes, and began to trade pigs and vegetables. A number appeared, belonging to 'a Chief named Terryaboo', who gave Cook a few pigs and left some of his people on board; they were later 'attended upon' by a double canoe that was towed behind the ship throughout the night. It is only the allusion to this 'attending' that hints that these were no ordinary chiefs, they were people who must have approached the *Resolution* with a good deal of grandeur and power. Cook did not know it, but his 'Terryaboo' was Kalani'opu'u, the ruler of a still more massive and more impressive Hawaiian island that came into view the following day. Kalani'opu'u remained on Maui, where he was fighting a war; Cook's ships crossed the passage towards the island of Hawaii itself, and all were surprised to see the volcanic cones of Mauna Kea and Mauna Loa covered in snow, 'so that these people know all the climates from the Torrid to the Fridgid Zones', Cook remarked. This convenient compression of the earth's environments was of less interest to him, though, than the ships' diminishing stores. Among the plants obtained through trade was sugar cane, the shortage of liquor was such that Cook made a trial 'decoction', which produced, he initially wrote in his journal, 'a very palatable and wholesome beer which was esteemed by every man on board'. But he was again crediting his crew with a willingness to entertain dietary innovations, which they in fact stolidly resisted. Just as the substitution of walrus flesh for salt meat had been deeply unpopular, this tropical cocktail was much resented, as Cook on this occasion acknowledged, in a rewritten journal entry.

I ordered some more to be brewed, but when the Cask came to broached not one of my Mutinous crew would even so much as taste it. As I had no montive for doing it but to save our spirit for a Colder climate, I gave myself no trouble either to oblige or persuaid them to drink it, knowing there was no danger of the Scurvy so long as we had plenty of other Vegetables; but that I might not be disapointed in my views I gave orders that no grog should be served in either Ship.

The crew complained by letter, and drew attention to the fact that they continued on reduced rations, despite their arrival at these islands; this Cook did not know and immediately rectified, but he remained inflexible on the subject of the beer, and had the cooper flogged a couple of days later, 'for starting yᵉ Cask of Decoction which was sour', the midshipman Watts reported. If Cook now felt still more remote from his company here – it is hard really to tell – the likelihood is that his estrangement was exacerbated by the sense that they had again betrayed him, through their reckless indifference to the communication of venereal disease.

In some island harbours a superabundance of food was succeeded by a shortage, Cook had found; he thought here that a supply of provisions was best assured, if the ships did not make a long stay in one bay, but tacked on and off the island, trading with canoes. The ships companies – officers as well as men – were frustrated to be so close, but so far from, a further Polynesian paradise, but their commander may well have wanted to restrain precisely the contacts they sought, even though the damage had already been done. In any case, the north and east coasts of Hawaii were beaten by the same sort of 'dreadfull surf' that had already been remarked upon: there was maybe no anchorage to be found. Over the following weeks, trade was sometimes interrupted when the ships moved too far off the land, but all that was needed was obtained, from people who seemed scrupulously honest, as well as very friendly. By the first days of 1779 the ships – albeit separated for a week – had rounded the island, and Cook had given up: 'It was not possible to keep the latter' – the women – 'out of the Ship and no women I ever met with were more ready to bestow their favours'. The seas on the south-western side were calmer, the rigging and sails were in need of attention, and finally on 16 January Cook sent Bligh to examine a likely looking bay. In the meantime thousands of canoes gathered about each ship; their numbers increased when the ships moved into what it transpired was a good anchorage.

If you look south from Kealakekua Bay, you see the even side of a volcanic cone that begins a great slide somewhere way out of view, up inland. It's as if a mountain of an average size had been inflated, blown out and up with hot air and lava. Its shell is up there green and fecund, and down here, at the ocean's edge, black, broken and harsh; and there is a sort of bite out of

51. John Webber, A View of Kealakekua Bay, 1779.

the edge of this eruption, small in relation to the mountain as a whole, enormous in itself, that is Kealakekua Bay, dominated by a lava cliff, pockmarked with caves, that gives way to the south to a gentler but still rocky slope, a space of gardens and villages. Those on Cook's ships who cared to be impressed by landscapes had seen many spectacular coastlines, but here, by any standards, was a harbour and a half. In keeping with its scale, the human welcome here was prodigious: 'I have no where in this Sea seen such a number of people assembled at one place,' wrote Cook. Between those in canoes, those swimming, and those on shore there were 10,000, King estimated.

The British were making their way into more than a topographic feature. They were also entering an indigenous domain, they were being recognized in native terms that they could neither predict nor control. This was no more than what had happened before, but here it happened differently. As in other parts of Polynesia, ideas of cosmos and creation ran parallel to ideas of society and politics. Genealogies linked the first gods with the ancestors of chiefs, and chiefs were intimately associated with deities, though neither Cook nor his companions had ever quite understood this. In Tahiti, Tonga, and many other places, the status of men such as Tutaha, Tu, Finau and Paulaho had more to do with religion than government; they stood for gods, they conquered and made demands like gods, they received sacrifices and tribute, and in return ensured fertility and abundance. Their largesse, their trappings, their appearances, and their performances were phenomena on the most spectacular scale that Islanders knew; chiefs had, in live and visible form, the look and the substance of divinity.

The Hawaiians knew many gods, but two were central to the islands' seasons, rites and rulers. Each year, for four months, the god of peace and productivity, Lono, was sovereign, and a sequence of ceremonies and sacrifices were offered by chiefs, priests and people, seeking and ensuring the reinvigoration of natural life and fertility. During this period, known as the Makahiki, an antagonistic god of war – Ku – was secluded, as were his living representatives, ruling chiefs like Kalani'opu'u and their families and associates. The worship of Ku, and the practice of war, with which he was pre-eminently associated, were likewise tabooed during this season, when an abstract figure of Lono – a sheet of white tapa mounted on a sort of mast and crosspiece – was carried on a procession around the island's coast, to receive offerings, to be at the centre of ceremonies, in one community after another. The ritual drama was inherently political, because Lono was identified with 'native' people – meaning not Hawaiians in general, but those descended from the island's earliest native settlers, who were most associated with the land, and who had been subdued by succeeding immigrants and warriors. Lono's priests, and their families and communities, were notionally if not actually the descendants of the defeated 'native' chiefs and commoners, those dominated in the present by the great ali'i, by the rulers closely identified with Ku. It was as though there was, in old England, a season when Saxons had to withdraw and defer to the gods of the Celts. But the ascendancy of Lono was short-lived. The sacrifices out of the way, the king and the cult of Ku re-emerged. The season came to an end when Lono's circuit of the island was complete; he returned to his principal temple, and on the same day the king and his attendants would arrive by canoe – as though once again invading the land. A sham fight followed, and a few days later the Lono edifice was taken apart, to be hidden, or at any rate stored, within the *heiau* precincts until the next year: figuratively, he was dispatched to the remote land known traditionally as Kahiki, the Hawaiian form of Tahiti. A canoe bearing samples of the fruits Lono had received was put to sea, to drift away – as though the god and his people were being displaced, and forced to take to canoes, as Polynesian refugees did. Meanwhile, Ku's temples were re-opened, and the war cult, which had been in abeyance, was resumed.

All this is germane because Cook's ships appeared just about at the time the Makahiki began. They met Kalani'opu'u off Maui as his campaign was concluding, as the taboos upon war came into force, and as he was obliged to withdraw. The *Resolution* and *Discovery* then crossed to Hawaii, and remarkably, made a circuit of the island in the same, right-hand direction that Lono was prescribed to pursue. As the vessels first approached the coast, they saw tapa streamers, which marked the taboos upon the land;

52. *The war god Kuka'ilimoku: feathers over wicker, dogs' teeth, pearl shell, and wood; probably among valuables presented to Cook and Clerke by Kalani'opu'u over 26–7 January 1779.*

still more fortuitously, the ships' masts and sails uncannily resembled the strut, cross-piece and sheet of white tapa that was the icon of Lono. In many parts of Polynesia, the British had been identified as new, strange, and powerful chiefs, who came in great canoes and were expected to behave as local chiefs did: they were accordingly resisted as invaders, treated gingerly as rivals, and welcomed as allies, according to the particular confluence of local ideas and circumstances. Here, although the advent of the British and the conventional Makahiki corresponded approximately rather than absolutely, the Hawaiians were prompted to receive the pre-eminent man among these visitors as an incarnation of Lono. The nature of this identification has been much debated and much misunderstood. Cook was not taken to be a god, not if a god is a supreme being, of a supernatural or transcendental nature, categorically distinct from any humans. Polynesians recognized no such gulf between the beings they called *atua* or in Hawaii *akua* and living men and women. Gods themselves had varied natures, ranging from the abstract and elemental, in the case of the original creator-beings, to the essentially human and historical, in that of deified ancestors of chiefs. But divinity and humanity always shaded together. From the perspective of a common person, a chief was so superior as to be divine, and certain priests were not just representatives of gods but embodiments of them, they were living *atua*, some sometimes, some all the time. Hence it is neither impossible nor even unexpected that Cook should be seen as a god in this sense, as a new incarnation of Lono, just as Kalani'opu'u was in his way a personification of Ku.

Those who landed in Kealakekua Bay – Cook, King, and others – on 17 January knew none of this. They stepped out of a boat on to a narrow beach that lay just before the great stone *heiau* of Hikiau, which – again fortuitously – happened to be the principal temple of Lono. Kalani'opu'u was nowhere to be seen, but Palea, one of his associates, had been managing trade and contact for Cook; it was he that brought the British ashore at this point, where they were met by the priest Koa who, Cook wrote, 'took me by the hand and conducted me to a large Morai' – he was using the Tahitian terms again – 'the other gentlemen with Parea and four or five more of the Natives followed'. With those words, Cook's Hawaiian log ends: whatever else he wrote was later lost. James King, however, tells us that as they arrived a few men 'who held wands tipt with dogs hair . . . kept repeating a sentence, wherein the word Erono [Lono] was always mention'd, this is the name by which the Captn has for some time been distinguish'd by the Natives'. Apart from these priests, the beach was deserted, which can only have been so because it was tabooed; at a distance, however, among coconut palms and thatch houses, many people prostrated themselves as Cook and his party were led up on to a paved stone platform that was not stepped, but was nevertheless hardly less impressive than the great *marae* of Mahaiatea, which Cook had visited ten years earlier. They paused and prayed before some carved gods, and Koa then led Cook up to what King called the 'Scaffolding' – a wooden tower for offerings – which they then climbed, 'not without great risk of tumbling'. A procession appeared, with a pig and a piece of red cloth; the bearers prostrated themselves, and the cloth was taken up by one priest and handed to Koa, who then wrapped Cook with it, the chanting proceeding all the time. In due course Cook and Koa descended; Koa addressed one carved god after another, and prostrated himself before a central figure, 'the only one covered with Cloth', he 'desird the Capt" to do the same, who was quite passive'. They then moved to the centre of the *heiau*, where Koa and King each supported an arm of Cook's, as if to stretch him out into the form of the Lono image. They received a second procession, headed by a priest with a pig, who 'kept repeating in a very quick tone some speeches or prayers . . . the Croud repeating the word Erono'. These chants concluded, Cook, King and Bayly were anointed with coconut, kava was drunk, and the British were fed pork. 'I had no objection to have the hog handled by Pareea,' King wrote, while recording that Cook was unable to eat, because he was to be fed by Koa, who had performed some 'offices' while handling a putrid pig, sacrificed earlier, that are not specifically described but that evidently disgusted him.

They departed as soon as they felt they could. Cook left some iron and trifles which he 'said was for the Eatooa'. This implies that he understood the event as a variant upon the Tahitian sacrifices he had witnessed. There, he had seen offerings received by priests on behalf of gods; here, he no doubt saw the gods embodied in the wooden images as the real recipients of the presentations; probably, he did not grasp that the second procession brought sacrifices *to him*, that he was the centre of an adapted version of a standard rite, the *hanaipu*, the welcoming or feeding of Lono. The Europeans made their way back to the beach, again led by two men who chanted the name Lono, and surrounded by people who prostrated themselves. If we recall Cook's pleasure and astonishment before the profound deference that ordinary Tongans exhibited in the presence of the Tongan king, we would expect that on this occasion too he was impressed and delighted, by the decorum and order manifest in this exaggerated respect. But it discomforted at least some among his companions. Whatever the ritual had involved, King was confident that 'it was highly respectful on their parts, & seemed to promise us every assistance they could afford us'. But he lamented 'the very Abject & slavish manner, in which the commonality shewd their respect', and for one would have preferred the noise and disorder of 'our friendly Islanders' – meaning the Tongans or perhaps Tahitians – 'with all its incumbrances'.

The impression that 'every assistance' would be forthcoming was soon reinforced. A plantation near the *heiau* looked like a good spot for tents and observatories; the people agreed to its use, and agreed to taboo it. Once this was done 'by the priests, sticking upon the Walls their Wands', no one ventured within it; it seemed that the Europeans would be entirely undisturbed. No canoe would land on the beach beside this place, and despite the most earnest solicitation, no women – who had been otherwise eager for sexual contact – would approach the tents. 'We enjoyd a tranquillity about our Dwellings that was the very reverse to other places in these Sea's,' wrote King, who had been placed in charge of this camp and remained there for the duration of the visit. At the same time, however, hundreds of people persisted in visiting the ships, which at first were so crowded that no work could be done. Palea assisted Cook and Clerke by making 'a Clearance', that is, by ordering or throwing everyone off, now and again. He went so far as to oblige them by swimming after a thief, whom he seemed to strangle underwater. The caulkers worked on the ship's sides, while the sailmakers were directed by the priests to work on the platform of Hikiau itself, probably because they took the sailcloth to be related to their own sacred barkcloth. Over subsequent days, further 'presents were made to the Erono'; the treatment of Cook 'seemd to approach to Adoration', King considered. He learned also that there 'was a great difference' between the priests of the district – the party that hosted them at Hikiau – and the chiefs who ruled over the coast further north, and were based particularly at the settlement of Ka'awaloa, at the north end of Kealakekua Bay: this was to register the opposition between the adherents of Lono, and those associated with Ku and the rulers. 'We began to attatch ourselves more strongly to the Priests,' he wrote, 'whose behaviour was remarkably obliging and modest; without however giveing any offence to the other Chiefs, who were very usefull on board the Ships by Keeping the Natives in order.' This sounds so simple and judicious. King had no notion that there was more going on here. He could not have known that a roughly regulated antagonism was on a timer, that an attachment to priests might mean one thing one week and another the next.

The British had not understood why Kalani'opu'u had stayed away. By 24 January, however, the Makahiki calender had moved on. Lono was no longer in the ascendancy, Ku and his representatives were no longer in seclusion, and the king appeared, 'whose presents & whose train was really Royal', James King thought, though he was surprised to discover that this was the same 'old immaculated infirm man' they had met off Maui. On 26 January a party of canoes, full of people singing, carved gods, pigs and vegetables, arrived at the beach beside Hikiau, and Cook, seeing Kalani'opu'u landing, himself visited, whereupon 'the King got up & threw in a graceful manner over the Capt^ns shoulders the Cloak he himself wore', and laid at his feet five or six further cloaks, 'all very beautiful, & to them of the greatest value'. Hawaiian feather cloaks were and are indeed beautiful, and were of supreme value. David Samwell's judgement was that 'A more rich or elegant Dress than this, perhaps the arts of Europe have not yet been able to supply.' But the cloaks were less garments of opulence, than the battledresses, at once practical and spiritual, of the very highest chiefs: the feathers were woven on to a matted support that physically protected wearers from stones and blows; the divine associations of feathers, and the ritually charged operations of tying and binding, provided a sacred as well as a material shield. The work that went into these fabrics was more-over incredible: most were made from the very small tuft feathers of a few species of forest birds, which produced a beautiful, even velvet texture. Some species were tracked through high rainforest enclaves, trapped by specialist hunters, selectively plucked, and released; others had to be killed. Cleaning, binding, and knotting was an intricate process; larger capes might contain up to half a million feathers, extracted from some 80,000 to 90,000 birds. Nothing like these cloaks could have been produced in any other Oceanic society, because chiefs nowhere else were able to demand so much of their subjects' labour.

In giving Cook these magnificent things, Kalani'opu'u deferred to Lono; Cook reciprocated with the best goods he could offer, which was to defer in his turn; he was used to making gifts of state, of this sort, but he did not appreciate that their flow now reflected the rise and fall of one god, and the fall and rise of another, an alternation of powers and principles that he and this deceptively 'infirm' king were caught up in. The priests of Lono made their own presentations to Kalani'opu'u, that were not reciprocated; there was indeed a tide in the affairs of these men, that was on the turn.

Much trade and gift-giving took place; parties off the ships explored inland, where they had the sense that they had nothing at all to fear from the people; they were impressed by vast and regular plantations; they were exhausted long before they reached the higher mountains they had hoped to climb.

The ships by now were pretty fully provisioned, though still short of fire-wood, which had to be brought, awkwardly, from well up the surrounding hillsides. Cook had King inquire whether the fence round the *heiau* might be purchased: they had seen the people themselves taking pales away, so 'we did not seem to run any risk in being look'd upon as impious to propose the purchasing of it'. The priests agreed readily, but sailors carried off some carved gods along with the rest of the timber; the whole transaction, the able seaman Heinrich Zimmermann later wrote, 'caused a good deal of indignation'. Yet King, who is more scrupulous and reliable than most of the voyage journal-keepers, and who was obviously troubled by the removal of the carvings, indicates that when he asked the priest Kao what should be done, the man wanted just one of the figures returned.

The following day, William Watman, a fondly regarded able seaman in his mid forties, died after suffering a 'paralytic stroke'. The Hawaiian chiefs wanted him buried on shore; and he was accordingly interred upon the *heiau* 'with as much solemnity & decency, as our situation permitted'. King was gratified that Kao and his fellow priests 'preservd the most profound Silence & regard' for the duration of the service, that they further 'shew'd their respect' by throwing pigs, coconuts and plantains into the grave as it was being filled; he, or someone, was maybe just a little disturbed when they too went 'thro their funeral prayers', so 'they were in some measure stop'd'. It sounds as though it became too obvious, that this ceremony became something other than a Christian burial, that rites were mixed up. What was in fact the case may even have become too obvious to Cook: that Watman's corpse was being treated rather as he knew human sacrifices were treated on Tahitian *marae*. This was certainly an improvisation – a man who had died naturally would not normally have been sacrificed – but sacrifices were in fact called for, at this time in Ku's ascendancy, and the Hawaiians appear to have seized the opportunity to cap the king's appropriation of British valuables and power with an appropriation of a British body. Now, on 2 February, 'Terreeoboo & the Chiefs became inquisitive as to the time of our departing & seemd well pleas'd that it was to be soon.' It was time for Lono to leave. The British witnessed a great presentation of tribute to Kalani'opu'u, thinking that it was a farewell gift to the ships; this misapprehension the king however made right by then giving them much of the food, in return for more iron from Cook. The sheer quantity of vegetables and pigs exceeded anything James King had seen before, confirming his sense that these people 'were under a more despotic Government than at the Society Islands'. If he was offended by this aspect of their society, King was otherwise awed, impressed, and delighted by these people; after the ships left the bay on 4 February, Samwell wrote the most extensive of the accounts of the place and people, and was just as hyperbolic in his account of their conduct and temperament. 'No quarrels could possibly arise in our intercourse with them,' he said, apart from those provoked by theft, which was not nearly the problem it had been at Tahiti.

Cook now hoped to examine the other islands of the group. But just a few days later, the ships were battered by a heavy gale and the *Resolution*'s mast was badly damaged. A place to repair it was needed and needed quickly; an open bay on the coast of Maui was investigated, which proved unsuitable; the decision was made to return to Kealakekua, the only secure anchorage that the Europeans had yet encountered in the whole archipelago. On 10 February they re-entered the harbour, and Samwell reflected that it was three years to the day since the ships had been commissioned. They were perhaps only half-way through the voyage; but all were in good health and spirits; they were faced with 'an arduous Undertaking', 'yet when we consider the Man who is to lead us through it we all agree that

> 'Nil desperandum
> Teucro Duce et Auspice Teucro.'' *

The ships resumed their anchorages on 11 February. 'Very few of the natives came to see us', which 'hurt our Vanity', King wrote. The coolness among the Hawaiians arose from the fact that Lono had reappeared not a year later, as he should have done, but at a time that could only have suggested a challenge to Kalani'opu'u. At first, however, it seemed that the quietness was due only to a taboo, the king visited the ships, the prohibition was relaxed, and a busy trade resumed. Yet – King later discovered – Kalani'opu'u was infuriated that the priests had again allowed the British to set up their tents besides Hikiau. If his anger stemmed from an opposition that existed in principle between the followers of Ku and Lono, this latent antagonism shifted, within forty-eight hours, into actual hostility. 'Ever since our arrival here upon this our second visit we have observ'd in the Natives a stronger propensity to theft,' Clerke lamented, 'every day produc'd more numerous and more audacious depradations.' He wrote, probably, on the evening of 13 February. That morning, a man had stolen the armourer's

---

* 'Never despair under the leadership and auspices of Teucer' (Horace, *Carmina*). Teucer was the brother of Ajax and a brave warrior, but may have seemed apt to Samwell because he also founded the Greek colony on Cyprus. Many thanks to Simon Schaffer for this information.

tongs, a large and no doubt a very attractive implement for Hawaiians still new to iron. This man was caught in the act, and Clerke had him given 'a very severe flogging', Samwell tells us, but in the afternoon another man 'had the boldness' to snatch the same tongs and a chisel from right in front of the armourer, who was at work at his forge. The thief leapt overboard before those on deck had grasped what was happening, and swam off. Edgar, in the pinnace, gave chase, but the man was picked up by a canoe. Palea, who was on board, followed, saying he would retrieve the tools. The canoe with the thief reached the shore. Another put off, and returned the tools to Edgar. He thought, however, that he ought to try to seize the offender and the canoe that had enabled his escape, though in Edgar's haste he'd brought no guns in the boat, which might have helped enforce such demands.

Cook was ashore at the time, and had seen the chase and the man land; presuming that some theft had been perpetrated, he tried to follow him, but was led astray by people who began to mock his threats to shoot if the thief was not surrendered. Meanwhile Vancouver, who was with Edgar, had got into the canoe in which the man had escaped, which he proposed to impound; he was on the point of paddling it back to the ship when Palea, who happened to own it, pulled it back out of the water. Edgar and Palea then struggled over a paddle; Palea was hit on the head with an oar; this assault on a chief incensed the gathering crowd of some hundreds of Hawaiian men, who began to shower the pinnace with stones. The crew abandoned the boat and swam off to some rocks, where they were picked up by the cutter, which had approached to assist. Edgar was in an unenviable situation: 'I not being able to swim had got upon a small rock up to my knees in water, when a man came up to me with a broken Oar, and most certainly would have knock'd me off the rock', presumably to drown, had not Vancouver stepped forward to protect him, and taken the blow himself. Another man began to beat Edgar with a piece of wood, but Palea then ordered everyone to desist, and told Edgar and Vancouver to take their boat away. The pinnace, however, by now had no oars, and while the chief went off to retrieve some, the people resumed their stoning. Edgar now tried to escape along the shore, but was seized and carried some way inland, where he and his captors met Palea, followed by a man carrying one intact and one broken oar. Bruised and humiliated, but at least alive, thanks I imagine to the even temper of the man they had assaulted, he and Vancouver beat a retreat. Cook, when he learned the details of the affair, was 'exceedingly angry'; he reprimanded those involved for attempting what they had, 'having no arms in the boat'.

For the duration of his Pacific voyaging, Cook's axiom had been that Islanders had always to be aware of the superior strength of the British. Little of this essential superiority remained evident: a set of his men had been unceremoniously thrashed, a valuable boat stripped of its fittings and only returned at the discretion of a native chief, and he himself had been mocked, by people unimpressed by the threat of fire. As Clerke put it, all this unfortunately 'increas'd the confidence of these People which before was too much bordering upon insolence'. At some stage during the day, Samwell tells us, some bold Hawaiian had asked Cook whether he was a *toa*, a warrior. Cook said that he was, and the man demanded to see his wounds. Cook showed him his right hand 'which had a large Gash upon it between the Thumb and fore finger, and the Indian Chief seemed satisfied'. He may have been, even though the old injury to Cook's hand had been caused by an accidental explosion in the course of one of his Newfoundland surveys. It had nothing to do with fighting, which was not an activity Cook had engaged in much, by Hawaiian standards. What kind of exemplary action could this 'warrior' now take?

Cook need not have wondered. The next step was not his. At first light on the morning of 14 February, James Burney, who was the officer of the watch, told Clerke that the *Discovery*'s large cutter, which had been at a mooring, was gone. Clerke himself examined its rope, which had been cut, and reported the theft to Cook. They discussed the problem, and Cook resolved to seize all the canoes he could in the bay, and hold these against the cutter's return. Both ships' boats would take up positions covering the bay, to prevent canoes from leaving. Clerke went back to the *Discovery* to give the appropriate orders. He then returned to the *Resolution*, hoping to discuss matters further with his commander, but found that Cook had already taken three boats to the town of Ka'awaloa, to see the king. Clerke was reassured that 'matters would soon be settled, for we were as yet by no means on bad terms either with Arees or anybody else'.

Cook landed with Lieutenant Molesworth Phillips and nine marines, just half of the twenty aboard the *Resolution*. They asked after, and were conducted to, Kalani'opu'u's house, where they waited a little while; Cook wondered whether the king was really there, and sent Phillips inside, where 'our old acquaintance' (Phillips called him) had just woken up. After speaking to Clerke, Cook must have decided that the seizure of canoes might not ensure the return of the cutter, or that taking the king hostage was in any case the better way to proceed, even though 'some little conversation' made it plain that he was 'quite innocent' of what had occurred. At first, it seemed that all would proceed smoothly; 'the old Gentleman . . . readily agree'd' and they began to walk back towards the boats. But then Kaneikapolei, one of Kalani'opu'u's wives, approached crying, and pleaded with the king not to go. Two chiefs seconded her and laid hold of him and sat him down; 'the old man now appear'd dejected and frighten'd'. The mood now took a turn for the worse. The population of the town – 'an immense Mob compos'd of at least 2 or 3 thousand People' – gathered about, and seemed to arm themselves. Phillips had the marines range themselves along the rocks, and people drew back to allow them to form a line. A priest sang, and seemed to be preparing some offering to Cook, or the king, or both. Phillips took this to be a diversionary nuisance, though it may have been a presentation soliciting the king's release. The multitude appeared to manoeuvre. 'Capt Cook now gave up all thoughts of taking Terre'oboo onboard with the following observation to me, "We can never think of compelling him onboard without killing a number of these People," and I believe was just going to give orders to embark', Phillips thought, when a man with a long iron dagger – one received from the British in trade – feinted at Cook, and threatened to throw his stone. Cook discharged a barrel of small shot, but the man was protected by a battle-mat, and was only further provoked; another chief tried to stab Phillips, who was able to fend him off with the butt end of his musket, but the crowd then began to throw stones, and one of the marines was knocked down. Cook fired, killed a man, ordered the marines to fire, and called out 'Take to the boats!'

Cook, Phillips, and just about every other participant in the voyage believed that Islanders would invariably retreat before gunfire. On this occasion, however, they 'acted so very contrary a part'. They rushed the marines, who were unable to reload, and might have killed all of them, but for the fire from the boats. The shouting of the crowd was deafening. 'The business was now a most miserable scene of confusion.' Phillips, stabbed in the shoulder, stumbled across the rocks into the water, but was then hit on the temple by a stone; had the pinnace not been very near, he would have drowned, but he managed to climb into the boat. He took a moment to recover, and then dived out of it, to rescue one of his drowning men. It was just eight o'clock.

An hour or so earlier that morning, Cook had sent King back to the camp at Hikiau with some instruments. He was told to keep the company there together, and be on his guard, but the lieutenant was not unduly concerned, and was 'for some time in the Observatory preparing to take equal Altitudes'. Hence he saw little of the boats moving about the bay. But then musket fire from Ka'awaloa 'so roused & agitated our Spirits, that it was impossible to keep on observing'. The firing ceased; but much to his annoyance, the *Discovery* discharged two cannonballs towards priests, men, women and children, seated along a wall beside the 'Taboo field', friends that King had not ten minutes earlier done his best to reassure. He sent a boat off to the ship to explain that they 'were on the best terms'. At a loss to understand what was happening, he watched boats going back and forth between the ships

& we for about 10 minutes or a quarter of an hour, were under the most torturing suspence & anxiety that can be conceiv'd; I never before felt such agitation as on seeing at last our Cutter coming on shore, with Mr Bligh, he calld out before he reachd the Shore, to strike the Observatorys as quick as possible, & before he announcd to us the Shocking news that Captn Cook was kill'd we saw it in his & the Sailors looks.

On board the *Resolution*, the boats from Ka'awaloa had returned with the news of the death of Cook. Just after Phillips lost sight of him, he had been hit with a club, stabbed, held under water, clubbed again, beaten with stones and stabbed repeatedly. Four of the marines, similarly, had failed to escape to the boats; though the Hawaiians had fallen back under fire, none of the bodies had been recovered. 'A general silence ensued throughout the ship, for the Space of near half an hour,' wrote George Gilbert, 'it appearing to us some what like a dream that we cou'd not reconcile our selves to for some time. Greif was visible in evry Countenance; Some expressing it by tears; and others by a kind of gloomy dejection: more easy to be conceived than described: for as all our hopes centred in him; our loss became irrepairable and the Sense of it was so deeply Impressed upon our minds as not to be forgot.'

Clerke, upon whom the command devolved, came aboard the *Resolution*. His first concern was with the astronomers and carpenters who were with King near Hikiau, who now appeared threatened by considerable numbers of people moving along the shore; he briefly considered, then set aside the idea of trying to hold their position, and instead ordered the observatories and foremast 'to be got off with all expedition'; by the middle of the day this had been done.

Already, argument had begun about what had happened, and why. It was clear that, at the critical moment, Lieutenant Williamson, in charge of the launch, had his men pull away, some fifty yards offshore; it was widely believed that his failure to instead approach the rocks, or maintain fire, decisively disadvantaged Cook and the marines who remained on the shore.

Williamson therefore asked Clerke to hold 'a public Enquiry into the affair'; and men belonging to that boat's crew were called to answer questions, 'but some of the mates seemed to prevaricate and dissent from their first Assertions, even expressly contradicting what they had said to the officer of Marines', that is, Phillips, 'when he blamed the Conduct of the third Lieu'', reported Samwell.

Just one of the participants – Molesworth Phillips – wrote about what happened, and it is his report for Clerke that I have drawn upon. But most of those who wrote logs wrote something, and they no doubt drew upon the stories of the surviving marines, as well as those in the boats, who knew little of what happened before the actual affray, but were close at hand then. 'But indeed,' wrote the master's mate, Alexander Home, 'they were so Exceedingly perplexed in their Accounts that it was a hard Matter to Colect Certainty.' Yet two distinct versions of events emerged, which overlapped in their account of the facts, but contradicted one another absolutely in their explanation; the divergence on the day prefigured argument that has, like an incurable wound, broken open from time to time ever since. In one view, an angry and aggressive Cook provoked the Hawaiian violence; in the other, an unfortunately restrained Cook was a victim of his own humanity. For Charles Clerke, who received Phillips's report, and talked over the tragedy with him, it was plain that the violence had not been premeditated, and could at the last moment have been averted. 'Upon the whole I firmly believe matters would not have been carried to the extremities they were had not Capt Cook attempted to chastize a man in the midst of this multitude'. Most logs agree that the violence in fact began with this attempt to 'chastize' – the moment when Cook fired small shot at the chief who either brandished a dagger, or was poised to throw a stone – but they did not all interpret this beginning in the same way. A mid-nineteenth-century reader of a journal of Phillips, later lost, made Clerke's implication explicit; Phillips's account, the writer thought, showed 'that *he*', that is Cook, 'not the Islanders' 'was the assailant'. This was the line, too, in influential nineteenth-century histories of Hawaii; it has been enlarged upon by recent critics who see Cook's death as the consequence of his own colonial violence.

But the balance of opinion was rather different. With respect to Cook's use of small shot, the midshipman Watts considered that 'this piece of ill timed humanity in the Capt only exaggerated the difficulty & increased the audacity of the Chiefs'. Harvey thought that Cook had failed to withdraw as promptly as he might have done, and instead 'premitted the greatest insults from them' until he was forced to shoot. King was unsure whether the marines had begun firing on their own accord, or whether Cook had ordered them to fire; in either case 'the Captn calld to them to cease fyirng & to come in with the boats . . . this humanity perhaps provd fatal to him . . .'

Samwell believed that even before Cook had been threatened by the chief with the stone, Phillips had sighted a man with a long dagger and asked Cook if he should fire upon him. 'But Capt. Cook who was ever too tender of the Lives of Indians' would not permit it; so Phillips instead hit the man with the butt of his gun. Moments later, Cook fired his small shot at the stone-bearing man, who was unhurt, who then flourished his spear, at which point Cook was 'still unwilling to take his Life' and similarly used the butt of his musket to beat the man back. When he and Phillips finally did shoot two men dead, the 'Indians' fell back, but threw a volley of stones, provoking the marines, and those in the boats, to fire in quick succession, 'On which Capt. Cook expressed his Astonishment, waved his hand to the Boats, told them to cease their fire and come nearer to receive the People.'

These accounts were inconsistent with Phillips's report, but they became more important than it. When it came to preparing the journals of the voyage for publication, it was natural to choose that of the literate and educated King to cover the period after Cook's own journal broke off; King's revision of his own manuscript therefore became the third volume of what would be called A Voyage to the Pacific Ocean, while Samwell produced a short book called A Narrative of the Death of Captain James Cook. The emphases of these accounts were still more forcefully distilled in the most ambitious picture that John Webber ever painted. The Death of Captain Cook, executed back in London between 1781 and 1783, was based on no personal observation, and there are no extant voyage sketches to suggest that Webber even tried to reconstruct the look of the event before he returned home. He did not attempt to depict the injured Cook, struggling to get himself out of the water, as one Hawaiian after another beat him: it is hard to imagine how this awfulness could have been represented in any remotely dignified way. Instead, Webber dramatized the moment just before Cook was struck. He transformed his 'wave' to his boats into a forthright signal that said: cease firing. The great navigator is, in effect, defenceless, surrounded by a mob of noble but evidently enraged savages, and about to be killed, yet his concern is to suppress the fire of his men. In less important respects, the painting was anyway an invention: the relation between beach and mountain looks ironically right for Hikiau, inhabited by Cook's allies, the priests of Lono, but bears no relation to the topography of the village of Ka'awaloa. No matter. It was engraved for publication in the Voyage to the Pacific Ocean and was reprinted in hundreds of later editions,

53. '*A victim of his own humanity*': *Webber's* The Death of Captain
Cook, *painted back in England between 1781 and 1783.*

abridgements, anthologies and translations. At the time, a print published
for separate sale carried the caption 'The Death of Captain Cook. In February 1779 by the murdering Dagger of a Barbarian at Carakakooa, in one of
the Sandwich Isles. He having there become a Victim to his own Humanity.'
The nuances and uncertainties that King had gone to some trouble to
acknowledge were wiped out by this picture, which would be less an image
than an icon, a definition of Cook's career, a definition of British exploration,
marked above all by a great, probably a misplaced, sacrifice to benevolence.

It has been argued that something in Cook snapped, prompting him to
shoot, and this led to his death. But there was nothing perverse or anomalous
in his behaviour on the morning of 14 February 1779. He had fired,
sometimes with small shot, and sometimes with ball, during both his first
and second voyages. It might even be claimed that when he fired first at
Ka'awaloa, shortly before eight in the morning, he fired in self-defence. As
men skulked about with daggers, as a breadfruit was thrown, as a stone was
levelled, he surely had no worse a reason to shoot than he had ever had.
More importantly, he had set out, that morning, to do something he had
done several times before, which was to take a high chief hostage. On each
of the occasions he had done this, at Tahiti, Raiatea and Tongatapu, he had

plainly done something dangerous that in each case people either thought of resisting, or tried to resist. The second time he had taken Tutaha, in Tahiti, two of his men were made counter-hostages; at Raiatea, a plan to take Cook himself and Clerke counter-hostages had been made but foiled; and at Tongatapu, what took place anticipated, up to a point, what happened at Ka'awaloa, a year and a half later: other chiefs had tried to prevent Paulaho from going aboard Cook's ship, as armed men began to gather behind the house that Cook and his hostages then occupied. Had Paulaho sat down dejected, had some argument led to insult, had a threat provoked a shot, matters might easily have been 'carried to the extremities' they were at Kealakekua, and this book would have been shorter.

If these situations were all similarly dangerous, the Hawaiian instance was distinct, and explosive. James King, Samwell and others had noticed that government in these islands was 'more despotic' than at Tahiti or even Tonga. To put it that way was to assimilate this Polynesian polity to a sort of barbaric absolutism. True, the great power and the great exactions of Hawaiian kings were sometimes resented by subjects; as the proverb had it, 'A chief is a shark that travels upon land.' But neither Cook, King, Samwell nor any other voyager appreciated the depth to which Hawaiians depended on *ali'i* – who were not simply political leaders, but embodiments of the lives of their communities. Ritually, they provided a sort of fecund grace, their sacrifices assured the prosperity of all; practically, their conduct of warfare provided loot, including lands, gardens, fishing-grounds, canoes and all the other things that Polynesians valued. We might say that a king such as Kalani'opu'u was a symbol of his society's being, but he was not an abstract symbol like a flag: his identity was intermingled with that of his subjects, he was a supreme expression of the vigour and power that – thanks to him – pervaded the gardens, the sexuality and the endeavours of the community as a whole. If this was true, in varied ways, throughout Polynesia, it was true in a powerfully accentuated way in the Hawaiian islands. Here chiefly status was awesome, and the trauma of a threat to a chief was magnified intolerably.

When Cook walked past the stone walls of Ka'awaloa, which still today are scattered across the site of this village, towards the house of Kalani'opu'u, he was thinking of taking one hostage too many. If what he contemplated was inherently problematic, it was still more so at that moment, given his own identification with Lono, the king's identification with Ku, and the threatening and destabilizing nature of his reappearance, his intrusion in the time of Ku's sovereignty. Perhaps, as this tall, strange and determined man with a gun was watched, making his way, by people who were puzzled but not yet unfriendly, there was no way out of the situation. The air was hot, and a fuse was ready: it may have been a further event that sparked it off.

King, Samwell and Edgar all mention a point that Phillips does not. King tells us that the Hawaiians were 'thrown into a great rage' when news reached Ka'awaloa that 'a Very principal Chief', one Kalimu, perhaps a brother of Palea's, had been killed in a canoe, fired on by Rickman's boat, on the other side of the bay. According to King, the event occurred and the news was transmitted after Cook had not only fired his small shot, but his ball, and shot another man dead: he is supposed then to have paused, to have heard gunfire from across the bay, to have expressed his concern to Phillips that King's party and the observatory were perhaps attacked. This does not make sense, especially because the canoe bearing the news was said to have called at both the ships first, in order to take a complaint to Cook; and all this would have taken time, a great deal more time than the bloody rush of moments that succeeded Cook's shots and concluded with him dead at the water's edge. Samwell and Edgar, on the other hand, agree that the news arrived just after the king had been pressed by those who loved him to sit down and stay where he was. Samwell wrote that at

About this time two men in a Canoe, having first called at the two Ships to tell the story, arrived with the News of a Chief called Ka-ree-moo having just been killed on the opposite side of the Bay by the Discovery's Boats that were stationed there; the Women who were sitting together on the rocks by the water side eating their Breakfast & talking in a friendly manner to some of our people in the Boats, on this immediately retired and a confused Murmur ran through the Croud.

His source, presumably, was one of the 'people in the Boats'. It is pure speculation, but my guess is that the person was Samuel Gibson, the sergeant of marines. He was on the spot, he had sailed on both the first and second voyages, he understood Tahitian and Maori better than just about anyone else, and he is the person Samwell would have trusted, as a witness. He would certainly have caught the gist of a remark such as 'They've killed Kalimu.' 'This intelligence seems to have Spread the Alarm, as they all begun to arm themselves,' Edgar added. 'At this time Capt. Cooke seemed to be in some Dilemma how to act as he fore-saw it would be impossible to carry the King on board without much trouble & probably blood shed.'

These reports are consistent with Phillips's account, though he says nothing of the news. If both the time of its arrival and its effect must remain uncertain – in so far as there is no direct testimony from anyone who was on the spot – these circumstances would do much to explain precisely how a tense stand-off broke down and sped up, as physical violence produced its own whirlwind of action and reaction. No one cared to do so, but an epitaph for this 'miserable scene of confusion' might have been taken from John Hawkesworth's much reviled *Voyages*: 'in such situations, when the command to fire has been given, no man can restrain its excess, or prescribe its effect'.

Late in the morning of 14 February, the better part of both ships' companies, including all the marines, were ashore to bring the mast and camp off as quickly as was possible. Though their landing was not generally resisted, there was 'now & then a shower of Stones', and a good deal of shooting back. 'Before our men were cool enough to obey Orders', King reported, some eight Hawaiians were thought killed. There was talk of an attack upon the crowd at Ka'awaloa, but concern above all to retrieve the bodies of Cook and the marines, and about four in the afternoon King – whose journal suggests that he was not comfortable with the duty – took a small boat supported by others, under a flag of truce, which was recognized and met with delight by the people on shore. A warrior known to King swam off, holding a piece of white cloth in one hand and a dagger in the other, 'as I never liked the man, I had the caution to hold the point while he was embracing me'. The man asked for a piece of iron, and promised that the body would be brought the next day. People on shore pressed King to land; he did not trust them and was 'inclin'd to find some occasion for breaking off all friendly terms'; another man known to them promised that the body would be returned; but King thought they 'were not sincere, nor sorry at what had happen'd, but perfectly content, as people who had gain'd an advantage'. As they rowed back, this impression was sustained by one man on a rocky point who 'had the Insolence to turn up his backside, & make other signs of Contempt'. King raised his gun to shoot, but James Burney, with him in the boat, 'desird me to stop, he said it was not right to overthrow all we had done, because of one Mans insolence'.

Back on board, argument continued. Clerke lamented his 'own unhappy state of Health which sometimes is so bad as hardly to suffer me to keep the Deck'. King agreed that his commander was incapacitated, and regretted that the discussion took the turn that it did. One party was for positioning the ships so that they might fire broadsides into the village; another was for 'mild measures' until the mast was repaired, then 'ample revenge' afterwards; and a third 'for endeavouring by all Means to become & to continue friends, as the injury was already done, & irreparable, & as some attention should be paid to their former good & kind behaviour'. King was for the first plan; Clerke was, if not for the third, more prudent, and did not want to risk further European lives.

The day after Cook's death, the messages from Ka'awaloa remained mixed: a few pigs were brought off, but the people continued to be 'insolent' and appeared to have no intention of bringing the body back. That night, however, two of the priests from Hikiau slipped out to the ship: they were at first fired upon, but called out King's name, and said they had something for them. They had been narrowly missed, were terrified, they 'shed abundance of tears at the loss of the Erono', and then produced a bundle. 'Our horror will be better conceiv'd, than can possibly be describ'd' – King resorted to one of the clichés of the period – when it was opened to reveal a piece of human flesh 'from the hind parts'. This, the priest explained, was all he had been able to obtain of Cook's body, which – they gathered – had been dismembered, burnt and distributed, though the skull and bones remained with Kalani'opu'u. Once again, the attachment of the priests of Lono to the British, and their fear and hatred of the chiefs, was manifest. And in this context it is not surprising that they hoped that Lono or Cook had not gone for good. 'A singular question was askd by them, & that was when the Erono would return, this was demanded afterwards by others, & what he would do to them when he return'd.' Later, these inquiries would reinforce King's inkling that Cook had been seen 'as a being of a superior nature', but at the time he and his companions were traumatically affected rather than intellectually inquisitive. According to Roberts, the sight of this portion of Cook's flesh left every officer and seaman horribly shocked, 'distraction & madness, was in every mind, and revenge the result of all'.

On the morning of the 17th, ostensibly because the *Discovery* 'wanted some water', a party did land, and was resisted, inasmuch as stones were thrown. Clerke says little more than that '5 or 6' were killed and the village later burnt. King, who had wanted quick reprisals, was now ashamed that

Our people in this days transactions did many reprehensible things; in excuse of which it can only be said that their minds were strongly agitat'd ... A common sailor with such a disposition, & sufferd to have its full operation, would soon equal the Cruelty of the most savage Indian.

What he meant, Samwell recorded. A couple of the Irish seamen had cut off the heads of two dead Hawaiians, which they hung from the bows of the boats. After one man, taken prisoner, had been brought on board the launch, 'they bound him up with Ropes & shaked the two heads of his

Countrymen which had just been killed & were yet reeking with blood in his face . . . this shocking piece of Cruelty was certainly a refinement upon savage barbarity and which no Provocation whatever can excuse'. One suspects that rather more than '5 or 6' were killed. King was ill, and took no part in the events; his thirst for revenge had diminished, and he regretted particularly that the vengeance had been substantially misdirected: it was the settlement of their allies, the priests beside Hikiau, not Ka'awaloa, that was fired.

In four days, men off Cook's ships killed more Islanders (at least thirty) than they had over the preceding ten years (about fifteen). Finally, on 19 February, a sort of truce was reached. The following day white flags and tapa pennants marked peace, offerings were made, and some remains were brought, 'decently wrapped', Samwell recorded, 'in a large quantity of fine new cloth'. The package was later opened in the great cabin of the *Resolution*, and found to contain Cook's thighs, calves, skull, scalp, arms and hands; 'we all knew the right [hand] by a large Scar on it', Samwell wrote; uncannily, the old injury was cited for the second time in a week. On the 21st, at ten minutes before six in the evening, these remains were 'committed to the deep'.

Cook's authoritative, even despotic command had been succeeded by a mix of anarchy and oligarchy: common men had briefly done as they pleased, and for the first time in the course of any of these voyages, there was sustained discussion among officers about how to act. Clerke's feebleness may, however, have been overstated. There is no suggestion that the tragedy prompted him, as the Grass Cove killings had prompted Furneaux, to think of taking the shortest route home. No one says so quite explicitly, but the sense appears to have been that the best memorial to Cook lay in the completion of his voyage. 'To prosecute these Discoveries which Captn Cook had in view is the intention of our present Expedition,' wrote Samwell in mid March, by which time he had spent a good deal more time with Hawaiian 'girls', and by which time the first part of Cook's plan – to examine and chart the whole chain of islands – had been effected. Kahoolawe, Maui, Lanai, Molokai and Oahu had been coasted; Kauai was revisited, and a further man killed after a pilfering incident. But after this the island's queen, Kamakahelei, was met, amicable relations were established, and a little learned, of genealogies, royal relationships, battles and histories within the islands. Here too, some women brought off the umbilical cords of their babies – perhaps fathered by members of the ship's crew during their first visit – which were wrapped in tapa, and which they wanted secreted in gaps and cracks in the ships' woodwork. This was to adapt customary action, which was to bury the cord on the lands of the progenitor: a claim to future rights was being made, which was recognizable only as an obscure 'Charm', or 'mystic Affair', by men such as Samwell, for whom the aim of sex was obviously pleasure, not procreation.

They shaped a course from the group towards Kamchatka. James King drew his observations on Hawaii and the Hawaiians together. If Tahiti was the queen of the South Sea isles, 'Owhyhee may be term'd the King,' he thought; by this time, too, his more characteristic feeling towards Polynesians had returned. 'We must I think allow the Natural dispositions of these people to be good,' he considered, 'I do not see that their conduct when we were at open hostilities ought to be brought as any Proof to the Contrary'; despite the killings at both Kauai and Kealakekua, people had made peace and given presents.

The ships sailed north for a month; the cruise was at first warm and despite leaks, pleasant. Bonito that would not go near baited European hooks were caught in abundance with Tongan trolling lures; extensive repairs to sails, rigging, gear and boats were made; in early April it became cold quickly, and the seamen, who had given away most of their clothes in trade with women, suffered. By the end of the month they reached the port of Petropavlovsk, still ice-bound, on the Kamchatka peninsula, the easternmost outpost of the Russian empire. From here, King, Gore and others travelled inland to make contact with the governor, Behm, who generously arranged supplies of beef and tobacco. Clerke sent copies of Cook's and his own journals and some charts to England via St Petersburg, and a smaller packet of letters 'by an express'. On 14 June, the *Resolution* and the *Discovery* sailed out of the harbour through fog and haze towards the Bering Strait. By early July they were through it, running in and out of loose ice again; by 21 July, they had added polar bear to the sorts of meat consumed by the crew, and the experience of the previous cruise was repeated: they had sailed east, the waters narrowed, and the mass of pack ice joined the American continent. It remained only to follow the ice edge back to the west, to confirm that there was neither a route through it, nor one to the north of Asia, 'during which time the Ship received many heavy blows on her Bows' from loose ice. On 27 July, at four in the afternoon, the Siberian coast was sighted and soon afterwards loose floes seen, 'which we saw join^g the Land. This put an end to our Navigation in these Seas in Search of North East and NWest Passage and here we may say that the Business of our Voyage is concluded', wrote Samwell. 'We now gave up the Expedition and stood from the Ice, to the great Joy of every one in the two Ships', who had been away from home for just over three years.

On 10 August, Clerke dictated a letter to Banks, reporting that he was unable any longer to turn himself in his bed, 'so that my stay in this world must be of very short duration'. He hoped his friends would 'have no occasion to blush in owning themselves such'; he hoped that he had served his country well; he hoped Banks liked the curiosities he had got him; he begged him to think of the surgeon's mate, William Ellis, and the two ships' clerks; because of Cook's death and 'very soon' his own, they would he feared be 'destitute of friends'. He died, aged thirty-six, just before they returned to Petropavlovsk; 'his happy convivial Turn & humourous Conversation' would be fondly remembered. Samwell judged him 'fitter to be second than first in Command', while acknowledging that his perseverance 'in pursuing the Voyage after the death of Captn Cook, notwithstanding his own bad state of Health, will ever reflect Honour upon his Memory'.

John Gore now became commander of the *Resolution* and of the expedition, and King took over the *Discovery*. Gore promptly abandoned Cook's practice of carefully sharing all fresh and desirable food, irrespective of rank, and bought a bullock, half of which was set aside for his own use, '& the remainder shared between the two Ships'. He followed Clerke in consulting his officers, to a greater degree than Cook ever had. On 2 October, 'having required the Officers of both Ships to give him their Opinions in writing of the Course we should take in our passage home', he examined their letters and found all agreed that the best route was via China and the East Indies. Before departing, they dined and danced with Kamchatkan and Russian women, 'Evashkin the Interpreter played the fiddle.' For all but six or eight of these men – George Vancouver and William Bligh among them – some remarkable South Seas years were over. In early December they reached Macao, where those who still had Arctic furs were able to sell them at a super-profit; they provisioned and refitted, and by mid February 1780 visited 'the hotest and most unhealthy place in the world'. Gore, William Harvey, Samuel Gibson and a few others can only have recalled Princes Island in the Sunda Strait as the source of the worst fevers they had experienced. But on this occasion the winds were good and there was no repetition of the awful malaise experienced during the homeward passage of the *Endeavour*. They reached Cape Town in early April. George Gilbert found the stay 'tedious', and the Atlantic voyage towards Britain 'very tedious'. Still worse, adverse winds in the channel forced the ships to the west of Ireland and north of Scotland; a period at Stromness on Orkney was 'exceeding tedious and disagreeable; for we cou'd get no more intiligence concerning our Friends that if we had been at Otaheite'. Gore was thought to dither, and compared unfavourably to Cook. King took a local boat to Aberdeen, to take papers and charts to the Admiralty from there; the *Discovery* received, in James Burney, her fourth captain in the course of the expedition. The visit was happy for at least one man: Samuel Gibson, the sergeant of marines, got married, but having survived all three voyages, then died on 23 September, just a week before the ships finally reached the Thames.

By the time they got to London, their news was old news. The packet that Clerke had sent from Siberia had arrived in early January. On the tenth, Sandwich had written an uncharacteristically distressed letter to Banks: 'Dear Sir what is uppermost in our mind allways must come first, poor captain Cooke is no more, he was massacred with four of his people by the Natives of an Island where he had been treated if possible with more hospitality than at Otaheite.' His brevity did not stop him noticing a paradox that had already been the cause of much argument, and that would sustain a great deal more. Who broke the news to Elizabeth Cook? She had been embroidering a waistcoat made of Tahitian tapa, for her husband on his return: on the 10th, 11th, or whenever, of January, 1780, she laid it aside, but would never throw it away.

Epilogue:
Cook's afterlives

In a warm and solid red-brick house at the edge of the market square in the village of Olney, north of London, in October 1783, the melancholy cat-lover, opponent of slavery and poet William Cowper found himself looking forward to the long winter evenings. 'I have two Ladies to read to; sometimes more, never less,' he wrote to a friend in Chancery Lane, in London. 'At present we are circumnavigating the globe.' He had read Hawkesworth before, but his memory was failing him, and the story was again fresh and new. He now wanted Cook's account of his second voyage. 'Have you it, can you borrow it, or can you hire it, and will you send it? I shall be glad of Forster's too.'

In June of the following year, he was looking forward to the *Voyage to the Pacific Ocean*, which had just appeared, after many delays – again edited by Douglas on the basis of Cook's journals, Anderson's enthusiastic accounts of Oceanic culture and nature, and King's narrative of proceedings after Cook's death. The book had been eagerly awaited, and the whole edition was sold out, it was said, within three days. But the poet was again able to borrow a set and by August was 'once more . . . a voyager in the Pacific Ocean'. 'In our last night's lecture we were made acquainted with the island of Hapaee where we had never been before.' The vivid accounts of Tongan dance were entrancing. It was extraordinary and delightful that these 'savages' equalled or perhaps excelled the most sophisticated of Europeans in this art, and could produce pleasant and harmonious music with the simplest of instruments. Cowper was prompted to wonder quite why the people of one island acquired a degree of politeness and elegance, while others no great distance away 'are as rude as we naturally expect'.

By October, he had read the three volumes. He and his ladies had been richly entertained, but there was a serious and spiritual lesson, Cowper felt, to be learned from the *Voyage to the Pacific Ocean*.

No observation . . . forced itself upon me with more violence, than one I could not help making on the death of Captain Cook. God is a jealous God, and at Owhyee the poor man was content to be worshipped. From that moment the remarkable interposition of Providence in his favor was converted into an opposition which thwarted all his purposes. He left the scene of his Deification, but was driven back to it by a most violent storm, in which he suffer'd more than in any that had preceded it. When he departed, he left his worshippers still infatuated with an Idea of his Godship, consequently well disposed to serve him. At his return he found them sullen, distrustfull and mysterious. A trifling theft was committed, which by a blunder of his own in pursuing the thief after the property had been restored, was magnified into an affair of the last importance. One of the fav'rite chiefs was killed too by a blunder. Nothing in short but blunder and mistake attended him, 'till he fell breathless into the water, and then, all was smooth again.

This – Cowper wrote, in a private letter to a friend – was the moral of Cook's end. But he had expressed himself in quite different terms in one of his most ambitious poems, which was already in print. 'Charity' dwelt upon the supreme virtue and just action that followed from recognition of common humanity, irrespective of difference 'in language, manners, or in face'. This virtue had its exemplar:

> When Cook – lamented, and with tears as just
> As ever mingled with heroic dust,
> Steer'd Britain's oak into a world unknown,
> And in his country's glory sought his own,
> Wherever he found man, to nature true,
> The rights of man were sacred in his view:
> He sooth'd with gifts and greeted with a smile
> The simple native of the new-found isle,
> He spurn'd the wretch that slighted or withstood
> The tender argument of kindred blood,
> Nor would endure that any should controul
> His free-born brethren of the southern pole.

This was inadequate and incomplete, as an account of Cook's dealing with indigenous peoples. But it, and idealizations like it, would be enduringly influential.

The goats and pigs Cook distributed throughout the Pacific multiplied quickly, but the cattle he left in the Society Islands never produced the stock that he hoped would be a monument to British benevolence. In Huahine, Mai got his chance to fight the warriors of Borabora, but is thought to have died young of illness, rather than on the battlefield. Tu founded a dynasty that controlled Tahiti, that used Christianity to dominate neighbouring islands, that endured until French annexation in the mid nineteenth century. Kamehameha took up where Kalani'opu'u left off, and created a native Hawaiian state, which was in due course stifled by American settlers.

Joseph Banks would be president of the Royal Society for almost fifty years. He dispatched hosts of botanists, explorers, and collectors to every continent of the world and was the single most powerful scientist of his epoch. George Forster argued about race with Immanuel Kant, became a revolutionary, was abandoned by his wife, and died in Paris in 1794. William Hodges would be the first professional European artist to visit India. He wrote a treatise on architecture and a travel book, but incurred the displeasure of the king, gave up painting, moved to Devon, invested his money in a bank, and lost the lot. He died, or, it was rather believed, he committed suicide, in 1797. William Wales taught at Christ's Hospital and gave one of his pupils, Samuel Taylor Coleridge, a few ideas for a poem about a mariner.

James King went to the south of France for his health, but died of consumption before his book and Cook's, the *Voyage to the Pacific Ocean*, made it into print. William Bligh was the target of the most famous mutiny in history. George Vancouver took up where Cook had left off, and charted the north-west American coast. Richard Pickersgill was given the command first of an unsuccessful voyage to search for a north-west passage, and then of a merchant ship. 'Liking ye grog' once too often, he slipped off some stairs into the Thames and drowned. Cook became a hero, and forgot how various and strange his life had been.

In 1902, the Commonwealth of Australia had just come into being. One of those charged with imagining a noble origin for the new nation was the painter Emmanuel Phillips Fox. His *Landing of Captain Cook at Botany Bay, 1770*, was painted on the monumental scale appropriate to a foundational event. It was evidently the product of first-hand study of the location, as well as some examination of the primary sources. The picture shows Cook, Banks, Solander, a group of ordinary seamen and some marines, confronted, as they in fact were, by two Eora men, brandishing or throwing spears in defence of the camp that lies behind them. Here, we see Cook's arm outstretched in a gesture of restraint; he is telling his men to hold their fire. This Cook is precisely the personification of British imperial charity that Cowper imagined, the 'humane conquistador' of a mid-twentieth-century Australian biographical poem, which I refrain from inflicting upon you.

Even the sand dunes and the water look about right, if you've walked the

56. *History's man:* Fox's Landing of Captain Cook at Botany
Bay, *1770, 1902.*

south shore of Botany Bay. The problem with the painting, considered as a historical document, is that there is no authority whatsoever for Cook's vitally significant signal. Fox borrowed it from John Webber, and John Webber invented it. Cook had not gestured in this way, just before his death in Kealakekua Bay, nor had he done so, so many years earlier, just after landing on the eastern Australian coast. He certainly was troubled, when violence that he thought was unnecessary did occur. But Cook had not restrained his men on this occasion; to the contrary, we have his own word for it that he fired the first shot, and did most of the shooting that followed.

A park now occupies the south shore of the Endeavour River, where the ship was beached to be repaired in 1770. There's a wharf, a fish and chip shop, and a place that rents aluminium boats to tourists and fishermen. There are several old monuments and one new one. The new structure is neither a statue nor an obelisk, but rather a low broad wall. Its sinuous form is that of the python whose body has left its trace, too, in the river's swerve. What is called the Milbi Wall, or story wall, distils the Aboriginal myth and history of the area, in narratives and pictures on ceramic tiles. You might have expected it to contradict the messages of the other edifices, which are like those of the local Cook museum, and Fox's painting. They make Cook's benevolence the beginning of a progressive history, but the Milbi Wall does not assert rather that his intrusiveness or violence inaugurated the devastating colonialism that Guugu Yimidhirr and neighbouring peoples in fact suffered. The story anyway begins not with Cook but with spirits, creator beings, bats, water-rats and snakes, and with pre-colonial life. The *Endeavour*'s arrival is said to have astonished locals, but 'Cook gained the confidence of the Aboriginal people without violence. Scientific recordings were made and the Gangurru was given the name Kangaroo.' Further contact was episodic and limited until 'the next invasion, the gold rush' which 'was not so amicable. Greed left no room for respect'; sacred places, food supplies and water sources were overrun; and between them guns and new diseases killed whole groups of people, and produced pervasive trauma among those who remained alive. Further stories outline the arrival of missions, twentieth-century experiences, and recent struggles for self-determination. In this representation, Cook's visit does not define what has happened since. It amounts, rather, to the exception that proves the rule. It figures as a respectful invasion, an anomaly that prefigured nothing. Though it is one important enough to re-enact annually for locals and tourists. If you ever get to Cooktown to watch Cook landing, your feelings might be mixed. Was it all for better or worse? Either way, whatever history is, it cannot be what it was.

Maps

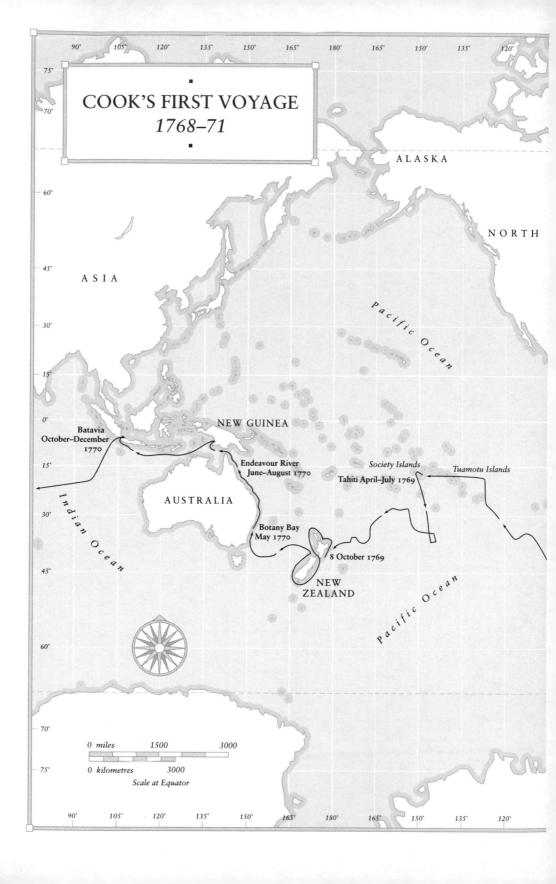

COOK'S FIRST VOYAGE
1768–71

ALASKA

NORTH

ASIA

Pacific Ocean

NEW GUINEA

Batavia
October–December
1770

Endeavour River
June–August 1770

Society Islands

Tahiti April–July 1769

Tuamotu Islands

AUSTRALIA

Indian Ocean

Botany Bay
May 1770

8 October 1769

NEW
ZEALAND

Pacific Ocean

0 miles   1500   3000

0 kilometres   3000
Scale at Equator

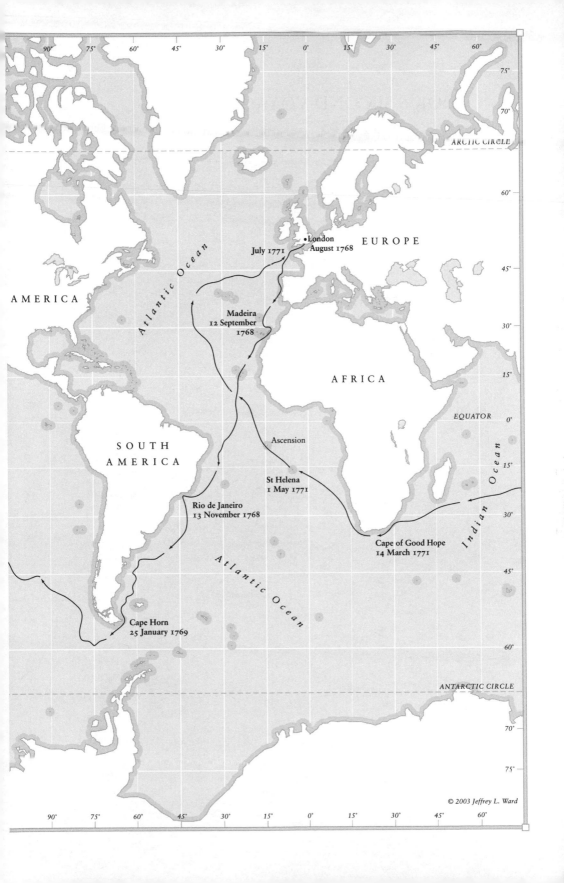

ARCTIC CIRCLE

70°

60°

•London
July 1771 August 1768

EUROPE

Atlantic Ocean

AMERICA

Madeira
12 September
1768

AFRICA

EQUATOR

Ascension

SOUTH
AMERICA

St Helena
1 May 1771

Indian Ocean

Rio de Janeiro
13 November 1768

Cape of Good Hope
14 March 1771

Atlantic Ocean

Cape Horn
25 January 1769

ANTARCTIC CIRCLE

© 2003 Jeffrey L. Ward

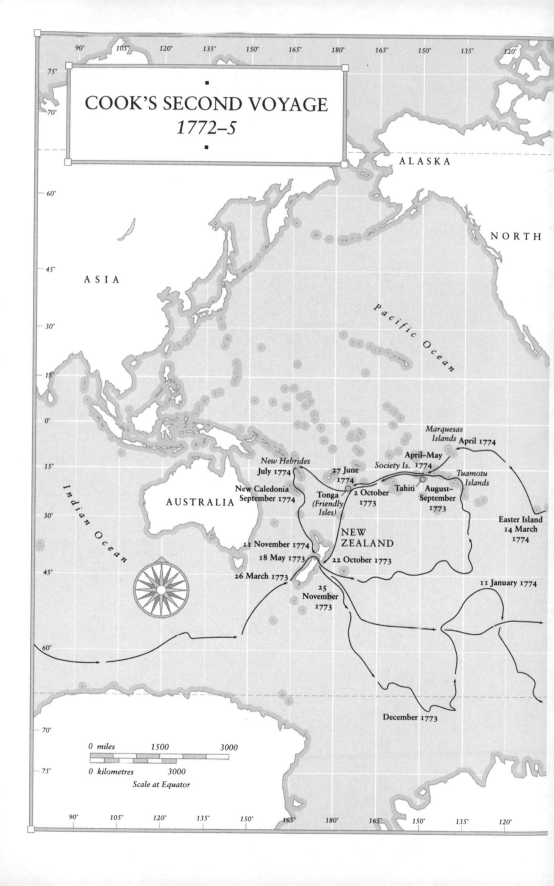

COOK'S SECOND VOYAGE
1772–5

ALASKA

NORTH

ASIA

Pacific Ocean

Marquesas Islands April 1774

New Hebrides July 1774

27 June 1774

Society Is. 1774

April–May 1774

Tuamotu Islands

New Caledonia September 1774

Tonga (Friendly Isles)

2 October 1773

Tahiti

August–September 1773

AUSTRALIA

Indian Ocean

NEW ZEALAND

Easter Island 14 March 1774

11 November 1774

18 May 1773

22 October 1773

26 March 1773

25 November 1773

11 January 1774

December 1773

0 miles 1500 3000

0 kilometres 3000

Scale at Equator

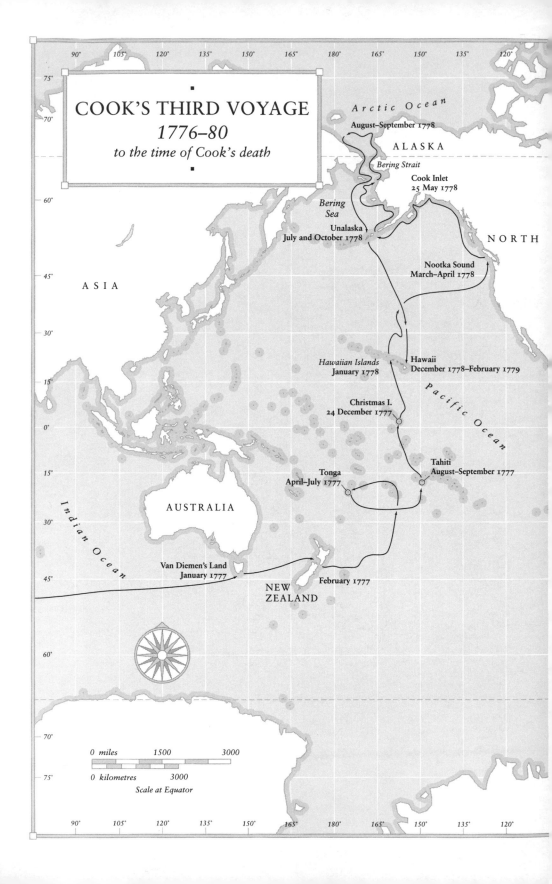

COOK'S THIRD VOYAGE
1776–80
to the time of Cook's death

Arctic Ocean

August–September 1778

ALASKA

Bering Strait

Cook Inlet
25 May 1778

*Bering
Sea*

Unalaska
July and October 1778

NORTH

Nootka Sound
March–April 1778

ASIA

Hawaiian Islands
January 1778

Hawaii
December 1778–February 1779

Pacific Ocean

Christmas I.
24 December 1777

Tahiti
August–September 1777

Tonga
April–July 1777

AUSTRALIA

Indian Ocean

Van Diemen's Land
January 1777

February 1777

NEW
ZEALAND

0 miles   1500   3000

0 kilometres   3000

Scale at Equator

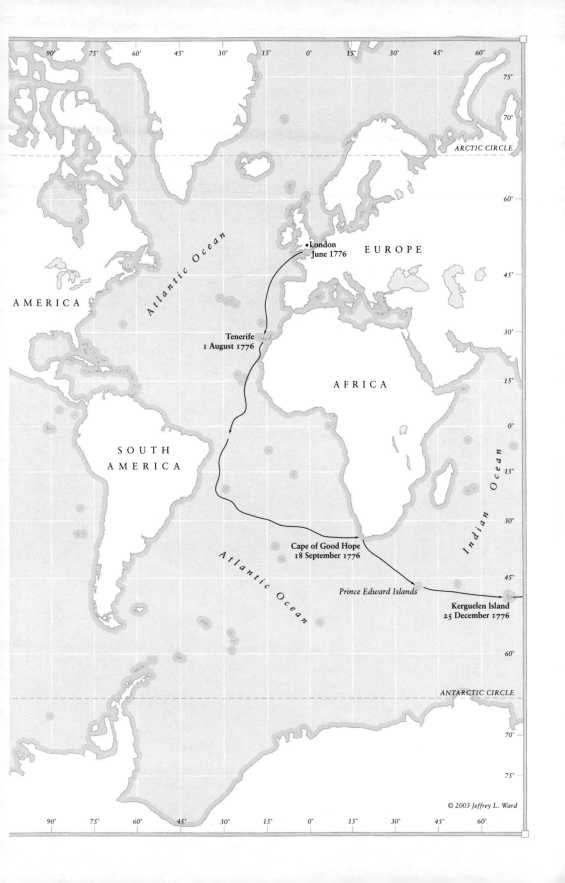

ARCTIC CIRCLE

•London
June 1776

EUROPE

Atlantic Ocean

AMERICA

Tenerife
1 August 1776

AFRICA

SOUTH
AMERICA

Indian Ocean

Atlantic Ocean

Cape of Good Hope
18 September 1776

Prince Edward Islands

Kerguelen Island
25 December 1776

ANTARCTIC CIRCLE

© 2003 Jeffrey L. Ward

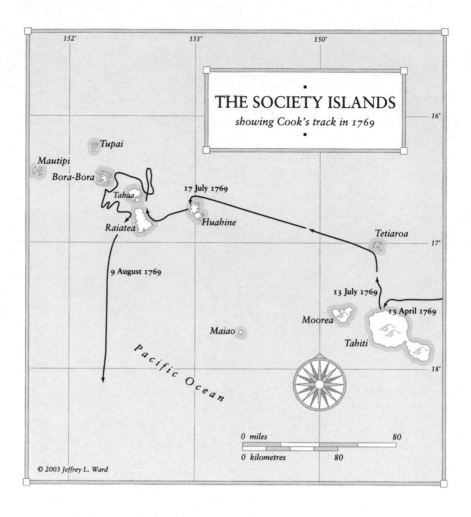

THE SOCIETY ISLANDS
showing Cook's track in 1769

152°   151°   150°

16°

Tupai

Mautipi

Bora-Bora

Tahaa

17 July 1769

Raiatea   *Huahine*

Tetiaroa

17°

9 August 1769

13 July 1769

13 April 1769

Moorea

Maiao

Tahiti

18°

Pacific Ocean

0 miles   80

0 kilometres   80

© 2003 Jeffrey L. Ward

NEW ZEALAND

showing the Endeavour's
circumnavigation of 1769–70

North Island

South Island

165°   170°   175°   180°

25 December 1769

North Cape
Bay of Islands

Pacific Ocean

35°

Mercury Bay

4 November 1769

Poverty Bay

8 October 1769

13 January
1770

40°

1 April 1770   24 March 1770

Cape Farewell

Cape Turnagain

Queen Charlotte Sound 16 January–6 February 1770

9 February 1770

Tasman Sea

South
Island

45°

0 miles   100   200   300

0 kilometres   300

Dusky
Sound

9 March 1770

Stewart Island

© 2003 Jeffrey L. Ward

166°   167°   168°   169°   170°   171°

*Maewo
(Aurora)*
17 July 1774

*Ombra
(Lepers I.)*

*Espiritu
Santo*

15°

*Pentecost or Raga
(Whitsuntide)*

— *Malo*

31 August 1774

**23 July
1774**

16°

Pacific Ocean

Ambrym

— *Paama*

*Malakuka
(Mallicollo)*

23 August 1774

— *Lopevi*
Epi

Shepherd Is.

17°

Mai —

Mataso —

— *Makura*

0 miles   100

0 kilometres   100

Coral Sea

*Efate
(Sandwich I.)*

18°

Traitor's Head
4 August 1774

Erromango

19°

Aniwa

•

VANUATU/
NEW HEBRIDES
ISLANDS

showing Cook's track in 1774

•

*Futuna
(Erronan)*

Tanna (Tana)

5–19 August 1774

20°

*Aneityum
(Annattom)*

© 2003 Jeffrey L. Ward

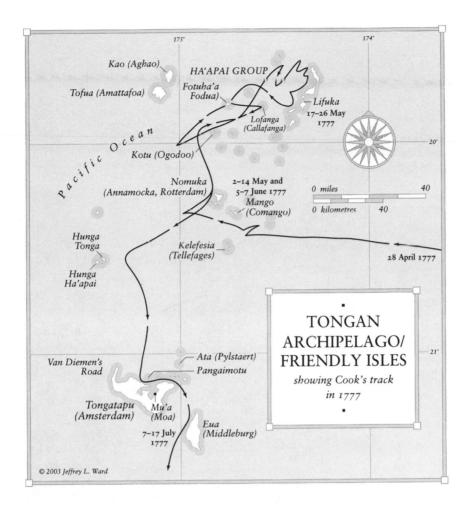

175°   174°

Kao (Aghao)   HA'APAI GROUP

Tofua (Amattafoa)   Fotuha'a
                       Fodua)   Lifuka
                                                   17–26 May
                                       Lofanga   1777
                                      (Callafanga)

                      Kotu (Ogodoo)
                                                               20°

Pacific Ocean

        Nomuka   2–14 May and
    (Annamocka, Rotterdam) 5–7 June 1777
                            Mango
                            (Comango)   0 miles   40

                                               0 kilometres   40

Hunga
Tonga   Kelefesia
             (Tellefages)
                                                    28 April 1777
Hunga
Ha'apai

                                          ▪

                                    TONGAN
                  Ata (Pylstaert) ARCHIPELAGO/
Van Diemen's   Pangaimotu   FRIENDLY ISLES
   Road   21°
                                   *showing Cook's track
                                         in 1777*
  Tongatapu   Mu'a
 (Amsterdam)   (Moa)   ▪
                        Eua
              7–17 July (Middleburg)
                1777

© 2003 Jeffrey L. Ward

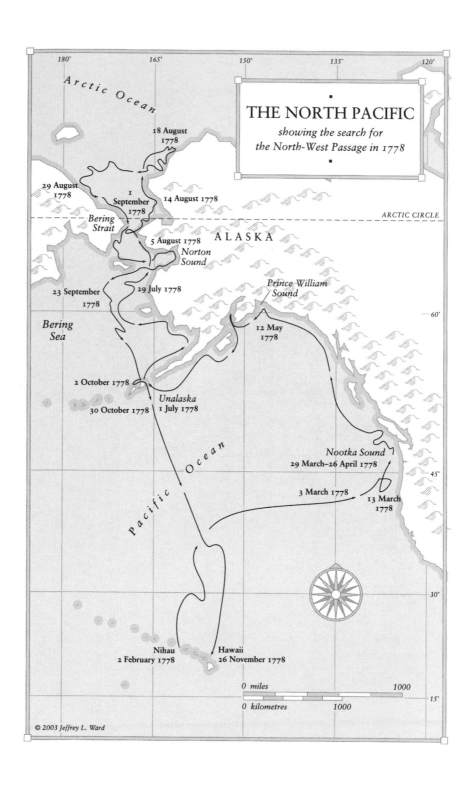

180°   165°   150°   135°   120°

Arctic Ocean

THE NORTH PACIFIC
*showing the search for
the North-West Passage in 1778*

18 August
1778

29 August
1778

1
September
1778

14 August 1778

ARCTIC CIRCLE

*Bering
Strait*

5 August 1778

A L A S K A

*Norton
Sound*

*Prince William
Sound*

23 September
1778

29 July 1778

60°

*Bering
Sea*

12 May
1778

2 October 1778

30 October 1778   *Unalaska*
1 July 1778

Pacific Ocean

Nootka Sound
29 March–26 April 1778

45°

3 March 1778

13 March
1778

30°

Nihau
2 February 1778

Hawaii
26 November 1778

0 *miles*   1000

0 *kilometres*   1000

15°

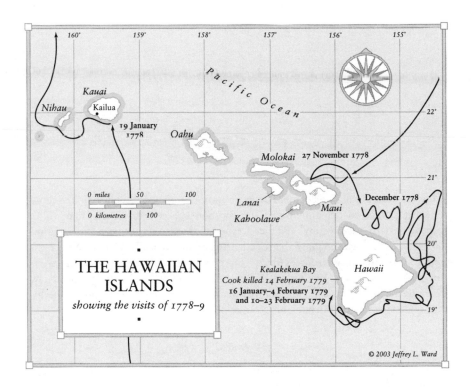

160° 159° 158° 157° 156° 155°

Pacific Ocean

Kauai

Nihau

Kailua

19 January
1778

Oahu

22°

Molokai 27 November 1778

21°

0 miles   50   100

0 kilometres   100

Lanai

Kahoolawe

Maui

December 1778

.

THE HAWAIIAN
ISLANDS

showing the visits of 1778–9

.

Kealakekua Bay
Cook killed 14 February 1779
16 January–4 February 1779
and 10–23 February 1779

Hawaii

20°

19°

© 2003 Jeffrey L. Ward

Sources and further reading

Most chapters of this book contain many quotations from Cook's journals and those of other voyage participants. I have not footnoted these individually; they are in general easy to trace by any reader concerned to do so because both my narrative and the various logs and journals are organized chronologically. Here I list the most important sources and resources for those interested in Cook, give specific references for passages that may not be easily located, and point, unavoidably selectively, towards the rich historical, anthropological and archaeological literature that helps one understand Cook's Britain, his voyages and the peoples he encountered.

General

Everyone interested in Cook owes an enormous debt to J. C. Beaglehole, whose editions of *The Journals of Captain James Cook* (Cambridge, 1955–67) were complemented by *The Endeavour Journal of Joseph Banks* (Sydney, 1963). Whatever reservations one may have about Beaglehole's idealization of Cook and occasionally opinionated pronouncements, these are great scholarly accomplishments that include invaluable introductions, authoritative annotations (for the first two volumes, largely the work of A. M. Lysaght) and the full texts of other significant journals such as those of Monkhouse, Wales, Anderson and Samwell. With similar thoroughness, Michael E. Hoare edited *The Resolution Journal of Johann Reinhold Forster* (London, 1982), the richest manuscript account other than Cook's own for the second voyage. Less significant but nevertheless interesting are *Captain Cook's Second Voyage: the Journals of Lieutenants Elliott and Pickersgill* (ed. Christine Holmes, London, 1984) and *With Captain James Cook in the Antarctic and Pacific: the Private Journal of James Burney* (ed. Beverley Hooper, Canberra, 1975). Many other logs and journals remain unpublished in archives such as the Public Record Office and the British Library in London, the State Library of New South Wales in Sydney, and the Alexander Turnbull Library in Wellington.

The early published accounts of the voyages are also of fundamental importance. The officially sanctioned books were: John Hawkesworth's *An Account of the Voyages Undertaken by the Order of His Present Majesty for Making Discoveries in the Southern Hemisphere* (London, 1773); James Cook, *A Voyage Toward the South Pole and Round the World* (London, 1777); and James Cook and James

King, *A Voyage to the Pacific Ocean . . . for Making Discoveries in the Northern Hemisphere* (London, 1784). In addition, there were unauthorized works, some dashed off with a view to a quick profit, others that add a great deal to our understanding. From the first voyage we have Sydney Parkinson's *Journal of a Voyage to the South Seas* (London, 1773) and a book attributed to James Magra, *A Journal of a Voyage Round the World* (London, 1771). From the second, the most remarkable is George Forster's *Voyage Round the World* (London, 1777; ed. N. Thomas and O. Berghof, Honolulu, 2000); Marra's *Journal of the Resolution's Voyage* (London, 1775) is also important, as are the works published much later by the naturalist Anders Sparrman. Johann Forster's *Observations Made During a Voyage Round the World* is the natural historian's synthesis of the findings of the voyage (London, 1778; ed. N. Thomas, H. Guest and M. Dettelbach, Honolulu, 1996). After the third voyage, Ellis, Ledyard, Rickman, Samwell and Zimmermann all brought out narratives that incorporate matter of some interest; details are given under specific chapters below. The early popularity of Cook made for a proliferation of pirated editions, abridgements and translations, published throughout Britain and in many north American and European cities. An extensive but by no means exhaustive listing appears in M. K. Beddie (ed.), *Bibliography of Captain James Cook* (Sydney, 1970), which also makes a heroic attempt to cover associated maps, illustrations, engravings, relics, secondary articles, children's books, fiction, music and films about the voyages.

The Art of Captain Cook's Voyages, ed. Rüdiger Joppien and Bernard Smith (New Haven, 1985–7) makes much of the extraordinary visual material accessible; Andrew F. David's *The Charts and Coastal Views of Captain Cook's Voyages* (London, 1988) does the same for the cartographic material. Adrienne Kaeppler's important '*Artificial Curiosities': an Exposition of Native Manufactures Collected on the Three Pacific Voyages of Captain James Cook, R.N.* (Honolulu, 1978) provides the single fullest listing of the Polynesian and other indigenous art and craft objects collected on the voyages. Since it was published some new material has been identified, and the locations of some objects have changed. *James Cook: Gifts and Treasures from the South Seas*, ed. Brigitta Hauser-Schäublin and Gundolf Krüger (Munich, 1998), is a beautifully illustrated catalogue of the Göttingen collection.

Other works that must be acknowledged include Beaglehole's *Life of Captain James Cook* (London, 1974); Bernard Smith's *European Vision and the South Pacific* (Oxford, 1960; 2nd edn, New Haven, 1985) was a pioneering effort of cultural history that paid particular attention to the connections between science and art on Cook's voyages; Marshall Sahlins's *Islands of History* (Chicago, 1985) offered a radical new approach to the interplay of history and anthropology, making use above all of Cook voyage encounters and the circumstances of Cook's death. Ray Parkin's *H. M. Bark Endeavour* (Melbourne, 1997) provides a sensitively technical account of the fabric of the vessel itself; John Robson's *Captain Cook's World* (Auckland, 2000) is a useful atlas of Cook's life and voyages.

Since the 1960s, there have been a number of relevant anthologies, including: Walter Veit (ed.), *Captain James Cook: Images and Impact* (2 vols, Melbourne,

1972, 1979); Robin Fisher and Hugh Johnston (eds.), *Captain James Cook and His Times* (Seattle, 1979); Jonathan Lamb (ed.), *The South Pacific in the Eighteenth Century: Narratives and Myths*, special issue, *Eighteenth Century Life*, 18 (3), (1994); Margarette Lincoln (ed.), *Science and Exploration in the Pacific* (London, 1998); and Alex Calder, Jonathan Lamb and Bridget Orr (eds.), *Voyages and Beaches* (Honolulu, 1999).

Introduction

Cook's famous passage on his confrontation with the Antarctic ice is in his *Journals*, II, 332–3; Forster's account of the storm is in his *Resolution Journal*, 446, and Elliott's description of the near miss is in Holmes (ed.), *Captain Cook's Second Voyage*, 26. William Hodges's Antarctic work is reproduced and discussed in Joppien and Smith, *The Art of Captain Cook's Voyages*, II, ch. 3.

For Banks's interests in transplantation and the transportation of animals, and science and empire in general, see John Gascoigne, *Joseph Banks and the English Enlightenment* (Cambridge, 1994) and David Philip Miller and Peter Hanns Reill (eds.) *Visions of Empire* (Cambridge, 1996). On the Chelsea Physic Garden (which approximately retains its eighteenth-century layout, and is a good place to visit), see Sue Minter, *The Apothecaries' Garden* (London, 2000). The early theoretical works referred to are Yves-Antoine de Goguet, *The Origin of Laws, Arts, and Sciences* (Edinburgh, 1761), Adam Ferguson, *An Essay on the History of Civil Society* (Edinburgh, 1767), and Henry Home (Lord Kames), *Sketches in the History of Man* (Edinburgh, 1774).

Concerns regarding sexually transmitted disease in the eighteenth century can be traced through many treatises, e.g. William Fordyce, *A Review of the Venereal Disease* (London, 1768). The passages relating to sexual contagion in Queen Charlotte Sound are: George Forster, *Voyage*, 121; Johann Forster, *Resolution Journal*, 308; Cook, *Journals*, II, 175; the censored, published text is Cook, *Voyage*, I, 130. The abridgement (from which many subsequent reprints derive) is George William Anderson, *A New, Authentic and Complete Collection of Voyages Round the World . . . containing a new, authentic, entertaining, instructive, full, and complete historical account of Captain Cook's first, second, third and last voyages* (London, 1784–6); it was published in fortnightly parts priced at sixpence each, and made the voyages accessible to a broad public, but was neither new, nor authentic nor complete. The account of the visit to Queen Charlotte Sound, omitting any reference to sexual transactions, appears over 131–2.

For Hodges's Cook portrait, see David Cordingly (ed.), *Captain James Cook, Navigator* (London, 1988), 108–9. Bernard Smith reviews 'Cook's posthumous reputation', dealing mainly with late-eighteenth- and nineteenth-century images, in *Imagining the Pacific* (New Haven, 1992); Jillian Robertson challenges *The Captain Cook Myth* (Sydney, 1981) from an Australian perspective, and is particularly good on the activities of the early twentieth-century Cook heroizer Sir Joseph Carruthers; Gananath Obeyesekere addresses what he calls 'the humanist myth' of Cook in New

Zealand history in *The Apotheosis of Captain Cook* (Princeton, 1992). A sense of the ongoing proliferation of Cook appreciations, souvenirs and spin-offs can be gained from the web pages and links of the Captain Cook Society, and the CCS newsletter, *Cook's Log*.

For indigenous Australian critiques of Cook, see H. J. Wedge, *Wiradjuri Spirit Man* (Sydney, 1996), Penny McDonald (producer/director), *Too Many Captain Cooks* (Ronin Films, Canberra, 1998), Deborah Bird Rose, *Dingo Makes Us Human* (Cambridge, 1992), and Chris Healy, 'Captain Cook: between black and white', in Sylvia Kleinert and Margo Neale (eds.) *The Oxford Companion to Aboriginal Art and Culture* (Melbourne, 2000), 92–6. Not all views are negative: for example, in *Koori: A Will to Win* (Sydney, 1985), James Miller juxtaposed Cook's idealization of Aboriginal society to the racism of the settlers who came later (20–22). The Hawaiian scholar Haunani-Kay Trask has written on 'Cultures in Collision: Hawai'i and England, 1778' in *Pacific Studies* 7 (1983), 91–117; for a more trenchant critique, see Lilikala Kame'eleihiwa, 'Review of *The Apotheosis of Captain Cook* by Gananath Obeyesekere', *Pacific Studies* 17 (1994), 111–18. Herb Kawainui Kane, *Voyagers* (Washington, 1991) is on the other hand sympathetic to Cook; see also his 'The Other Attack on Captain Cook', *Honolulu Star-Bulletin*, 2 October 1999, which argues that Hawaiian perceptions have been enduringly influenced by anti-Cook propaganda produced by nineteenth-century missionaries; on this point, J. F. G. Stokes, 'Origins of the Condemnation of Captain Cook in Hawaii', *Report of the Hawaiian Historical Society for 1930*, is interesting.

PART 1

I

Cook's maps

My description of the Tower draws on R. and J. Dodsley, *London and Its Environs Described* (London, 1761), VI, 155f., 191–2. The productions of the maritime publishers Mount and Page can be traced through the English Short Title Catalogue (an electronic resource accessible through research libraries). Cook's *Directions for Navigating the West Coast of Newfoundland* (London, 1768) was sold not only by Mount and Page but by N.Gill, said to be a naval officer, in St Johns, Newfoundland. For the most informative accounts of Cook's Newfoundland work, see R. A. Skelton, *James Cook Surveyor of Newfoundland* (San Francisco: David Magee, 1965) (a set of facsimiles of Cook's charts, with an introduction) and in Beaglehole, *Life*, chs. 3–4. Cook's *Grenville* log is ADM 52/1263 in the Public Record Office; most entries are of the cursory 'wind and weather' sort with which readers of naval logs will be familiar.

The Moravian missionary quotation is from the journal of C. F. Hill *et al.*, 10 September 1765, in *Joseph Banks in Newfoundland and Labrador, 1765*, ed. A. M. Lysaght (London, 1971), 211. I quote Banks's Newfoundland diary entries for August 1765 from the same volume, 132–3. For a useful later synthesis of sources concerning Beothuk, see James P. Howley, *The Beothucks or Red Indians: the Aboriginal Inhabitants of Newfoundland* (Cambridge, 1915).

The text of the poet laureate's effort, the reports of people being frozen, and the riots, are from the *St James Chronicle*, nos. 1067, 1068 and 1069, of 1–6 January 1768; no. 1070, of 9 January, carried the Northamptonshire suicide. On the broader themes of liberty and Britishness, see Linda Colley, *Britons: Forging the Nation* (New Haven: Yale University Press, 1992); on Wilkes, see George Rudé, *Wilkes and Liberty* (Oxford: Oxford University Press, 1968), esp. ch. 6. Rioting and dissent are much reported in all the newspapers of the time, and the main developments summarized in the *Annual Register*.

For the description of the Painted Hall (which remains open to public view in what is now the defunct Royal Naval College), see Anon., *An Explanation of the Painting in the Royal Hospital at Greenwich by Sir James Thornhill* (Greenwich, n.d. but *c.*1730), 20. The quotations regarding impressment are from: Captain John Blake, *A Plan for Regulating the Marine System of Great Britain* (London, 1758) i–ii; N. A. M. Rodger, *The Wooden World: an Anatomy of the Georgian Navy* (London, 1988), 150; *The Narrative of William Spavens*, ed. N. A. M. Rodger (London, 1998, orig. 1796), 20; Rodger's *Wooden World* is the most informative revisionist study of the navy. I quote from William Falconer, *An Universal Dictionary of the Marine* (London, 1768) (unpaginated).

The Walker family house is now the Captain Cook Memorial Museum in Whitby and ships' timbers and doors can still be seen there. There are few good accounts of Whitby for the period of Cook's intermittent residence (1748–55), but the following are useful: Lionel Charlton, *History of Whitby* (York, 1779), George Young, *History of Whitby* (Whitby, 1817), and S. K. Jones, 'A maritime history of the port of Whitby, 1700–1914', PhD thesis, University of London, 1982. My brief evocation of Cook's experience on Walker's ships is informed by the autobiography of an approximate contemporary: *The Memoirs of Henry Taylor* (North Shields, 1811).

2

Banks's books

The observations on opportunities to shop, and on the global character of tea-drinking are from *The Macaroni Jester* (London, 1773), 27. The passage on the peculiar characters of seamen is from Anon., *The London and Westminster Guide* (London: W. Nicoll, 1768), XV; it was republished in similar London descriptions of the 1770s, and has been attributed to Sir John Fielding, magistrate and half-brother of the novelist Henry.

Banks cites de Brosses in the journal that he kept on board the ship (Banks, *Endeavour Journal*, e.g. I, 230 and 370); though I like to think he referred to the copy now in the British Library, he may well have owned more than one. Byron's instructions are quoted from *Byron's Journal of His Circumnavigation*, ed. Robert

E. Gallagher (Cambridge, 1964), 3. A copy of Banks's letter to Falconer of early April 1768 is in the Banks Archive at the British Museum (Natural History); it is reference JSB 920324/004.0368. De Brosses's observations on human variety in the South Seas are in his *Histoire des navigations aux terres australes* (Paris, 1756), II, 348. For Dampier on Australians, see William Dampier, *A New Voyage Round the World* (London: James Knapton, 1697–1703) (extracts in Jonathan Lamb, Vanessa Smith, and Nicholas Thomas (eds.) *Exploration and Exchange: A South Seas Anthology 1680–1900* (Chicago: University of Chicago Press, 2000), 12–13). The report of Wallis's visit to Tahiti appeared in the *St James Chronicle, or the British Evening Post*, 26 May 1768. The richest account of the voyage is published as *The Discovery of Tahiti: A Journal of the Second Voyage of the Dolphin . . . written by her master George Robertson*, ed. Hugh Carrington (London, 1948).

For naval hierarchies and naval society, see N. A. M. Rodger's *Wooden World*, cited above. For scurvy and Anson, see Glyn Williams, *The Prize of All the Oceans* (London, 1999), and Jonathan Lamb, *Preserving the Self in the South Seas* (Chicago, 2001), 116–31. For Byron's account of Takapoto, see *Byron's Journal of His Circumnavigation*, ed. Robert E. Gallagher (Cambridge, 1964), 95–100. For the Patagonians, see Charles Clerke, 'An Account of the Very Tall Men, seen near the Streights of Magellan, in the year 1764', *Philosophical Transactions* 57 (1768), 75–9, reprinted in *Byron's Journal of His Circumnavigation*, 210–13; Helen Wallis's appendix to this volume, 'The Patagonian Giants', provides an authoritative review.

On the *Endeavour*'s natural history equipment, I quote from a letter from Ellis to Linnaeus, printed by Beaglehole in Banks, *Endeavour Journal*, I, 30. The account of Banks's last evening in London is from Douglas W. Freshfield, *Life of Horace Benedict de Saussure* (London 1920), and is quoted by Beaglehole in Banks's *Endeavour Journal*, I, 31.

PART 2

The basic sources for Cook's first voyage are: J. C. Beaglehole (ed.) *The Journals of Captain James Cook . . . I. The Voyage of the Endeavour 1768–1771* (Cambridge, 1955), which includes the Earl of Morton's important *Hints* (in appendix II), and the full text of the surviving section of W. B. Monkhouse's journal (in appendix IV), among much other material; Beaglehole (ed.), *The Endeavour Journal of Joseph Banks* (Sydney, 1963); and Sydney Parkinson, *A Journal of a Voyage to the South Seas* (London, 1773 and 1784). No manuscript of Parkinson's book appears to survive. The *Journal of a Voyage Round the World* (London, 1771) attributed to Magra contains a little of interest; I have drawn also on other logs such as that of Gore (PRO Adm 51/4548/145–6), Pickersgill (PRO Adm 51/4547/140–41), Wilkinson (PRO Adm 51/4547/149–50) and Briscoe (Dixson Library, State Library of New South Wales, MS 96).

3

Punished Henry Stephens Seaman

For Anson see Glyn Williams (ed.), *A Voyage Round the World . . . by George Anson* (Oxford, 1974) and Glyn Williams, *The Prize of All the Oceans* (London, 1999). For 'hideous' Madeira see Anon., *A Description of the Island of Madeira* (London, *c*.1760), 50. For the suggestion that Cook was 'jealous' of Gore, see 'Notes by Charles Blagden, *c*.1780–2, from conversation with Solander', Osborn Collection, C.114, Beineke Library, Yale University; copy in Banks Archive, BM(NH). The document adds that 'Gore had a sort of separate command in the vessel being appointed Master Hunter, which gave him superintendence over all the transactions with the Indians. He made use of this sometimes to disobey Cooke; & therefore they hate each other.' Blagden mixes up Gore's nickname ('Master Hunter') with an official status; yet, if his notes are somewhat scrambled, it seems unlikely that there was no basis to his report.

For Charles Fletcher's account of sailors' diversions, see Fletcher, *A Maritime State Considered, as to the health of seamen, with effectual means for rendering the situation of that valuable class of people more comfortable* (Dublin: Mills, 1786), 181–2. The account of the horrific storms is in Williams (ed.), *A Voyage*, 85–6; Cowper's poem, 'The Castaway', is included in most editions of his verse.

4

As miserable a set of People as are this day upon Earth

My sense of indigenous Fuegian life is informed above all by Anne Mackay Chapman, *Drama and Power in a Hunting Society: the Selk'nam of Tierra del Fuego* (Cambridge, 1982), which deals with the immediate neighbours of the Haush. Earlier major works include Martin Gusinde, *Die Feuerland-Indianer* (Vienna, 1931), and Robert Fitz-Roy, *Narrative of the Surveying Voyages of his Majesty's Ships Adventure and Beagle* (4 vols., London, 1839).

For the full series of Buchan's drawings of Haush ornaments, see Joppien and Smith, *The Art of Captain Cook's Voyages*, I, ch. 3 and 88–92. The journals of Banks's surviving footmen, Peter Briscoe and James Roberts, suggest a reproachful attitude towards the mountain tragedy excursion (compare the various entries under 17 January 1769).

5

As favourable to our purpose as we could wish

The sources for the political conflict involving Purea, and for Tahitian history, society and culture in general, are rich and complex. One of the key early works is the description by the *Bounty* mutineer James Morrison, *The Journal of James Morrison*

(London, 1935); Henry Adams, *Tahiti: The Memoirs of the Arii Taimai* (New York, 1947) publishes, in possibly distorted form, oral history obtained late in the nineteenth century; Teuira Henry, *Ancient Tahiti* (Honolulu, 1928) drew together missionary records of Tahitian history, myth and ritual. Douglas L. Oliver synthesized material from these works and many others in *Ancient Tahitian Society* (Canberra, 1974); for a more recent appraisal, see Anne D'Alleva, 'Shaping the Body Politic: Gender, Status and Power in the Art of Eighteenth-century Tahiti and the Society Islands', PhD dissertation, Columbia University, 1997. For an important early treatment of voyagers' violence in Tahiti, see W. H. Pearson, 'European intimidation and the myth of Tahiti', *Journal of Pacific History* 4 (1969), 199–217.

Until recently, the drawings of the *marae*, chief mourner, village and so on discussed here were assigned to 'The Artist of the Chief Mourner' who was thought to be Joseph Banks (see Joppien and Smith, *The Art of Captain Cook's Voyages*, I, ch. 10). But in the mid 1990s, Harold B. Carter, Banks's biographer, located an 1812 letter from Banks which referred to Tupaia learning to draw and referring specifically to the sketch of a European (Banks himself) buying a lobster from a Maori (see Anne Salmond, *Between Worlds*, Auckland, 1997, 16). This is unambiguous, and can only indicate that the whole group of drawings, which are both stylistically homogeneous and unlike the output of any other voyage draughtsmen, are Tupaia's work.

For Polynesian tattooing and European mariners' adoptions of it, see Alfred Gell, *Wrapping in Images: Tattooing in Polynesia* (Oxford, 1993) and Harriet Guest, 'Curiously marked: tattooing, masculinity and nationality in eighteenth-century British perceptions of the South Pacific', in John Barrell (ed.) *Painting and the Politics of Culture* (Oxford, 1992).

6

In order to seize upon the people

The oral traditions cited are from Rongowhakaata Halbert, *Horouta: The History of the Horouta Canoe, Gisborne and East Coast* (Auckland, 1999); for other aspects of traditional history and society in the Poverty Bay area, see Anne Salmond, *Two Worlds: First Meetings between Maori and Europeans 1642–1771* (Auckland, 1991), esp. ch. 5. This book and its sequel, *Between Worlds* (Auckland, 1997), are of tremendous value for their synthesis and reappraisal of early Maori encounter histories. There is an extensive earlier literature detailing Maori customs, rites and myths that can inform interpretation of the eighteenth-century encounters, e.g. Eldson Best, *Notes on the Art of War* (Auckland, 2001; orig. 1902–4) is good on the martial culture that generated the 'defiance' Cook so often encountered. For surveys of the Maori arts that so impressed the visitors, see S. M. Mead (ed.), *Te Maori: Maori Art from New Zealand Collections* (New York, 1984), and D. C. Starzecka (ed.), *Maori Art and Culture* (London, 1996). The objects collected on Cook's voyages are catalogued and reproduced in part in Kaeppler, 'Artificial Curi-

osities'. Despite the art's global fame, there is still no satisfactory publication on Maori tattooing: H. G. Robley's *Moko* (London, 1896) is rich in examples and commonly cited, but carries many of the prejudices of the colonial ethnologist.

7

He was laughed at by the Indians

For Parkinson's and Spöring's canoe pictures, see Joppien and Smith, *The Art of Captain Cook's Voyages*, I, 30–31, 176ff. The child's body obtained by Monkhouse may have passed to Banks after both Monkhouse and his younger brother died at a later stage of the voyage, but I have found no reference to an infant's body in his collection, or to the remains entering any museum subsequently. The proposition that 'cannibalism is what the English reading public wanted to hear' is advanced by Gananath Obeyesekere in ' "British Cannibals": contemplation of an event in the death and resurrection of James Cook, explorer', *Critical Inquiry* 18 (1992), 630–54, quotation from 635.

8

An alarming and I may say terrible Circumstance

'Eora' was probably not a term of tribal identification at the time of Cook's visit, but has since been adopted by some Sydney region Aboriginal people. Societies in the area were rapidly destroyed after the establishment of the Port Jackson colony in 1788, and the evidence for early culture is therefore far more fragmented than for many other parts of Australia. See J. L. Kohen and R. Lampert, 'Hunters and fishers in the Sydney region', in D. J. Mulvaney and J. Peter White (eds.), *Australians to 1788* (Sydney, 1988); important primary sources include David Collins, *An Account of the English Colony in New South Wales* (London, 1798–1802); Melinda Hinkson, *Aboriginal Sydney* (Canberra, 2001), is informative.

The story of Dyirimadhi and Mungurru is from Tulo Gordon and John B. Haviland, *Milbi: Aboriginal Tales from Queensland's Endeavour River* (Canberra: Australian National University Press, 1980), 1–2. The fullest materials on Guugu Yimidhirr are included in W. E. Roth, *The Queensland Aborigines* (Victoria Park, Western Australia, 1984; a reprint of various government ethnography bulletins of 1897–1910); Roth conveys something of the complexity of local property relations and social arrangements (which, for example, lay behind the turtle dispute) that entirely eluded Cook. On the word 'kangaroo' and other linguistic issues, see John B. Haviland, 'A Last Look at Cook's Guugu Yimidhirr Wordlist', *Oceania* 44 (1974), 216–32.

Beaglehole finds Cook's remarks on Guugu Yimidhirr shocking at several points in his commentary, see, for example, his *Life of Captain James Cook*, 251–2. In an important essay Glyn Williams has shown that Cook's observations are likely to have been inspired by a book known to be on the *Endeavour*, George Shelvocke's

Voyage Round the World (London, 1726), which included similar evocations of a 'perfect tranquility' among native Americans (Williams, 'Reactions on Cook's voyage', in Ian Donaldson and Tamsin Donaldson (eds.), *Seeing the First Australians*, Sydney, 1985).

10

My intentions certainly were not criminal

Early news items concerning the voyage are in the *London Evening Post*, 27–9 July 1771, and the *General Evening Post*, 27 August 1771; the same material appeared in a number of other newspapers. On Cook's marriage I quote from Ray Parkin, *H. M. Bark Endeavour* (Melbourne: Melbourne University Press, 1997), 65.

The main sources for Banks's personal affairs are two letters from Daines Barrington to Thomas Pennant, 24 August 1771, Alexander Turnbull Library, Wellington; printed by Beaglehole in Banks, *Journal*, I, 55–6. Cook's letter to Walker is printed in *Journals*, I, 506–8. Elliott's 'Memoirs' are published in *Captain Cook's Second Voyage: The Journals of Lieutenants Elliott and Pickersgill*, ed. Christine Holmes (London, 1984); the quotations are from 2–5. For Banks's interests in flax, see Carter, *Sir Joseph Banks*; for Hodges, see Smith, *European Vision*; for Forster, see Michael E. Hoare, *The Tactless Philosopher: Johann Reinhold Forster, 1729–1798* (Melbourne: Hawthorn Press, 1976). For Hawkesworth see Beaglehole's 'Textual Introduction' to Cook, *Journals*, I; W. H. Pearson, 'Hawkesworth's *Voyages*', in R. F. Brissenden (ed.), *Studies in the Eighteenth Century*, Canberra, 1973; and Jonathan Lamb – to whom I am especially indebted – 'Circumstances surrounding the death of John Hawkesworth', in Lamb (ed.), *The South Pacific in the Eighteenth Century*. Hawkesworth's mangling of Cook's Aboriginal observations (and their inappropriate transmission to Tierra del Fuego) is discussed by Williams (in 'Reactions', 46) and Smith (*European Vision*, 38). For another perspective on the Point Venus scene, see Neil Rennie, *Far-fetched Facts* (Oxford, 1995). Charlotte Hayes's 're-enactment' is described in *Nocturnal Revels* 2 (1779), 24–5, which (I understand from the late Roy Porter) may reprint a 1774 publication, *The Whore-Mongers Guide to London*, which I have been unable to trace. William Wales's comments are from his *Remarks on Mr Forster's Account of Captain Cook's Last Voyage . . .*, printed in Forster, *Voyage Round the World*, ed. Thomas and Berghof, 724. For Diderot's and Voltaire's responses see John Dunmore, 'The Explorer and the Philosopher', in Walter Veit (ed.), *Captain James Cook: Image and Impact*, I.

PART 3

The key sources for Cook's second voyage are Beaglehole, *Journals*, II; Hoare, *The Resolution Journal of Johann Reinhold Forster*, and the logs, journals and memoirs of Wales, Pickersgill, Clerke, Elliott and Burney, some printed in part or in full by Beaglehole. George Forster's *Voyage Round the World* was based on his father's journal but includes independent material.

11

The Inhospitable parts I am going to

John Atkins's reflections are in *A Voyage to Guinea, Brasil, and the West Indies* (London, 1737), 19, 21. Cook's letter to John Walker is quoted from *Journals*, II, 689. For the longitude issue, see Dava Sobel, *Longitude* (New York, 1995). For Jeanne Baret, see Bougainville, *Voyage autour du monde*, ed. Jacques Proust (Paris, 1982), 293–5. Anders Sparrman's hesitations are set out in his *Voyage to the Cape of Good Hope*, ed. V. S. Forbes (Cape Town, 1975), 109. This book, dealing primarily with Sparrman's southern African researches, was first published in Swedish in 1783; a separate account of the voyage on the *Resolution* appeared only much later, in two parts in 1802 and 1818, and was published in English as *A Voyage Round the World* (London, 1956); the description of boxing is at 12–16 of this edition. For further discussion of the Dusky Sound encounters, see A. Charles Begg and Neil C. Begg, *Dusky Bay: In the Steps of Captain Cook* (Christchurch, 1966), and Mark Adams and Nicholas Thomas, *Cook's Sites: Revisiting History* (Dunedin, 1999); which includes the various reworked 'family of Dusky Bay' prints.

12

Mingling my tears with hers

For Totaranui communities, Anne Salmond's *Between Worlds* is again very useful. For Tahitian politics and events, the sources listed earlier are again relevant. Oliver, *Ancient Tahiti Society*, III, deals with the growing power of the dynasty Tu founded, the Pomares.

13

We are the innocent cause of this war

Bougainville's *Voyage autour du monde* had appeared in Paris in October 1771, but Cook almost certainly was reading the English translation by the Forsters that was published in London early in 1772. For early Tongan society, see Elizabeth Bott, *Tongan Society at the Time of Captain Cook's Visits* (Wellington, 1982). Cook's main source for Tasman (and for that matter various earlier voyages, such as those of Quiros) would have been Alexander Dalrymple's *Historical Collection of the Several Voyages and Discoveries in the South Pacific Ocean* (London, 1771).

14

The varieties of the human species

The Elliott quotation is from Holmes (ed.), *Captain Cook's Second Voyage*, 25–6. This probably refers to the change of course back to the south-east on 11 January, which might have stuck in Elliott's mind because it was his sixteenth birthday, though the chronology of his account is otherwise muddled: he has a near miss with an iceberg occuring after this, when he seems to be referring to the incident of 15 December 1773. For Rapanui, see Jo Anne Van Tilburg, *Easter Island Archaeology, Ecology and Culture* (London, 1994); for the Marquesas, see Greg Dening, *Islands and Beaches* (Melbourne, 1980), and Nicholas Thomas, *Marquesan Societies* (Oxford, 1990). For more extended discussion of the Forsters' responses to Tahiti and related matters, see the editorial material in the recent editions of *Observations* and *A Voyage Round the World*, cited earlier; and David Bindman, *Ape to Apollo* (London, 2002). For the significance of feathers in Polynesian art and culture, see N. Thomas, *Oceanic Art* (London, 1995), ch. 7. For the abortive attempt to land on Niue, see T. F. Ryan, 'Narratives of encounter: the anthropology of history on Niue', PhD thesis, University of Auckland, 1993, and (for a novelistic treatment), John Pule, *The Shark That Ate the Sun* (Auckland, 1994). For Vanuatu, see Ron Adams, *In the Land of Strangers: A Century of European Contact with Tanna* (Canberra, 1984), and Margaret Jolly, ' "Ill-natured comparisons": racism and relativism in European representations of ni-Vanuatu from Cook's second voyage', *History and Anthropology* 5 (1992), 331–63. For New Caledonia, see Bronwen Douglas, 'A contact history of the Balad people of New Caledonia, 1774–1845', *Journal of the Polynesian Society* 79 (1970), 180–200.

15

The Southern Hemisphere sufficiently explored

There have been a number of recent reappraisals of the Grass Cove killings; see, for example, Salmond, *Between Worlds*, and Ian G. Barber, 'Early contact ethnography and understanding', in Calder, Lamb and Orr (eds.), *Voyages and Beaches*. Clerke's letter on arriving home is quoted in Beaglehole, *Journals*, II, 953.

16

Now I am going to be confined

The reports cited are *Lloyds Evening Post* (no. 2826), 7–9 August, 1775; 'Harlequin' in the *London Magazine* (September 1775), 441; and 'An Authentic Account of the Miserable Fate of Ten Men, belonging to the *Adventure*', *Middlesex Journal and Evening Advertiser* (no. 1006), 5–7 September 1775. The standard study of Mai is E. H. McCormick, *Omai: Pacific Envoy* (Auckland, 1977); *Cook and Omai: The Cult of the South Seas* (Canberra, 2001) includes several useful essays. For the issue of the Northwest Passage, and Daines Barrington's role, see Glyn Williams, *Voyages of Delusion: The Search for the Northwest Passage in the Age of Reason* (London, 2002). For Forster and the publishing of Cook's second voyage, see, again, Hoare, *The Tactless Philosopher* and the introductions to the 1996 and 2000 editions of Johann Forster's *Observations* and George Forster's *Voyage Round the World*. For Hodges's *Landings*, see Joppien and Smith, *The Art of Captain Cook's Voyages*, II, 92–5. The set of portraits presented, apparently by Cook himself, to Paul Henry Ourry were with Maggs Bros., London, as of 2002. For Webber, see *The Art of Captain Cook's Voyages*, III. The rumour that Cook's third voyage might transplant breadfruit to the West Indies is reported by Daniel Wray, see John Nichols, *Illustrations of the Literary History of the Eighteenth Century* (London, 1817), I, 154. I quote from George Forster's *Voyage*, 90–91 (the cascade), 123 (on Maori women; cf. 612), 548–51 (on Tanna); and from Wales's *Remarks*, printed as Appendix B in Forster's *Voyage*, 701 (on Johann Forster's character), 735 (Erramanga), and 739–41 (Tanna).

PART 4

Cook's third voyage journal is published in Beaglehole, *Journals*, III; the edition includes the full texts of Samwell's and Anderson's accounts, and extensive extracts from Clerke, King, Gore and Williamson among others. Edgar's log is also important: there are two versions, PRO Adm 55/21 and 24, and BM Add MS 37528. George Gilbert's post-voyage memoir, published as *Captain Cook's Final Voyage: the Journal of Midshipman George Gilbert* (ed. Christine Holmes, London, 1982), is useful and lively. In addition to the official account, Cook and King's *Voyage to the Pacific Ocean* (London, 1784), there are several important early published works. John Rickman, *Journal of Captain Cook's Last Voyage to the Pacific Ocean* (London, 1781) is unreliable but interesting, as is John Ledyard's book of more or less the same title (Hartford, 1783), in part a plagiarization of Rickman. William Ellis, *An Authentic Narrative of a Voyage Performed by Captain Cook* (London, 1782) is less fanciful but adds little that is distinctive. Heinrich Zimmermann's *Reise um die Welt, mit Capitain Cook* (Mannheim, 1781) is brief but interesting on a number of points, and appeared in English as *Zimmermann's Account of the Third Voyage of Captain Cook*, trans. U. Tewsley, Wellington, 1926.

17

I allow because I cannot prevent it

For Kerguelen, see Jean Paul Kauffmann, *Voyage to Desolation Island* (London, 2001). For John Webber, see Joppien and Smith, *The Art of Cook's Voyages*, III, 171–204. For Tasmania, the best general account is Lyndall Ryan, *The Aboriginal Tasmanians* (St Lucia, Queensland, 1981).

18

An act that I cannot account for

I am grateful to Michael Reilly of Otago University for showing me his manuscript, 'The Children of Tangaroa', which deals in part with Mangaian traditions of Cook's visit. For Tonga, the sources cited above remain relevant; the story of the plot is from John Martin, *An Account of the Natives of the Tonga Islands* (Edinburgh, 1827), II, 71–3; on the *'inasi* rite that Cook witnessed, see Arne Aleksej Perminow, 'Captain Cook and the roots of precedence in Tonga', *History and Anthropology* 12 (2001), 289–314.

19

They may fear, but never love us

For Beaglehole's observation on Cook's supposed lack of interest in seeking out Fiji, see his Introduction to *Journals*, III, cvii-cviii, restated in the *Life of Captain James Cook*, 547–8, and repeated, for example, by Sir James Watt, 'Medical aspects and consequences of Cook's voyages', in Fisher and Johnston (eds.), *Captain James Cook and His Times*, 155. The Spanish visits to Tahiti are usefully reviewed by O. H. K. Spate in *Paradise Found and Lost* (Canberra, 1988), ch. 6; the main primary accounts are translated in B. G. Corney (ed.) *The Quest and Occupation of Tahiti by the Emissaries of Spain* (London, 1913–19). As before, early accounts such as those of Morrison and more recent works such as those of Oliver and D'Alleva help one understand the transactions of Cook's visit. I am grateful to Anne D'Alleva for drawing my attention to the point, attested to by Edgar, that Poetua was pregnant at the time of her captivity.

20

Squalls and rain and so dark

For the general background to Hawaiian culture and society, the major sources include works by nineteenth-century Hawaiians such as David Malo's *Hawaiian Antiquities* (Honolulu, 1951) and Samuel M. Kamakau's *The Works of the People of Old* (Honolulu, 1976). Among recent anthropological studies, Valerio Valeri's *Kingship and Sacrifice* (Chicago, 1995) provides a detailed and insightful account of cosmology and ritual; Jocelyn Linnekin's *Sacred Queens and Women of Consequence* (Ann Arbor, 1993) foregrounds the power of women in the Hawaiian kingdoms. Kaneoneo's assertion of precedence over his followers is discussed by Marshall Sahlins, *Historical Metaphors and Mythical Realities* (Ann Arbor, 1981), 33–5.

For the Nuu-chah-nulth, see Alan L. Hoover (ed.) *Nuu-chah-nulth Voices, Histories, Objects and Journeys* (Victoria, 2000); the modern native view I quote is from the 'Yuquot Agenda Paper' in this volume. See also Martha Black, *Out of the Mist: Treasures of the Nuu-chah-nulth Chiefs* (Victoria, 1999), and Robin Fisher, 'Cook and the Nootka', in Fisher and Johnston (eds.), *Captain James Cook and His Times*. Williams, *Voyages of Delusion*, ch. 9, is useful for this phase of the voyage. The book Cook consulted was David Crantz, *The History of Greenland, Containing a Description of the Country and Its Inhabitants* (London, 1767). Modern Inuit perspectives are accessible via **www.inuit.org**, the site of the Inuit Circumpolar Conference.

Cook's increasing fatigue over the course of the third voyage is the theme of Beaglehole's commentary in his edition of the *Journals* and in relevant sections of the *Life*. Sir James Watt, in a tendentious section of his essay, 'Medical Aspects and Consequences', attributes this decline to a deficiency of vitamin B; Gananath Obeyesekere, citing much of the same evidence, argues that the explorer was increasingly violent and increasingly detached from reality (*Apotheosis*, 41–4 and *passim*). I do not dispute that there are changes in Cook's behaviour and apparent disposition over the decade of the three voyages, but these changes are more complex than these accounts suggest. Certain shifts – Cook's diminishing empathy towards his men – date from the middle of the second voyage rather than some point in the course of the third. And while Cook indeed punished Polynesians for theft to a degree that he had not done before, fewer Islanders were actually killed during the third voyage, up to the time of Cook's death, than on either the first or second expeditions.

21

A dream that we could not reconcile ourselves to

For Hawaii's population trends and the real tragedy that venereal disease was part of, see David Stannard, *Before the Horror* (Honolulu, 1989). It is not surprising that David Samwell was among those who insisted that the British were not responsible: his *Narrative of the Death of Captain Cook* (London, 1786) included *Observations*

Respecting the Introduction of the Venereal Disease into the Sandwich Islands,
which made extended but not very convincing arguments for its pre-existence in the
archipelago.

The suggestion that Cook was identified with Lono, in some way that accounted
for his death, has long been expressed in a variety of ways; a longstanding and
popular belief had it that Cook was killed when Hawaiians realized that he was not
a god. In a brief essay, Gavan Daws made the more ethnohistorically sensitive
suggestion that the timing of the Makahiki festival was crucial in prompting the
identification of Cook and Lono, while the subsequent ascendancy of Ku played a
part in causing the shift towards hostility ('Kealakekua Bay revisited: a note on the
death of Captain Cook', *Journal of Pacific History* 3 (1968), 21–3). This argument
was elaborated on by Marshall Sahlins, who drew together the fragmented evidence
for parallels between rites of Lono and the treatment of Cook from the voyage logs,
while presenting, with much interpretative virtuosity, a fresh anthropological theory
of the nature of cultural change (*Historical Metaphors and Mythical Realities*, Ann
Arbor, 1981; *Islands of History*, esp. ch. 4). Both the theory and the example were
challenged: the approximation of Cook's arrival with the Makahiki calender was,
for example, questioned by Steen Bergendorff, Ulla Hasager and Peter Henriques
in 'Mythopraxis and history: on the interpretation of the Makahiki', *Journal of
the Polynesian Society* 97 (1988), 391–408; Sahlins responded with fuller
documentation in 'Captain Cook in Hawaii', *Journal of the Polynesian Society* 98
(1989), 371–425.

These somewhat specialized debates erupted into a widely publicized controversy
in the early 1990s with the publication of Gananath Obeyesekere's *Apotheosis of
Captain Cook*, which generally ignored earlier criticism of Sahlins, while arguing
that the Hawaiian deification of Cook was a self-congratulatory myth of European
colonization, which Sahlins's anthropological account perpetuated. Obeyesekere's
book was engaging, and was written with much verve; but it attracted more praise
than it deserved, and anyone who took the trouble to read it in parallel with its
sources became increasingly dismayed by a cavalier historical method. Much of the
polemic moreover responds to a mistranslation or non-problem, in the sense that
the proposition that is offensive to Obeyesekere, and implausible for many others,
is that Cook was taken to be 'a god' – a European category that only roughly
corresponds with Polynesian *akua*. For Polynesians, divinity was manifest in a variety
of living things and people as well as in supreme deities; for them there was therefore
nothing exceptional or outrageous in the identification of a priest, a chief or a
powerful foreigner such as Cook with Lono or Ku.

Sahlins's response, *How 'Natives' Think, About Captain Cook for Example*
(Chicago, 1995), amounted to a relentless counter-critique and comprehensive vindi-
cation of his own arguments (which were however revised in a number of ways).
While the partial nature of the ethnohistorical record is such that eighteenth-century
events, perceptions, and especially indigenous categories can never be interpreted
with certainty, the case for an identification between Cook and Lono, and a deterio-
ration of British–Hawaiian relations associated with the ascendancy of Ku, is now

compelling. For a useful review of the controversy, see Rob Borofsky, 'Cook, Lono, Obeyesekere, Sahlins', *Current Anthropology* 38 (1997), 255–82. Those interested in references to the extensive Hawaiian historical and anthropological literature will find many works listed (and their merits debated) by Obeyesekere and Sahlins, as well as by Valeri (*Kingship and Sacrifice*) and Linnekin (*Sacred Queens*).

For the argument that Cook 'snapped', see Beaglehole, 'Introduction', *Journals*, III, cxlvi–clvii. This is an extension, or the rationale, for the thesis of increasing fatigue (see above). Rupert T. Gould, 'Some unpublished accounts of Cook's death', *Mariner's Mirror* 14 (1928), 301–19, reproduces fuller extracts from certain logs than Beaglehole, and instances the propensity to blame Williamson.

Clerke's dying letter to Banks, and Sandwich's with the news of Cook's death, are reproduced in *Journals*, III, 1542–3, 1552–3. The waistcoat of Tahitian tapa that Elizabeth Cook embroidered is among the Cook relics in the State Library of New South Wales.

Epilogue

I quote from James King and Charles Ryskamp (eds.), *The Letters and Prose Writings of William Cowper* (Oxford, 1981), II, 172, 270–71, and 282–3. 'Charity' is in John D. Baird and Charles Ryskamp (eds.) *The Poems of William Cowper* (Oxford 1980), I, 337ff., as well as in other Cowper selections.

The Milbi Wall in Cooktown is complemented by new displays in the recently renovated and extended James Cook Museum. For the first time local Aboriginal perceptions are represented in this institution; elder Eric Deeral's account of Cook's visit is presented, including the great ship's strange arrival, and the anger over the visitors' refusal to pass on any of the turtle they had caught. 'The sharing code was broken. They should have got permission from us as the owners or custodians.' But 'diplomacy was used by both sides' and 'may be caution on the part of Guugu Yimithirr saved Cook's life . . . Before leaving to board their canoes, our bama agreed between themselves that the things that the strangers gave were to be got rid of and that no further contact was to be made . . . Then, finally, one day they watched the ship sail out of the Wahalumbaalbirri [the Endeavour River estuary] and away from our Guugu Yimithirr land. Although contact had been limited, it had for the most part been surprisingly friendly. These strangers showed respect for us and our families and it was very sad to see them go.'

Acknowledgements

Over the last twenty years I have had the luck to live for periods in the Marquesas Islands, Fiji and New Zealand, and to visit Hawaii, Tahiti, Vanuatu and New Caledonia among other places in the Pacific. Everywhere I have been overwhelmed by people's generosity. In most cases I did not visit to research Cook, but my sense of the contexts of his voyages owes more than I can say to the help and the imaginations of many Pacific Islanders. Although it is awkward to single anyone out, I must specifically thank Herb Kawainui Kane for an unforgettable guided tour of Kealakekua Bay in April 2002, and John Pule for taking me to Niue in 1999, as well as for his long-term friendship.

I have a similarly profound but quite different debt to the dozens of librarians, archivists and museum curators who have supported my research in Oceanic cultures and European maritime histories. I would especially like to thank staff at the State Library of New South Wales, the National Library of Australia, the State Archives of Hawaii, the Provincial Archives of British Columbia, the Staatsbibliothek in Berlin, the Institute for Ethnology at the University of Göttingen, the British Library, the British Museum, the Cambridge University Museum for Archaeology and Anthropology, the Public Record Office, the National Maritime Museum, the Banks Archive at the British Museum (Natural History) and the Captain Cook Memorial Museum in Whitby. I have a different debt again to Goldsmiths College; I appreciate the support of colleagues, and particularly the allocation of a sabbatical term in 2001.

I have long gained much from Cook-related conversations with academic friends, including Anne D'Alleva, Harriet Guest, Jenny Newell, Nigel Rigby, Bernard Smith and Glyn Williams. I have especially appreciated the personal support of Bronwen Douglas, Jonathan Lamb and Anne Salmond. Marshall Sahlins's brilliant anthropology inspires me today, as it did when I became an undergraduate student in 1979.

Since 1995 I have worked with Mark Adams on a photographic project documenting the Pacific places visited by Cook and the European sites associated with his memory and his collections. Tracking and talking Cook together from north Yorkshire to north Queensland has been great fun; and I have learned a lot from Mark's reflections and his visual intelligence.

I thank Anna Cole and Makiko Kuwahara for a great deal of practical assistance, especially with obtaining pictures; Rachel Eggleston helped me access Australian microfilm among other materials. Dan Clayton, Niel Gunson, Alex Perminow, Roslyn Poignant, Michael Reilly and Cliff Thornton all kindly gave me advice and/ or access to their writing. I am very grateful to John Lutz for organizing a memorable visit to Nootka Sound in February 2002, and to Margarita James of the Mowachaht/ Muchalaht First Nations for hosting us.

I owe a great deal to my agent and publishers. Peter Robinson, Simon Winder and George Gibson have all been wonderfully encouraging; only I know how much their suggestions have helped shape and improve this book. Both Annie Coombes and Keith Thomas read draft chapters and provided much stylistic and otherwise crucial advice.

Henrietta Moore has been an unfailingly supportive friend; I thank her here specifically for introducing Annie Coombes and myself to a small village in south-western France, where much of this book was in the end written. On the south coast of New South Wales, the Christmas company of Anna, Jeannine, Julian, Sam, Matilda, Morgan, Julia and Keith has made a huge difference to me. Without Annie Coombes I would not have had a place or space or reasons to write this book; I thank her for giving and sharing more than I thought life had to offer.

446

Index

Figures in italics indicate illustrations.